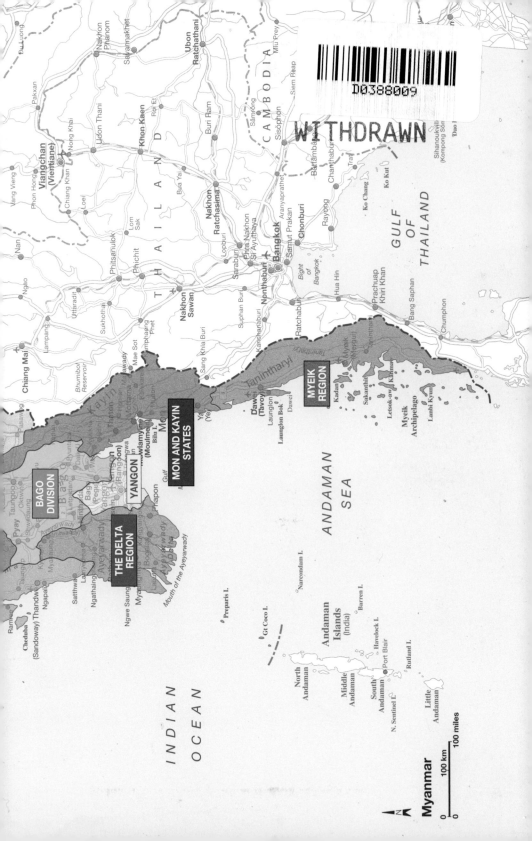

INSIGHT GUIDES
MYANMAR
(BURMA)

APA PUBLICATIONS
Part of the Langenscheidt Publishing Group

The unmissable sights of this fascinating country range from awe-inspiring ancient treasures to timeless landscapes, rewarding treks and river cruises.

The first Insight Guide pioneered the use of creative full-colour photography in travel guides in 1970. Since then, we have expanded our range to cater for our readers' need not only for reliable information about their chosen destination but also for a real understanding of the culture and workings of that destination. Now, when the internet can supply inexhaustible (but not always reliable) facts, our books marry text and pictures to provide those much more elusive qualities: knowledge and discernment. To achieve this, they rely heavily on the authority of experts.

How to use this book

Insight Guide: Myanmar (Burma) is structured to convey an understanding of the country and its people as well as to guide readers through its attractions.

The **Features** section, indicated by a pink bar at the top of each page, covers the natural geography and the eventful history of Myanmar as well as aspects of its culture: its people, religions, performing arts, crafts, cuisine and architecture.

The main **Places** section, indicated by a blue bar, is a complete guide to all the sights and areas worth visiting. Places of special interest are coordinated by number with the maps.

The **Travel Tips** listings section, with a yellow bar, provides full information on transport, restaurants, hotels and activities, an A–Z section of essential practical information and a short guide to the Burmese language and further reading recommendations.

The contributors

This new edition of *Insight Guide: Myanmar (Burma)* was commissioned by **Tom Le Bas**, managing editor at Insight's London office. The book has been completely restructured and updated with the invaluable help of a number of people.

Freelance travel writer **David Abram** grew up in south Wales, Somerset and the Middle East. He became an Asia specialist after studying anthropology, and has since worked on more than a hundred books worldwide, produced travel articles for numerous magazines and newspapers,

and worked as a radio presenter for the BBC. Having respected the NLD tourism boycott for two decades, David made his first trip to Myanmar in the year Aung San Suu Kyi was released from house arrest. Current publishing projects include a book on the British annexation of the country and its legacy.

Andrew Forbes, of the Chiang Mai-based CPA Media, wrote the chapters on history, festivals, temple architecture and the poppy trail, as well as picture stories on Myanmar's ethnic minorities and Buddha images, for the previous edition of the book. Food and travel writer **Wendy Hutton** wrote the original chapter on Burmese cuisine. Other contributors to earlier editions have included **David Henley**, **Tan Chung Lee**, **Oliver Hargreave** and **Bertil Lintner**.

The original edition was the work of **Wilhelm Klein** and photographer **Günter Pfannmüller**, who put together the first edition of the book at a time when most regions in Myanmar were closed to foreigners.

New photography was provided by **Corrie Wingate**. Picture research was done by **Tom Smyth**, the book was proofread by **Jan McCann** and indexed by **Penny Phenix**.

Map Legend

International Boundary
Province Boundary
National Park
Ferry Route
Swamp
City Wall
Airport: International/Regional
Bus Station
Tourist Information
Church/Ruins
Castle/Ruins
Mosque
Viewpoint
Pass
Beach
Cave
Statue/Monument
Place of Interest
Main post office

The main places of interest in the Places section are coordinated by number with a full-colour map (eg ❶), and a symbol at the top of every right-hand page tells you where to find the map.

Contents

THE BEST OF MYANMAR (BURMA): TOP ATTRACTIONS

From the glittering pagodas and downtown bustle of Yangon to the splendid setting of Inle Lake, the temple-strewn plains of Bagan and the forested hills of Shan State, prioritise with our selection of Myanmar's must-see sights.

△ **Shwedagon Pagoda, Yangon.** The supreme symbol of Burmese Buddhism and national pride, the gigantic golden stupa rising from the midst of Yangon (Rangoon) is a sublime spectacle, especially at dawn and dusk. See page 122.

△ **Sagaing, Mandalay.** Encrusted with literally thousands of gold and whitewashed stupa spires, this holy hilltop overlooking the Ayeyarwady near Mandalay rests on the site of one of several ancient Burmese royal capitals. See page 185.

△ **Inle Lake, Shan State.** "One-legged" Intha rowers, floating gardens and markets, pretty stilt villages, ancient Shan stupa complexes and beautiful scenery are just some of the attractions of serene Inle Lake in the Shan Hills. See page 243.

▷ **Bagan, Mandalay Division.** Around 2,200 ancient religious buildings dating from the 11th and 13th centuries litter the arid Plains of Bagan – one of Southeast Asia's greatest archaeological sites and Myanmar's principal visitor attraction. See it from the air on a magical balloon flight. See page 205.

△ **Golden Rock Pagoda, Kyaiktiyo, Mon State.** Teetering on the rim of a clifftop high in the coastal hills of Mon State, this extraordinary gilded monument ranks among the country's most magical pilgrimage sites. Getting to it involves a stiff hour-long hike up a sacred stairway. See page 291.

▷ **Mount Popa.** Climb the sacred steps leading from Popa's famous Nature Spirit *(Nat)* temple to the Buddhist shrine clinging to the volcanic plug above it for a matchless view of the Bagan plains. See page 232.

◁ **Mrauk-U, Rakhaing State.** Hidden away in the remote west of the country, Mrauk-U is an amazing lost city of ruined temples, palaces and shrines, set amid scrub-covered hills. Boats leave Sittwe daily to reach the site – an unforgettable six-hour river trip. See page 273.

△ **Cruising the Ayeyarwady.** Whether you travel by luxury cruiser or cronky government ferry, a journey along Myanmar's mightiest river takes you deep into the country's rural heart – a watery world of shifting sand banks, remote jetties and bamboo-built villages. See pages 177, 305.

▽ **Hill-tribe treks, Shan State.** The hill-tribe trekking scene in Myanmar is nowhere near as commercialised as in neighbouring Thailand. Kalaw, a former British retreat near Inle Lake, and Hsipaw, further northeast, are the two main hubs. See page 249.

△ **Ngapali Beach, Rakhaing State.** Kick back at Myanmar's premier beach resort, whose brilliant turquoise water, golden sand and superb seafood offer a welcome respite from the heat and dust of inland travel. See page 281.

THE BEST OF MYANMAR (BURMA): EDITOR'S CHOICE

Unique attractions, colourful markets, fabulous temples and pagodas, quiet backwaters, beautiful scenery and beaches ... here are our recommendations.

The reclining buddha at Bodhi Tataung.

BEST BUDDHIST MONUMENTS

Shwedagon Pagoda, Yangon. Thousands of pilgrims stream daily around the precincts of Myanmar's most splendid religious monument – a structure of otherworldly beauty. See page 122.

Chantha Abhaya Labha Muni, Yangon. Quarried and sculpted in Mandalay from a single block of marble, this milky white Buddha is a modern masterpiece.See page 137.

Shwemawdaw Pagoda, Bago. Bago's magnificent stupa, smothered in gold and precious stones, outstrips even the Shwedagon for size, if not national importance. See page 149.

Shwethalyaung Buddha,

Bago. Dating from the zenith of Burma's Second Empire, this colossal reclining Buddha is regarded as the one that best expresses the Master's attainment of Nirvana. See page 151.

Maha Muni, Mandalay. Myanmar's number one Buddha, a serene-faced giant, was brought to Mandalay from Rakhaing (Arakan) as war booty in the 18th century. See page 175.

Shweshandaw Pagoda, Pyay (Bago Division). Though a provincial backwater now, Pyay (Prome) was once a wealthy river port – as the scale and splendour of its great gold stupa testify. See page 155.

Bodhi Tataung, Monywa (Mandalay). Among the most surreal sights in Southeast Asia are the two vast Buddhas – one standing, one reclined – on this hilltop to the east of Monywa. See page 191.

Pho Win Taung Caves, Monywa (Mandalay). An ancient complex of hand-hewn caves containing rows of antique sculptures and murals, buried deep in the countryside west of the Chindwin River, central Myanmar. See page 192.

Shwezigon Pagoda, Bagan. The most revered of Bagan's two-thousand-odd surviving shrines. Pilgrims pour through it year-round, but in

particularly large numbers during the annual festival. See page 218.

Win Sein Taw Ya, nr Mawlamyine (Mon State). The country's largest reclining Buddha rests on a ridgetop near the former colonial capital of Mawlamyine (Moulmein) – a diorama inside recounts moral tales and stories from the Master's life. See page 294.

Golden Rock Pagoda, Kyaiktiyo (Mon State). An historic monument of breathtaking beauty perched on the rim of a precipice, the exquisite Golden Rock Pagoda can only be reached after a tiring, hour-long climb. See page 291.

Verdant landscape near Kalaw.

BEST WALKS & TREKS

Kalaw–Inle Lake (Shan State). The country's most popular trekking route winds from the hill station of Kalaw to the shores of Inle Lake via a string of pretty minority villages and tracts of forest. See page 249.

Inle Lake–Pindaya (Shan State). Hike over the hilly western fringes of the Shan Plateau – home to several ethnic minority communities – to the Buddha-filled cave complex at Pindaya. See page 249.

Hsipaw (Shan State). Numerous day walks out of Hsipaw take you to Palaung minority villages such as Pankam, renowned for its tea cultivation, teak houses and traditions of nature-spirit worship. See page 252.

Kengtung (Shan State). The market town of Kengtung, near the Chinese border, serves as a springboard for a choice of routes to Eng, Akha, Palaung and Wa settlements. See page 251.

Nat Ma Taung (Chin State). A distinctive "sky-island" summit with its own peculiar jungle flora and fauna, Nat Ma Taung – aka "Mount Victoria" (3,053 metres/10,016ft) – is the target for a superb six-day trek from Bagan. See page 283.

Hkakabo Razi base camp (Kachin). Close encounters with spectacular forest, abundant wildlife and some awesome snowy-mountain scenery characterise the trek to the foot of Burma's highest peak, Hkakabo Razi (5,889 metres/ 19,321ft). See page 265.

Gemstones at Bogyoke Aung San Market in Yangon.

BEST JOURNEYS

Mandalay–Bagan. You can chug in a relaxing day between Mandalay and Bagan – on a rusty old government tub, or shiny, state-of-the-art, retro cruise boat. See page 177.

Mawlamyine–Hpa-an. The karst limestone mountains and outcrops of Kayin State make the ferry trip up the Thanlwin (Salween) River one of the loveliest in Asia. See page 297.

Pyin U Lwin to Lashio, via the Gokteik Viaduct. It takes longer than by road, but the stop-and-start train ride through northwest Shan State is worth making for the crossing of the spectacular Gokteik Viaduct. See page 199.

Myitkyina–Mandalay. A series of natural defiles gouged by the river is the stand-out feature of the week-long journey by government ferry along the northern stretch of the Ayeyarwady. See page 262.

Mandalay–Mingun. A short and sweet river trip lasting an hour takes you from Mandalay through some idyllic countryside to the mighty ruined stupa at Mingun. See page 188.

The Gokteik Viaduct.

BEST MARKETS

Bogyoke Aung San Market, Yangon. Known for its colonial architecture and stone-lined backstreets, Bogyoke is the country's best source of antiques, handicrafts, jewellery and – famously – jade and rubies. See page 121.

Sittwe. You'll have to get up before dawn to catch Sittwe's quayside fish market firing on all cylinders. An amazing array of Andaman seafood is on sale here each morning. See page 272.

Five-Day Floating Markets, Inle Lake. Every five days, the towns encircling Inle take it in turns to host the local market, where you can pick up lotus silk textiles, Shan bags and other handicrafts. See page 246.

Hsipaw. This weekly bazaar in the Shan Hills is a great place to see local tribal villagers dressed in traditional finery. See page 251.

Bhamo. Head to the south end of Bhamo's lively riverfront market area for the town's main ceramic centre, where pots of all sizes and shapes are laid out for sale beside the water. See page 258.

BEST SOUVENIRS

Laquerware. Imported from Siam in the 16th century, *yun* laquerwork has since been refined into a distinctively Burmese art form. Myinkaba in Bagan is its major centre. See page 83.

Htamein & longyis. The backlanes of Amarapura, near Mandalay, are filled with the sound of handlooms making the elegant *longyis* and *htamein* (sarongs) worn by Burmese men and women. See page 236.

Marionettes. Delightful string puppets, representing characters from much-loved myth and folk tales, are a common sight at souvenir stores in Yangon, Mandalay and Bagan. See page 86.

Parasols. Capital of the Ayeyarwady Delta region, Pathein holds a dozen or more workshops where traditional paper and resin parasols are made in dazzling day-glo colours. See pages 84, 145.

Kalaga tapestries. Beads, silver thread and sequins are used to make padded *kalaga* tapestries, featuring scenes from Buddhist scriptures. Mandalay is the main focus for this popular craft form. See page 87.

BEST BEACHES

Ngapali (Rakhaing State). Ngapali is far and away Myanmar's most appealing resort, with a string of high-end hotels behind a bay of soft white sand and blue water. See page 281.

Chaungtha (Delta). Chaungtha, on the western rim of the Ayeyarwady Delta, is where middle-class Yangonites come on weekends to party and eat seafood; during the week it's much quieter. See page 145.

Ngwe Saung. Just down the coast from Chaung Tha, this is the more upmarket and peaceful of the Delta's two resorts and has a better choice of accommodation. See page 145.

Myeik Archipelago. Superb beaches and fabulous diving are waiting to be discovered in Myanmar's deep south. See page 300.

Ngwe Saung beach.

Mountains in the Phonkan Razi National Park.

BEST SCENERY & VIEWS

Mandalay Hill (Mandalay). Expansive views over the Konbaung Dynasty's former palace and across the city to the Ayeyarwady River extend from the hill where the Buddha is said to have preached in his lifetime. See page 168.

Sun U Ponya Shin, Sagaing (Mandalay). This whitewashed pagoda, crowning the top of sacred Sagaing Hill, affords an iconic vista over gilded stupa spires and monasteries to the river below. See page 185.

Mingun (Mandalay). The flat top of Mingun's gigantic stupa could have been purpose-built for admiring the glassy expanse of the Ayeyarwady as it flows south to Mandalay. See page 187.

Shwesandaw Temple, Bagan. The upper terraces of this pyramidal stupa offer famous sunset views over the Bagan Archaeological Zone – though you'll have to jostle for space to photograph them. See page 225.

Mount Phonkan Razi (Kachin). Climb this 3,630-metre (11,900ft) snow-dusted summit in the far north for a superb view over the eastern arm of the Himalayas, including the country's highest peak, Hkakabo Razi. See page 265.

Mount Zwegabin, Hpa-an (Kayin State). Spend a night in the monastery at the summit of Mount Zwegabin, the largest of the limestone mountains near Hpa-an, to watch the sun rising over the coastal plain. See page 296.

Kyaikthanlan Pagoda, Mawlamyine (Mon State). This was the stupa that entranced Kipling in his poem *Mandalay*, and the panorama from its terrace across the port city and Andaman Sea is stupendous. See page 293.

BEST HOTELS

Bayview Resort, Ngapali Beach. Right on the sand, the sea-facing teak chalets in this sleek boutique place are the perfect base from which to enjoy Myanmar's dreamiest beach. See page 317.
Governor's Residence, Yangon. The last word in retro-colonial chic. Sip a gin sling on the verandah of this immaculately restored 1920s mansion, Yangon's most stylish place to stay. See page 309.
Hotel by the Red Canal, Mandalay. Blending sumptuous Burmese style with international boutique chic, this small hotel in the suburbs of Mandalay is a haven befitting the city's former royal connections. See

page 311.
Hotel @ Tharabar Gate, Bagan. Luxuriously furnished brick and thatch chalets set amid flower-filled gardens, only a short cycle away from some of Bagan's most striking landmarks. See page 313.
Inle Princess, Inle Lake. Relax in regal fashion on the sunny northeastern shore of Inle Lake, with unbroken views over the water from its elegant pagoda-roofed buildings. See page 314.
Strand, Yangon. Dating from 1903, the Strand is the granddaddy of Myanmar's luxury hotels, where the likes of Somerset Maugham and Rudyard Kipling stayed at the twilight of the British Empire. See page 310.

Governor's Residence

Playing chinlone in Nyuang U.

ONLY IN MYANMAR

White Elephants. Burmese royalty traditionally considered white elephants as auspicious – a superstition maintained by their military successors today, who collect albino pachyderms for good luck in elections. See page 196.
Thanaka. To protect themselves from the burning effects of the sun, Burmese women and children smear their faces in fragrant *thanaka* paste made from aromatic trees. See page 237.
Chinlone. Myanmar's own version of "keepy-uppy" is *the* national sport. You'll see it played informally on the streets and in competitions at temple festivals across the country. See page 327.
Nat Pwe, Taungbyon (Mandalay). Drink-fuelled oracle rituals, music, dance and general

mayhem accompany Myanmar's largest *nat* nature spirit festival. See page 192.
Thingyan festival. Welcoming in the Burmese New Year in mid-April, this three-day water festival is basically an excuse for teenagers to soak each other to the skin at specially erected stalls, or *pandals*. See page 74.
Mohinga pavement cafés. A spicy noodle broth flavoured with tasty fish stock is the quintessential Burmese breakfast, served at pavement cafés in all the major cities. See page 79.
Lahpet. No special occasion is considered complete in Myanmar without a bowl of the national delicacy, fermented or pickled tea leaves, which may be drunk or eaten in a complex salad. See page 80.

Pottery workshop, Kyaukmyaung.

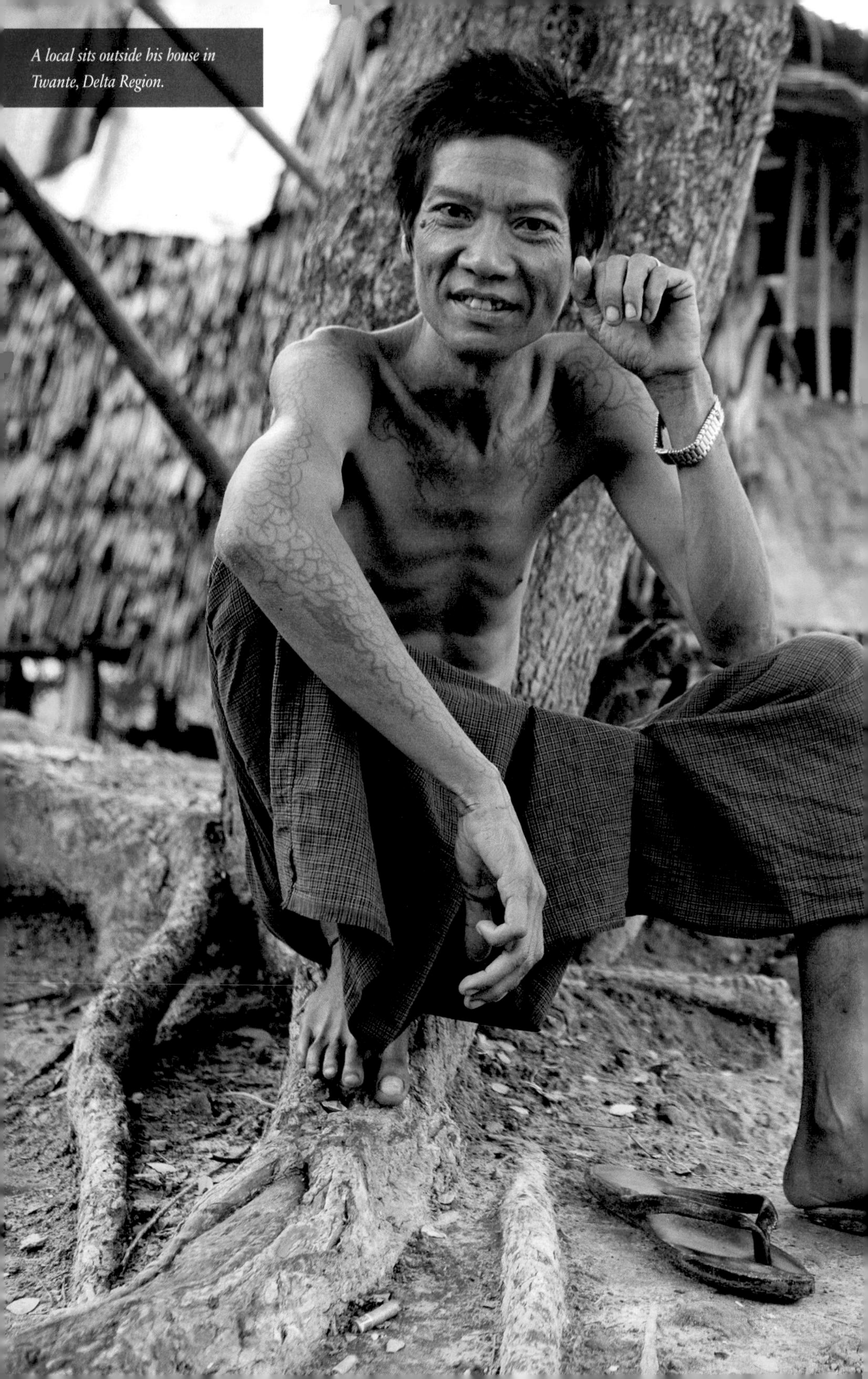

A local sits outside his house in Twante, Delta Region.

Making cheroots in Yin Myo Aung
cheroot factory, Nampam village,
Inle lake region.

Walking across U Bein bridge at sunrise, Amarapura.

To visit Kakku pagoda you need to be accompanied by a guide.

INTRODUCTION

One of the least-known and least developed countries in Southeast Asia, Myanmar is on the threshold of long-overdue change. Now is the perfect time to visit.

*A monk crosses
Taungthaman lake
by boat.*

Myanmar – or Burma as it was named before 1989 – is the most enigmatic country in Southeast Asia. Enfolded by jungle-clad hills, its central river valleys were for centuries the heartland of a classical civilisation about which very little was known by the outside world – a tantalisingly exotic culture of gilded stupas, red-robed monks and elaborately carved teak palaces. Not until the British invasion of 1885 did foreign traders penetrate far beyond its tropical coastline. Since then, constant wars, civil unrest, devastating cyclones and – in recent decades – chronic economic mismanagement by a repressive military junta have compounded the country's isolation.

However, the democratic reforms which ushered in Aung San Suu Kyi's release from house arrest in 2010 look set to bring about dramatic change. With economic sanctions eased and long-running civil wars mostly at an end, the future is looking bright.

Even so, after fifty years in the economic doldrums Myanmar remains locked in a kind of time warp. The former capital, Yangon (Rangoon), may be sprouting skyscrapers, but elsewhere people live in dilapidated low-rise towns and villages made of mud brick and bamboo. Bullocks plough the paddy fields, horse-carts outnumber cars.

*Stupa detail, Mahabodhi
temple, Bagan.*

From a foreign traveller's point of view, this quirky, hand-made, old-world atmosphere makes Myanmar a charismatic place to travel. Traditions of the past remain very much to the fore. Walking the streets of Mandalay in the early morning , you'll see hundreds of shaven-headed monks queuing for alms, young women with fragrant *thanaka* paste smeared over their faces, elderly vegetable sellers puffing on oversized cheroots, and all manner of exotic headgear, from conical straw hats to burgundy turbans. *Htameins* and *longyis*, beautifully patterned batik sarongs, are worn by nearly all women – and most men. The everyday smells in the street can be just as strikingly unfamiliar, along with the wonderful flavours of Burmese cooking, with its pungent mix of spices, seafood sauces and coconut milk.

Just how well this unique way of life will withstand the onslaught of modernity that's waiting in the wings remains to be seen. But for the time being, despite its manifold problems, Myanmar is ripe for exploration, with more world-class monuments than you could possibly see on a 28-day tourist visa, a wealth of vibrant arts and crafts traditions and, not least, inhabitants whose resilience, gentleness and hospitable attitude to foreigners impress every visitor to the country.
Note: we have used Myanmar instead of Burma, except for historical references. The adjective "Burmese" has been retained throughout.

Taking goods home from Taung Tho
market by ox and cart, Inle Lake
region.

LAND OF RICE AND RIVERS

Myanmar is roughly kite-shaped: a diamond with the long Tanintharyi as its tail and the Ayeyarwady as the controlling string.

As the centre of the rice culture on which Myanmar's economy has always been based, the Ayeyarwady (Irrawaddy) is the lifeblood of the land. Rising in the Himalayas, the river crosses the country from north to south for 2,170 km (1,350 miles), emptying into the Andaman Sea through a nine-armed delta. Called "the Road to Mandalay" by British colonialists, the broad river has traditionally been the major transport artery, though in more recent times road, rail and now air travel have played an increasingly important role.

Travellers following the Ayeyarwady's entire course may experience the full range of Myanmar's climatic zones. Beginning at the far north, the river runs through the rugged Kachin Hills, outliers of the Himalayas. At Bhamo, the furthest point to which the Ayeyarwady is navigable by steamer (1,500km/ 930 miles from the delta), it enters the forested valleys and hills of the Shan Plateau. Further downstream, the waters emerge onto the broad dry plain of central Myanmar, the centre of classical Burmese civilisation. The Ayeyarwady then flows past sandbars to the ruins of Bagan and Sri Ksetra (Thayekhittaya), and enters the more fertile southern stretch of its course.

In terms of surface area, Myanmar is the largest country in mainland Southeast Asia. Its population is estimated at about 60 million, of whom about 70 percent live in rural villages. After Yangon, with its population of around 5 million, the major population centres are Mandalay (1 million), Mawlamyine (Moulmein; 500,000) and Pathein (Bassein; 225,000).

Canoeing around Nampam village, Inle Lake region.

Three season cycle

Myanmar is at its best during the dry and relatively cool period from late November to late February. This is the peak tourist season. From March onwards, humidity levels start to build ahead of the annual monsoons, with thermometers soaring well above 40°C (104°F) in the Ayeyarwady Valley around Mandalay by late April. The rains proper erupt in mid-May and last through to October – low season in tourism terms. Travel anywhere in the country at this time is problematic: roads are routinely washed away, rail lines flooded and cyclones wreak havoc on the coastal plains and delta area.

Myanmar's festival calendar is jam-packed and you're sure to come across some kind of celebration during your trip, whenever you choose to come. The biggest events are Yangon's Shwedagon Pwe in February and raucous Thingyan in April, a nationwide knees-up when lots of drinking, singing, dancing and throwing of water marks the start of the Burmese New Year.

Inland navigation

Two rivers besides the Ayeyarwady are important to Myanmar's inland navigation and irri-

economy – as the route by which teak was rafted from the Shan Plateau to Mawlamyine, its export harbour – but now teak is exported via Yangon.

The lie of the land

Geographically, Myanmar can be divided up into several zones. In the far north, are the Kachin Hills, reaching heights of 3,000 metres (10,000ft) on the southeastern edge of the Himalayas. On the Tibetan border is Hkakabo Razi, the highest peak in Southeast Asia at 5,887 metres (19,314ft). Deep valleys, many of them with subtropical vegetation and terraced

Fertiliser made from lake-bed weeds is used to feed these floating gardens in the Inle Lake region.

gation. One, the Chindwin, is a tributary of the Ayeyarwady, flowing through the northwest and joining the larger river about 110km (70 miles) downstream from Mandalay. Readily navigable for 180km (110 miles) upstream from its confluence, it opens up remote stretches of the Sagaing region.

In the east of the country, the Thanlwin (Salween) River slices through Shan State in a series of deep gorges. It has few tributaries between its source in the Himalayas and its exit to the Andaman Sea at Mawlamyine (Moulmein). It is navigable only for about 160km (100 miles) upstream due to its fast current and 20-metre (65ft) fluctuations in water level. It used to play an important role in the

rice fields, separate the mountain ridges. The chief inhabitants are the Kachin; Lisu are also common in the Chinese border region. The administrative centre of Myitkyina is the terminus of the railway from Yangon and Mandalay.

The Kachin Hills link with the Shan Plateau in the south, a vast area averaging 1,000 metres (3,200ft) in elevation. Deep valleys intersect the undulating surface of the plateau, and the Thanlwin (Salween) flows through it like an arrow. Once popular as a site for hill stations, the region still offers the flavour of a bygone era in its administrative centres of Taunggyi, Pyin U-Lwin (Maymyo) and Kalaw. A tourist centre has been developed around Inle Lake in the southwestern part of the plateau. With a European-like climate, fruit, citrus crops and vegetables thrive, as does timber. Myanmar is the world's leading exporter of teak, most of which is harvested in the Shan State. Other crops include rice, peanuts, potatoes, tea, tobacco, coffee, cotton and opium. The "Golden Triangle" encompasses much of the eastern part of the plateau.

East of the Gulf of Mottama (Martaban), Myanmar narrows into a long, thin strip of land called *Tanintharyi* (formerly Tenasserim), with the forested Tanintharyi hills forming the natural border with Thailand. The coastland which follows this range down to the Isthmus of Kra is not easily accessible, for various reasons, but the coastal areas of Mawlamyine and Dawei (Tavoy) are home to pockets of densely populated agricultural land.

Scattered off this southern coast are the isles of the Myeik (Mergui) Archipelago, one of Southeast Asia's least developed island groups. For security reasons it is still off-limits to most Burmese and foreign visitors, although it has begun – slowly – to open up.

West of the Ayeyarwady Delta, on the seaward side of the Rakhaing Yoma hills, is the state of Rakhaing. The flat, fertile coastal strip is characterised by small rivers flowing out of mountains to the north, the highest of which is Mount Victoria at 3,053 metres (10,016ft). Several long and sandy beaches, many undeveloped, run along the coastline.

The central belt of the nation extends around the Ayeyarwady. With its tributary the Chindwin, and the Sittaung, this is the core settlement area of the dominant Bamar (Burman) people. The region is subdivided into two parts – Upper Myanmar, the area surrounding Mandalay, north of Pyay (the former Prome, also called Pyi), and Taungoo; and Lower Myanmar, which focuses on Yangon, and south of the Pyay–Taungoo line.

Rice cultivation

Upper Myanmar is a region of scant rainfall, with farmers using traditional methods of irrigated and dry cultivation in rice-growing. A complicated system of lakes and canals allowed the earliest Burmese civilisations to exist here. Today, more than 8 million hectares (20 million acres) of land are devoted to irrigated rice farming across the country. Crop failures occur at least once a decade, and before rice was available from Lower Myanmar, famine was common. As the delta is now Myanmar's major rice-producing area, an impressive 1.5 million hectares (3.7 million acres) of irrigated land in the so-called Dry Zone is devoted to the farming of cotton, tobacco, peanuts, grain sorghum, sesame, beans and corn.

If Upper Myanmar's agricultural area is impressive, that of Lower Myanmar is astounding. The Ayeyarwady Delta contains 3.6 million hectares (9 million acres) of irrigated rice farms, with a yield great enough to feed the entire population of the country. The delta is expanding into the Andaman Sea at a rate of about 5km (3

Ploughing the fields around Bagan's Dhammayangyi temple.

miles) a century as a result of silt deposits.

When the British arrived in the mid-19th century, the delta region was an uncultivated expanse of jungle. Colonists from the Dry Zone moved south and cleared the jungle to make way for wet-rice fields. For most of the 20th century, until 1962, Burma was the world's largest exporter of rice. The population, though, has grown faster than production, so that the annual amount exported – more than 3 million tonnes in the pre-war years – dropped to 600,000 tonnes by 1976. In recent decades, however, export levels have revived again, peaking at 350,000 tonnes in 2011, a figure that looks set to rise with the introduction of high-yield strains, land reclamation,

Gem Stones

Myanmar's rich natural bounty includes some of the world's largest deposits of precious stones, notably rubies and jade

Gem stone

Ludovico di Varthema, an Italian who visited Burma in 1505, was the first European to report the existence in the country of a seemingly prodigious quantity of gem stones, among them sparkling star rubies which were at the time unknown to the rest

Polishing jade in Mandalay city's jade market.

of the world. Di Varthema was also the first Westerner to prosper from dealing in them. He presented the King of Bago with a gift of corals, and was rewarded with 200 rubies – worth about 100,000 ducats (about US$150,000) in Europe at that time. Today, it is not so easy to get rich in the gem business, but each February hundreds of dealers from all over the world gather in Naypyidaw to try their luck at the famous Gems and Pearl Emporium, where lots are sold by bidding.

Myanmar still holds a world monopoly in rubies. Stones the colour of pigeon blood fetch the highest prices. However, fakes abound these days too. Synthetic stones (often deceptively labelled) are popular at tourist markets. The largest ruby mines

are situated in Mogok, 110km (70 miles) northeast of Mandalay. In earlier times, the kings of Burma appropriated much of the wealth recovered here, leaving the miners with only the smaller stones. When the British annexed Upper Burma in 1886, a year of frenzied digging ensued. But the colonials were able to occupy the Mines District in 1887, and the London firm of Messrs Streeter & Co received sole buying rights for whatever the ground yielded. It made the company's shareholders wildly rich. Today, the nationalised mines provide a steady flow of foreign currency for Myanmar's government.

Naypyidaw also has a major stake in the mining of jade, carried out in the hinterland to the west of Myitkyina in Kachin State, near the town of Mogaung. The riches of this region were well known to the Chinese as long ago as 2000 BC.

As most of Myanmar's natural resources are found where minority ethnic groups live, the way the proceeds are distributed is of crucial importance to the country's future – and has been a major source of controversy, fuelling much of the conflict of the past decades. Opposition groups cite the fact that while the trade has generated phenomenal wealth for the former military junta and its cronies, few, if any, of the benefits have trickled down to ordinary Burmese people in the regions affected by the mining. Illegal trade in gem stones and jade has also provided the main source of income for various ethnic rebel groups fighting the government for greater autonomy.

Since peace has come to Kachin State, the jade mining district has been experiencing a California-style Gold Rush. Prospectors from all over the country have flocked north in search of instant wealth. Some have succeeded, but most end up as day labourers in the larger pits often controlled by ethnic Chinese. Stories of lawlessness and exploitation are rife in this "off limits" area.

Rubies and jade are the most evident examples of Myanmar's precious mineral wealth, but sapphires, oriental aquamarine and emeralds, topaz, amethysts and lapis lazuli are among other stones which attract international buyers to the country.

improved irrigation and more mechanised farming methods.

Minerals and forests

Myanmar has huge, largely untapped mineral reserves. Oil, found mostly in the Ayeyarwady basin, is most important; in recent years, test drilling for natural gas in the Gulf of Mottama has also generated increased revenues for the government-owned Myanmar Oil and Gas Enterprise (MOGE), largely through deals with China. Licences for further oil and gas exploration, both on- and off-shore, should bring badly needed foreign currency into Myanmar over the coming decade

Iron, tungsten, lead, silver, tin, mercury, nickel, plutonium, zinc, copper, cobalt, antimony and gold are found in significant quantities around the country. The famed rubies and sapphires are mined in Mogok in western Shan State, and fine jade is extracted near Mogaung in Kachin State.

Myanmar's vegetation varies according to regional rainfall. Almost half of the country is covered by forest; 13 percent of this is given over to teak and other hardwoods. In wetter districts, tropical rainforests climb the hills to 800 metres (2,625ft) above sea level; bamboo, used in house construction, is common. From this elevation to the snow line at about 3,000 metres (9,842ft), oaks, silver firs, chestnuts and rhododendrons thrive. In the central Dry Zone, cacti and acacia trees are common.

Taunggya (slash-and-burn) cultivation used through much of upland Myanmar has resulted in the depletion of the original forest cover, now replaced by a second growth of scrub forest. In *taunggya* agriculture, large trees are felled and the jungle burned to prepare for planting – often with 40 or more different crops.

When crops and torrential rains have depleted soil fertility (within a year or two), the clearing is abandoned and the land left to fallow for 12 to 15 years. Villages therefore often change sites when the accessible land has been exhausted. About 2.5 million inhabitants still follow this agricultural method.

Burmese wildlife

The great variety of Myanmar's landscapes,

Collecting palm sugar to make jaggery.

climates and habitats – and a relative lack of exploitation – should be reflected in a rich and abundant biodiversity. But the truth is, no one is entirely sure how many species survive, and in what numbers. Wars in remote border areas, in particular, have prevented naturalists from undertaking wide-ranging surveys. The one certainty is that over the past century, increased population, poaching and destruction of natural habitats by loggers and big agro businesses have, inevitably, had a negative impact on the local wildlife.

The willingness of the Burmese government to demarcate national parks and reserves in the 1990s and 2000s was a cause for optimism among conservationists, even if it is generally acknowledged that

OPENING UP

After more than 30 years of restrictive policies and limited access, Myanmar's military rulers have at last opened their doors to international tourism, welcoming everybody from independent travellers to group tours. Visas to visit Myanmar – unobtainable for much of the 1960s, limited to 24 hours in the early 1970s and to one week throughout the 1980s – are now readily available and relatively easy to extend. Geographical restrictions on travel are also being swept away as one closed area after another has been opened up to foreigners. As a consequence, in terms of freedom of movement, there has rarely been a better time to visit.

the junta's motivation stemmed less from a desire to save endangered species than to wrest control of peripheral zones – and their natural resources – from the enemy insurgent groups who formerly occupied them. One of the great hopes for wildlife conservation in Myanmar therefore rests with tourism. Generate sufficient income for local people (and the government) in parks – or so the argument runs – and the poaching, illegal mining and timber extraction will cease – though wildlife tourism as yet barely exists.

The gradual easing of travel restrictions in the remote corners of the country is particularly wel-

Red Panda

comed by wildlife experts because Myanmar's unspoilt forests keep turning up hitherto unknown species. A prime example is the snub-nosed monkey, only discovered in 2010. Local hunters produced carcasses of the rare primate, which they claimed loathed the rain and spent wet days with its head between its knees to stop water dripping in its trademark upturned nose.

Another totally new species, unknown until 1997, is the leaf muntjac – the world's smallest deer, which weighs just 11kg (25lbs). And there have been numerous examples of species appearing that were thought to have become extinct, among them Gurney's pitta, a striking yellow bird with an electric-blue crown, and the Arakan forest turtle, which was believed to survive only in a few

zoos until one was found in the Rakhaing Yoma Elephant Sanctuary in 2007 (see page ###).

The species most likely to attract wildlife tourists, however, is rather better known. An estimated 50 tigers inhabit an area of pristine forest in the Hukawng Valley, in the far north, which the American conservationist, Alan Rabinowitz, successfully lobbied to have turned into a reserve in 2004. At 13,602 sq km (8,452 sq miles), it's the largest tiger reserve in the world, though one under threat from logging, oil and gas exploration, uranium and gold mining – as well as poachers.

One of the principal drivers for illegal hunting in Myanmar is the existence in the east of the country of a booming market for exotic animal parts. In the casino town of Mong La in Shan State, Chinese tourists like to fortify themselves with libido-enhancing tiger's penis or bear's bile soup ahead of sex sessions with local prostitutes.

Apart from tigers, other critically endangered species still present in Myanmar are the Asiatic two-horned Sumatran rhinoceros and one-horned Javan rhinoceros, both of which inhabit the jungle region along the Thai border in the far south. At the opposite end of the country in the Kachin Hills, the red panda is another great rarity that's been spotted in recent years.

Asian elephants are present in safer numbers in Chin and Rakhaing states, where a special sanctuary has been created to protect them. Habitat destruction by illegal logging and capture to work in the timber trade are the main culprits.

With most tourism confined to the river valleys of central Myanmar and western fringe of Shah State, it's unlikely you'll spot any of the region's Big Five mammals in the wild: elephant, tiger, leopard, bear or gaur (Indian bison). You may, however, be lucky enough to encounter the critically endangered Irrawaddy dolphin. Resembling a small beluga with a distinctive round nose, this small cetacean has suffered terribly in recent decades from gill-net fishing and water pollution from gold mining in its stronghold area – a 45km (28-mile) stretch of the Ayeyarwady around Kyaukmyaung (see page 261), where a special dolphin reserve has been created. Only around 30 pairs survive today, though your chances of sighting one are good while cruising the river by ferry.

Environmental issues

Myanmar is one of the least environmentally protected countries in the world, and since 1988, when its military government opened the door to foreign investment in exchange for quick cash, threats to the country's forests, water, soil and biodiversity have spiralled out of control. Moreover, because most Burmese people are ignorant of the problems (the junta has long suppressed any reports of environmental issues), opposition is negligible, although this is now starting to change.

Laws to protect the environment do exist, but they're rarely enforced if there's a profit to be made. As a consequence, logging companies have decimated Myanmar's teak forests. Between

by the government to produce hydroelectricity, dozens of barrages, including a handful of gigantic "mega-dams", are scheduled to be built with Chinese help over the coming decade. Opponents claim the schemes are merely a ruse to earn foreign exchange for the government and its cronies (most of the electricity generated will be exported to China), and will result in the forcible relocation of hundreds of villages, as well as the destruction of important fisheries and fragile ecosystems.

Opposition to the dam-building projects, however, began to gain the upper hand as the

Boats arriving at Nampam market, Inle Lake region.

1990 and 2005, an estimated 18 percent of the country's jungle disappeared. Most of it went illegally across the Chinese border, in exchange for cash to prop up the ailing regime (the trade is worth $250 million annually). But due to the low levels of electrification, vast quantities of wood are also burned for fuel. Deforestation due to population growth is a particular problem in the Dry Zone south of Mandalay, home to around one third of the country's inhabitants.

Further north along the banks of the Ayeyarwady, gold and gem-stone mining are having a disastrous impact on water quality, as tonnes of cyanide, mercury and other chemicals are spilled into the rivers. Dam projects pose another threat to the river system. Promoted

democratic reform process has gathered pace: work on the largest and most controversial scheme, at Myitson in the Upper Ayeyarwady region, was suspended in 2012 in the face of pressure both from Burmese activist groups and foreign governments.

In the rice-growing regions, soil depletion has become a major issue. For the past three decades the military government has forced farmers to double or treble outputs, claiming the lion's share of the harvest at reduced prices for itself, and then selling the rice on the world market for huge profits. As a result, traditional crop rotation has fallen by the wayside, and yields are these days only maintained by costly, and environmentally damaging, inputs of fertilisers.

DECISIVE DATES

A British lithograph (1825) of Shwedagon Pagoda shows the British occupation during the First Anglo-Burmese War.

Early empires

5000–3000 BC
The lower-Palaeolithic Anyathian culture flourishes in northern Burma.

3rd century BC
The Mon, immigrants from Central Asia, settle the Sittaung Valley and establish Buddhism.

1st century AD
The Pyus arrive in the Ayeyarwady Valley, founding their capital near present-day Pyay (Prome).

9th century AD
Known as the Bamar, the Myanmar people from the China-Tibet border settle in the rice-growing area around Bagan, from where they control trade between China and India.

The Burmese dynasties

1084–1113
The Golden Age of Bagan under King Kyanzittha, the great pagoda builder.

1287
Fall of the first Burmese empire following an invasion by the Mongol warlord, Kublai Khan.

1430
Mrauk-U, the last capital of independent Arakan, is established upriver from Sittwe in northwest Burma.

1519
The Portuguese gain the first foothold of any European power in the region, founding a trading post at Mottama (Martaban) in southeast Burma.

1550–81
Bayinnaung, third king of the Taungoo Dynasty, subdues all of the country's rival dynasties and founds the largest empire in the history of Southeast Asia.

1599
Thanlyin falls to Arakan forces led by the Portuguese mercenary, Filipe de Brito e Nicote.

1784
The Burmese annexe Arakan, looting religious relics including the famous Maha Muni statue, and destroying much of the city.

Colonial period to World War II

1824–26
The First Anglo-Burmese War.

1852
In the Second Anglo-Burmese war, Britain annexes all of southern Burma, establishing their capital at Yangon (Rangoon).

1885
The British take the Burmese capital, Mandalay. King Thibaw and his family are sent into exile in India. All of Burma falls under British control.

1886–95
Insurgency breaks out across the country, but the guerrilla uprising is quashed with brutal force by the British.

1941
The Japanese occupy Burma, forcing the Allies northwest into India.

1945
The Burma National Army starts an anti-Japanese uprising as the Allies re-take Burma.

1947
Aung San signs an independence agreement with the UK, but is assassinated,

British World War II soldiers on patrol in the ruins of Bahe town during the advance on Mandalay.

along with six other members of the interim government.

Independence

1948

Burma formally regains independence, unleashing civil war and regional rebellions. U Nu becomes prime minister.

1962

Ne Win sweeps to power in near bloodless coup. He appoints a Revolutionary Council to rule by decree, and implements the economically disastrous "Burmese Road to Socialism".

1964

All political parties are banned and media strictly censored.

1988

Following a period of civil unrest fuelled by economic hardship, major demonstrations are staged at Yangon University. On 8 August 1988 hundreds of thousands mount further protests calling for democracy – the so-called "8888 Revolution".

The SLORC takes power

18 September 1988

A military coup places the State Law and Order Restoaration Council (SLORC) in power and a massive crackdown is launched by the military. Aung San Suu Kyi and colleagues form the National League for Democracy (the NLD).

1989

Burma's name is changed by its military government to Myanmar. Some Western powers refuse to recognise the change.

1990

Aung San Suu Kyi placed under house around while general elections are held.

1991

SLORC refuses to accept the election results. Aung San Suu Kyi is awarded the Nobel Peace Prize.

1992

Myanmar condemned for serious human rights violations.

1993

The Kachin Independence Organisation (KIO) signs a ceasefire agreement with the government, ending a 30-year war in the north.

1995

Aung San Suu Kyi is temporarily freed from house arrest, but returned to confinement five years later.

2003

70 members of the NLD are murdered by a government-sponsored mob in what would become known as the "Depayin Massacre".

2006

The military junta inaugurates a brand-new planned capital called Naypyidaw ("city of kings"), 320km (200 miles) north of Yangon.

The "Saffron Revolution" and beyond . . .

2007

A hike in the price of fuel leads to widespread anti-government protests, which are violently suppressed. Thousands of monks spearhead a growing

Aung San Suu Kyi speaks at a National League for Democracy demonstration near Sule Pagoda, Yangon.

campaign of civil resistance, dubbed the "Saffron Revolution".

May 2008

Cyclone Nargis wreaks devastation across the Ayeyarwady Delta, killing an estimated 200,000 people.

2010

As part of a raft of constitutional reforms, national elections are held, but the NLD condemn the result as fraudulent. Further reforms see a wind down of press censorship and the release of hundreds of political prisoners – among them NLD leader, Aung San Suu Kyi.

2012

Aung San Suu Kyi is one of 44 NLD representatives who enter the Burmese parliament following by-elections across the country. Tourist numbers increase rapidly as the tourism boycott is lifted.

Nat are spirits worshipped by many Burmese in conjunction with their Buddhist beliefs.

FROM EARLIEST TIMES

Settlement by the Mon, the Pyu, the Tai and the Bamar eventually led to a Burmese empire that would in turn fall prey to European imperialism.

According to *The Glass Palace Chronicle of the Kings of Burma* (see below), the first kingdom on Burmese soil was founded in pre-Christian times by Sakyan immigrants from India. However, ethnologists generally agree that the present Bamar (Burman) inhabitants of Myanmar are the descendants of people who originally migrated south from the Sino-Tibetan borderlands.

The "land of gold"

The Mon may have been the first historic group to occupy what is now Myanmar, over 2,000 years ago. These people, whose language belongs to the Mon-Khmer family and who are still to be found in parts of Thailand and Cambodia today, may have come from Central Asia or from eastern India. They settled on the estuaries of the Thanlwin (Salween) and Sittoung (Sittang) rivers, and their civilisation, which Indian chronicles call *Suvannabhumi* ("Land of Gold"), is also mentioned in ancient Chinese and Arab chronicles.

Legend says it was the Mon who laid the foundation stone of the Shwedagon Pagoda as far back as 2,500 years ago. While this is difficult to prove, it is known that the Mon first established the Buddhist tradition in Burma. By the 3rd century BC, the Mon already enjoyed close ties with the realm of King Ashoka in India through the port of Thaton on the southeast coast.

About two millennia ago, the Pyu settled in Upper Burma, and set up their first capital at Sri Ksetra (Thayekhittaya) (see page 156), close to present-day Pyay (Prome). The brick ruins here still clearly show extensive evidence of their brand of religious architecture – mainly

Vishnu is the Supreme god in the Hindu pantheon.

Buddhist in style, but with a noticeably strong Brahman influence. Some time around the 8th century AD, the capital was relocated north to Halin, in the region of Shwebo.

At about the same time, the Tai people were pressing southward from their ancestral home in Yunnan, southwest China. They subjugated Upper Burma in the 9th century, capturing Halin in 832, and assimilating the population.

The First Burmese Empire

It was also in the 9th century that the Bamar people first made their appearance. Moving southwards from the China-Tibet border area, they travelled down the Ayeyarwady and quickly

Despite his attempts to defend his empire, Narathihapate was branded Tarok-pyemin, which means "the king who ran away from the Chinese".

established themselves as the major power in the rice-cultivating region of Upper Burma. From the fortified town of Bagan, they controlled the Ayeyarwady and Sittoung river valleys and the trade routes between China and India, which passed through their territory.

Anawrahta established the First Burmese Empire in 1057 when he suddenly and over-whelmingly conquered the Mon capital of Thaton. He returned to Bagan with 30,000 prisoners, including the Mon royal family and many master builders. Other Mon and Pyu settlements submitted to Anawrahta's dominance over Burma, and the king reigned for 33 years.

Ironically, despite the Mon's defeat, their culture became dominant in the Bamar capital. The Mon language replaced Pali and Sanskrit in royal inscriptions, and the Theravada Buddhist religion became the state religion (the Bamar

Four of the 28 Buddhas in the Dhammacakka Mudra, Payathonzu Temple.

THE GLASS PALACE CHRONICLE

In 1829, King Bagyidaw of Burma appointed a committee of scholars to write a chronicle of the Burmese monarchy, which became a 19th-century history and mythology of the entire country. The committee consisted of "learned monks, learned brahmans and learned ministers" who compiled a record "which they sifted and prepared in accordance with all credible records". The resulting chronicle, which takes its name from Bagyidaw's Palace of Glass where the compilation was made, recounts the story of Buddhism and of the Buddhist kings of ancient India, as well as the history of the early Burmese kingdoms to the fall of Bagan.

having previously practised animism). Through the close relations maintained by the Mon with Sri Lanka, at that time the centre of Theravadin culture, "the way of the elders" spread throughout most of mainland Southeast Asia. Under this new influence, especially that of the monk Shin Arahan, Anawrahta became a devout Theravada Buddhist. He commissioned the building of the Shwezigon Pagoda in Nyaung U (near Bagan; see page 218), as well as other shrines on the plain.

Bagan's golden age

Having defeated the Mon, the Bamar were now in control of much of lowland Burma, and a golden age of pagoda building began, with a great deal of construction taking place during the reign of Anawrahta's second successor, Kyanzittha (1084–1113). Kyanzittha, whose name means "soldier lord", came to power after defeating a Mon rebellion during which Anawrahta's son and successor, Sawlu, was killed. Like Anawrahta, Kyanzittha was a deeply religious man. He ordered the construction of the Ananda Temple and – an indication of his vast wealth – sent a ship filled with treasures to India to assist in the restoration of the Mahabodhi Temple in Bodhgaya, the place of Buddha's enlightenment. Kyanzittha gave his daughter away in marriage to a Mon prince, and chose their son, Alaungsithu, as successor to preserve the unity of the Burmese Empire.

Bagan's golden age came during the 12th century, when it acquired the name "city of the four million pagodas". In common with the other great civilisation in the region at the time – Angkor – the kingdom was supported by rice cultivation, made possible by a highly developed system of irrigation canals. But in the middle of the 13th century, the empire began to crumble as the Tai – known to the Bamars as Shan – threatened from the northeast.

The end of the empire

The end of the Bagan empire was hastened when the Mongol armies of Kublai Khan appeared on the scene. Fresh from overrunning the Nan-Chao Empire in Yunnan, Kublai Khan now demanded payment of tribute by the Bagan emperors. King Narathihapate, overestimating the strength of his own forces, refused.

When the Mongol forces invaded Burma in a series of battles in the late 13th century, advancing as far as present-day Bhamo, it is said that, in desperation, Narathihapate pulled down 6,000 temples to fortify Bagan's city walls. He died soon after, poisoned by his own son, the ruler of Pyay. The end result was the conquest of Bagan by the Mongols in 1287.

After the fall of Bagan, Burma was divided into several small states for almost 300 years. In Lower Burma, the Mon founded a new kingdom centred on Bago (Pegu). Although they lost their grip on Tanintharyi (Tenasserim) during a mid-14th-century invasion by the Thai (Siamese) from Ayutthaya, they managed to hold the rest of their realm together. In Upper Burma, meanwhile, the Shans established

sovereignty over a kingdom with its capital at Inwa (Ava). And in the west, along the Bay of Bengal, the Rakhaing spread north to Chittagong in what is now Bangladesh.

The Portuguese period

It was in the 15th century that Europeans first appeared in Burma. In 1435, a Venetian merchant named Nicolo di Conti visited Bago and remained for four months. Six decades later, in 1498, the Portuguese seafarer Vasco da Gama discovered the sea route from Europe to India. His countrymen were very quick to

Kublai Khan invaded the Bagan Kingdom of Burma in 1277, 1283 and 1287.

take advantage of his great success: Alfonso de Albuquerque conquered Goa in 1510, and within a year Malacca, the spice centre of the Orient, was in his grasp.

It was from these two ports that the Portuguese sought to establish a monopoly over the commerce of the Indian Ocean. Antony Correa arrived in Mottama (Martaban) in 1519 and signed a trade and settlement treaty with the town's viceroy which gave the Portuguese a base from which to trade with Siam.

The most remarkable character from the Portuguese era in Burma was Philip de Brito y Nicote. He came to Asia as a cabin boy and later accepted a post in the court of King Razagyi of

Rakhaing, who had conquered Bago. De Brito was entrusted with the job of running the customs administration in Thanlyin (Syriam). But before long, he had built forts and placed the town under Portuguese sovereignty. After a trip to Goa, during which he married the viceroy's

Filipe de Brito, Portuguese mercenary and governor of Syriam, c. 1600.

daughter, he returned to Thanlyin with supplies and reinforcements to withstand native sieges – which had already been attempted by the rulers of Bamar and Rakhaing – and proclaimed himself king of Lower Burma.

De Brito's superior naval power forced all seagoing trade through his port of Thanlyin. He displayed utter contempt for Buddhist beliefs and destroyed and plundered monuments: during his 13-year reign, 100,000 native people are said to have converted to Christianity.

In 1613, Anaukhpetlun of Taungoo stormed Thanlyin with 12,000 men. Around 400 Portuguese defended the town for 34 days but de Brito was captured and impaled: it took him three days to die.

In north Burma, meanwhile, hill tribes razed the Shan capital of Inwa in 1527. The Bamar population withdrew to the town of Taungoo, where Tabinshweti established his empire before moving it to Bago. Bamar control then extended down the coast to Dawei (Tavoy) and west to Pyay, before overwhelming the Shan and conquering the Thai kingdoms of Lan Na and (briefly) Ayutthaya far to the west, thus extending Burma's boundaries to the maximum.

During the 17th century, the Dutch, British and French set up trading companies in Burma's coastal ports. When the country's capital was transferred back to Inwa, it was retaken by the Mon in 1752 with the help of French arms. As a result, the Second Burmese Empire foundered and dissolved. Soon afterwards, however, Alaungpaya, a Bamar from Shwebo, founded the Third Burmese Empire. He defeated the Mon, deported the French to Bayingyi, and got rid of British trading posts. Mon resistance ceased entirely, and the Mon people either fled to Siam or submitted to Bamar rule.

British control

Alaungpaya's second successor, Hsinbyushin, attacked Ayutthaya in Siam in 1767 and returned to Inwa with artists and craftsmen who gave a fresh cultural impetus to the Burmese kingdom. Bodawpaya, who took the throne in 1782, conquered Rakhaing, bringing the borders of his kingdom right up against the British sphere of influence in Bengal. On the advice of his soothsayers, he moved his capital to Amarapura, not far from Inwa. Because Burma and British India now shared a common boundary, the number of border incidents increased.

Serious conflict was sparked after King Bagyidaw came to the throne in 1819. The Raja of Manipur, who had previously paid tribute to the Burmese Crown, did not attend Bagyidaw's coronation. The subsequent punitive expedition took the Burmese into the Indian state of Cachar, and this intrusion was used by the British as a pretext for what is now called the First Anglo-Burmese War.

The Burmese underestimated the strength of the British, and were soundly defeated. In the Treaty of Yandabo (1826), the Burmese were forced to cede Rakhaing and Taninthayi, plus the Assam and Manipur border areas they had controlled since 1819, to the European victors. The British thereby succeeded in making secure their exposed flank on the Bay of Bengal.

The Burmese were without a capable ruler through the first half of the 19th century, and this weakened the kingdom just at the wrong time. When British and French interests collided in Southeast Asia, Burma's independence was rapidly nearing an end. In 1852, two British sea captains registered a complaint about unfair treatment in a Burmese court.

Synod of Buddhism, during which the great Buddhist scripture, known as the *Tipitaka*, was committed to stone. Mindon wanted the sacred scriptures to be conserved in a way that they would be available until the coming of the Maitryea Buddha. Some 2,400 scribes worked on the text, which was then chiselled onto 729 tablets of stone and a pagoda was built over each of the tablets at the base of Mandalay Hill. But even this appeal for a return to the values of Buddhism, which would thereby sustain the Burmese state and people, could not alter the course of history.

The original Mandalay Palace compound was constructed between 1857 and 1859.

The British Empire responded by sending an expeditionary force to Burma. In the Second Anglo-Burmese War, this force quickly conquered Lower Burma.

Mindon's Mandalay

It was about this time that King Mindon (1853–1878) came to power in Amarapura. His was a relatively enlightened rule, and he was the first Burmese sovereign to attempt to bring the country more in line with Western ideas. In 1861, commemorating the 2,400th anniversary of the Buddha's first sermon, Mindon transferred his court to the new city of Mandalay.

Mandalay was sacred to the Buddhist faith, and in 1872 Mindon hosted the Fifth Great

KING MINDON

The king of Burma between 1853 and 1878, Mindon deposed his brother Pagan Min in 1852, occupying Amarapura in 1853. In 1857, he transferred his capital to Mandalay. Sources characterise Mindon as a man of high moral standards who did his best, in difficult circumstances, to preserve Burmese independence while maintaining relations with Britain. A pious Buddhist, he welcomed Christian missionaries to his country and sent missions to the courts of Britain, France and Italy. In 1861, he introduced coinage and reorganised the tax system, greatly improving Burmese state finances. He died at the age of 64, without choosing a successor.

Supayalat, pictured centre, was the last queen of Burma (r.1878–85).

BRITISH RULE AND WORLD WAR II

In the late 19th century, Burma was annexed as a province of British India, a move that still has repercussions today.

King Mindon was succeeded by Thibaw in 1878, and the new sovereign wasted little time in alienating the British. Most provocatively, he was negotiating an agreement with the French – who were seeking a direct trade route to China – for shipping rights on the Ayeyarwady. This was clearly contrary to the interests of the British. The final straw came when a British timber company became embroiled in a dispute with Thibaw's government; the king was given an ultimatum which he chose to ignore. In no time, British troops had invaded Upper Burma: encountering almost no resistance, they easily overwhelmed the capital.

British Burma

On 1 January 1886, Burma ceased to exist as an independent country. Thibaw and his queen, Supayalat, were sent into exile, and Burma was annexed as a province of British India.

To facilitate their exercise of power over all of Burma, the British permitted the autonomy of the country's many racial minorities. As early as 1875, they had enforced the autonomy of the Kayin (Karen) states by refusing to supply King Mindon with the arms he needed to put down a Kayin revolt. The repercussions of this and other similar political moves by the British are still influencing the country today.

Throughout Upper and Lower Burma, the British assumed all government positions down to district officer level. In the bordering states where Chin, Kachin, Shan and various other minorities predominated, they relied on indirect rule, permitting the respective chieftains to govern in their place. Military forces were

British Army officers pose at the base of a pagoda at Wuntho, c.1891.

largely recruited from India and the northern hill tribes. During most of the colonial period the Bamar were barred from admission to the armed forces.

British interest in Burma was principally of an economic nature. So it is understandable that an economic upswing took place after 1886. The Ayeyarwady Delta had been opened up for rice cultivation and colonised following the British occupation of Lower Burma in 1852. A generation later, this move began to pay significant dividends. Economic growth was to the advantage both of the British, who controlled the rice exports, and Indian moneylenders and merchants, who were far more sophisticated than the Burmese in their familiarity with a money economy. In particular, the *chettyars*, a caste of moneylenders from south India, profited greatly from Burma's agricultural expansion.

In the five years following annexation of Upper Burma, a quasi-guerrilla war tied up some 10,000 Indian troops in the country. The guerrillas were led by *myothugyis*, local leaders of the old social structure. This resistance declined after 1890, however, and from this time on the Burmese attempted to adjust to the far-reaching social and economic changes that were taking place.

Following World War I, India was granted a degree of self-government by its British rulers, but Burma remained under the direct control of the Colonial Governor. This led to extensive opposition within the country, highlighted by a lengthy boycott of schools beginning in December 1920. Eventually, in 1923, the same concessions granted to India – known as the "dyarchy reform" – were extended to Burma.

The British embassy in Amarapura.

SCOTT OF THE SHAN HILLS

Sir James George Scott, who is also known by his Burmese pseudonym Shway Yoe, was a prominent British administrator, soldier, explorer and writer who lived in Burma during the latter half of the 19th century. Scott was chiefly remarkable for his ability to assimilate Burmese customs and language, as well as for his love of the country and its people. The founder of Taunggyi (a place of respite for the British from the tropical heat) and one of the most respected colonial officers in the history of British Burma, Scott was a personal friend of King Thibaw, but later became a colonial administrator following the annexation of the Shan States in 1890. He is credited with introducing football to Burma, as well as for such major academic endeavours as producing the multi-volume Gazetteer of Shan State. His most famous work, *The Burman: His Life and Notions* (1882), published under the pseudonym "Shway Yoe – Subject of the Great Queen", presented so authentic an image of Burma that some contemporary reviewers mistakenly believed it to be the work of a prominent Bamar scholar. Scott went on to serve as British Commissioner of India in 1897. The book has been republished many times, and still remains an invaluable sourcebook for all those wishing to understand Bamar life cycles, society, religion and culture.

The rise of nationalism

A major revolt took place in the Tharrawaddy region north of Yangon between 1930 and 1932. Saya San, a former monk, organised a group of followers called *galon* (after the mythical bird Garuda), and convinced them that British bullets could not harm them. In a subsequent battle, 3,000 of his supporters were killed and another 9,000 were taken prisoner, of whom 78, including Saya San, were executed.

Throughout the early 1930s, opinion was split in Burma as to whether the country should be separated from British India or not. The question was resolved in 1935 when the "Government of Burma Act" was signed in London. Two years later, Burma became a separate colony with its own legislative council. This council dealt only with "Burma Proper", however, and not with the indirectly administered border states.

However, as Burma was granted greater autonomy, the underground nationalist movement gathered momentum. In 1930, at the University of Yangon, the All Burma Student Movement emerged to defy colonial rule. The young men who spearheaded this group studied Marxism and called each other *Thakin* ("master"), a term generally used to address Europeans. In 1936, the group's leaders – Thakin Aung San and Thakin Nu – boldly led another strike of university and high-school classes in opposition to the "alien" educational system.

The success of their movement in bringing about major reforms helped to give these men the confidence in the following decade to come to the forefront of the nationalist movement.

Meanwhile, however, war was brewing. The "Burma Road" made that inevitable. Built as an all-weather route in the 1930s to carry supplies and reinforcements to Chinese troops attempting to repulse the Japanese invasion, it was of extreme strategic importance. As Allied forces moved to defend the road, Japan planned an all-out attack on the Burmese heartland.

The colonial government unexpectedly played into Japanese hands when it arrested several leaders of the Thakin group in 1940. Aung San escaped by disguising himself as a Chinese crewman on a Norwegian boat. He arrived in Amoy seeking contact with Chinese communists to help in Burma's drive for independence. But the Japanese arrested him, and although his movement was opposed to Japan's war on China, his release was negotiated on the grounds that he

> In Burmese the term shikoe means the act of touching one's head to the floor before the presence of an honoured person, a Buddha image or a Buddhist monk.

and other members of the Thakin organisation would collaborate with the Japanese.

In March 1941, Aung San returned to Yangon aboard a Japanese freighter. He secretly picked out 30 members of the Thakin group (the "Thirty Comrades") to be trained

Japanese soldiers in Moulmein, 1942.

by the Japanese on Hainan Island in guerrilla warfare.

A brutal battlefield

In December 1941, the Japanese landed in Lower Burma. Together with the "Burmese Liberation Army" led by Aung San, they overwhelmed the British, drove them from Yangon four months later, then convincingly won battle after battle. British, Indian, Chinese and American troops suffered heavy casualties and were forced to retreat to India. While World War II raged in fury in Europe and the Pacific, the fighting was nowhere more bitter than in the jungles of Southeast Asia. Hand-to-hand combat was a frequent necessity, and tens of thousands of

Allied soldiers were killed, along with hundreds of thousands of Burmese. The 27,000 Allied graves in the Htaukkyan cemetery near Yangon are but one testimony to the horrors that took place. Survivors of this conflict emerged from the jungle with stories of suffering, sacrifice and heroic deeds. They made household names out of such warriors as "Vinegar Joe" Stilwell, "Old Weatherface" Chennault, Wingate's Chindits and Merrill's Marauders.

In February 1942, Joseph Warren Stilwell was sent by the US government as the senior military representative to the China-Burma-India theatre.

every major town along the escape route. There were hundreds of thousands of civilian casualties, and only 12,000 British-Indian troops reached Assam safely. Some 30,000 perished.

All 114 of Stilwell's charges reached the haven of India, just as the general had pledged. But "Vinegar Joe" was riled. "I claim we got run out of Burma," he told a press conference in Delhi some days later. "It is humiliating as hell. I think we ought to find out what caused it, go back and retake it." Stilwell's words helped guide the Allied war effort in Burma from that point on. He and British General William Slim retraced

A group of Chindits having crossed a river on their march into Burma, c.1943.

Within two months of his arrival, Stilwell was struggling through Upper Burma, a mere 36 hours ahead of Japanese troops, trying desperately to reach the safety of the British lines in India.

Stilwell's retreat

There were 114 soldiers, mainly Chinese, in Stilwell's party. "Vinegar Joe" promised each one of them they would reach India. His retreat – which he called "eating bitterness," citing a Chinese proverb – involved 1,500km (930 miles) of trekking through formidable jungles with no hope of outside assistance. At about the same time, 42,000 members of the British-Indian army began to withdraw. The Japanese were right on the tail of the Allied retreat, burning

their steps along the same difficult route – out of Assam, across the Chindwin River to Myitkyina, and down the Ayeyarwady River to Mandalay. Yangon was finally recaptured on 3 May 1945.

Wingate's Chindits

While Stilwell is perhaps best remembered for his retreat, others gained their greatest fame on the offensive. One of these men was General Orde Charles Wingate, a Briton whose deep penetration teams used guerrilla tactics to slip behind the Japanese lines and block supplies. Known as Chindits – after the mythological *chinthe*, the lions that guard temples throughout Burma – the troops were an amalgam of British, Indian, Chin, Kachin and Gurkha units.

The return to Burma of a large land force to combat the Japanese depended very much on a usable road. US Army engineers undertook the task with a unit consisting mostly of Americans. Called the Ledo Road, the new route was to reach from Assam to Mong Yo, where it would join the Burma Road and then continue into Chinese Yunnan.

For more than two years, several thousand engineers and 35,000 native workers laboured in one of the world's most inaccessible areas. The war was almost over by the time the 800km (500-mile) road was completed. Japanese snip-

to be known, was one of the most hazardous passages of the war. Between Dinjan air base in Assam and the town of Kunming in Yunnan lay 800km (500 miles) of rugged wilderness. Planes had to fly over the Himalayan outliers with its 6,000-metre (20,000ft) peaks, as well as the 3,000-metre (9,843ft) -high Naga Hills, the 4,500-metre (14,700ft) -high Santsung range, and the jungle-covered gorges of the Ayeyarwady, Thanlwin (Salween) and Mekong rivers.

About 1,000 men and 600 planes were lost during the operation. In fact, so many planes went down on one of the many unnamed peaks of "The

A soldier guards a line of American P-40 fighter planes painted with the shark-face emblem of the Flying Tigers.

ers killed 130 engineers, hundreds more lost their lives through illness and accidents, and the Ledo Road became known as "the man-a-mile road". Built down deep gorges and across raging rapids, it traversed a jungle where no road had passed before.

Despite the immense effort that went into the building of this vital link between India and Southeast Asia, today it is overgrown and virtually impassable to motor traffic. For more on the Ledo Road, see page 45.

Flying "The Hump"

Until the Ledo Road was completed, supplies had to be flown to the Allied forces in western China. The air link over "The Hump", as it came

ROYAL PALACE OF MANDALAY

The palace is located at the centre of a royal enclosure within Mandalay City, built by King Mindon in 1857. The former royal city is a mile square, surrounded by a moat 70 metres (225ft) wide and 3 metres (11ft) deep. The surrounding walls are 8.5 metres (27ft) high and 3 metres (10ft) thick. After annexation by the British, it was renamed Fort Dufferin, and parts of the wall were demolished to permit railway tracks to pass through the enclosure. In March 1945, the palace buildings were badly damaged by fire during fighting between Allied and Japanese forces. Now restored, the former royal palace is set amid lands used by the Burmese Army.

Hump" that it was nicknamed the "Aluminum Plated Mountain". The C-46, the workhorse of the transport operation, was often overloaded, and its pilots, flying up to 160 hours a month, were overworked. During 1944, three men died for every 1,000 tonnes of cargo flown into Yunnan.

Chennault's "Flying Tigers"

Another air unit which achieved fame in the Burma war were the "Flying Tigers" of "Old Weatherface" Chennault. Volunteer pilots from the US Army, Navy and Marine Corps fought for only seven months under Chennault. But

Before they were incorporated into the 14th US Air Force, this band of heroic volunteers – who made their planes look like airborne sharks and who painted Japanese flags on their planes' bodies for every enemy aircraft shot down – built a legend which lingers even today.

Merrill's Marauders

While the US provided an estimated 50 percent of the air strength to the Allied counteroffensive in Burma, there was only one US ground unit involved in the theatre. It had an unmemorable name: the 5307th Composite Unit. But

Tombstones and the memorial at the Taukkyan British war cemetery.

during that period they became so feared by the Japanese that a Tokyo radio broadcaster called them "American guerrilla pilots" for their unorthodox tactics.

These same tactics, masterminded by Chennault, put him in head-on conflict with General Stilwell. While Stilwell pressed for an infantry-led reconquest of Burma, Chennault intended to win the war through air superiority. Ironically, both men had to leave the Asian theatre before the war had ended, but not before Chennault had left his unforgettable mark.

During their brief offensive, the "Flying Tigers" destroyed as many as 1,900 Japanese aircraft, while losing 573 planes themselves.

behind this title was one of the toughest volunteer fighting teams the US Army has ever assembled.

The troops called themselves "Galahad Force" but they were better known as "Merrill's Marauders", after their commander General Frank Merrill. Originally intended to join Wingate's Chindits, General Stilwell designated them for his own deep-penetration operations.

From the border of Assam to Myitkyina, these soldiers went head-to-head with Japanese forces. It was a formidable task. By the time the unit was disbanded in the summer of 1944, there were 2,394 casualties out of an original 2,830 men.

The Ledo Road

The Upper reaches of the Hukawng Valley may be a wilderness zone today, but in World War II the region was crossed by one of Asia's busiest transport arteries: the infamous Ledo Road.

One of the most impressive mountain routes in Asia snakes across the jungle-covered hills lining Myanmar's border with India – though no one has used it to traverse the international boundary for decades. Beginning at the Indian railhead town of Ledo in Assam, the unsurfaced track snakes 61km (38 miles) uphill to crest the jungle-covered Patkai Range at the Pangsau Pass (3,727m/1,136ft), on the frontier, and from there runs via an impressive series of switchbacks to Tan-Nai in Myanmar. You can just about trace its muddy course on Google Earth, but access is extremely difficult in this politically unstable region.

The extraordinary road was a key component in US General Joseph "Vinegar Joe" Stilwell's plan to build a year-round, all-weather land link between northeast India and southwest China. The aim was to help supply Chinese armies fighting the Japanese, who would otherwise have been cut off behind a wall of mountains for nine months of the year. Through the early phases of the war, the Chinese Nationalist Army (Kuomintang) had to be re-provisioned via a massive, and perilous, airlift over the treacherous eastern arm of the Himalayas,

U.S. Army trucks wind along the Ledo Road.

nicknamed "the Hump". More than a dozen planes and their crews were lost flying this notoriously difficult route, and Stilwell was desperate to replace it. Churchill, however, disagreed, claiming the plan would prove "as immense, laborious task, unlikely to be finished until the need for it has passed."

In the event, the British prime minister's prediction proved spot-on. Of the 15,000 US troops and 35,000 local Burmese coolies drafted in as a labour force, 1,100 American servicemen and a considerably greater number of Burmese lost their lives to landslides, disease and Japanese snipers before the track was declared open for business in

The twists and turns of the Ledo Road.

January 1945 – by which time the Japanese were in full retreat. More gallinwg still for Vinegar Joe must have been the fact that the airlift proved capable of carrying ten times more supplies per day to the Chinese armies than could be carried by truck on the Ledo Road.

In spite of the suffering and death toll required to build it, the route gradually fell into disuse after the war. Traversing a region long held by Naga and Kachin rebels, it's closed to regular traffic today, but may well open in future if the 2011 cease-fire holds, allowing tourists to visit the beautiful "Lake of No Return", close to the border – a serene body of water whose name derives from its wartime reputation among airmen as Burma's Bermuda Triangle.

INDEPENDENCE AND MILITARY RULE

Post-war independence led to dictatorial leadership, economic hardships and conflict between the government and minority groups. Hard-won political changes, however, are finally bringing a measure of freedom to the long-suffering population.

By 1943, it was evident that the Japanese wanted to see Burma's government, which they had helped establish, become subordinate to the Imperial Japanese Army. Burma was declared "independent" in August of that year, with Dr Ba Maw, former education minister, as head of the puppet state, Thakin Aung San was named minister of defence, and Thakin Nu was chosen as foreign secretary.

The Burmese nationalists, however, were not pleased with the arrangement. In December 1944, Aung San established contact with the Allies, and in March 1945 he switched sides, with his 10,000-man army now ready to fight the Japanese. Now called the "Patriotic Burmese Forces", they helped the Allies recapture Yangon. The Japanese surrender was signed in Burma's capital on 28 August.

Results of war

The war had completely devastated Burma. That which had not been destroyed during the Japanese attack was laid to waste during the Allied onslaught. There were, however, two positive results for the Burmese: their experience of nominal self-government, and the weakening of British power and prestige. It was clear Burma could no longer remain under the former colonial constitution. Yet the British, climbing back into the driver's seat after the wartime hiatus, had other ideas, having planned a three-year period of direct rule for Burma.

Meanwhile, Aung San was quietly building up two important nationalist organisations. One of these was the Anti-Fascist People's Freedom League, a Marxist-oriented group better known by its acronym (AFPFL). As the military wing of this political league, Aung San

U Nu pictured in 1962 during his time under house arrest.

founded the People's Volunteer Organisation (PVO), which, as early as 1946, claimed 100,000 (mostly unarmed) members.

Despite the growth of nationalist sentiment behind the AFPFL, the British remained firmly in control of Burma until September 1946. Then, a general strike, first by the police, then by all government employees plus railway and oil workers' unions, brought the country to a standstill. The colonial government turned to the AFPFL and other nationalist groups for help. A moderate national council was formed, and the strike ended in early October.

The AFPFL took advantage of the weakened position of the British to seize the political

The term "U" is added to the names of senior figures in Myanmar to convey honour and respect.

initiative. Aung San presented a list of demands to the British Labour government, which included the granting of total independence to Burma by January 1948.

A conference was promptly called in London in January 1947. Burma was awarded its independence as demanded, but there were several difficult questions to resolve in nego-

Watched by Indian soldiers, Japanese officers surrender their swords (1945).

tiations, especially concerning ethnic minorities. The AFPFL representative insisted upon complete independence for all of Burma, including the minority regions; the British were concerned about the consequences of continual friction between the Bamar and other groups.

In February, however, Aung San met with minority representatives at Panglong in Shan State. The result was a unanimous resolution that all the ethnic groups would work together with the Burmese interim government to achieve independence for the minority regions in a shorter space of time. After a period of 10 years, each of the major groups that formed a

state would be permitted to secede from the Union if they so desired.

National independence

National elections for a Constituent Assembly were held in April 1947 and Aung San and his AFPFL won an overwhelming majority of seats. But on 19 July, as the new constitution was still being drafted, tragedy struck. A group of armed men burst in on a meeting of the interim government and assassinated nine people, including Aung San and six of his ministers. U Saw, right-wing prime minister of the last prewar colonial government, was convicted of instigating the murders and later executed.

Thakin Nu, one of the early leaders of the All Burma Student Movement, and later of the AFPFL, was asked by the British colonial government to step into Aung San's shoes. Thakin Nu (now known as U Nu; see panel) became prime minister when on 4 January 1948, at the astrologically auspicious hour of 4.20am, the "Union of Burma" became an independent nation. In so doing, Burma became the first former British colony to sever ties with the Commonwealth.

No sooner had Burma been thrust into solving its own problems than it came face-to-face with the bitter realities of nationhood. The first three years of independence were marked by violent domestic confrontations and a militarisation of daily life. No less than five separate groups, including the Kayin, opposed to membership in the "Union of Burma" took up arms against the newly founded state.

Lieutenant General Ne Win was appointed commander-in-chief of the armed forces, and soon thereafter minister of defence. The Bamar, who had not been allowed in the armed forces since the British took over in 1886, assumed all the high-ranking military posts, and all mutinous Kayin were discharged from active service. Under Ne Win, the army gained an upper hand in the early 1950s.

Economic disaster

In economic terms, the first few years of independence were disastrous for Burma. Income from rice exports plummeted and tax revenue diminished, yet the expenditure that was needed to maintain the oversized military machine continued to grow.

U Nu and the AFPFL kept a firm grip on power during the 1951 national elections. But a schism within the party soon disrupted the government's programme of economic development. The Eight-Year Plan of 1953, produced by a team of US experts and called Pyidawtha (Happy Land), had to be abandoned in 1955 due to the increasing intra-party disputes.

In 1958, the squabbling had become so serious that the government was virtually paralysed. U Nu was forced to appoint a caretaker government, with General Ne Win at its helm. The 18-month administration was stern, but made progress in cleaning up the cities, modernising the archaic bureaucracy and establishing free and fair elections.

The elections were held in February 1960, and the U Nu faction of the AFPFL, renamed the Pyidaungsu (Union) Party, regained power. U Nu's campaign promises inspired scepticism, however. He sought to have Buddhism recognised as the state religion. He also promised the Mon and Rakhaing people semi-autonomy. The promises spurred the Shan and Kayah to demand the right of secession granted them in the 1948 constitution, and again the U Nu government was thrown into turmoil. There was little resistance when Ne Win swept into power in a nearly bloodless coup on 2 March 1962.

The road to socialism

Ne Win's first move was to appoint a Revolutionary Council made up entirely of military personnel. On 30 April, the council published its manifesto, which was titled *The Burmese Way to Socialism*.

For 12 years, Ne Win ruled by decree, with all power vested in the Revolutionary Council. Foreign businesses were nationalised, and the state took control of all businesses, including banks. The army was put in charge of commerce and industry. A foreign policy of self-imposed isolation and neutrality was pursued.

In May 1970, U Nu announced the formation of a National United Liberation Front (NULF), an alliance between his followers, the Mon and Kayin, as well as a smattering of Shan and Kachin. He claimed to have an army of 50,000, although that figure may well have been exaggerated. In 1971, the rebels launched successful raids from the Thai border, and, for a while, held territory inside Burma.

In Burma, meanwhile, Ne Win was reforming the government structure and introducing a constitutional authoritarianism. First, in an effort

to "civilianise" the system, he dropped his military title. On 2 March 1974, the Revolutionary Council was officially disbanded and the "Socialist Republic of the Union of Burma" was born. Ne Win became president of the nation and chairman of the Burma Socialist Program Party; various leaders of the armed forces filled 16 of the 17 ministerial posts.

In foreign affairs, Burma shocked much of the world in September 1979 when it became the first country to withdraw from the 88-member Non-Aligned Movement. Impatience with "big powers engaged in a behind-the-scene struggle

General Ne Win, the first military commander to be appointed prime minister of Burma.

for exerting their influence on the movement" was the official government explanation for the decision to pull out.

Ne Win stepped down from the presidency in November 1981. U San Yu, a loyal disciple, was elected to succeed him. Ne Win, then already 71, continued as Burma Socialist Program Party (BSPP) chairman, and retained behind-the-scenes power. In December 1987, the United Nations general assembly approved LDC (Least Developed Country) status for Burma.

A year of turmoil

Frustrated by a lack of freedom and the deteriorating economy, students started to stage demonstrations in early 1988. These soon escalated, and heavy-handed government retaliation prompted the flight of thousands across the Thai border. In June 1988, a curfew was imposed in Yangon. In July, while proposing a referendum on a multi-party system, Ne Win announced his retirement as BSPP chairman. Sein Lwin became, for a short while, chairman of the Council of State.

On 8 August, a huge popular demonstration was crushed by the *tatmadaw* (military), with thousands of demonstrators shot dead on the streets of Yangon. Sein Lwin was succeeded by Dr Maung Maung, a civilian, who was then made president and BSPP chairman. However,

> *China is the Burmese regime's principal ally, and its backing has been a factor in the generals' hold on power. How this plays out in the face of newly won Burmese freedom remains to be seen.*

were dissolved. Opposition leaders formed the National League for Democracy (NLD). The general strike collapsed and thousands of students crossed the borders into neighbouring countries, later forming the Democratic Alliance of Burma

A student anti-government protest.

after huge country-wide demonstrations, he lifted martial law and promised a referendum.

At an emergency session on 10 September, however, the BSPP instead proposed general elections under a multi-party system. Soon after, Aung San Suu Kyi (see page 53), daughter of the national hero Aung San, proposed the formation of an interim government. But this was not to be.

The SLORC in power

On 18 September, the Chief of Staff, General Saw Maung, announced over the radio that the military had assumed power and set up the State Law and Order Restoration Council (SLORC), with himself as prime minister. The next day the Pyithu Hluttaw and other organs of power

(DAB) in which 10 ethnic resistance armies and 12 underground student groups united under the leadership of the Kayin leader Bo Mya.

In 1989, the English name of Burma was officially changed to that of Myanmar and the SLORC promulgated a new election law for the Pyithu Hluttaw. Aung San Suu Kyi, who had assumed the leadership of the NLD (National League for Democracy), was barred from participating in the elections and was placed under house arrest (she received the Nobel Peace Prize in September 1991 while still in captivity).

When the general elections finally took place on 27 May 1990, the NLD captured 82 percent of the vote. However, the military demanded that a new constitution should first be drafted in which different groups, including the military, should have a say. In spite of the free elections and the clear democratic vote, the Pyithu Hluttaw could not be convened and the military remained in control of the government. In 1993, under pressure from China, the Kachin Independence Organisation (KIO) signed a cease-fire agreement with the Yangon government, thus ending a 30-year war in the north of the country. This was soon followed by agreements with 14 other insurgent groups. Another factor was the disintegration of the BCP, once an eminent contender for power and the best-armed foe of the *tatmawdaw*.

As if to underline these successes, and in a cosmetic bid to improve its overseas image, in 1997 the SLORC reconstituted itself as the State Peace and Development Council (SPDC).

The wait for democracy

Despite the quasi-boycott of Western nations barring Myanmar from World Bank loans and International Monetary Fund assistance, the SPDC managed to speed up the economy by attracting Southeast Asian, Chinese, Japanese and French capital, often in the form of joint ventures channelled through the regime. In the 1990s GDP grew by around 4 to 5 percent a year, but by 2003 the economy was in recession once again.

Meanwhile, the opposition became fractured and weak. Armed resistance lapsed into total disarray, with the Kayin rebels divided into mutually hostile Buddhist and Christian factions. The Thai government – long discreet supporters of the Kayin cause – were angered by the actions of "God's Army", a breakaway Kayin faction led by child soldiers, who in 1999 seized the Burmese Embassy in Bangkok, and in 2000 hit international headlines when they took more than 400 Thai nationals hostage at a hospital in Ratchaburi.

The following year, after lengthy negotiations with the UN, NLD leader Aung San Suu Kyi was released from house arrest and permitted to travel around the country. In May 2003, her convoy was attacked by pro-government forces in the north of the country – in which 70 of her supporters were killed – and this resulted in another period of incarceration, which would last another seven years.

While the opposition considered its next move, Senior General Than Shwe embarked on one of the barmiest initiatives ever ordered by

the regime: the construction of a completely new capital 320km (200 miles) north up the Sittaung Valley from Yangon. Named "Naypyidaw" ("Abode of Kings"), the city cost an estimated $4 billion to build and required the relocation of tens of thousands of government workers.

The Saffron Revolution

Before it was officially completed, however, a decision to remove fuel subsidies, which saw the price of gasoline double, led to one of the worst outbreaks of civil unrest in modern history. Initially a series of non-violent demonstra-

The military has a strong presence in Myanmar.

tions led by students, the campaign escalated in September 2007 to a mass movement spearheaded by Buddhist monks, whence its popular name, "the Saffron Revolution". The demonstrations were put down with characteristic brutality by the junta, which raided monasteries across the country, imprisoning at least 6,000 monks.

Disturbances rumbled on for another year but internal politics took a back seat in May 2008 after Cyclone Nargis wrought devastation across the Ayeyarwady Delta. An estimated 200,000 people were killed and billions of dollars' worth of damage caused in the worst natural disaster ever to afflict the country. The Burmese government were criticised by international agencies for hampering the emergency aid effort.

Armed rebellions intensified in Shan State a year later, when ethnic Chinese, Wa and Kachin minorities took up arms against the Burmese army – an insurgency dubbed the Kokang Incident, in the wake of which 30,000 refugees fled across the border to China. Elsewhere in Burma, however, armed groups were fast losing ground in a series of military incursions by the army aimed at subduing the rebel forces once and for all. The crackdown bore fruit in 2010, when in exchange for assurances of representation in a future democratic government, insurgent leaders in Mon, Shan and Chin regions signed historic accords to end the violence.

The path to democracy

The move was part of a broader initiative by the military to stimulate foreign investment and a relaxation of economic sanctions against Burma. Constitutional reforms were central to the project, led by the new, reformist Burmese President Thein Sein, who ordered the release of Aung San Suu Kyi from house arrest in the run-up to national elections held in 2010.

Nominally won by the military-backed Union Solidarity and Development Party, the elections were condemned by the NLD as fraudulent. Yet the reform process gathered momentum nonetheless, with a relaxation of press censorship and the release of hundreds of political prisoners. Visits to Naypyidaw by Hillary Clinton and UK Prime Minister David Cameron underlined support for the reforms by the international community as by-elections in 2012 finally handed Aung San Suu Kyi and 43 other NLD candidates seats in the Burmese parliament.

Although at the time of writing (late 2012) the political situation in Myanmar looks more promising than it has for several decades, the problems facing the country remain considerable. With a per capita GDP of around $1,324, this is the poorest state in Southeast Asia. Infrastructure and energy provision are chronically inadequate, inflation is rampant and corruption endemic at all levels of government. At the same time, foreign investment is on the rise amid widespread hopes that with increased democracy will flow the prosperity and individual liberty denied so many Burmese for so long.

Buddhist monks march in Yangon as part of an anti-government protest, 25 September 2007.

GENERAL NE WIN

The strongman of Burmese politics for over 30 years, and a powerful force behind the SPDC, Ne Win was born at Pyay in 1910. He took the name Bo Ne Win or "Sun of Glory General" at the time of the formation of the association of the "thirty comrades". Educated at Yangon University, he left without a degree in 1930. He worked for the post office while becoming an early member of the "Our Burma" Association. In 1943, he became commander of the Burma National Army with the rank of Japanese colonel, and in 1945 became commander of the Patriotic Burmese Forces. After the war Ne Win became second in command and later CO of the 4th Burma Rifles. He became an MP in 1947, then Commander-in-Chief of the Burmese Army in 1949.

In the 1950s he served as Minister for Defence and Home Affairs, before seizing power in a military coup in 1958. In 1960 he was replaced by U Nu in general elections, but in 1962 he seized power again through a military coup. Since that time the military grip on the country has remained absolute.

Ne Win resigned the presidency in 1981 and stepped down as BSPP chairman seven years later. He retained an influence over the military junta until his death in 2002.

Aung San Suu Kyi

Also known by her supporters as "The Lady", Aung San Suu Kyi has come to be seen both in Myanmar and abroad as a symbol of implacable but peaceful resistance to military oppression.

Young and old protest over electricity cuts at a National League for Democracy demonstration.

Born in 1945, Aung San Suu Kyi is the daughter of the late Burmese nationalist leader, General Aung San, whose resistance to British colonial rule cul-

Aung San Suu Kyi before embarking on her European tour to collect the Nobel Peace prize, 2012.

minated in independence in 1948. After attending school in Yangon, Suu Kyi lived in India before going to Britain for her higher education. There she met and married her late husband, Michael Aris, an Oxford University professor specialising in Tibetan Studies. Aris accepted that his wife's destiny might ultimately lie in Myanmar. "Before we were married I promised my wife that I would never stand between her and her country," he said.

Suu Kyi first came to prominence when she returned home in August 1988 to visit her ailing mother. She became the leader of a burgeoning pro-democracy movement in the aftermath of the brutal repression of the uprising. Inspired by the non-violent campaign of Mahatma Gandhi, Suu Kyi organised rallies and travelled the country, calling for peaceful democratic reforms and free elections. The movement quickly grew into a political party, the National League for Democracy (NLD), which went on to win 51 percent of the national vote and 81 percent of seats in parliament, by which time she had already been under house arrest for a year. The military regime, however, refused to relinquish power and stepped up intensified repression of the NLD.

Aung San Suu Kyi spent 15 of the next 21 years under house arrest, restricted in her movements and slandered by the pro-government media as a political opportunist and even a "genocidal prostitute". This last unlikely phrase derived from the military regime's obsession with her marriage to Michael Aris, who died of prostate cancer in Oxford in 1999 at the age of 53. Throughout Aris's final illness, the Yangon authorities denied him permission to visit Myanmar. Fearing that she would not be allowed to re-enter the country, however, Suu Kyi declined the option of leaving and remained separated from her husband and two sons at the time of his death.

Finally, decades of international pressure and sanctions bore fruit on 13 November 2010, when the woman regarded by most of the world as Myanmar's leader-in-waiting was released "for good conduct" from her Yangon home. The end of her detention came only six days after a widely criticised national election.

For most of the following year, the NLD leader campaigned for her party in the run-up to a key by-election in which her party won 43 of the 45 seats it was allowed to contest. In its wake, Aung San Suu Kyi took her seat in the Pyithu Hluttaw, the lower house of Myanmar's parliament, for the first time, and met with US Secretary of State, Hillary Clinton. The event signalled the start of what most impartial observers hope will be full rehabilitation into political life. Whether the perennially paranoid, corrupt and megalomaniac military government will allow the NLD to dominate the country's political life remains to be seen.

Pa-O women heading home through Taung Tho Kyaung.

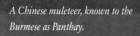

THE POPPY TRAIL

In spite of international attempts to curb poppy
growing in the region, Myanmar's Golden Triangle
remains the hub of Southeast Asia's opium belt.

During the past half century, the remote and
often lawless badlands where the borders of
Myanmar, Laos and Thailand intersect has
become known as the "Golden Triangle". Originally
a Western term applied to the area due to its wealth
in gems, teak and, above all, opium, this tract of
deep, roadless valleys and jungle-covered hills in
eastern Shan State is still largely dominated by drug
warlords, arms dealers and insurgent armies.

Myanmar is the second-largest producer of
opium in the world after Afghanistan (a distant
second, in fact, as Afghanistan is responsible
for around 90 percent of international output).
Yields have soared in recent years due to a col-
lapse in the price of substitute crops, coupled
with a dramatic 50 percent rise in the market
price for opium: another factor is that production
in Thailand has been cut back to almost nothing.

Much of the harvest is grown by poor farmers in far-flung minority villages. Perennially
troubled by political instability and food inse-
curity, smallholders in Shan State stand to make
five times more per day labouring in poppy
fields than cultivating rubber, tea or fruit.

Opium poppies are still grown in Myanmar.

Growth of the Golden Triangle

The rise of the Golden Triangle as an opium production centre dates back to 1948 when, in the
wake of Independence, Burma was swamped by
the defeated remnants of China's Nationalist
government, the Kuomintang (KMT). Within a
few short months, the KMT established itself as a
major force in Shan State, attracting to the region
a dozen other armed groups – communist, separatist and warlord – with one thing in common: the
need to finance their continued struggle against
the authorities, whether Chinese or Burmese. The
obvious source of revenue was opium.

Armed with sophisticated weaponry, the KMT
soon developed a stranglehold on the trade.
Speaking in 1967, General Tuan Shi-wen, commander of the KMT's 5th Army, made no bones
about where the money came from. "Necessity
knows no law," he informed a visiting journalist. "We
have to continue to fight the evil of communism.
To fight you must have an army, and an army must
have guns, and to buy guns you must have money. In
these mountains the only money is opium."

The growing influence of renegade KMT
soldiers over the opium business in the Golden
Triangle was mirrored by a sustained offensive against drug trafficking and manufacture
within China. After the founding of the People's

Republic in 1949, illicit heroin manufacture in Shanghai or Tianjin became all but impossible. It made sense for the heroin technicians to relocate in Hong Kong, or better yet in KMT-controlled sectors of the Golden Triangle itself.

By manufacturing heroin in the hills where the opium was actually grown, costs could be cut appreciably – refined heroin takes up less than 5 percent of the space of raw opium and is therefore easier to both transport and conceal. The trade received another major boost during the first and second Indochina Wars, as both the French and subsequently the Americans used opium and its derivatives to fund anti-communist armies in Laos and Vietnam, while more than half-a-million US troops in Indochina were encouraged both by miserable circumstances and communist enemies to use hard drugs. Many US servicemen who were first exposed to heroin in Indochina took their habit home with them. This in turn led to increased demand in Southeast Asia, and especially in the key production areas of Myanmar's Shan State.

A lucrative industry

While long a favoured cash crop of certain hill

Khun Sa, dubbed the Opium King.

BAMAR DISAPPROVAL

Despite Myanmar's infamous reputation as a major illicit opium-producing nation, most ordinary Bamar view opiates and all intoxicants with strong disapproval. A 19th-century observer noted that "opium use among the better class of Burmese is extremely rare" and that "a respectable Burman would hesitate to be seen around a government liquor shop". He adds that "Burmans have no taste for (cannabis)". This disapproval is based on long-standing Buddhist injunctions against taking intoxicants. Perhaps as a result of these injunctions, tea drinking became popular among Buddhist Burmese from around the 14th century.

tribes – notably, the Wa, Hmong, Akha, Mien, Lahu and Lisu – opium has not greatly benefited these peoples; their reward has been government suspicion, widespread addiction and social disruption. Instead, most profits from the drug trade accrue to international syndicates and major traffickers. In the 1950s and 1960s, the KMT controlled the Golden Triangle narcotics business, but during the 1970s and 1980s they were replaced by private warlords such as the notorious Shan-Chinese "freedom fighter" Khun Sa and allies of the Burmese junta such as Lo Hsing Han. Today, the Wa National Army – heavily armed and with an estimated 20,000 troops – rules the roost.

After a marked fall-off in production through the 1990s, poppy production has risen steadily again in recent years. An estimated 48,000 hectares (118,600 acres) of land were given over to opium growing in Myanmar in 2011 – a 16 percent increase on the previous season. This dramatic upsurge has occurred despite promises by the reformist government under President Then Sein to stamp out the trade by 2014.

Behind the trend lies the enduring poverty of Shan's ethnic minority farmers. The past few years have seen a marked drop in demand for their traditional crops of fruit, tea and rubber from the Chinese; the price of raw opium, meanwhile, has rocketed by 48 percent to record highs of over $300/kg, tempting many small farmers back into poppy production.

The one ray of hope for the region is the new cease-fire agreement signed between the Wa separatist armies and the Burmese government. With the decades-old conflict now at an end in Shan State, the guerrilla forces should in theory no longer need income from the drug trade to buy arms and munitions, though the trade has a habit of enduring as long as there remains a demand – something unlikely to change as long as addicts in New York, London and Paris need their fix.

A soldier stands guard during the destruction of seized narcotics in Lashio, 2007.

TRADERS OF THE GOLDEN TRIANGLE

The rugged, indomitable Chinese muleteers known to the Burmese as Panthay were – and to some extent still are – the masters of the Golden Triangle. In the 19th century, they made the remote settlement of Panglong in the Wa region of Shan State their base. From here, their caravans laden with precious stones, jade and guns, but above all opium, traded as far as Mawlamyaing in Burma, Luang Prabang in Laos, Dali and Kunming in Yunnan, and Chiang Mai in northern Thailand.

Wherever they went they were protected with the best weapons money could buy, and they used these to good effect – to ensure the respect of the law-abiding and the fear of the lawless. When the British first arrived in Shan State in 1886, they were amazed to discover the Panthay armed with Remington repeater rifles better, in most cases, than those of their own troops. During World War II, Panglong was looted and burned by marauding Japanese soldiers, but the Panthay – now armed with newer AK47s – survived to help generations of drug-smugglers transport their opium.

Today, most Panthay are respectable and increasingly prosperous, having settled in the larger towns of Shan State and in Mandalay. Their reputation as traders survives, however, and they are still considered to be the hard men of the Golden Triangle.

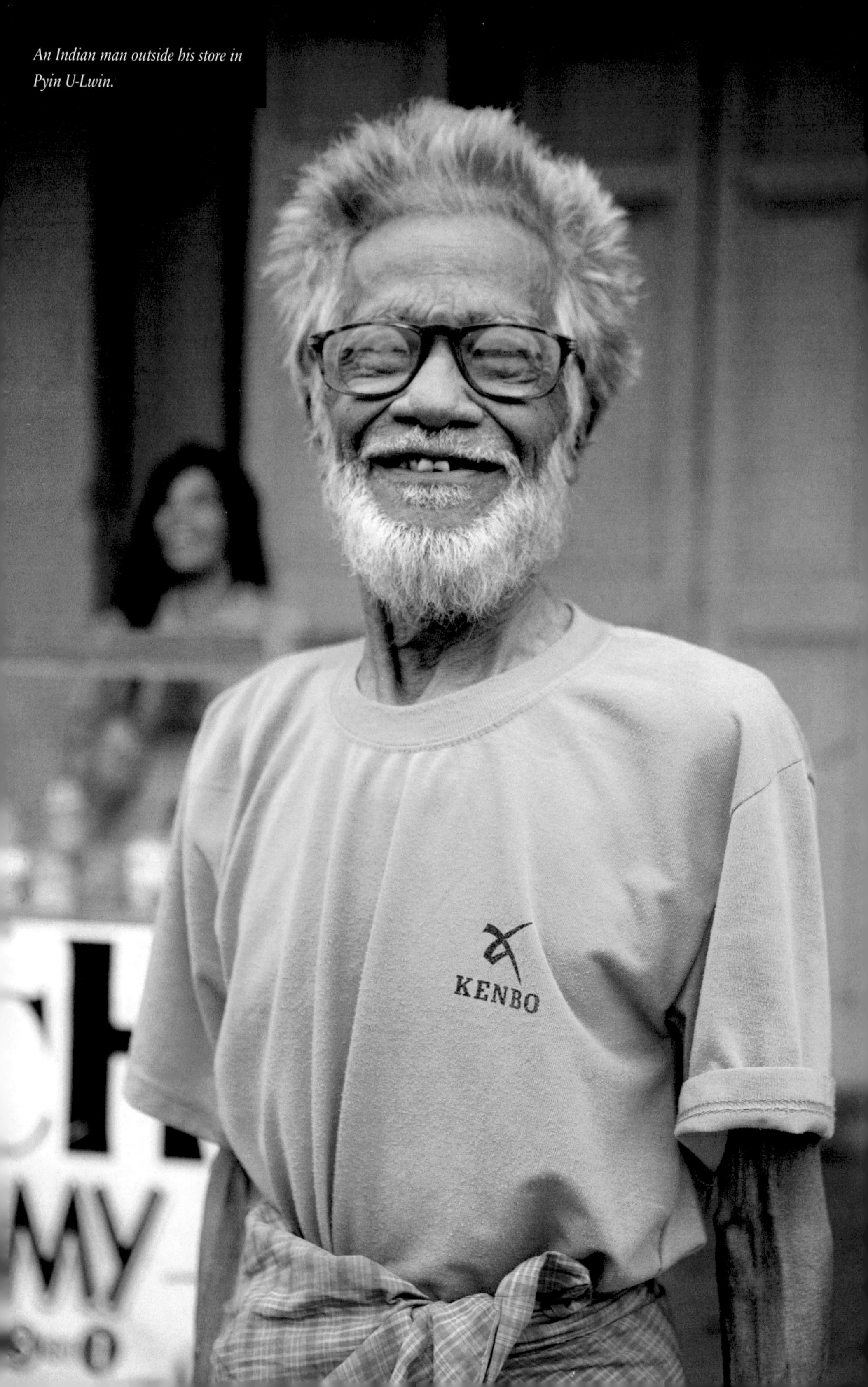

An Indian man outside his store in Pyin U-Lwin.

THE PEOPLE OF MYANMAR

No fewer than 67 indigenous racial groups inhabit Myanmar, and as many as 242 languages and dialects are spoken.

The Burmese are not a homogeneous people. This simple fact has caused many problems over the years, but it also enriches the cultural life of the country and enhances its appeal to visitors. The present population is a little over 60 million, the majority of which live in the fertile Ayeyarwady delta region, in Rakhaing, and along the southeastern coastline. The Burmese authorities presently recognise no fewer than 135 separate nationalities living within the union. Of this number the Bamar (Burman) majority, taken together with the six main ethnic minority groups – each of which has its own state – constitute about 92 percent.

Ethnologists divide Myanmar's indigenous population into four main groups: Tibeto-Burman, Mon-Khmer, Austro-Tai and Karennic. The Tibeto-Burman group, which includes the predominant Bamar, the Rakhaing, Kachin and Chin, constitutes around 78 percent of the total. Mon-Khmer peoples include the Mon, the Wa and the Palaung, while the major Austro-Tai group are the Shan. Karennic peoples include the Kayin (Karen) and the closely related Kayah. Major non-indigenous groups, who are predominantly urban-based, are relatively recent migrants (in the past 150 years) from South Asia and China.

The Bamar

Traditional holders of power since they displaced the Mon more than a thousand years ago, the Bamar – also known as Burmans – today constitute around 68 percent of the total population. Originally migrants from the Tibetan Plateau, they are a wet-rice farming people, Theravada Buddhist by religion, whose tonal, Tibeto-Burman tongue – Burmese – has long been the

The bride at a Pa O wedding ceremony.

national language. As the majority racial group and predominant landholder, as well as the group holding the reins of government, the Bamar are often viewed with suspicion and even hostility by other groups. Their main areas of settlement are in the predominantly lowland divisions of Yangon (Rangoon), Ayeyarwady, Pathein (Bassein), Bago (Pegu), Magway (Magwe), Mandalay and Sagaing, as well as the Rakhaing (Arakan) State, Mon State and Tanintharyi (Tenasserim).

Most of the cultural forms described in later sections of this book are broadly representative of the Bamar, who live typically in thatched dwellings and work as rice farmers. Perhaps their greatest distinguishing trademark is the pale yellow powder, made from *thanaka* bark (see page 237), which Bamar women apply to their faces as protection against the sun. Their traditional dress is the wrap-around *longyi*, which is similar to the Malaysian sarong.

The Shan

At just over 9 percent of the population, Myanmar's 3.9 million Shan, or Tai Yai as they call themselves, are close relatives of the Thai and the second-largest nationality in Myanmar. Inhabitants of the upland plateaux and rolling hills of northeast Myanmar, they are mostly wet-rice farmers, and practise Theravada Buddhism.

Other *sawbwas* and their followers founded the Shan Independence Army (SIA), and in the ensuing years attempted to wrest territory away from the government. It was because of U Nu's apparent inability to deal with this problem that Ne Win staged his military coup in 1962, subsequently imprisoning the Shan leaders who had failed to flee Burma. Some are now in self-imposed exile; others, highly educated scholars, teach at universities in Yangon; while those who responded to the 1980 amnesty have returned to Shan State.

The Shan make their homes in valleys and on high plains and this, plus their Buddhist

Young men sitting outside a market in Shan State.

From the 15th century – when they were pushed back onto the Shan Plateau after early success in establishing an Ayeyarwady kingdom – until 1959, 34 *sawbwas* (hereditary princes) ruled separate feudal principalities in medieval splendour, with serfs, slaves and concubines. Their alliance of small states was recognised by the 1948 constitution, and granted the right to withdraw from the "Union of Burma" after 10 years of membership.

However, in 1959 many of the *sawbwas* sold out, signing an agreement with the Ne Win government to renounce all their hereditary rights and privileges. In exchange, the Shan princes accepted a payment of 25 million kyat, a sum roughly equal to their income over a 15- to 25-year period.

religion, distinguishes them from animist or Christian hill peoples, who generally occupy the mountain tops and steep slopes.

Shan are recognisable by the turbans worn by men and married women. Men usually dress in baggy, dark-blue trousers rather than in Bamar-style *longyi*. Girls wear trousers and blouses until the age of 14, at which time they don colourful dresses. As they get older, their costumes grow less colourful until, at about the age of 40, the women start to wear sober black clothing for the rest of their lives.

The Kayin and Kachin

The fiercely independent Kayin (Karen), who constitute about 7 percent of the population, live scattered throughout central and southern Myanmar, but mainly in their own Kayin State, which they call "Kawthoolei". Many Kayin are Christian, and this – together with the favoured status they enjoyed over the majority Bamar during the British period – has exacerbated their already poor relations with the Bamar-dominated Yangon government. Closely related groups are the Kayah and the "long-neck" Padaung of Kayah State.

Comprising around 2.5 percent of the population and the dominant minority of northern Myanmar, the Kachin are skilled dry-rice farmers and hunters. They have been widely Christianised, chiefly by American Baptist missionaries, but retain a complex and wide-reaching kinship system. Like the Kayin, the Kachin were widely employed as soldiers by the British and have fought a long struggle for independence. Sometimes called the "Gurkhas of Southeast Asia", they are renowned for their military prowess. At war with the military authorities from the early 1960s, the Kachin Independence Organisation (KIO) and its military wing, the Kachin Independence Army (KIA), have proved perhaps the most intractable of Yangon's opponents. In 1994, the Kachin rebels signed a cease-fire agreement with the Burmese *tatmadaw* which lasted until June 2011, when fighting broke out once again in the region between Bhamo and Myitkyina, the capital.

The Rakhaing and the Chin

Closely related to the Bamar, the Rakhaing (Arakanese) inhabit Rakhaing (Arakan) State and constitute about 4 percent of the total population. Although of the same Tibeto-Burman stock as the Bamar, the Rakhaing are slightly darker in complexion, an indication of the region's 2,000-year history of contact and intermarriage with Indian traders, sailors and Brahman settlers. There are several significant differences between the lifestyles of the coastal Rakhaing and the Bamar of the Ayeyarwady basin.

Around 75 percent are devout Buddhists, but significant numbers of Muslim Rakhaing live in the capital city of Sittwe (Akyab), and along

A Padaung (or "Long Neck" tribe) woman at a handicraft workshop at Inle Lake.

MANNERS AND ETIQUETTE

Burmese society is characterised by *onana*, the all-pervasive avoidance of doing anything that would offend, cause someone to lose face or become embarrassed. This is allied with the concept of *hpon*, "power", used to justify socioeconomic differences between people. *Hpon* is a Buddhist concept, a result of merit (or otherwise) earned in previous lives.

Age is considered synonymous with experience and wisdom, and children are taught from a young age to venerate their elders. It is considered rude to touch a person's head, because it is the "highest" point of the body. It is also considered taboo to touch another's feet, but worse still to point with the foot or sit with feet pointing at an older person. Shoes are always taken off upon entering homes, monasteries and pagoda compounds.

Physical demonstrations of affection in public are common between friends of the same gender or between members of the family. It is thus common to see friends walking together holding hands or with arms round each other.

It is considered polite to refer to people by their full title and full name. There are many different honorific titles in the Burmese language (see page 65).

the northern coast, ancestors of people who settled in the region during the British colonial era, when movement between India and Burma was not restricted.

The Chin, together with the related Naga people, make up about 3 percent of Myanmar's population, numbering around 1.5 million in total. They live in the far northwest, where they inhabit the dense forest close to the India and Bangladesh borders. Traditionally animist, most Chin have converted to Christianity, having been evangelised by American and Australian missionaries.

Young Muslim boy in downtown Yangon.

Slash-and-burn agriculture has for centuries furnished land for dry-rice growing, though the resulting soil erosion has depleted the amount of cultivable land to less than is required to sustain the population in recent decades. Some Chin along the banks of the Kaladan River, to the north of the ruined former Arakan capital of Mrauk-U, also practise subsistence fishing alongside settled farming. Among these, and throughout the jungle region to the north, may be seen senior women with elaborately tattooed faces, though the custom is rapidly dying out.

Armed insurgent groups, under the umbrella leadership of the Chin National Army (CAN), have been active in the Chin heartland since

Independence in 1948, but the fighting intensified following the 1988 uprising, since when the minority has been persecuted by the Burmese army. Chin State is officially the poorest in the country, with the least infrastructure: 70 percent of its population live below the poverty line and 40 percent live without adequate food. As a consequence, and to flee the violence perpetrated by the *tatmadaw*, hundreds of thousands of Chin have fled across the Indian frontier to neighbouring Mizoram – a cause of political controversy between the two countries.

The ongoing problem of food shortages in Chin State reached crisis proportions in 2006, after the region's bamboo forest flowered – a natural event that occurs only once every 50 or so years. The fruit produced by the bamboo causes a spike in the rodent population, but when the feast is over the rats and mice target local grain stocks. Famine ensued, forcing still greater numbers or refugees across the border.

The Mon

Possessors of a proud, ancient civilisation which preceded that of the Burmans, the Mon – at about 2 percent of the population – have their own state centred on Mawlamyine (Moulmein) in the southeast of the country. Though largely assimilated into Burman culture, they continue to use their own distinct language, and have retained their own state within the Burmese union. Traditionally, they have preferred to live in rainy lowland areas to pursue wet-rice growing. As Buddhists, they observe their own calendar of Theravadin festivals.

The Indians

Myanmar has an influential migrant Indian community, particularly in Yangon and Mandalay. The Indians and their culture have a 2,000-year history in Burma, predating the presence of the Bamar majority, although it was not until the 19th century, when Burma became a part of the British Raj, that they began to settle in large numbers. At one stage in the early 20th century the population of the capital was almost 60 percent Indian, though this figure has since declined drastically.

Some Indians were well educated and occupied middle and higher levels of administration and business during the colonial era. Those with less education came to Burma as contract labourers for government construction projects, and to work in teak camps. Many of the immigrants were from southern India, and brought with them their beliefs and regional village social structure, which included the caste system, Hindu deities and professional moneylenders (*chettyars*), who quickly became so entrenched in Burmese society that they bought up more than half of the arable land in the Ayeyarwady Delta region.

Many were forced to return to India during the Japanese occupation. In what would become the one of the most desperate and difficult mass evacuations in history, an estimated quarter of a million made the journey on foot via the leech-infested, jungle-covered mountains of the northwest – 4,268 are recorded to have died en route, but the true death toll was probably much higher. Those who remained faced the land reforms of the new government. Businessmen who stayed during the U Nu years staged a mass migration when Ne Win installed his nationalisation programme.

Besides Hindus, there is a small South Asian Muslim population in major towns. Many trace their ancestry back to areas that now form part of Pakistan and Bangladesh. Others, known as *zerbadi*, are the result of unions between migrant Muslim men and Bamar women.

The Chinese

The number of Chinese in Myanmar today is estimated at around 1.3 million. In broad terms, there are two groups, with very different histories and lifestyles. The first is mainly rural, comprising the Shan Tayok and the Kokang

Chinese. They came across the border of Yunnan during the time when the Shan principalities were under British administration, and are still concentrated in the northeast, close to Yunnan province from where many originate. In the Kokang area of northern Shan State they form more than 80 percent of the population, so that Kokang is known as Myanmar's "Little China".

The urban Chinese, on the other hand, have an entirely different background. A large number arrived in Yangon to work as merchants or restaurant owners during the colonial era.

A priest inside Sri Devi temple, Yangon.

BURMESE NAMES

There are no family names in Burmese culture: women keep their maiden names upon marriage, and a child can have a name which bears no relation to his parents' names. A Burmese has a name of one, two or three syllables, given shortly after birth at a naming ceremony. Parents consult an authority in astrology and supernatural knowledge in selecting the name.

Burmese can change their name as often as they like, for example to bring about financial success.

Only by way of address can one tell the gender or social status of a Burmese. For example, a Burmese named Kau Reng, if a man, might be addressed as "U Kau Reng", "Ko Kau Reng" or "Maung Kau Reng." The title "U" indicates superiority of social or official position, or of age. "Ko" is commonly used among men of similar standing in addressing each other. "Maung" generally is used with persons who are younger or of an inferior status, and among children and teenage boys. Sometimes the dual title "Ko Maung" is used if the Burmese has a monosyllabic name.

Superiors are often addressed "Ah Ko Gyi," "Ko Gyi" or "Saya" (teacher). "Saya" is also used in reference to medical doctors. Monks are addressed as "Sayadaw" ("Venerable"), "Ashin" ("Reverend") or "Kodaw" ("Your Reverence"), the latter used most often by a layman addressing a monk. Military officers are called "Bo".

By grafting hard and sending their children to be educated in Western-type schools and universities, they soon occupied the middle and higher strata of modern society. Far from being "overlanders" from Yunnan, most were Overseas Chinese originating from the coastal provinces of Guangdong, Fujian and Hainan Island. Despite nationalisation under Ne Win, and the vicious anti-Chinese riots in Yangon in 1967, the urban Chinese remained strong commercially, and with a market economy now becoming established in Myanmar, many are once again in business.

Streetside café, downtown Yangon.

Another Chinese group found in remote parts of Shan State, as well as in large towns like Yangon and Mandalay, are the Panthay. This group is essentially identical with the Hui minority in Yunnan. The descendants of Uzbek soldiery who fought for the Mongol dynasty, their ancestors settled in Yunnan over six centuries ago and intermarried with local Han Chinese. Today, there is little to distinguish them from other Chinese except for their Muslim faith.

Other minorities

Inle Lake, in Shan State, is the adopted homeland of the resourceful Intha minority, whose "one-legged" rowing style, stilted villages, floating gardens and beautiful handicrafts make them one of the more distinctive among Myanmar's ethnic groups. An immigrant tribe from the southeast coast who left their former homeland in the 18th century to flee wars between the Burmese and Thais, the Intha now number around 70,000, most of whom live in villages clustered around the lush, paddy-filled shores of Inle Lake.

Another minority you'll encounter in these parts are the Kayan-Lahwi, better known as the "Padaung", whose prominence on the tourist circuit derives from the custom adopted by their women of wearing brass rings around their necks to depress their collar bones and make their necks appear longer. Originally from the Golden Triangle region of northeastern Shan State, the Kayan-Lahwi number around 60,000; the majority are Roman Catholics. You'll see numerous "long-necked" or "giraffe-necked" women, as they're sometimes referred to, selling trinkets and handicrafts, and posing for photographs with foreign tourists.

The homeland of the Kayan-Lahwi, straddling the borders of Laos, Thailand and Myanmar, has long been an area associated with lawlessness and insurgency. On the northwestern frontier with India, the Naga people inhabit the thick forests sweeping from the Chindwin River. Notorious for their former practice of head hunting, the Naga are today all but completely Christianised, although they continued to resist Burmese rule until 2011, when a peace accord was struck with the *tatmadaw* guaranteeing Naga leaders representation in the national government. This followed the creation three years earlier of a Naga Self-Administered Zone, formerly part of Sagaing Division. With militancy on the decline, tourism has made its first tentative steps in the region. A handful of Burmese tour operators now run trips to remote Naga towns where the various tribes celebrate their New Year – a great opportunity to see Naga traditional dress and dance in its authentic context. Among the more distinctive elements of Naga attire are the colourful shawl and black kilt worn as everyday garb, and the conical head gear with boars' teeth and feathers donned on ceremonial occasions.

Further north from Naga territory sprawls the most remote, impenetrable region of Myanmar, around the foothills of the Hukaung Valley and Hkakabo Razi massif. As well as harbouring a viable tiger population, the forest here is also home to an array of obscure tribes, including a race of pygmies known as the Taron. The outside world was ignorant of their existence until the American conservationist Alan Rabinowitz, while conducting a wildlife survey in the area in 1996, was introduced to members of the community. Enslaved for generations by the dominant Kachins, the Taron had dwindled to a vestigial population of a dozen individuals who, beset by deformities and other health problems resulting from inbreeding, had made a pact not to have children.

Although not approaching extinction, the Moken of the far south are another ethnic group struggling to survive on the margins of modern Myanmar. Often dubbed "Sea Gypsies" because of their nomadic lifestyle, the Moken spend eight or nine months of the year at sea, rarely touching dry land except to re-provision and trade. For the rest of the year, when the rough conditions of the rainy season make life in their hand-built *kabang* boats too dangerous, they reside in stilted villages at remote sites on the coast of Tanintharyi (Tenarassim) Division, particularly in and around the Myeik Archipelago. Diving and beachcombing the shores of these remote islands, the Moken fish and collect sandworms and molluscs to eat, and shells and oysters to trade with the Malay and Chinese market people in the area's ports.

CULTURE AND SOCIETY

Myanmar's decades as a pariah state have ensured that it ranks today among the most staunchly traditional nations in Asia. And it's not just the peripheral, remote and mountainous regions where picturesque, antiquated traditions still hold sway. Even in the cities, adherence to traditional values remains to the fore – something you'll notice from the minute you step off the plane. Traditional dress is ubiquitous, and the Burmese are remarkably polite and deferential towards their elders and strangers. Conventions of hospitality remain strong, as do the beliefs and practices of Theravada Buddhism, fervent adherence to which is a fact of daily life in a country where monks queue in the street each morning to accept alms from lay people and the terraces of huge gilded pagodas throng from sunset to sunrise with pilgrims and worshippers.

Because they comprise by far the largest and most dominant cultural group in Myanmar, the following account refers principally to the Bamar and Mon, the overwhelming majority of whom are Buddhists.

Dress

The Burmese emphasise their national identity through the clothes they wear. Most evident is the longyi, introduced by immigrant families from southern India. Similar to the Malaysian sarong, it consists of a kilt-like piece of cloth worn from the waist to the ankle. Together

Working the silk-weaving looms in Phaw Khone weaving village.

with the *eingyi*, a transparent blouse which is worn with a round-collared, long-sleeved jacket, the longyi still takes precedence over Western-style garments. For more on longyis, see page 236.

The Burmese Premier, General Than Shwe, and other members of the ruling junta caused a stir in February 2011 when they appeared on national television wearing women's acheiks and longbon headscarves – an act political observers were quick to interpret as superstition, or yadaya. Fortune tellers have repeatedly predicted that a woman will rule Myanmar one day, and so the generals' cross-dressing was seen as an attempt to confound the pundits and forestall the rise of NLD leader, Aung San Suu Kyi.

Marriage

By and large, and unlike their Indian cousins across the Andaman Sea, Burmese choose their own life partners. Traditions of romantic love are strong. Couples meet, court and decide to marry themselves, albeit in a style that appears very old-fashioned and demure to Western eyes. Should the parents disapprove of the match there's little they can do about it. Parental opposition to any marriage in Myanmar will typically result in an elopement, followed by a gradual rehabilitation of the couple if the marriage proves a success.

Local lady outside Mingun Paya, near Mandalay.

WOMEN IN MYANMAR

Women, despite their lower status in Buddhist doctrine, have historically enjoyed high levels of social power, being appointed to high office by the Burmese kings and allowed to inherit the position of village head. Their rights are today almost always equal to those of men, guaranteed by simple divorce laws.

That said, the country's economic difficulties have seen an erosion in the status of women among poorer sectors of society. Burmese women have also been targeted in the nation's numerous ethnic conflicts, recruited as porters and unpaid labourers for the military, and in some cases becoming victims of slavery, murder, torture and systematic rape.

The ceremony itself is considered *lokiya*, or "earthly", in the Buddhist tradition, and as such is not officiated over by a monk or abbot (although to gain merit, monks may well attend the betrothal dinner or wedding reception). Instead, a Brahmin priest presides over the ritual, which begins with the blowing of a conch shell as the couple have the palms of their hands bound together in cloth and placed in a silver bowl (the Burmese for marriage is "*let htat*" or "join palms"). Sanskrit verses are intoned by the Brahmin, who then raises the couple's hands and unties them, to more blasts from the conch shell. Afterwards, there will be entertainment and speeches, and with more affluent families, perhaps a reception dinner at a smart hotel.

Throughout, traditional dress is worn by the participants and those attending, even among more sophisticated urbanites – though with wealthier families the bride's dress tends to be an extravagant modern designer twist on the traditional *htamein* featuring embroidery, pearls, sequins and even on some occasions gold. Upper-class brides will also wear a pearl- and jewel-encrusted tiara, and an opulent necklace.

Burmese get married expecting it to be for life; comparatively few marriages end in divorce, but those that do see the common property divided equally. If the marriage fails, women can return to their parents.

Birth and family life

One hundred days after the birth of a child, the parents invite family and friends to a naming ceremony at the local monastery, where the baby is given a name by a senior monk based on astrological calculations; it need bear no relation to that of the parents. After the ritual, a grand feast is held at the family home or in a functions venue to mark the event.

Children are sent to school at the age of five. However, despite a system of compulsory education and strenuous efforts by the government since independence to ensure education for all, there are still areas with no state schools. In these places, the local *kyaung* (monastery) takes charge of elementary education.

When a boy is nine years old, his *shin-pyu* takes place (see page 73). This is an initiation ceremony marking the end of childhood and the start of a period of monkhood. Girls of the same age participate in an ear-piercing ceremony called the *nahtwin*, which also symbolises a farewell to the unburdened life of the child.

As two-thirds of the population still work on the arable land, the transition from school to adult life is relatively easy for most young people: during their school years, they help out with the harvest in their parents' fields.

Death

When the Burmese die they are either buried or cremated. A special coin called a *gadaw ga* is put in the mouth of the deceased so they can pay the "ferryman" who will transport them

home to be fed and recite blessings for a rite that ends with a water libation ceremony marking the formal end to the funeral..

Business etiquette

It is now commonplace for businessmen to greet each other with a handshake. It is, however, considered rude to offer one's hand to a woman. If a business woman offers you her hand first it is acceptable to shake it, but usually all contact will be avoided. A small bow would be the acceptable form of greeting. Business cards are used widely in Myanmar and should

Yangon schoolchildren.

"across the river" into the next life. Relatives and friends of the dead person are invited to the funeral, where an offering of turmeric-coated rice is made to please the *bhumazo*, or guardian deity of the earth, and paper fans bearing the deceased person's name and Buddhist scriptures are handed to the attenders. Among better-off families, wreaths may also be placed around the grave, although in poorer communities more functional gifts are made to the grieving family.

For a week, the windows and doors of the house in which the person died remain open to allow the deceased's spirit, or *leippya*, to fly away. A nocturnal vigil by close family members may also be held at this time. On the seventh day, known as *yet le*, monks arrive at the

be exchanged upon greeting. Always use both hands to present and receive cards as this shows respect, as does taking a few seconds to read the card. Do not immediately place the card in your pocket as this is also considered disrespectful.

Attire should be conservative and formal. The tropical climate means lightweight suits for men are acceptable, if worn with a tie. Women should wear either a skirt suit or a blouse and skirt. Ensure that the skirt is of a conservative length (below the knee is preferable) and avoid bright colours. Most business people in Myanmar will dress similarly when dealing with foreigners, but some may still wear the traditional sarong-type garment with a Western shirt or blouse.

BURMESE BUDDHISM

The ancient faith permeates the everyday lives of the people, placing great emphasis on individual achievement.

Although Christianity and Islam are practised by some minority communities in Myanmar, the overwhelming majority of the population – around 90 percent – are Buddhists. Going by the proportion of monks in society and the amount given as alms, Myanmar is the most fervently Buddhist country in the world, and the influence of the faith is all-pervasive. Moreover, the brand of Buddhism practised is unique, blending the precepts of the ancient Theravada school (which adheres most closely to the Buddha's original teaching) with indigenous forms of nature spirit, or *nat*, worship, inherited from the animistic beliefs of the hill tribes as well as by the Hindu-Brahmanism of early traders.

Burmese Buddhist cosmology has also been shaped by millennia of influences from other cultures, particularly that of India's Brahmans. According to the Burmese, the European-Asian continent is called Jambudvipa. It is the southernmost of four islands situated at the cardinal points surrounding Mount Meru, the centre of the world. This southern island is considered to be a place of misery compared to the other abodes of this universe, and the only place where future Buddhas can be born.

There are 31 planes of existence on, above and below Mount Meru. They can be divided into three main groups: the 11 planes of *Kama-Loka*, the realm of the sensuous world; the 16 planes of *Rupa-Loka*, the realm of subtle material matter; and, finally, the four planes of *Arupa-Loka*, the realm of formlessness.

Simplifying Buddhism

King Anawrahta, founder of the first Burmese empire in the 11th century AD, devoted his attention to simplifying spiritual beliefs. When he introduced Theravada Buddhism into Upper

Frieze on the walls of Kaba Aye Pagoda, Yangon.

Burma as the national religion, he was unable to eliminate the animistic beliefs of his people. Despite radical measures, 36 of the countless nature spirits, or *nat*, continued to be venerated. For the Burmese, these 36 *nat* serve a similar purpose to the saints of the Catholic Church, and are called upon in times of need. So Anawrahta introduced a 37th figure – Thagyamin – and made him king of the *nat*. He thereafter tolerated the popular worship of these 37 *nat*, once it had been established that they were also followers of the Buddha's teachings.

Teachings of the Buddha

The division between the Theravada and Mahayana styles, while already developing for some time, actually occurred in 235 BC when King Ashoka convened the Third Synod at Pataliputra, India. The Buddhist elders (Theravada means "the way of the elders") held tight to their literal interpretation of the Master's teaching. They were opposed by a group which sought to understand the personality of the historical Buddha, and its relationship to one's salvation. The Theravada branch of Buddhism is actually a more conservative, orthodox form of Buddhist thought. The latter group became known as the Mahayana school. It established itself in Tibet, Nepal, China, Korea, Mongolia, Japan and Vietnam, where its further development varied greatly from region to region. The Theravada school, meanwhile, has thrived in Sri Lanka, Myanmar, Thailand, Laos and Cambodia.

The Buddha denied the existence of a soul. There is no permanence, he explained, for that which one perceives to be "self". Rather, one's essence is forever changing. The idea of rebirth, therefore, is a complicated philosophical question within the structure of Buddhism. When a Buddhist (or any person, for that matter) is reincarnated, it is neither the person nor the soul which is actually reborn. Rather, it is the

Inside one of the meditation alcoves at Botataung Pagoda, Yangon.

THREE JEWELS, FOUR NOBLE TRUTHS AND THE EIGHTFOLD PATH

As there is no true form of worship in the Theravada style of Buddhism, the only true ritual to which both monks and laity submit themselves is the recitation – three times a day – of the "Three Jewels", or the *Triratna*: "I take refuge in the Buddha. I take refuge in the Dhamma. I take refuge in the Sangha."

The formula of the "Three Jewels" offers solace and security. These are needed for strength, if one understands the "Four Noble Truths" expounded upon by Gautama Buddha in his first sermon:

Life always has in it the element of suffering

The cause of suffering is desire

In order to end the suffering, give up desire and give up attachment

The way to this goal is the Noble Eightfold Path. This consists of right view, right intent, right speech, right conduct, right means of livelihood, right endeavour, right mindfulness and right meditation. This "path" is normally divided into three areas: view and intent are matters of wisdom; speech, conduct or action, and livelihood are matters of morality; and endeavour, mindfulness and meditation are matters resulting from true mental discipline.

sum of one's karma, the balance of good and evil deeds. One is reborn as a result of prior existence. A popular metaphor used to explain this transition is that of a candle. Were a person to light one candle from the flame of another, then extinguish the first, it could not be said that the new flame was the same as the previous one. Rather, in fact, its existence would be due to that of the previous flame. The Noble Eight-fold Path, therefore, does not lead to salvation in the traditional Judeo-Christian sense. By pursuing matters of wisdom, morality and mental discipline, one can hope to make the transition into *nibbana* (nirvana), which can perhaps best

of all possessions, except eight items: three robes, a razor for shaving, a needle for sewing, a strainer (to ensure that no living thing is swallowed), a belt, and an alms bowl. Second, a vow to injure no living thing and to offend no one. Finally, the vow of complete sexual celibacy. The monk must make his livelihood by seeking alms, setting out two hours before dawn and going from door to door. The food received is the monk's only meal of the day. A young Burmese begins his novitiate at around the age of nine. For the majority of Burmese, this does not last long. Most would have left the monkhood before their 20th birthday.

Nuns collecting alms, Pyin U-Lwin.

be defined as the extinction of suffering, or cessation of desire. It is not heaven, nor is it annihilation – simply a quality of existence.

The monk

There are no priests in Theravada Buddhism. But the faithful still need a model to follow on the path to salvation and this is provided by monks. In Myanmar, there are about 400,000 monks (and 75,000 nuns). Most of these are students and novices who don the saffron robe only temporarily; nearly all male Burmese devote a period – from just a few weeks to several years – to the monkhood (*sangha*).

There are three fundamental rules to which the monk must subscribe. First, the renunciation

BURMESE BUDDHIST TERMINOLOGY

Gyo-daing – small Buddha shrines in temples.
Kyaung or *pongyikyaung* – Buddhist monastery.
Parabaik – folded palm-leaf manuscript.
Paya – generic term for Buddha images and stupas.
Pongyi – a Buddhist monk.
Pyat-that – multi-roofed pavilions.
Samsara – cycle of birth and death (rebirth).
Sayadaw – Abbot of a Burmese monastery.
Tazaung – a Buddhist shrine.
Thabeit – a monk's bowl.
Thilashin – a Buddhist nun.
Zedi – a stupa.

Shin-Pyu

The most important moment in the life of a young Burmese boy is his *shin-pyu* – the initiation as a novice in the order of monks.

Until a Buddhist has gone through the *shin-pyu* ceremony, he is regarded as being no better than an animal. To become "human", he must for a time withdraw from secular life, following the example set forth by the Buddha when he left his family to seek enlight-

The night before a *shin-pyu*, a feast is prepared for all the monks whose company the young boy will join. The following morning, the novitiate's head is shaved in preparation. The boy's mother and eldest sister hold a white cloth to receive the falling hair, and later bury it near a pagoda.

In the weeks before the ceremony, the boy would have been familiarised with the language and behaviour befitting a monk. He would have learned how to address a superior; how to walk with decorum, keeping his eyes fixed on a point 2 metres (6ft) in front of him; and how to respond to the questions put to him at the ceremony. During his novicehood, he will not take any food after noon, sing or play, use cosmetics,

Young monks at Kaba Aye Pagoda, Yangon.

enment. Unlike his illustrious predecessor, the novice will probably carry his alms bowl for a short period, then return to his normal lifestyle. But his time spent studying scriptures and strictly following the code of discipline makes him a dignified human being.

During the period between his ninth and twelfth birthdays, a boy is deemed ready to don the saffron-coloured robes of the *sangha* and become a "son of the Buddha". If his parents are very pious, they may arrange to have the *shin-pyu* staged on the full moon day of Waso (June/July), the start of the Buddhist Lent. Once the ceremony has been arranged, the boy's sisters announce it to the whole village or neighbourhood. Everyone is invited, and contributions are collected for a festival which will dig deep into the savings of the boy's parents.

sit on any elevated seat, possess any money, interfere in the business of other monks or abuse them. He must not kill, steal, lie, get drunk or have sex. He must not blaspheme or listen to heretical doctrines.

When the boy's request to enter the monkhood is approved, he prostrates himself three times. He is robed, and now he is ready to walk the path of perfection first trodden by the Buddha. If he is steadfast enough, he might even reach nirvana. Once the *say-adaw* – the abbot who has presided over the ceremony – hangs the novitiate's *thabeit* alms bowl) over his shoulder, the boy's childhood is left behind. He has been accepted as a monk. During his time in the monastery, his parents must address him in honorific terms. He will call them "lay sister" and "lay brother", the same names he calls others not in the monkhood.

FESTIVALS

Solemn Buddhist Lent in July is flanked by the frivolous water dousing of New Year in April, and the incredible Festival of Lights in October.

Myanmar's traditional year is based on a 12-month lunar calendar, and this determines the dates of festivals and Buddhist holidays, beginning with Thingyan, the Burmese New Year, in March or April. Whenever the full moon waxes, it's time for a *pwe*, or festival, of one sort or another. Some *pwe* are solemn; others are occasions for fun and frivolity. All are worth experiencing.

Htamein, Manao and Tabaung

The Htamein (rice harvest festival) – a joyous celebration when rice is offered to the monasteries and elaborate meals are cooked in Burmese homes – takes place between January and February. A special dish of rice, sesame, peanuts, ginger and coconut is eaten.

In Kachin State, the predominantly Christian minority people celebrate their annual thanksgiving ceremony in early January with masked and costumed Manao dances around a decorated pole. The largest such event takes place in the stadium of the regional capital, Myitkyina, and brings together all several branches of the traditional Kachin tribe in a week of dancing, games and all-round merriment.

The last month of the traditional Burmese year, March, is considered a time of romance and tranquillity. On the full moon day of the festival of Tabaung, Burmese travel to lakes or rivers where they play music, sing and recite poetry, often in the company of a loved one.

Tabaung also signals the start of Myanmar's largest temple festival, the Shwedagon Pagoda Festival in Yangon, held in February and March of 2012 for the first time since the uprising of 1988. Thousands of people dress in ceremonial costumes and descend on the shrine for

A Buddhist devotee lights a candle at the full moon festival.

the event. Traditional puppet shows and dance recitals also take place.

Thingyan

The hot season from March to April brings Thingyan ("changing over") water festival, Myanmar's biggest party, marking the traditional New Year's Day held at full moon during the lunar month of Tagu. The festival goes on for three or four days, the length of the celebration determined by *ponna* or Brahman astrologers. Water is poured from delicate silver vessels, sprayed from water pistols, hurled from buckets, and even blasted from fire hydrants to wash away the old year and welcome the new. The drenching stops each day at 6.30pm, and is followed by an evening of feasting and partying. For the duration of the festival, government buildings and businesses are closed.

Pandals – pavilions or stages made from bamboo and beautifully decorated with flowers and papier mâché – are erected in which lines of garlanded girls dressed in identical suits of colourful material perform carefully rehearsed song and dance routines while boys douse them with water. More overtly suggestive versions spring up in the liberal, upper-class neighbourhoods of Yangon, where hot pants,

floats parade up and down the streets of the cities and larger towns. But there are also moments of tranquillity in the midst of this exuberance. Most revellers find time to make offerings at pagodas and at the homes of their elders, and Buddha images are washed by the devout.

Kason

Kason (the birthday of Lord Buddha) is celebrated between April and May. Water is poured over the roots of sacred Banyan trees, beneath the branches of which the Buddha attained enlightenment. Kason is a time of anticipation – the monsoon

People throw buckets of water onto a car during the water festival, Thingyan.

crop tops and Western-style dancing replace the traditional elegance.

Thagyamin

Thingyan also celebrates the descent to earth of Thagyamin, the king of the 37 *nat*, to bring blessings for the new year. He brings two books with him: one bound in gold to record the names of children who have been well behaved in the past year, and one bound in dog skin to record the names of any naughty children. Thagyamin rides a winged golden horse and bears a water jar, symbolic of peace and prosperity. Households greet Thagyamin with flowers and palm leaves at the front door. Guns are fired and music is played in salute. Gaily decorated

could break at any time. At the full moon, the birth, enlightenment and death of the Buddha are celebrated. The devout join a procession of musicians and dancers to the local pagoda.

During the full moon of Nayon (May to June), after the rains have begun and the hot, dry months are at an end, Burmese students are tested on their knowledge of the Tripitaka (the Buddhist scriptures). Abbots lecture before large crowds, schools operated by monasteries are opened to the public, and eminent scholars exhibit their knowledge to public acclaim.

Buddhist Lent

Dhammasetkya (the beginning of Buddhist Lent), held during June–July, is a solemn

> *So popular are the Phaung Daw U and Thadingyut festivals held at Inle Lake each September that celebrants often spend all their savings on new clothing.*

religious occasion, during which all monks go into a period of deep retreat for study and meditation. This is an auspicious time for young men to have their *shin-pyu* initiation into the monkhood (see page 73). For the next three months the country is soaked in water as

One layman will have drawn a paper containing the name of the Gautama Buddha and he has the honour of hosting the Buddha.

Tawthalin, Thadingyut Tazaungmone

By mid-September the rainy season is at its height, and Myanmar's waterways, from the mighty Ayeyarwady to the smallest stream, are full. To celebrate this bounty, Tawthalin (boat races) are held all over the country. The most impressive take place in Shan State, at the Phaung Daw U Festival on Inle Lake.

The majestic royal barge, along with a boat carrying female dancers, during the Phaung Daw U festival on Inle Lake.

the monsoons gain strength. During this time monks are not permitted to travel, and the devout will enter a period of fasting.

Wagaung

The Wagaung ("Draw-a-Lot") Festival is held in July or August. Since no marriage or other secular celebration is permitted during Buddhist Lent, the full moon of Wagaung is observed as a festival of merit-making. The name of each member of the local *sangha* is written on a piece of paper, which is then rolled up and deposited into a large basket. A representative from each household of the community draws a slip of paper from the basket, and, the next day, provides an elaborate feast for the monk named on the piece of paper.

Heralding the end of Buddhist Lent and the approach of the cool season, the Thadingyut (Festival of Lights) celebrates the Buddha's return from heaven to earth, and means weddings and other secular celebrations can now take place. To symbolise the radiance of the Buddha on his return, millions of candles and oil lamps illuminate monasteries, pagodas, houses and trees throughout the land.

The festival of Tazaungmone (the Weaving Festival) takes place between October and November. Under the full moon, unmarried women work at their looms all night to make new robes for the monks. These are then presented to the monks at the local temple early next morning.

Nat festivals and Pyatho

In Nadaw (November/December), when the full moon arrives, villages dedicate celebrations to the spirit world; this is the time most *nat* festivals take place. National or regional *nat* celebrations, however, are held in other months over a period of several days, before, during and after the full moon. Among the most important are the Mount Popa Festival in Nayon (May/June), the Taungbyon Festival held in the town of Wagaung, 30km (19 miles) north of Mandalay, and the traditional Shan Festival in Kyaukme in Tabaung (February/March).

Pyatho (December/January), the month of temple festivals, was formerly a time when Burmese royalty displayed its strength with military parades. Today, this period is reserved mostly for local pagoda festivals. These are essentially religious, with gifts presented to monks and offerings made for temple upkeep. But even more so, they are occasions for merrymaking, lasting three or more days. A few major temple festivals are held in Pyatho. The Ananda Temple festival in Bagan also falls at this time.

Other festivals

National holidays of a secular nature are dated according to the Western (international) calendar. Independence Day, a secular holiday, is held on 4 January and celebrated with week-long festivities. Boat races are staged on the Royal Lake in Yangon and the palace moats in Mandalay.

On 12 February, Union Day marks national unity with flag-bearing, feasting and celebrations. Peasant's Day is celebrated on 2 March, and on 27 March, fireworks and parades mark the annual Armed Forces Day, or Resistance Day, commemorating the World War II struggle against Japanese imperialism. The first day of May is Worker's Day, and 19 July is Martyr's Day, which commemorates the assassination of Bogyoke Aung San and his comrades in 1947.

Minority festivals include the spectacular Kachin Manao – a celebration to placate Kachin *nat* and ensure peace, plenty and prosperity. It's difficult to predict with any accuracy the exact date on which a *manao* may be held. The decision to hold a *manao* is taken by the *duwa* (Kachin elders). The *sup manao* looks to the future, while the *padang manao* celebrates a past success or victory. The festival involves the sacrifice of cattle or buffalo to placate and honour the *nat*, with traditional Kachin music and dance centred around a

In Shan State each November sins are floated away in giant hot-air balloons. These spectacular two-storey-high leviathans are fired by coal braziers and drip with hundreds of candles.

manao taing (totem pole). The festival may go on for 24 hours, and a lot of locally brewed alcohol is drunk. The most fixed of *manao* is held on 10 January at Myitkyina, the capital of Kachin State, to celebrate Kachin State Day. The Kayin New Year is based on the lunar calendar and held in

Procession of the villagers of Kyauk Se Gome during Nat Pwe, the spirits festival.

December and January. Celebrated by Kayin people throughout Myanmar, but especially in Kayin State and the Ayeyarwady Delta, it's a time of vibrant celebration.

Other widely celebrated festivals include Divali, the Hindu "Festival of Lights", as well as the Muslim celebrations of 'Id al-Fitr to celebrate the end of the fasting month of Ramadan, Maulid al-Nabi to commemorate the Prophet Muhammad's birthday, and 'Id al-Adha to celebrate the conclusion of the annual Haj Pilgrimage to Mecca. The Chinese community mark (discreetly) Chinese New Year, the Festival of Hungry Ghosts and the annual Moon Cake Festival, while Myanmar's Christians celebrate Christmas and Easter.

A FEAST OF FLAVOURS

Although influenced by the culinary traditions of neighbouring India and China, Burmese dishes retain a character as distinctive and flamboyant as the country's Buddhist architecture.

Sharing borders with two culinary giants, India and China, and with the Southeast Asian nations of Laos and Thailand, Myanmar has inevitably been influenced by the spices, seasonings and cooking styles of its neighbours. Yet it is the way that these shared ingredients are combined which makes the cuisine of Myanmar different.

You'll find Chinese foodstuffs, particularly soybean products such as soy sauce, bean sprouts and bean curd, as well as a distinctive local variation of bean curd made from chickpeas which is popular among the Shan people. Chinese noodles have become a staple, but appear in purely Burmese dishes such as *mohinga*, a noodle soup that starts with fish stock and simmered banana stem and finishes with a host of garnishes you'd never find in China. The Chinese wok is used for frying, along with traditional terracotta pots, modern metal saucepans and the ubiquitous banana leaf, used as a wrapper for steaming or grilling everything from rice to meat to fish and cakes.

Indian influence is also noticeable, especially the use of chickpeas – not just whole, but toasted and ground to make a nutty powder which is sprinkled into soups, noodle dishes and over salads. The Burmese use only a few Indian spices, most notably turmeric, cumin and coriander, preferring to flavour their curry-style dishes with huge amounts of crushed onion, garlic and ginger, often slowly cooked to a rich brown. Indian curry leaves, very popular in the south of the subcontinent, are also used in parts of Myanmar, and a number of traditional Indian recipes have been adapted to local tastes.

The food of Myanmar is perhaps most similar to that of its Southeast Asian neighbours. Herbs, such as lemon grass and kaffir lime, pungent

Frying snacks at a local tea stall, Taung Tho market, Inle lake

fish products and creamy coconut milk are frequently used, not forgetting an abundance of fresh, dried and powdered chillies. In the central and southern parts of the country, fish sauce and *ngapi* (dried shrimp paste) are as common as salt in a Western kitchen. Fruity sour tamarind, various types of ginger, including common ginger and fresh turmeric, and butterscotch-sweet palm sugar all add their character to countless dishes.

Regional diversity

The well-watered Ayeyarwady Delta and Isthmus of Kra, "Lower Myanmar", is the nation's rice bowl. With rivers, estuaries, canals and coastal waters, it's not surprising that fish and other seafood is the main source of protein in this part of the country. Much of it is dried. Small prawns are used in salads, soups, main dishes and spicy side dishes or in condiments such as the indispensable Burmese *balachaung*, a combination of pounded dried prawns, deep-fried garlic and onions, vinegar and chilli powder. Sour, hot, salty and crisp, it can very quickly become addictive to lovers of emphatically flavoured food.

The central plains around Mandalay are the driest part of the country. Being far from the coast, the people of this region rely on freshwater fish. Thanks to irrigation, crops including various beans and lentils are grown, and some of them fermented to make seasonings substituted for the fermented fish products of the south.

The third geographic region encompasses the mountainous regions of the Shan area to the east, the western Chin Hills and Kachin State in the north. Because many of these mountainous areas are poor, the local diet might well include items not found elsewhere, such as insect larvae, ants and grasshoppers. Parts of the Shan Plateau are a fertile exception, where hill rice, beans and lentils are grown and Lake Inle provides a variety of freshwater fish. As they lack the abundant fish and prawns of the southern regions of Myanmar, the Shan have developed fermented bean pastes that replace dried shrimp paste as a seasoning, and also make fermented soybean cakes similar to the Indonesian *tempeh*.

The staple diet

Allowing for some regional differences, what constitutes the average meal in Myanmar? A main meal – as opposed to breakfast or a between-meal snack – is based on rice, with the accompanying dishes chosen to provide a contrast of flavours and textures. There will usually be a thin soup (*hingo*), often slightly sour and with leafy greens floating in it, which is eaten throughout the meal to "help wash down the rice". Then there should be at least one curry of either meat, poultry, fish or even egg; you can tell by the colour roughly what the flavour will be like in advance, with red signifying lashings of chilli, white, a milder coconut gravy, and yellow, plenty of turmeric.

There will also be a cooked vegetable dish, maybe some lentils, a salad, a chilli-hot condiment and almost certainly *balachaung*. When it comes to vegetables, the Burmese living outside the major cities or towns depend on a huge range of wild plants. These include aquatic

The Burmese have a sweet tooth, especially in the afternoons, when they snack on moun – made from coconut, sticky rice, tapioca and fruit. Bein moun, pancakes made from rice flour and palm sugar, are another favourite.

plants gathered from rivers, canals and lakes, as well as various leaves, tubers, shoots, buds, seeds, and fungi found in the forests or along the edges of the rice fields. The young leaves of many shrubs and fruit trees such as papaya and mango

Eating mohinga, Downtown Yangon

BREAKFAST NOODLES

Myanmar's morning chorus is the sound of slurping as the "national dish" is devoured at food stalls throughout the country. Known as *mohinga*, this starts with pungent fish broth seasoned with lashings of dried shrimp paste, lemon grass, ginger, onion and garlic. This is added to a bowl of rice vermicelli, then topped off with the "small accompaniments" so beloved by the Burmese: crunchy wafers of dried soybean cake, chilli powder, fried garlic, coriander leaf, sliced fish cake, ground roasted chickpeas, egg and spring onions. Forget your breakfast rolls and coffee – *mohinga* is what real men (and women) eat for breakfast.

are also edible, as are the leaves of a number of root vegetables.

Salads and noodle dishes

The creativity of Burmese cooks is perhaps at its best when it comes to salads and noodle dishes. Salads – called *thoke*, which means "mixed by hand" – begin with raw vegetables, either a single vegetable or a wide range of leaves. For a salty flavour, fish sauce, salt or soy sauce are added, and for greater pungency, some dried shrimp paste or soybean powder.

Sourness comes in the form of tamarind,

Tasty street food

lime or vinegar, or perhaps some shredded sour fruit. To absorb the moisture of the sour juice, pounded dried shrimp, peanuts, roasted chickpea powder, sesame seeds or soybeans are added. To blend everything together, vegetable oil and sesame oil are added. The final garnishing comes in the form of crisp fried onion and garlic, roasted chilli and herbs such as mint, coriander, kaffir lime leaf or lemon grass.

Noodle dishes, too, can be dazzlingly complex in flavour and texture. Take, for example, the popular *mishee* from Mandalay, which begins with rice noodles. These are put into a bowl and topped with some deep-fried pork in batter, deep-fried beancurd puffs, a pickle made from fermented mustard greens and some crisp

bean sprouts. A ladleful of shredded pork in rich stock is added, then a dollop or two of garlic sauce, chilli sauce and a salty sauce made from preserved chilli bean curd. The finishing touch comes in the form of a sprinkle of chopped spring onions.

A more simple but equally tempting noodle dish – and one which has been adopted by northern Thais – is *kyauk shwe*, which consists of chicken simmered in a spicy coconut milk gravy made with plenty of onion, garlic, ginger and chilli. This fragrant mixture is poured over egg noodles, with slices of boiled egg, crisp-fried onions, chilli flakes, fresh coriander and a wedge of lime.

Snacks and stimulants

Burmese of all ages love to snack, and along the streets and the markets, *longyi*-clad cooks stand or squat over a single burner holding a wok full of bubbling oil, into which fritters of spiced lentils, dried beans, prawns, and mixtures of pork or chicken and vegetable are plunged. Hawkers offer spiced nuts, salted broad beans, banana chips, pancakes with sweet fillings, brightly coloured squares of sweet jelly, preserved dried fruits coated in sugar and spiked with chilli powder… it is truly a snacker's paradise.

Only in Myanmar can you drink your tea and eat it, too. You will, of course, find the usual beverage (better known as Indian or Ceylon tea) as well as Chinese tea. If you're lucky, you might also get the chance to sample tea-leaf salad or *lahpet* (also spelt *lepet*), made with young tea leaves packed into bamboo tubes and left to ferment. The leaves are mixed with salt and sesame oil, then served surrounded by lime juice, chilli and garnishes including fried garlic, dried shrimps, toasted sesame seeds, fried broad beans or dried peas. The secret is to take a pinch of two or three seasonings, together with some tea leaves, and discreetly pop it into your mouth.

The *lahpet* is supposed to act as a stimulant, and eating it is traditionally accompanied by as much ritual as the preparation of betel. This old custom, now dying out, involves smearing betel leaf with lime paste, wrapping it around sliced areca nut and spicing it to taste with fennel seeds, cloves or some shredded dried liquorice.

Tropical fruits

Myanmar offers all the luscious fruits of the tropics, many of them available year-round.

You'll find juicy mangoes; sweet pineapples; papayas; bananas of different sizes, skin tones and flavours; pomelos (massive citrus fruits reminiscent of but far superior to grapefruit); giant jackfruit which can weigh up to 25kg (55lbs), and the purple-skinned mangosteen, which has a translucent white flesh with a perfect balance of sweetness and acidity.

And then there is the durian, whose foul-smelling spiky exterior encloses large seeds covered with a buttery flesh that tastes, to the initiated at least, like heaven. Sir James George Scott, who wrote *The Burman His Life and Notions*, said: "Some Englishmen will tell you that the flavour and the odour of the fruit may be realised by eating a "garlic custard" over a London sewer; others will be no less positive in their perception of blendings of sherry, delicious custards, and the nectar of the gods…"

Eating out in Myanmar

Finding indigenous Burmese cuisine isn't as easy as you might expect. Particularly in the major cities, migration of ethnic Chinese and Indians has resulted in many restaurants offering Chinese or Indian food, without a Burmese dish in sight. In Yangon and Mandalay, and tourist centres such as Bagan and Inle Lake, you'll have a choice of the usual five-star restaurants in hotels – which serve Western-style and pan-Asian menus – and more modest pizza-pasta-curry places pitched at independent travellers. However, with the recent increase in tourism, true Burmese cuisine is increasingly available in elegant restaurants in Yangon and in upmarket hotels elsewhere.

Alternatively, if you want to sample real local cuisine, try the simple, semi-open-air restaurants and food stalls, especially those clustered around the markets. And in the more out-of-the-way locations, you're likely to be limited to Burmese eateries. The surroundings are usually basic – with cement floors, Formica tables and dining halls opening straight onto the street – but the food is invariably fresh and delicious, though it helps if you've some familiarity with the routine.

First off, order your main-course curries from the hot plates or pots on display. When you sit down, an array of little side dishes and condiments will usually be brought to your table, to be replenished when they're empty: a dhal-style soup or sour broth for dipping; various plates of steamed seasonal veg; *balachaung*; pickled tea leaves; green tea; and lumps of jaggery

> The two main kinds of tea you'll encounter are the standard Burmese variety, which is loaded Indian-style with milk and sugar, and lighter Chinese tea, which is weaker and comes without milk.

(un-refined cane sugar). Food is usually eaten with the fingers or by using a fork and spoon, unless it is a noodle soup when a spoon and pair of chopsticks are used.

The curries forming the centre of the meal

Mangoes for sale in downtown Yangon

will be of fish, chicken, prawn or mutton, or sometimes vegetables; and they'll invariably be swimming in oil. This unctuous covering, intended to help keep the dish fresh and insects at bay, can be spooned off. The sauce beneath, featuring copious amounts of ginger, garlic and tomatoes, will be highly spicy, but not hot. The Burmese are nowhere near as fond of chillies as their Bangladeshi or Thai neighbours. Curries tend to be mild, but flavoursome.

Out on the streets in the evenings, rows of grab-and-go stalls offer plates of freshly prepared fried and noodle dishes, which you can eat on little plastic chairs. Locally brewed Mandalay Beer often accompanies the food. For more on eating out in Myanmar, see page 318.

Scratching patterns in lacquerware, Myinkaba village, Bagan.

ARTS AND CRAFTS

The time-honoured skills of lacquerware, metalwork, woodcarving and embroidery are still much in evidence in modern-day Myanmar.

From Yangon's Bogyoke Aung San Market to Mandalay's Zegyo, and at all local bazaars beyond and between, visitors to Myanmar will find a remarkable variety of native handicrafts. Stalls display lacquerware, metalwork, brass and marble sculpture, woodcarvings, embroidered textiles and more. Burmese craftsmen may not have achieved the same international renown as artisans from other parts of Southeast Asia, but they are no less skilled.

Lacquerware

Burmese lacquerware has developed into an art form of refined quality. Its history can be traced to China's Shang dynasty (18th to 11th century BC). The craft reached the area of present-day Myanmar in the 1st century AD by way of the Nan Chao Empire (modern Yunnan), and is believed to have been carried to Bagan during King Anawrahta's conquest of Thaton in 1057. Today, it thrives in northern Thailand and Laos, as well as in Myanmar.

Raw lacquer is tapped from the thitsi tree (*Melanorrhoea usitatissima*) in the same way as latex is taken from the rubber tree. As soon as the sticky-grey extract comes in contact with the air, it turns hard and black. In the past, extraordinarily fine lacquerware bowls were produced around inner cores made of a mixture of horsehair and bamboo, or even pure horsehair. This gave such flexibility that one could press opposite sides of the bowl's rim together without the bowl breaking or the lacquer peeling off. Today, two other techniques of manufacture prevail. Inferior products have a gilded lacquer relief on a wooden base. Better-quality wares have a core of light

The finest attention to detail.

bamboo wickerwork, which assures elasticity and durability.

This basic structure is coated with a layer of lacquer and clay, then put in a cool place to dry. After three or four days, the vessel is sealed with a paste of lacquer and ash, the fineness of ash determining the quality of the work. It may come from sawdust, paddy husk or even cow dung. After this coating has dried, the object is polished until smooth. Over time, it is given several successive coats of lacquer to eliminate irregularities. At this stage, the ware is black – ornamental and figurative designs must still be added. Cheaper articles are simply painted, while expensive ones are embellished

Brightly painted paper and resin parasols are a speciality of Pathein. You'll see these exquisitely painted items on sale at souvenir shops in most tourist areas, but it's best to buy in Pathein, direct from the dozen or so workshops dotted around the town.

by means of engraving, painting and polishing. A similar effect can be produced with coloured reliefs, which are painted and partially polished. Red, yellow, blue and gold are the most frequent colours used. The production of

A woman prepares gold leaf in the Gold Pounders district of Mandalay.

BURMESE SILK

Before the influx of imported textiles in the colonial period, silk was an important product of Henzada and Amarapura. Henzada silks were heavy and brocade-like, while Amarapura specialised in shot silks in red, green and yellow, with the weft (the threads that lie across the cloth) colours generally lighter than those of the warp (the threads that run lengthways). Certain colour combinations such as two shades of green were considered unlucky, while rose-pink was much sought-after. All textiles were made on simple frame looms in Burmese households. Today, expensive silk *longyi* often display peacocks or floral designs.

such multi-coloured lacquerware takes about six months, involving 12 or more stages of manufacture.

Generally, the designs represented in lacquerware are of Buddhist origin, derived from the *Jataka* Buddha life-cycle stories, images of the Buddha, and celestial animals from Hindu-Buddhist mythology. Among the most common icons are the *chinthe* or lion, the *hintha* or goose, the *naga* or serpent, the *galoun* or eagle, and – unlikely, perhaps, in such distinguished company – the unassuming *youn* or rabbit.

Metalwork

The most frequently seen evidence of Burmese metalwork is probably the gold leaf, pasted by Buddhist devotees on pagodas and Buddha images all over the country. The industry is especially prevalent in Mandalay.

The gold comes from the north of the country in nuggets, which are flattened on a slab of marble until paper-thin. These sheets are then alternately cut and pounded between layers of leather and copper-plate until they are almost transparent. Then they are picked up with pincers, placed between sheets of oiled bamboo paper, and neatly packaged in 2cm (1-in) -long stacks of 100 leaves, for sale at pagodas and bazaars. An ounce of gold can produce enough gold leaf for an area of 10 sq metres (12 sq yds).

Burmese silverwork dates back to the 13th century, when palace bowls, vases and betel-nut boxes, as well as daggers and sheaths, were made. Today, the craftsmanship at Ywataung village near Sagaing rivals that of the earlier artisans. While silverwork is not as prominent as it once was, work in copper and brass has never seriously declined in importance and it remains a major cottage industry in Mandalay for about 300 families. Bago (Pegu) is another important centre. Here, Buddha images, orchestral gongs, bells for pagodas and monasteries, and small cattle bells are in constant demand.

Bronze Buddha images

Foundry workers cast bronze Buddhas and ritual implements using the ancient "lost wax process" in the Tampawaddy district of Chanmyathazi, just outside Mandalay (between Maha Muni and the airport). The process is a complex one and requires real skill. The artisan begins by making a mould in three stages. First, a mix is made of dust, manure, ochre clay and rice husks, which is blended with water to make a fine clay-like mixture. The Buddha image-to-be is then moulded with consummate skill from the clay mixture, before being allowed to dry and then covered with layers of wax. Finally, the wax is covered with two further layers of clay, and the whole is fired, allowing the wax to melt and run away – hence the "lost wax process".

Cast Buddha images are generally made from a mixture of copper and zinc. Smelting takes place over a large pit filled with coal or charcoal; this is fanned to a great heat, permitting the metals to melt and blend in a huge clay crucible. The molten metal is then poured into the inverted mould through one of two small holes left there to permit egress of wax and ingress of molten bronze. The bronze is poured into one hole, taking the place of the lost wax, until it begins to emerge from the other hole. After a day or two solidifying and cooling, both the outer layers and inner core of clay are removed with a hammer and chisel. Finally the Buddha image is filed, polished and generally made perfect. It may then be decorated, often with a crown or flame-like halo.

At the marble Buddha workshops near Maha Muni pagoda, Mandalay.

WHERE TO SHOP

Nearly everywhere you visit in Myanmar will have markets selling traditional handicrafts and other potential souvenirs, and these are great places to spend your money, as you can be sure most of it will reach the local people who most need it. In addition, upscale hotels nearly all have souvenir boutiques, selling similar merchandise at inflated prices. Either way, don't count on being able to pay with plastic.

For sheer variety, you can't beat the country's two largest shopping areas: Bogyoke Aung San Market in Yangon, and Mandalay's Zegyo Market. Both offer a vast selection of antiques, fake antiques, arts and handicrafts, in all price brackets.

Another rich source of things to take home is the concessions lining the stairways to Buddhist pagodas, which specialize in quintessentially Burmese religious paraphernalia, from incense to mini Buddhas and prayer beads. Worth looking out for here too are *kammawa* – traditional "books" of Buddhist manuscripts written on slats of wood, cane or cloth with gilded borders. Beautiful floral motifs and images of birds and animals often embellish the lines of script – rendered in a square style known as "tamarind seed" *(magyi-zi)*. In a similar vein are *parabaik* palm-leaf manuscripts, which are bound together concertina fashion.

> *"Money scales and weights are all fabricated at the capital, where they are stamped and afterwards circulated throughout the empire."*
> Symes, Account of an Embassy to the Kingdom of Ava (1795).

Buddha images may be the most obvious and the best-known products of Burmese bronze-making artisans, but they are far from being the only product. Other items cast or beaten in bronze include huge bells – the best example

Teak carvings at Shwenandaw Kyaung Monastery, Mandalay.

of which is the mighty bell cast on the orders of King Bodawpaya in 1790, and reputedly the second largest in the world after the cracked monster at the Kremlin. Burmese bells cast in this fashion have no hanging central clapper as in Europe, but instead are designed to be hit on the outside with a wooden club.

Also made of bronze, the small "opium weights" that were once used throughout the country are now produced on a large scale for sale to visitors as souvenirs. Properly sold in sets of 10, these weights are kept with a set of scales in a specially carved wooden box, usually stained black. The earliest known weights date back to the 14th century, and today's reproductions have changed little. The weights are often in the form

of mystical animals or birds from the Hindu-Buddhist pantheon, such as the *hintha* (celestial goose) and the *karaweik* (Indian cuckoo).

Woodcarving

Woodcarving is among the oldest of Burmese handicrafts, although evidence of the ancient artisans' skills has been destroyed. Significant 19th-century works still survive in Mandalay, particularly in the ornamentation of monasteries. Today, *nat* images are among the objects most commonly made. The artisans first sketch the figures they wish to carve on a solid block of wood, using charcoal and chalk, then shape an outline with chisel and saw. Details are completed with knives and other fine instruments.

Marionettes have traditionally been made for *yok thei pwe* or the marionette theatre. Often exquisitely carved and colourfully clad, these hinged, wooden figures make excellent gifts, and are now manufactured for sale at shops and bazaars all over the country, but especially in Yangon and Mandalay.

Up to a metre (3ft) in height, the marionettes are controlled by as many as 60 strings, although 10 would be a more usual number. The function of the strings, together with skilful jointing, is to enable the puppets to portray basic human movements such as walking, dancing and stylised gesturing. Characters featured in traditional marionette theatre include Thagyamin, the King of the Nat, a human king, queen, prince and princess, a regent, two court pages, an elderly couple, a sage, a villain, four ministers and two clowns.

A typical troupe of marionettes includes 28 such traditional characters. Animals, real and mythological, also feature in the troupe – for example, horses, elephants, monkeys and *makara* sea serpents.

Painting

Painting has long been an esteemed art throughout Myanmar, with the subject matter often derived from Buddha birth stories and related themes. The temples of Bagan were richly adorned with painted murals, many of which have survived to the present day, albeit in a faded and dilapidated state. In these early examples of temple decoration, Indian influence – and especially that of the Ajanta school – is apparent. Most murals were painted directly onto plaster made from a mix of clay, with sand and rice husks to provide a binding agent.

By the 19th century murals had become more indigenous in style, with the faces, costumes and buildings all taking on a distinctly Burmese quality. Buddhist themes remain predominant, and are almost always drawn from the Theravada tradition, although Mahayana subject matter – for example, representations of Avalokitesvara or Guan Yin – and some Hindu iconography drawn from the *Ramayana* are also found. During the British colonial period, a school of Burmese watercolour painting devel-

Makers of marble religious works of art in southern Mandalay get their raw materials from a quarry at Sagyin 34km (21 miles) north of Mandalay.

able to adorn themselves with precious gold and fine clothes.

Court dress in ancient periods often featured expensive silks and cloth embroidered with gold and silver threads, and adorned with fine lacework. Some court costumes from the days

At work in a parasol workshop in Pindaya.

oped, which combined Western and Burmese artistic traditions and frequently features nationalistic subjects such as the exile of King Thibaw and the perceived uncouth mannerisms of the British. Examples can be found in a few galleries and art shops, especially in Yangon.

Embroidery

Dress and ornamentation have long been an important part of Burmese life, from the former royal court down to simple *pwe* festivities. The elaborate ornamentation of the Burmese court is mentioned as early as the 9th century AD in Chinese sources, while King Kyanzittha of Bagan felt able to boast in a 12th-century inscription that even his poor subjects were

of King Mindon and King Thibaw were particularly elaborate.

Related to the art of embroidery and popular as souvenir items among visitors to the "Golden Land" are the hangings known as *kalaga* or "Indian curtains". These are elaborately sequined and padded wall hangings on black velvet, featuring scenes from the Buddha's life, Hindu-Buddhist mythology and – at least in recent years – more secular subjects such as elephant fights, warriors and princesses, flowers, trees and scenic views. The technique used for making *kalaga* is ancient but adaptable; today's artisans incorporate the art form into clothing, blankets and even gaily coloured bags and caps.

THE PERFORMING ARTS

Most musical theatre and dance in Myanmar is
inspired by ancient myths and legends, and by
Brahman-Buddhist beliefs.

"The description of the Burmese as a happy
and smiling person is borne out on the
stage more than one would think possible."
– James R Brandon, *Brandon's Guide to Theatre
in Asia*, 1976
To the Burmese, a festival or fair of any kind
means a *pwe*. It is a time to gather the entire
family together and go along to watch a mixture of dance, music, comedy and the recrea-
tion of epic drama. Burmese theatre often has
its audience shrieking, sobbing and rolling with
laughter. No one visiting the country, especially
between November and May, should miss an
opportunity to take in at least one form of the
Burmese performing arts.

Shan traditional dance.

Understanding pwe

There are several types of *pwe*. Most popular
is the *zat pwe*, the ultimate mélange of music,
dance and dramatics. *Anyein pwe* is a more
"folksy" theatrical form presenting episodes
from daily life, along with dancing and sto-
rytelling. *Yein pwe* is pure dance, solos alter-
nating with group numbers. *Yok thei pwe*, or
marionette theatre, is a uniquely Burmese theatrical form not so often seen today. *Nat pwe*
is ritual spirit-medium dance, only performed
in public at animistic festivals, and rarely seen
by visitors.

Among other forms of theatre, *pya zat* is
often seen before *zat pwe* performances. A
dance-play with mythical themes, it is generally set in a fantasy world where a heroic prince
must overcome the evil-doings of demons and
sorcerers.

From the mid-18th to the mid-19th centuries,
a masked dance-drama called *zat gyi* flourished
in royal courts under the patronage of Burmese

kings. Today, public performances are rare,
although papier-mâché replicas of *zat gyi* dance
masks can be purchased at souvenir stalls along
the stairs leading to the Shwedagon Pagoda.

Myanmar has a National Theatre, a company of 14 dancers and musicians who, due to
sanctions on the Burmese regime, have been
sadly absent from the international scene
– although that may be about to change.
Other troupes are trained in the State Schools
of Music and Drama in Yangon and Mandalay.
Countless troupes travel around villages and
during pagoda festivals, staging performances
throughout the countryside during the dry
season.

These troupes present their repertoire to throngs of villagers, performing on temporary bamboo stages, under a makeshift awning or (more often than not) in the open air. Large audiences sit on mats spread in front of the stage. Many bring their children, as well as picnics. Performances often last from sunset to sunrise; many spectators doze off for a couple of hours in the middle of the show, hoping to be nudged awake for their favourite dance sequence or story.

Dance-drama

The history of Burmese dance troupes dates

Konbaung dynasty era in Mandalay. Although some stylistic leaps and turns of Western ballet were introduced and assimilated during the years of British colonial rule, enthusiasm for dance went into a period of decline. Efforts have been made to revive theatre arts, and while the programme has been quite successful, it's also been very inward-looking.

Setting the mood is an orchestra, called the *saing*, akin to the Javanese *gamelan* and dominated by percussion instruments. Its centrepiece is a circle of 21 drums, the *patt-waing* (smaller orchestras have only nine drums).

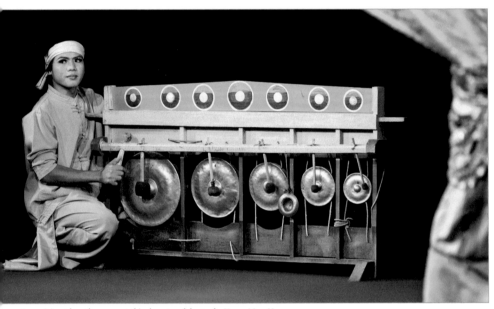

A musician plays the gongs at this show to celebrate the Karen New Year.

back as far as 1767, when King Hsinbyushin returned to Ava after his conquest of the Thai capital of Ayutthaya. Among his captives were the royal Siamese dancers. It was from these exquisitely trained performers that the Burmese developed the dance movements which prevail on stage today.

During the pre-eminence of Bagan from the 11th to the 13th centuries, a form resembling Indian dance had been popular at pagoda festivals and royal audiences. This had disintegrated into popular drama after the fall of Bagan, and took a back seat to the highly refined Thai classical dance. But it still wielded some influence in shaping a uniquely Burmese dance form. Burmese dance reached its zenith in the late

PERFORMING PWE

Pwe is a generic Burmese term for theatrical performances and dramatic shows. It embraces all kinds of plays, dramas and musical operas. Dancing is inevitably part of a *pwe*, and performances generally last for at least eight hours, and often right through the night. It's possible to make a loose classification of different types of *pwe*, thus a *zat pwe* is a religious performance based on the various Jataka, or Buddha life-cycle stories, while a *yama zat pwe* is based on the great Hindu epic, Ramayana. *Anyein pwe* are plays without plots, usually accompanied by clowning, ironic repartee and dancing. Finally, *yein pwe* feature group singing and dancing.

Around this are a gong section, a single large drum, cymbals, bamboo clappers, an oboe-like woodwind instrument, a bamboo flute and a bamboo xylophone.

Occasionally, an orchestra will employ the most delicate of all Burmese instruments, the 13-stringed harp. Shaped like a toy boat covered in buffalo hide, with silk strings attached to a curved wooden "prow", it is a solo instrument usually played by a woman, unlike other musical instruments, which are all played by men. When used in a *pwe*, it accompanies solo singing.

> Burmese dance emphasises double-jointed suppleness. Wrists, elbows, knees, ankles, fingers and toes are bent in stylised directions with seeming effortlessness.

preceding Buddhahood are seen as especially important.

As the stories are well known beforehand, it is up to the troupe and its individual dancers to bring them to life for audiences. The highlight of a *zat pwe* performance usually

A performance of a traditional Kachin dance.

Legendary tales

Ancient legends permeate all aspects of theatre in Myanmar. Nearly all performances are based on the Hindu epics (the *Ramayana* in particular), or on the *Jataka* tales of the Buddha's 550 prior incarnations. The *Ramayana* is the best-known saga in South and Southeast Asia; it tells the story of the capture of the beautiful Princess Sita by the demon king Dasagir, and of her heroic rescue by her husband, Prince Rama. The *Jataka*, meanwhile, are familiar to every Burmese schoolchild and adult. The tales relate, in a quasi-historical moral fashion, how the Buddha overcame the various mortal sins to attain his final rebirth and enlightenment. The 10 tales of incarnations immediately

comes in the early hours of the morning at about 2am, when the stars of the show let go with a breathtaking exhibition of their skills.

Marionette theatre

An exception to all other forms of theatre is the *yok thei pwe*, or marionette theatre. A single master puppeteer manipulates 28 dolls, some with as many as 60 strings. He presents the dialogue simultaneously, while getting help from only two stage assistants.

Puppet theatre in Burma had its foundation not long after Hsinbyushin's return from Ayutthaya with the Siamese court dancers. The king's son and successor, Singu Min, created a Ministry for Fine Arts, and gave his minister, U Thaw, the task of developing a new art form.

In 18th-century Burma, and to some extent even today, modesty and etiquette forbade the depiction of intimate scenes on the stage. Further, many actors refused to portray the future Buddha in the *Jataka* tales, considering this to be sacrilegious. U Thaw saw a way around these obstacles. What human beings could not do in public, wooden figures could do without prohibition. And thus the *yok thei pwe* was born.

The orchestra opens with an overture to create an auspicious mood. Then two ritual dancers appear, followed by a dance of various animals and mythological beings to depict the first stage in the creation of the universe. Next, making its appearance alone, is the figure of the horse, whose heavenly constellation brings order to the primeval chaos. Then (in order) a parakeet, two elephants, a tiger and a monkey come on stage.

The imagination of the audience is stirred with the entrance of two giants, a dragon as well as a *zawgyi* (sorcerer) who always flies on stage. These figures prepare onlookers for the magical world of Brahman-Buddhist belief, which provides the

Wa dancers in Yangon dance in honour of the Karen New Year.

THE MAHA GITA

The complete body of Burmese classical songs is generally referred to as the *Maha Gita*, meaning "Great Song" or "Royal Song". These are the songs and music of the various Burmese royal courts, which today form the basis of Burmese classical music. The impact of the *Maha Gita* on the performance of Burmese music can hardly be overstated. It forms the basis of both the chamber music ensemble, the *hsaing* ensemble and also of solo musical instrument performances such as the piano. The *Maha Gita* also provides much of the basis for music in the theatre, both that of the puppet tradition and that which employs live actors.

plot for almost all puppet plays. According to traditional Buddhist doctrine, each organism consists of 28 physical parts. U Thaw, seeking to be consistent with this belief, directed that there should be precisely 28 marionettes. Each of these is almost a metre (3ft) tall, faultlessly carved and with costumes identical to the originals that U Thaw specified. The two principal characters are a prince and princess – Mintha and Minthami – around whom the romantic plot of the performance always revolves.

The *yok thei pwe* is fast disappearing in modern Myanmar. It can occasionally be seen at temple festivals, including the Shwedagon Pagoda festival in Yangon, and regularly in Mandalay at tourist-oriented marionette theatres.

Musical performances

The structure of Burmese music is little known outside the country. There has been little systematic study of it and writings by Burmese scholars are even today extremely rare. It is generally related to the music genres of Southeast Asia and often uses gong and chime instruments similar to those found in neighbouring countries.

Burmese music lacks a chromatic scale, or even chords. But the melody pounded out on drums and gongs is mellowed by the other instruments, and love songs are as touching as they would be if they were played on violins. There are two distinct modes of performance: a chamber music ensemble which prominently uses the Burmese harp or *saung gauk*, and the outdoor gong and drum ensemble known as *hsaing*. Both ensembles share a single vast repertoire. This body of music is known as the *Maha Gita*, or great song.

Burmese music consists of a series of seven tone scales referred to as *athan*. In theory, a series of seven tones is recognised as basic. Each of these seven pitches can be used as a starting tone for one or more "modes" (a form of tonal sequence that preceded scales in the West).

Unless you're lucky enough to catch a performance at a venue in Yangon or Mandalay, the place you're most likely to experience traditional Burmese music is at your hotel. Most of the five-stars employ musicians to serenade diners, or as evening entertainment.

The contemporary music scene

While traditional Burmese folk and classical music have been actively promoted by the military regime since the 1960s, with slots on state-controlled TV and radio, the same is not true of the new generation of popular music coming out of Yangon and Mandalay. Heavily influenced by trends in Korea, Europe and the US, Myanmar pop music is dominated by so-called "copy tracks" – covers of foreign hits sung in Burmese, or a mixture of Burmese and English.

Queen of the copy scene is the flamboyant Phyu Phyu Kyaw Thein, who belts out chart toppers such as Queen's "You've Got to Break Free" and Celine Dion's "I Am Your Lady" while dressed in peacock-feather hats or figure-hugging pink-lamé jump suits.

Much less acceptable to the authorities are the numerous hip-hop acts which have dominated the country's underground music scene since the early 2000s. More masculine, aggressive and

> "The girl began to dance... a rhythmic nodding, posturing and twisting of the elbows... like a jointed doll, and yet incredibly sinuous." George Orwell Burmese Days.

materialistic in tone, they adopt the familiar style of US hip-hop – low-slung jeans, baggy T-shirts and baseball caps – but are just as likely to rap about political and social issues as girls-ganja-and-good-times. Others resort to obscure meta-

A ceremony on the road between Yangon and Mount Popa.

phors to express their anger at oppression and poverty. The upshot has been heavy censorship, and in some cases imprisonment of artistes.

With YouTube as a platform to bypass state-controlled media, popular music is one of the main ways in which established attitudes to gender and sexuality are being challenged in Myanmar. Short skirts, high heels and dyed hair are nowadays commonplace in the world of girl singers and bands.

One of the ironies of modern Burmese pop, however, is that while many of its most high-profile stars and promoters are seen as opposing the establishment, a large proportion are children of top members of the military regime or its cronies – this ensures them a degree of immunity from persecution, while fomenting feeling against the regime their parents remain part of.

THE MANY IMAGES OF BUDDHA

Buddha images have been integral to Burmese fine arts for almost 1,500 years, reflecting the creative skill of artisans and their deep religious beliefs.

Images of the Buddha in Myanmar come in many styles. Experts divide them into various groups, distinguished either by historical period or by region of origin. The earliest major group derives from Bagan and dates from the 11th to 13th centuries. Bagan-style Buddhas, whether of bronze, alabaster or wood, are usually heavy-set with broad shoulders and large faces. The head, set on a short neck, often tilts slightly forward.

An equally distinguished but separate tradition developed across the Rakhaing Yoma in and around Mrauk U. This Rakhaing style, which favoured stout Buddhas with square faces, joined eyebrows and often elaborate crowns, was responsible for the famed Maha Muni image taken from Rakhaing in 1784 and now displayed in the Maha Muni Pagoda in Mandalay. This image, the most revered in Myanmar, is coated in so much gold leaf that the lower part of the body is difficult to distinguish.

Mon images, by contrast, are often slimmer and more etiolated in design, with fuller faces, downcast eyes and very long ears. Again quite distinct, Shan Buddha images tend to have semi-triangular-shaped faces narrowing towards the chin. A broad forehead arches over narrowed eyes, partly open. Earlobes are long, noses fairly pronounced, and necks shortened. Mandalay-style images are common. Earlier images dating from the Inwa (Ava) period are often carved from alabaster, while later images are made of bronze or gilded wood. Eyebrows are slightly raised, and nostrils flared.

The Shweyattaw Buddha statue, Mandalay Hill.

Buddha at Sun U Ponya Shin Pagoda, Sagaing, near Mandalay

Buddha statues embellish the exterior of Kaba Aye Pagoda in Yangon

Row upon row of Buddhas at Bodhi Tataung, in the Monywa area.

ASANA AND MUDRA

The Buddha is invariably depicted in one of four traditional basic postures, or *asana*. These are standing, sitting cross-legged, walking or reclining. In the first three of these postures, the Buddha is perceived as teaching or meditating. In the fourth *asana*, by contrast, the Buddha's death and attainment of *parinirvana* (nirvana beyond death) is celebrated. Equally important and conventional are the various hand postures or *mudra* of the Buddha. In the *bhumisparsa mudra*, or "calling the earth to witness" posture, the right hand of the seated Buddha image touches the ground while the left rests on the lap. In the *dhammachakka mudra* or "turning the wheel of dharma", the thumb and forefinger of the image form a circle while the other fingers fan out to symbolise the preaching of the First Sermon. In the *abhaya mudra*, or "displaying no fear" posture, the palm of the right hand is raised and turned outwards to show the palm with straight fingers. In the *dhyana mudra* or "meditation" position, the hands rest flat on the lap, one on top of each other, while in the *dana mudra* or "offering" position the right hand is palm up and parallel to the ground.

Seated Buddha at Nga Htat Gyi Pagoda, Yangon.

Buddha statues inside the Dhammayangyi temple, Bagan.

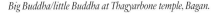

Big Buddha/little Buddha at Thagyarbone temple, Bagan.

Stairs leading up the side of Shwesandaw temple, Bagan.

TEMPLE ARCHITECTURE

The Burmese landscape is scattered with dazzling pagodas, shrines and stupas – a legacy of the country's Buddhist merit-making traditions.

Myanmar possesses a singularly wide range of Buddhist architectural styles, and one of the reasons for this is the eclectic nature of Burmese Theravada Buddhism, which incorporates elements from a range of sources.

In times past the dominant Bamar people have borrowed cultural traditions and traits from other groups such as the Mon and the Rakhaing. The country's religious and cultural traditions have also been influenced by conquests abroad, most notably in the former Kingdom of Lan Na (now northern Thailand) and in Siam (Thailand). From the extinction of the Mon Kingdom of Thaton in the 10th century, through the long occupation of Lan Na (1564–1774), to the destruction of Ayutthaya in 1767, it was common practice for skilled artisans and religious scholars to be taken back to enrich and embellish the Burmese court of the time.

Buddhist builders

The wide diversity of temple styles in Myanmar is also a consequence of the oft-repeated habit of new rulers of moving the royal court. New temples and religious edifices would then be built to compliment and serve the new palace and royal court, a process that encouraged a constant updating of religious architecture.

The sheer number of Buddhist structures scattered throughout the country leaves a lasting impression on visitors. Many are of exquisite beauty – most famously at the golden Shwedagon Pagoda in Yangon. Their ubiquity is a result of the seemingly endless desire of all Burmese to build temples, shrines and, above all, *stupas* or *zedi*. In spiritual terms, this has everything to do with merit-making, the possibility of an improved rebirth and compensation for

Dhammayazika temple is lit up at sunset, Bagan.

transgressions committed in the present life. Raising funds to build *paya* (pagodas) of any sort also brings the sponsor respect and status in the current life, and leaves a fitting memorial for the family to be proud of after the builder has passed on to the next life.

Zedi styles

The most common *paya* seen throughout Myanmar is the *zedi*, more commonly known in Western literature as the stupa. There are numerous variations in *zedi* style, but the basic concept and structure remain the same.

The stupa in its present form evolved more than 2,500 years ago in India following the death of

> *Hti refers to the umbrella-shaped pinnacle at the top of Buddhist stupas. The hti is often gilded and jewelled, and bears small bells.*

Gautama Buddha, when relics of the "Enlightened One" were taken by his disciples and enshrined within solid structures, usually of brick and stucco. In Southeast Asia, and especially in Myanmar, hollowed-out stupas – which could be entered by devotees – evolved to house Buddha images. *Zedi* are found everywhere in Myanmar, marking passes, raised mounds and hilltops, and sacred places of

View of Hsinbyume Paya from the top of Mingun Paya, near Mandalay.

all kinds. Commonly, however, they form part of an extended *paya* complex comprising a *kyaung* or *pongyikyaun* – that is, a Buddhist monastery.

Generally speaking, most Burmese *zedi* consist of square or octagonal terraces supporting a bell-shaped dome which is often likened to a *thabeiq* or monk's bowl, or sometimes to an *anda* or temple bell. Above the dome, the *zedi* narrows to a tall spire supported by concentric rings shaped like lotus petals and banana buds.

At the top of the spire rests the *hti*, decorated umbrellas (usually gilded and bejewelled) near the top of which is attached a metal, flag-like vane. The topmost part of the *hti* is surmounted by an orb, symbolising enlightenment, release from the cycle of rebirth and the attainment of nirvana.

Temple and monastery buildings

Typically, a Burmese monastery forms the spiritual centre of the village or district in which it may stand. Traditionally, it functions as a place of worship for monks and lay people alike, as well as a school, social centre and even a hospital.

Temples tend to be built around *zedi*, but include other buildings such as a *thein* or consecrated assembly hall for the ordination of novices, a *vihara* where the faithful assemble to pray and listen to sermons, living quarters for resident and itinerant monks, a library and a bell tower or gong.

The central *zedi* is often surrounded by several smaller shrines or *gyo-daing* which may house Buddha images, or equally may be dedicated to the local tutelary spirit or *bo bo gyi*. Sometimes there is also a *zayat*, a hall where lay people may rest by day or sleep overnight during pilgrimages and festivals.

Another common feature of Burmese temples is the *pahto*, a building which sometimes substitutes for, but more usually compliments, a *zedi*. *Pahto* tend to be square or oblong, often massively built with low passageways and small windows, sometimes with several floors and passages leading to outer terraces. The *pahto* represents a symbolic Mount Meru, the home of the gods, which worshippers can climb and venerate.

Pyu

The oldest surviving remains of religious buildings in Myanmar date from the pre-Bamar Pyu Kingdoms of Beikthano, Thayekhittaya (Sri Ksetra) and Halin (approximately 3rd to 10th centuries). Brick-built structures at Beikthano,

---

THE WORDS OF NORMAN LEWIS

"The special sanctity of the Shwedagon arises from the fact that it is the only pagoda recognised as enshrining relics not only of Gautama, but of the three Buddhas preceding him. Those of the Master consist of eight hairs, four of them original… and four others, miraculous reproductions generated from them in the course of their journey from India. These, according to the account… flew up, when the casket… was opened, to a height of seven palm trees. They emitted rays of variegated hues, which caused the dumb to speak, the deaf to hear, and the lame to walk. Later, a rain of jewels fell, covering the earth to knee's depth." – *Golden Earth* (1952).

to the southeast of Bagan, which have been dated to between the 1st and the 5th centuries AD, are clearly based on Indian prototypes. The Beikthano Monastery complex is said by experts to be similar to that of Nagarajunakonda in South India and is believed to date from the 2nd century. Later structures at Thayekhittaya, also known as Sri Ksetra, near Pyay, have been dated to the 5th and the 9th centuries and include three bulbous stupas evincing clear Indian influence.

Also attributed to the Pyu, stupa-like brick structures at Halin, a short distance southeast of Shwebo, are thought to date from between

Today, little of ancient Thaton remains apart from sections of a ruined city wall. Even less remains at another former Mon capital, Bilin, just south of the famous balancing boulder *zedi* of Kyaikto. Over the past millennium, the Mon have been substantially absorbed by the dominant Bamar, leaving little evidence of distinct architectural styles.

It seems clear, however, that Mon traditions were not destroyed, but rather embraced with enthusiasm by Anawrahta when he conquered Thaton in 1057. The victorious Bamar monarch took back to his capital at Bagan not just the

The Shwedagon's main stupa at dusk.

the 9th and 11th centuries. Skeletons excavated here are aligned to the southeast, commonly considered the direction of the locality spirit or *ein-saung nat*, indicating that the religious beliefs of these early Burmese were probably as much animistic as Buddhist.

Mon

Well established in and around Mon State and the Ayeyarwady Delta by the 6th to 9th centuries, the Mon were the first indigenous people on the east side of the Bay of Bengal to embrace Buddhism. The early Mon kingdom centred on Thaton, which according to legend was visited by Buddhist missionaries of the Indian Emperor Ashoka as early as 300 BC.

Mon king, but most of his court, including architects, painters and artisans. The style of temple which emerged at Bagan was therefore as much Mon as Bamar, and may be described as the first authentically "Burmese" tradition.

Bagan

Had Bagan been known to classical European antiquity, it would doubtless have been famous as one of the Wonders of the World. In its prime, the city would have bustled with tens of thousands of people, and the greater part of the buildings would have been made of wood and bamboo. These structures have long since disappeared, leaving behind the immensity of Bagan's Buddhist architectural heritage.

The Bagan plain is studded with a plethora of temples and stupas, constructed mainly of brick and decorated with stucco on the outside, and mural paintings within. Archaeologists often distinguish between the earlier, one-storey temples dating from the 10th to 12th centuries, which are sometimes ascribed to the Mon craftsmen of King Anawrahta. Many have Mon inscriptions, and they are distinguished by being smaller and darker than the later temples.

Clear evidence exists that the building of *paya* was considered an act of merit-making during the Bagan era just as it is now, and that their construc-

Art historians recognise two distinct features of Rakhaing temples: the combined use of brick and stone, and the enclosure of temples by massive walls, giving a fortress-like appearance. It appears that Rakhaing temples often functioned as places of safe refuge during times of war. Within the massive walls, the narrow corridors and passages were often elaborately decorated with both painted murals and carvings. The inspiration for the Rakhaing temples, such as those found at Mrauk U, can be traced to distant Bihar, across the Bay of Bengal in India, rather than to the nearby but generally inaccessible Burmese heartlands.

Shop selling hti (temple umbrellas) outside Maha Muni pagoda, Mandalay.

tion was not limited to the great and the powerful. Bricks were donated by kilns in surrounding villages, and sometimes these were stamped with a village name. When finished, the temples were decorated on the inside with elaborate murals, generally featuring *Jataka* Buddha life-cycle stories.

Rakhaing

Isolated from the rest of the country by the coastal Rakhaing Yoma range of hills, and enjoying good seaway communications with neighbouring Bengal, Rakhaing – formerly known as Arakan – was an independent kingdom until its conquest by King Bodawpaya in the 18th century. For this reason, its architecture is distinct from that of the rest of Myanmar.

THE SPELL OF THE PAGODAS

The beauty of Myanmar's pagodas casts a spell over visitors that is hard to break. Ralph Fitch, the first Englishman to visit (in 1586) and record his impressions, described the Shwedagon as "the fairest place, as I suppose, that is in the world".

And Somerset Maugham on first seeing Bagan wrote: "A light rain was falling and the sky was dark with heavy clouds when I reached Bagan. In the distance I saw the pagodas for which it is renowned. They loomed, huge, remote and mysterious, out of the mist of the early morning like the vague recollections of a fantastic dream".

– *The Gentleman in the Parlour* (1930).

Amarapura and Mingun

Amarapura, the "City of Immortality", was founded by King Bodawpaya in 1783 and remained the capital of Burma until 1857, with a hiatus between 1823 and 1841, when the city of Inwa (Ava) was briefly re-established.

The religious architecture of Amarapura is essentially a continuation of the Avan tradition. Marble was increasingly used in temple construction, and the period is also marked by the extravagant use of stucco in *paya* decoration, notably at the elaborate Nagayon shrine. Various Chinese and European architectural influences became apparent perhaps for the first time in Burmese history. Murals surviving on the walls of the Kyauktawgyi Pagoda (completed in 1847) are particularly interesting, providing the visitor with some vivid examples of mid-19th-century wooden monastic architecture.

Although never a Burmese royal capital, the city of Mingun, on the west bank of the Ayeyarwady River about 11km (7 miles) upstream from Mandalay, was singled out by King Bodawpaya (1782–1819) as the site of the huge Mantara Gyi (Mingun) Pagoda. Work was

Shwenandaw Kyaung Monastery, Mandalay.

REFINED INWA (AVA)

Ava – officially named Inwa – functioned as the centre of the Shan Kingdom in the 14th to 16th centuries before becoming capital of Burma during the 17th and 18th centuries. As with Bagan, many religious and secular buildings were made of wood, but, unlike Bagan, in Ava a few wooden *paya* have survived, most notably the *Bagaya kyaung*, though in its present form this dates from the early 20th century. During its infancy, the religious architecture of Ava was distinguished by the use of stucco decoration, the refined elegance of its stupas – by now less bulbous and more tapering – as well as very elaborate *pyat-that* or multi-roofed pavilions.

started in 1816, but Bodawpaya died before the project was completed, coming to a halt when the *zedi* was a "mere" 50 metres (160ft) tall, one-third of the height intended. It was subsequently damaged in the earthquake of 1838.

Mandalay

The last royal capital of Burma, Mandalay was established by King Mindon in 1857. The architectural style adopted by Mindon was in direct continuation with the Ava-Amarapura tradition, but if anything it was even more elaborate than the latter. Richly ornamented in stucco and marble, temples also benefited from a wealth of elaborate and highly skilled woodcarving, much of which has survived.

Sunset over pagodas in Bagan.

Fisherman on Inle Lake.

Ananda festival gathering in Bagan

PLACES

A detailed guide to the entire country, with principal
sites clearly cross-referenced by number to the maps.

*Inscribed marble slabs at
Kuthodaw Paya, Mandalay.*

The 28 days granted to foreign visitors by the standard
tourist visa are nowhere near enough to see the whole
of Myanmar. By catching planes rather than trains and
buses, however, you can sample its chief highlights in a couple of weeks, gaining along the way a vivid sense of what
makes this such a distinctive country.

Myanmar certainly has its fair share of astounding landscapes and monuments. For most visitors to the country, however, the warmth and traditional
culture of the Burmese themselves, miraculously intact despite the events
of the past fifty years or so, are what make a journey here so memorable.

Point of arrival for most international flights, Yangon (Rangoon) serves, as
it has for centuries, as Myanmar's main gateway. Though no longer
the capital (an honour now conferred on the recently erected city
of Naypyidaw, 320km/200miles north), it remains a pulsating, charismatic city whose crowning glory, the gilded Shwedagon Pagoda,
ranks among the world's most enthralling religious monuments.

From Yangon, an hour's flight north takes you to Bagan where,
between the 11th and 13th centuries, the Bamar kings embellished
an arid plain on the banks of the Ayeyarwady River with lavish temples, palaces and monasteries. Bagan can also be reached by cruise
boat from Myanmar's second city and cultural hub, Mandalay,
whose lacklustre modern architecture is more than offset by a profusion of Buddhist shrines, crafts workshops and music and dance venues, and
by the evocative vestiges of former royal capitals crumbling on its outskirts.

*A typical street in
Downtown Yangon.*

East of Mandalay rises the mighty Shan plateau, a tract of deep river valleys, rocky gorges and denuded hills rippling to the Chinese border. Boat
trips to markets, floating gardens and stilt settlements of the local Intha
people are the main incentive to visit this region's tourist centre, Inle Lake,
along with the famously serene sunsets, and the chance to trek to the neighbouring hill villages. With its waterside boutique hotels and souvenir markets, Inle has blossomed into a fully fledged international resort. The same
is true of Ngapali beach, in the northwest, where you can relax in luxurious
Thai-style beach hideaways under the palms.

The rest of the country's great sights, however, require more resilience
to explore – notably the atmospheric ghost city of Mrauk-U in Rakhaing
State, whose weed-infested stupas and monasteries soar above a landscape
of jungle and rice fields, and the southeast of the country, where the famous
"Golden Rock" temple of Kyaiktiyo gleams on a forested mountain top.

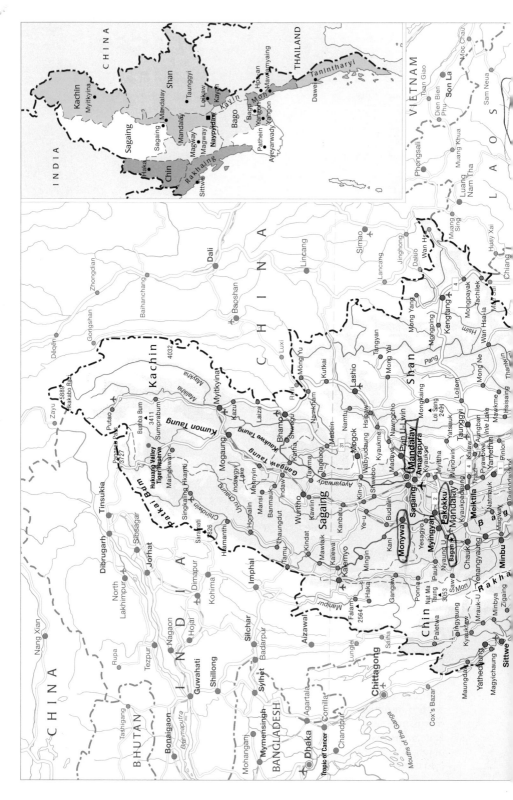

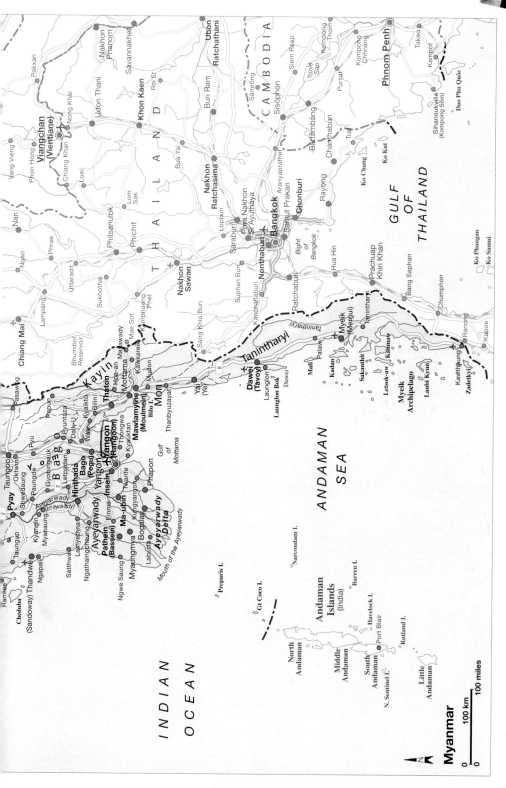

Myanmar

INDIAN OCEAN

ANDAMAN SEA

GULF OF THAILAND

THAILAND

CAMBODIA

Phnom Penh

Bangkok

Nonthaburi

Ubon Ratchathani

Nakhon Ratchasima

Khon Kaen

Viangchan (Vientiane)

Chiang Mai

Andaman Islands (India)

North Andaman

Middle Andaman

South Andaman

Little Andaman

N. Sentinel I.

Havelock I.

Rutland I.

Port Blair

Barren I.

Narcondam I.

Preparis I.

Gt Coco I.

Kayin

Mon

Mawlamyine (Moulmein)

Thaton

Mottama

Hpa-an

Bilu I.

Tanintharyi

Dawei (Tavoy)

Myeik (Mergui)

Myeik Archipelago

Kadan

Lanbi Kyun

Kawthaung

Zadetkyi

Yangon (Rangoon)

Insein

Bago (Pegu)

Bago

Ayeyarwady (Irrawaddy)

Ayeyarwady Delta

Pathein (Bassein)

Hinthada

Pyay

Taungoo

Ma-ubin

Ngwe Saung

Myaungmya

Bogalay

Labutta

Mouth of the Ayeyarwady

Gulf of Mottama

Cheduba

Ramree

Taungup

Ngapali

Thandwe (Sandoway)

Viangchan (Vientiane)

Pakxan

Nakhon Phanom

Savannakhet

Udon Thani

Nong Khai

Chiang Khan

Loei

Phon Hong

Vang Vieng

Nan

Ngao

Lampang

Phrae

Uttaradit

Sukhothai

Phitsanulok

Phichit

Nakhon Sawan

Lom Sak

Roi Et

Buri Ram

Siem Reap

Tonlé Sap

Samrong

Sisophon

Battambang

Pursat

Kompong Thom

Kompong Chhnang

Takeo

Kampot

Sihanoukville (Kompong Som)

Dao Phu Quôc

Ko Kut

Ko Chang

Trat

Chanthaburi

Rayong

Aranyaprathet

Chonburi

Samut Prakan

Bight of Bangkok

Phra Nakhon Si Ayutthaya

Lopburi

Saraburi

Suphan Buri

Kanchanaburi

Ratchaburi

Phetchaburi

Hua Hin

Prachuap Khiri Khan

Bang Saphan

Chumphon

Ranong

Kapoe

Ko Phangan

Ko Samui

Ratchathani

Bua Yai

Ban Phai

Kamphaeng Phet

Sang Khla Buri

Mae Sot

Tak

Myawady

Kawkareik

Mudon

Thanbyuzayat

Ye

Palaw

Mali

Sakanthit

Letsok-aw

Kanmaw

Kawthaung

Laungion Bok

Laungion

Dawei

Tanintharyi

Tanintharyi

Yai (Ye)

Kadan

Pakhan

Bilin

Kyaikto

Waw

Daik-U

Pyuntaza

Papun

Thongwa

Kyauktan

Twante

Kungyangon

Phapon

Letpadan

Pyu

Paungde

Gyobingauk

Swedaung

Oktwin

Myanaung

Kyangin

Kyaukpadaung

Satthwa

Lanyethna

Ngathaingchaung

Pasawng

Bhumibol Reservoir

0   100 km
0   100 miles

N

Fabrics for sale at Bogyoke
Aung San Market, Yangon.

YANGON AND THE AYEYARWADY DELTA

Beyond the old-world charms of Myanmar's largest city sprawls the vast Ayeyarwady Delta, a region of winding rivers and lush rice paddies.

The Shwedagon Pagoda is reflected in Kandawgyi Lake.

Despite having lost its capital status to Naypyidaw in 2005, Yangon remains Myanmar's principal city: with a population of around 5 million it is by far the largest urban area in the country. Few visitors spend more than a couple of nights sampling its distinctive atmosphere, but the faded colonial charm of the downtown district and resplendent Shwedagon Pagoda – just one among a wonderful crop of impressive Buddhist monuments – warrant at least a couple of days' sightseeing.

For centuries a lowly fishing village, Yangon rose to prominence only in 1755 after King Alaungpaya founded a harbour overlooking the confluence of the Yangon and Bago rivers. Under the British, who annexed the port in 1852, the city, renamed "Rangoon", became for a time one of the most prosperous and cosmopolitan in Southeast Asia. Grand fin-de-siècle administrative buildings were erected along its broad avenues and waterfront, reflecting the booming teak and gem-stone trade.

However, with the economic isolation of the independence era, the city entered a kind of time warp, defined by its dilapidated colonial architecture, dusty streets, vintage Wolseley cars and ageing fleet of trishaws – not to mention the pro-democracy demonstrations, military crackdowns and repeated incarcerations of NLD leader, Aung San Suu Kyi, at her Raj-era home in the northern suburbs. Signs of modernisation began to appear in the mid-1990s; with

Farming the land in the lush Ayerarwady Delta.

the city renamed Yangon, the vintage cars began to give way to shiny Japanese hatchbacks, and a handful of international-chain hotels sprang up in the centre. With the recent political changes, this process is now starting to accelerate, but the old-world charm remains in the city's old-fashioned teashops, sidewalk *mohinga* stalls, shabby old buildings and traditional street markets.

West of Yangon is the lush Ayeyarwady Delta, Myanmar's "rice bowl" heartland. The inhabitants of these watery lowlands, ravaged in recent years by a succession of devastating cyclones, still travel mainly by boat, through a labyrinth of canals and rivulets. The few foreign visitors who venture into the Delta tend to do so en route to Pathein, the country's fourth city and springboard for the beach resorts of Chaungtha and Ngwe Saung, a favourite weekend escape for Yangon's affluent classes.

Yangon

Pazundaung Creek →

PAZUNDAUNG

KYAUKTADA

BOTATAUNG

LATHA

PABEDAN

CHINA-TOWN

LANMADAW

Yangon →

Pazundaung

Shwe Bone Pwint Zedi

Nyaung-Gon Monastery

Sri Devi (Hindu Temple)

St Mary's Cathedral

Prime Minister's and Ministers Offices

Natural History Museum

Aung San Stadium

Yangon Central

Sakura Tower

Immanuel Baptist Church

Central Telex Office

Supreme & High Court

Strand Hotel ❹

Central P.O.

City Hall ❷

Sule Pagoda ❶

MTT ⓘ

❸ ❶

Independence Monument
MAHA BANDOOLA GARDEN

Botataung Pagoda ❺

Yangon Duty-Free Shop

FMI Centre

Bogyoke Aung San Market ❽

New Bogyoke Market

Sri Kali (Hindu Temple)

Theingyi Zei (Indian Market) ❼

Moseah Yeshua

Kon Zay Dan

English Methodist Church

Holy Trinity Cathedral

Defence Services Museum

Lanmadaw

Yangon General Hospital

Kheng Hock Keong (Chinese Temple)

❻

Dargah of Bahadur Zafar Shah ❶❷

National Theatre

MYOMA GROUND

New Yangon General Hospital

Ein Daw Yar Pagoda

National Museum ❾

Governor's Residence

Shwedagon Pagoda

Zoological Garden

GARDENS

Twante →

Pathein →

N

0   500 m
0   500 yds

YANGON

In Yangon, high-rises tower over ancient monuments in a city poised on the brink of sweeping change.

I n *Letters From the East* (1889), Rudyard Kipling wrote: "Then, a golden mystery upheaved itself on the horizon – a beautiful, winking wonder that blazed in the sun, of a shape that was neither Muslim dome nor Hindu temple spire. It stood upon a green knoll…'There's the old Shway Dagon,' said my companion… The golden dome said, 'This is Burma, and it will be quite unlike any land that one knows about.'"

It's more than 100 years since Kipling sailed up the Rangoon River to the Burmese capital, but the glistening golden stupa of the Shwedagon continues to dominate the city's skyline. The massive pagoda, said to be around 2,500 years old, is not only a remarkable architectural achievement; it is also the perfect symbol of a country in which Buddhism pervades every aspect of life.

The Shwedagon may be the undisputed show stealer, but this city holds plenty of less celebrated attractions. Spend a couple of days here and you'll have time to wander the tree-lined avenues and narrow backstreets of the colonial district downtown, with its court house, city hall and famous Strand Hotel, and to take in a few more pagodas, including the majestic Botataung Paya near the riverside. Re-fuel in a traditional Burmese teahouse before sampling the priceless treasures on show at

the National Museum, or mingle with the crowds milling around Bogyoke Aung San market.

The city's vivid street life makes a lasting impression: the street-side *mohinga* stalls, where diners dressed in traditional *longyis* and *htameins* tuck into bowls of steaming noodles; the ancient, overloaded, green-, cream- and red-painted buses jostling for space at junctions with the streams of trishaws, cycles and taxis; and the open-air markets, whose traders squat beside piles of fresh produce, an outsize cheroot

Main Attractions
Shwedagon Pagoda
Botataung Pagoda
The Lion Throne, National Museum
Bogyoke Aung San Market
Kyauk Htat Gyi Pagoda
Thanlyin
Ye Le Pagoda, Kyauktan

Crickets for sale in Bogyoke market.

Colonial buildings, Downtown Yangon

wedged in their mouth, and *thanaka* paste smeared over their cheeks.

With the country poised on the brink of rapid economic change, modernity is making its presence felt these days, particularly around the striking Sule Pagoda, whose gilded profile is dwarfed by the nearby skyscrapers. Yet the overriding impression of Yangon remains one of a city that has altered little since the British slow-marched to their waiting steamers in 1948.

Just across the river, the provincial towns of Thanlyin and Kyauktan hold other splendid Buddhist monuments in striking settings, and provide a welcome respite from the headlong rush of downtown Yangon, while the superb medieval stupas at Bago, a daytrip northwest, tempt many travellers to extend their stay.

Getting your bearings

Home to around 5 million people – the population has increased fivefold in three decades – Yangon is surrounded on three sides by water. The Hlaing or Yangon River flows from the Bago Yoma (hills) down its

western and southern flanks, past the Shwedagon and picturesque artificial lakes created by the British, which today form the focus of affluent residential districts. The river then continues through the Delta to the south, dumping its silt-laden waters in the Gulf of Mottama (Martaban).

Sri Lankan chronicles indicate that there was a settlement in the area 2,500 years ago known as Okkala – probably a fishing village or a minor Indian trading colony which grew in fame after the building of the Shwedagon Paya. For centuries, its history was inextricably bound to that of the great pagoda, and the nearby town of Syriam (Thanlyin), across the Bago and Hlaing rivers, which was Burma's main port well into the 18th century.

King Alaungpaya set Yangon on its modern path in 1755, when he captured the village from the Mon, destroying Syriam (Thanlyin) the following year. The British then conquered the town during the First Anglo-Burmese War in 1824, after which its port began to flourish again. Fire caused devastation in 1841 and,

A tricycle rider takes a break

in 1852, Yangon was again almost completely destroyed in the course of the Second Anglo-Burmese War, but thrived after the British annexation of the rest of Burma in 1885, largely on the back of the lucrative trade in teak and other natural resources procured in the north of the country.

Although the city today lies 30km (20 miles) from the open sea, Yangon's river is easily navigable, and the vast majority of the country's import and export trade is still handled in the docks at nearby Thanlyin. Industrial suburbs have mushroomed to the north and east, providing work for many of the immigrants flocking to the Yangon area. There is a sizeable Indian community – a hangover from the time when Burma was still a part of British India – as well as a large number of people of Chinese descent, and indigenous ethnic minorities.

EXPLORING YANGON

The old heritage district downtown is compact enough to explore on foot, albeit with frequent heat-beating pit stops in teahouses and cafés along the way. Motorbikes and scooters are not permitted in this area, making it a lot quieter and more relaxing for pedestrians than other cities such as Mandalay. However, quite a few of Yangon's sights lie further afield and are best reached by taxi. Cabs, identifiable by the signs on their roofs, come in a variety of shapes and sizes, but offer great value for money, with few trips across town costing more than K2,000–2,500 ($3–4). Moreover, the drivers themselves are considerably more courteous and honest than their counterparts in other Asian cities. That said, few speak fluent English, so it can help if you have the name of your destination written in Burmese.

Sule Pagoda

The most logical place to begin any tour of Yangon is the **Sule Pagoda** ❶ (open daily; charge), the shining stupa at the city's heart which the British used as the centrepiece of their Victorian grid-plan system in the mid-19th century. For centuries a focus of social and religious activity, the richly gilded monument rises from

TIP

There's no better way to kick-start a day's sightseeing in Yangon than breakfast in a traditional teahouse (see page 319).

Detail of houses and shops, Downtown Yangon.

TIP

Sule Pagoda is the point from which all distances to and from the former capital are officially measured.

the middle of a busy intersection, surrounded on all sides by shops, swirling traffic and a proliferating number of high-rise hotels and office blocks – a location that belies the stupa's great antiquity.

Its origins are believed to date back to 230 BC, when a pair of monks, Sona and Uttara, were sent from India as missionaries to Thaton after the Third Buddhist Synod. The King of Thaton gave them permission to build a shrine at the foot of Singuttara Hill in which the monks preserved a hair of the Buddha. The name "Sule Pagoda" itself, however, comes from a later period and is linked to the Sule Nat, or guardian spirit, of Singuttara Hill, who local legend claims showed the monks the site where the relics of three previous Buddhas had been buried. Inside, the pagoda's shrines and images include four colourful Buddhas with neon halos behind their heads. As with all stupas, visitors should walk around it in a clockwise direction.

As well as its religious significance, the Sule Pagoda is iconic among the Burmese as the venue for several famous political demonstrations over the past three decades, most notably the rally of 1988 when the military opened fire on unarmed protesters, killing and injuring dozens. The monument also formed the focal point of mass gatherings during the Saffron Revolution of 2007.

Downtown

The orderly blocks of late 19th- and early 20th-century buildings erected by the British on the banks of the Yangon River today comprise the largest collection of colonial architecture in Southeast Asia – a fact all the more remarkable for the virtual absence in their midst of modern, high-rise constructions. By turns elegant, pompous and flamboyant, the buildings perfectly epitomise the imperious self-confidence of the Raj at its zenith, and lend to the area as a whole an old-world grandiloquence that's rare for Asian cities of comparable size.

Having been occupied by squatters for decades, many of the structures have lapsed into an advanced state of

Sule Pagoda seen from the sky bar at the top of the Sakura tower.

disrepair, with mildew-streaked walls and peeling plasterwork. The grandest of all, owned by the Burmese government, were deserted completely when the administration decamped to Naypyidaw in 2005. Help, however, may be at hand. A group led by historian Thant Myint-U recently secured a moratorium on the demolition of all buildings over fifty years old, the eventual aim being to preserve and restore the area as a "heritage enclave" to attract foreign businesses and tourists.

The perfect primer for any tour of Yangon's colonial district is the massive **City Hall ❷** on the northeast corner of Sule Pagoda Road and Mahabandoola Street. Erected in 1924, it fuses typically British style with Burmese elements, such as traditional tiered roofs and a peacock seal high over the entrance.

On the southeastern corner of the same intersection stands **Maha Bandoola Garden ❸** (open daily; charge), named after a Burmese general of the First Anglo-Burmese War. In the centre of the park, the 46-metre (150ft) **Independence Monument** is an obelisk surrounded by five smaller, 9-metre (30ft) pillars. Formerly known as Fitch Square (after the 16th-century chronicler and trader, Ralph Fitch, who was the first Englishman to visit Burma), the park is popular in the early mornings with t'ai chi practitioners. Facing the square on the east side stands the Queen-Anne-style **Supreme Court**, dating from 1911, and similarly grand **High Court** building.

Southeast of the square on Strand Road, it's impossible to miss the famous **Strand Hotel ❹**, patronised by visitors from Rudyard Kipling and Somerset Maugham to Mick Jagger. After decades in the doldrums, the building was lavishly restored in the mid-1990s, though its timeless elegance endures, with colonial-style wicker furniture in the lounge and corridors of polished marble. Even if you can't afford the room rates, it's worth stepping into the teak-furnished lounge, where you enjoy high tea to the accompaniment of local harp music during the afternoon.

Afternoon tea is served at the Strand hotel.

The red-brick high court and the Independence statue, Mahabandoola Gardens.

TIP

Relive the old colonial days at the Strand Hotel by propping up its bar. Happy hours are from 5pm to 8pm daily.

The Botataung Pagoda

Heading east on Strand Road for several blocks brings you to the **Botataung Pagoda** ❺. It is said that when eight Indian monks carried relics of the Buddha here more than 2,000 years ago, 1,000 military officers (*botataung*) formed a guard of honour at the place where the rebuilt pagoda stands today. The original structure was destroyed by an Allies' bomb in November 1943.

During the clean-up work, a golden casket in the shape of a stupa was found to contain a hair and two other relics of the Buddha. In addition, about 700 gold, silver and bronze statues were uncovered, as well as a number of terracotta tablets, one of which is inscribed both in Pali and in the south Indian Brahmi script, from which the modern Burmese script developed. Part of the discovery is displayed in the pagoda, but the relics and more valuable objects are locked away. Among these is the tooth of the Buddha, which Alaungsithu, a king of Bagan, tried unsuccessfully to acquire from Nan-chao (now China's

Monsoon rain at Botataung pagoda.

Yunnan province) in 1115. China eventually gave it to Burma in 1960. The 40-metre (130ft) bell-shaped stupa is hollow, and visitors can walk around the interior. Look out for the glass mosaic, and the many small alcoves for private meditation. The small lake outside is home to thousands of terrapin turtles; you can feed them with food sold at nearby stalls, thereby acquiring merit for a future existence.

The markets

West of the Sule Pagoda are Yangon's main street markets. Before World War II, most of the inhabitants of the city were Indian or Chinese, and their influence is still reflected in this jam-packed district. Take a stroll through **Chinatown** ❻, stretching from Shwedagon Pagoda Road, west over 24th, Bo Yawe, Latha and Sint Oh Dan roads, where the cracked sidewalks are piled high with all manner of goods – bamboo baskets, religious images, calligraphy, peanut candy, melon seeds, flowers, dried mushrooms, handmade rice paper, caged songbirds, tropical

fish for aquariums and live crabs. In the evening these streets turn into a rambling outdoor restaurant, with stalls offering delicious soups, curries and other local dishes.

A few blocks back towards Sule Pagoda, the pungent aroma of curry powder and other ground spices emanates from the Indian Quarter. **Theingyi Zei ❼** (Indian Market) offers mounds of red chillies and fragrant cinnamon bark, boxes of tropical fruits such as mangosteen and durian, dried fish and seafoods, medicinal herbs, bottled concoctions and local snacks. The market is at the side of a Hindu temple on Anawrahta Street.

The largest and most interesting of Yangon's bazaars, however, is the **Bogyoke Aung San Market ❽** (formerly the Scott Market) to the north of the Indian and Chinese quarters at the corner of Sule Pagoda Road and Bogyoke Aung San Street. Stalls sell a wonderful range of Burmese handicrafts, a wide variety of textiles and craft objects, woodcarvings, lacquerware, dolls, musical instruments,

colourful longyis, Shan bags and wickerware. It's also a good place to shop for jade and gems, with nearly the entire ground floor taken up by ruby sellers. Opposite the Bogyoke Market, the New Bogyoke Market specialises in imported textiles, household appliances and medicines.

The National Museum

A short taxi ride northwest of the market district on Pyay Road, the **National Museum ❾** (open daily 10am–4pm; charge) stands in a neighbourhood lined with foreign missions. The museum's undisputed showpiece is King Thibaw's Lion Throne, originally from Mandalay Palace – one of many valuables carried off by the British in 1886 after the Third Anglo-Burmese War. Some items on show here were shipped to the Indian Museum in Calcutta; others were kept in London's Victoria and Albert Museum. The artefacts were, however, returned to Burma as a gesture of goodwill in 1964 after Ne Win's state visit to Britain. The wooden throne, 8 metres (27ft)

Temple offerings for sale outside Botataung Pagoda.

Jewellery for sale at Bogyoke Aung San Market.

TIP

Avoid changing money at the absurd official rate of exchange, which is more than 100 times less than you get from most banks. For more on changing money, see page 334.

tall and inlaid with gold and lacquerwork, is a particularly striking example of the Burmese art of woodcarving. Among the Mandalay Regalia are gem-studded arms, swords, jewellery and serving dishes. Artefacts from Burma's early history in Beikthano, Thayekhittaya and Bagan in the museum's archaeological section include an 18th-century bronze cannon and a crocodile-shaped harp.

THE SHWEDAGON PAGODA

"The Shwe Dagon rose superb, glistening with its gold, like a sudden hope in the dark night of the soul of which the mystics write glistening against the fog and smoke of the thriving city."
– W. Somerset Maugham, *The Gentleman in the Parlour* (1930)

Few religious monuments in the world cast as powerful a spell as Yangon's **Shwedagon Pagoda ❿** (open daily 4am–9pm; charge, tickets are not sold to foreigners before 6am), the gigantic golden stupa rising on the northern fringes of the city. The holiest of holies for Burmese Buddhists, it's also a potent symbol of national identity,

and in recent decades has become a rallying point for the pro-democracy movement.

Its unique sanctity derives from the belief that the stupa enshrines relics not merely of the historical Buddha, Gautama, but also those of three of his predecessors. No one, however, has been able to confirm whether or not the eight hairs of the Master actually lie sealed deep inside the stupa, as the structure would have to be partly destroyed to reach its solid core – something the shrine's custodians will never permit.

It's tempting when you arrive in Yangon to head straight for the mesmerising gilded spire on the horizon, but resist the urge if you can until early evening, when the warm light of sunset has a transformative effect on the gold-encrusted pagoda and its myriad subsidiary shrines.

The complex can be entered through four different gateways, each approached via elegant flights of covered steps (see below). Whichever stairway you use, be sure to remove your footwear at the bottom of the steps.

Sugar cane being pressed into juice, Bogyoke market.

The stairways (zaungdan)

The passageway most commonly used by visitors to the Shwedagon is the **Southern Stairway** Ⓐ *(zaungdan)*, which ascends from the direction of the city centre. Its 104 steps lead from Shwedagon Pagoda Road to the main platform. The entrance is closely guarded by a couple of statues representing two fearful mythological creatures – the *chinthe*, or leogryph, is a half-lion, half-griffin; the ogre, or giant, is a man-eating monster. If you're not up to the climb, note that this stairway also boasts a lift, the fare for which is covered by your entry ticket.

The **Western Stairway** Ⓑ, which leads up from U Wisara Road, was damaged during the Second Anglo-Burmese War and kept closed by soldiers from the British garrison. In 1931, a stall at the foot of the stairs caught fire. The blaze raced up and around the northern flank of the Shwedagon, causing severe damage to the precincts before being halted on the eastern stairway; unfortunately not in time to save many ancient monuments.

The Western Stairway is the longest *zaungdan* with 166 steps. The landing on the platform bears the name **Two Pice Tazaung** because of the contribution of two *pice* (a small copper coin) given daily by Buddhist businessmen and bazaar-stallholders for the stairway's reconstruction.

The **Northern Stairway** Ⓒ was built in 1460 by Queen Shinsawbu, and has 128 steps, with decorative borders shaped like crocodiles. Two water tanks can be seen to the north of the stairway; the one on the right is called *thwezekan*, meaning "blood wash-tank". The name derives from a popular legend recounting how, during King Anawrahta's conquest of the Mon capital Thaton, his commander-in-chief, Kyanzittha, used the tank to clean his blood-stained weapons. The northern entrance also features a public lift.

The **Eastern Stairway** Ⓓ is much like an extension of the Bahan bazaar, which lies between the Royal Lake and the Shwedagon. You might want to take a break at one of the teahouses on the stairway near the **Dhammazedi Stones**, placed there by the king in

TIP

To experience sailing down the Yangon River, go to the Pansodan Street Jetty, near the Strand Hotel, and board one of the frequent ferries for Dalah. It's about a 15-minute ride costing K2,000/US$1 (for tourists) for the round trip.

Novice monk at the Shwedagon.

TIP

Visit Bogyoke Aung San
Park at night when
open-air restaurants
offer barbecued food –
and in some cases,
folkloric performances –
in cool surroundings.

1485. This flight of 118 steps suffered particularly heavy damage during the British attack on the pagoda in 1852.

The upper terrace

A magnificent spectacle greets visitors emerging from the half-darkness of the covered stairways. In Somerset Maugham's words: "At last we reached the great terrace. All about, shrines and pagodas were jumbled pell-mell with the confusion with which trees grow in the jungle. They had been built without design or symmetry, but in the darkness, their gold and marble faintly gleaming, they had a fantastic richness. And then, emerging from among them like a great ship surrounded by lighters, rose dim, severe and splendid, the Shwe Dagon."

The terrace was created in the 15th century when the rulers of Bago levelled off the top of the 58-metre (190ft) -high Singuttara Hill. The main platform is inlaid with marble slabs, which can be very hot under unaccustomed bare feet, so a mat pathway is laid out for visitors. Walk around to discover the various prayer pavilions (*tazaung*) and resting places (*zayat*) sporting traditional roofs of five, seven or nine tiers.

The Shwedagon still dominates the city skyline.

The stupa

From the centre of the platform rises the gold-covered stupa itself, the reflected light from which casts an ethereal glow over the forest of subsidiary shrines, temples, pavilions and elaborately roofed halls below. Rising to a height of 99 metres (325ft) and with a circumference of 433 metres (1,421ft), the *zedi* adheres to traditional Burmese design, divided into distinct sections, each with its particular symbolic significance.

The base, or plinth (*paccaya*) rising from the main terrace is octagonal and on each of its eight sides rest eight smaller stupas – 64 in all. The four larger stupas opposite the stairways mark the cardinal points. At each of the platform's four corners are *manokthiha* (sphinxes), each surrounded by several *chinthe* (half-dragon, half-lion guardians).

The stepped terraces of the base, which only monks are permitted to

HISTORY OF THE SHWEDAGON

Although the origins of the Shwedagon are shrouded in legend (see page 39), it is known that the site was well-established on the pilgrimage circuit by the 11th century. Queen Shinsawpu (r.1453–72) is revered for giving the pagoda its present shape and form. She established the terraces and walls around the stupa, and donated her weight in gold (40kg/90lbs) to be beaten into gilt leaf and used to plate the pagoda.

King Hsinbyushin of the Konbaung dynasty raised the stupa to its current height of 99 metres (325ft) after a devastating earthquake in 1768 brought down the top of the spire. His son, Singu, had a 23-tonne bronze bell cast; known as Maha Gandha, it can be found today on the northwest side of the main pagoda platform. The British pillaged Shwegadon during their 1824–26 wartime occupation and tried to carry the bell to Calcutta, but the ill-fated object fell into the river. A third bell weighing more than 40 tonnes was donated by King Tharrawaddy in 1841: it sits today on the northeast side of the pagoda enclosure.

In 1931 the pagoda was seriously damaged in a fire, and has suffered from the effects of several earthquakes in recent years. Yet for all the Shwedagon's roller-coaster history, the Burmese are convinced no lasting damage can befall it.

access, merge into the stupa's elegantly curved "bell" *(khaung laung bon)*, which is divided from the so-called "inverted alms bowl" *(thabeik)* by the "turban band" *(baungyit)*. Above the bowl rests one of the most delicately embellished elements, representing 16 lotus petals *(kyahlan)*, which in turn give way to the uppermost section, or conical spire. This begins with a distinctively shaped banana bud *(hnget pyaw bu)* on which sits the 10-metre (33ft) *hti*, or umbrella, decorated with 1,485 gold and silver bells, 5,448 diamonds, and 2,317 rubies, sapphires and other precious stones. An enormous emerald sits in its centre to catch the first and last rays of the sun. Finally, crowning the very top of the monument is the golden orb *(seinbu)*, tipped with a single, exquisite 76-carat diamond.

Around the terrace

A constant swirl of activity surrounds the great stupa, as worshippers perform their ritual circumambulation of the monument, pausing to pray and perform rituals at the numerous shrines and planetary posts along the way. The circuit is always performed in a clockwise direction.

Directly opposite the top of the southern stairway stands the **Temple of the Konagamana Buddha ⓔ**. Its collection of Buddha statues includes some of the oldest on show at the pagoda. On either side you will see the **Planetary Post for Mercury**, one of eight planetary posts around the stupa, which worshippers venerate according to the day of the week on which they were born. A gilded alabaster Buddha figure is to be found beside each one.

On the southwestern side of the stupa is the **Chinese Community's Tazaung ⓕ**, a pavilion housing 28 small Buddha figures representing the Buddhas who have so far lived on earth, and nearby is a **Commemorative Column ⓖ**, inscribed in Burmese, English, French and Russian, honouring the 1920 student revolt which sparked Burma's drive for independence from Britain.

Continuing down this side of the platform, you'll soon reach the **Rakhaing Tazaung ⓗ**, built by two

Key rings depicting Aung San Suu Kyi.

The Shwedagon Pagoda.

TIP

Try not to limit yourself to a single visit to the Shwedagon Pagoda, whose appearance and atmosphere changes mysteriously with the shifting light.

wealthy merchants, next to which sprawls an 8.5-metre (28ft) reclining Buddha. Pictures on the rear wall depict the legend of the founding of the Kyaiktiyo Pagoda (see page 291). The pavilion is inlaid with beautiful, intricate woodcarvings.

Opposite stand **Statues of Me La Mu and Sakka ❶**, two legendary figures said to be the parents of King Okkalapa, the founder of the Shwedagon, and situated under white umbrellas, the symbol of royalty. The homeland of Sakka (or Thagyamin), king of the *nat*, is in the heavenly province of Mount Meru, the centre of the universe.

In an open area to the northwest of the stupa is a small octagonal pagoda known as the **Pagoda of the Eight Weekdays ❶**, whose sides hold niches containing small Buddha images, each with the figure of an animal placed above it, corresponding to the eight Burmese weekdays. Behind it is the huge bronze **Maha Gandha Bell ❻**, which King Singu had cast in 1779 and which was raised from the Yangon River in 1825 after the British

attempted to steal it. The bell weighs 23 tonnes and is 2.2 metres (over 7ft) tall. The **Assembly Hall ❶** opposite houses a 9-metre (30ft) Buddha image. Lectures on Buddhist teachings are frequently held in this *tazaung*.

There are a number of small stupas in the northwestern corner of the terrace. In one of these is the **Wonder Working Buddha Image**, which is nearly always decorated with flowers and surrounded closely by the faithful. The gilded Buddha in the stupa's niche has the reputation of being able to fulfil wishes and work miracles.

In the far northwest corner of the terrace are two **Bodhi Trees** decorated with flowers and small flags. The smaller of the pair grew from a cutting taken from the holy Bodhi tree in Bodhgaya, India, under which the Gautama Buddha gained enlightenment.

Returning to the main part of the pavilion, you'll notice an especially busy area. This is known as the **Wish Fulfilling Place**, where devotees kneel, facing the great stupa, and earnestly pray that their wishes will come

The Shwedagon at dusk, seen from the Northern exit.

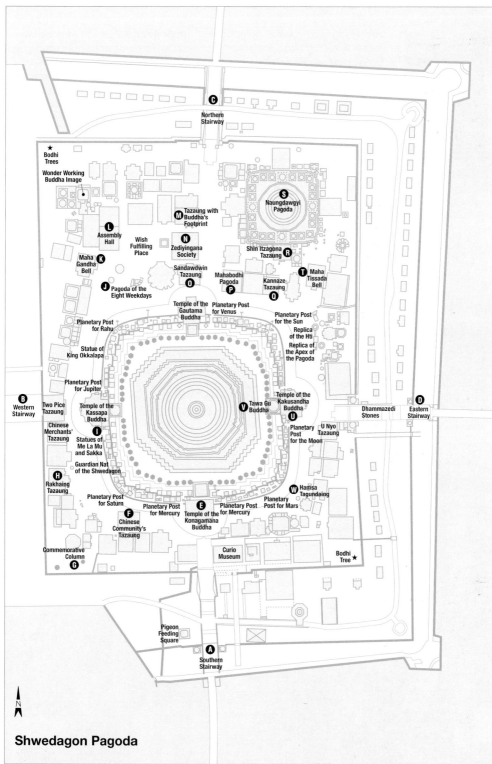

★ Bodhi Trees

Wonder Working Buddha Image

C Northern Stairway

S Naungdawgyi Pagoda

M Tazaung with Buddha's Footprint

L Assembly Hall

Wish Fulfilling Place

N Zediyingana Society

Shin Itzagona Tazaung **R**

K Maha Gandha Bell

Sandawdwin Tazaung **O**

Mahabodhi Pagoda **P**

Kannaze Tazaung **Q**

T Maha Tissada Bell

J Pagoda of the Eight Weekdays

Temple of the Gautama Buddha

Planetary Post for Venus

Planetary Post for the Sun

Planetary Post for Rahu

Statue of King Okkalapa

Replica of the Hti

Replica of the Apex of the Pagoda

Planetary Post for Jupiter

Temple of the Kakusandha Buddha

B Western Stairway

Two Pice Tazaung

I Temple of the Kassapa Buddha

V Tawa Gu Buddha

Dhammazedi Stones

D Eastern Stairway

Chinese Merchants' Tazaung

Statues of Me La Mu and Sakka

Guardian Nat of the Shwedagon

U Planetary Post for the Moon

U Nyo Tazaung

H Rakhaing Tazaung

Planetary Post for Saturn

W Hamsa Tagundaing

Planetary Post for Mercury

F Chinese Community's Tazaung

Planetary Post for Mercury

E Temple of the Konagamana Buddha

Planetary Post for Mars

Commemorative Column

G

Curio Museum

Bodhi Tree ★

Pigeon Feeding Square

A Southern Stairway

N

Shwedagon Pagoda

Architectural detail of Shwedagon, the gilded stupa also known as the Golden Pagoda.

Washing the Buddha statue on the planetary post for the moon, Shwedagon.

true. In a nearby cluster of pavilions not far from the north entrance is the **Tazaung with Buddha's Footprint ⓜ**. Life-sized statues of Indian guards stand in front of this hall, and a dragon protects a representation of the Buddha as prince. In front of the "prince" is a *chidawya*, or footprint of the Buddha, divided into 108 sections, each of which has a special significance. To the south is the library of the **Zediyingana Society ⓝ**, which has more than 6,000 books, many of them rare texts on religion and Burmese culture.

Between the library and the stupa is the **Sandawdwin Tazaung ⓞ**, built in 1879 over the spring in which, according to legend, the Buddha's eight hairs were washed before they were enshrined. The spring is said to be fed by the Ayeyarwady (Irrawaddy) River.

On the north side of the main stupa you will find the Temple of the **Gautama Buddha**, dedicated to the Buddha whose world dominion, it is believed, will last until the 45th century. Across the platform stands the **Mahabodhi Pagoda ⓟ**, a replica of the original pagoda of the same name

in Bodhgaya. You will notice that it is very different from all the other pagodas in the Shwedagon precincts, which are built in distinct Bamar (Burman) or Mon styles.

Across from the northeast corner of the stupa is the **Kannaze Tazaung ⓠ**. According to legend, it was here that King Okkalapa prayed for relics of the Gautama Buddha. The Buddha figure in this shrine is thus called Sudaungbyi, meaning "Buddha grants the prayer of the king". In front of it resides the "wish-granting stone", a sort of Delphic oracle. The etiquette is to bow before Sudaungbyi and lift the stone, saying, "May this stone seem light to me, if my wish is to be fulfilled." If the stone still feels heavy, the request has not been successful and the applicant's wish will presumably remain unfulfilled.

North of this pavilion is the **Shin Itzagona Tazaung ⓡ** housing a Buddha statue with large eyes of different sizes which is said to have been erected by, or for, Shin Itzagona, a *zawgyi* (alchemist) from Bagan's early period. According to legend,

Itzagona's obsession with discovering the Philosopher's Stone, the mythical substance said to be able to change base metals to gold or silver, plunged the country into poverty. When his final experiment was about to end in failure, he poked out both his eyes to satisfy the king. In his final casting, however, Itzagona did produce the Philosopher's Stone, and immediately sent his assistant to the slaughterhouse to obtain two eyes that would, with the stone's help, allow him to regain his sight. The assistant returned with one eye from a goat and another from a bull; from that time on, Shin Itzagona was known as "Goat-Bull Monk".

Just to the north is the **Naung-dawgyi Pagoda** Ⓢ, situated in the place where the eight hairs of the Buddha, carried by the merchants Tapussa and Bhallika, were originally kept. Nearby is the **Maha Tissada Bell** Ⓣ, commissioned by King Tharrawaddy in 1841. It weighs almost 42 tonnes, is 2.55 metres (8ft 4in) tall and has a diameter of 2.3 metres (7ft 6in) at its mouth.

Opposite the Eastern Stairway is the **Temple of the Kakusandha Buddha** Ⓤ, built by Ma May Gale, the wife of King Tharrawaddy, though later destroyed by the fire of 1931. The temple was rebuilt in its original style in 1940. The Buddha figure in this *tazaung* is unusual in that the palm of its right hand is turned upwards; three of the four smaller Buddha figures in front of the niche are also depicted in this unfamiliar posture. Behind the temple, in a niche on the eastern side of the upper platform, is the **Tawa Gu Buddha** Ⓥ statue, which is said to be able to work miracles.

Descend the Eastern Stairway just a short distance to arrive at the **Dhammazedi Stones**. The *tazaung* which originally housed these stones was one of the last buildings destroyed by the 1931 fire before the blaze was finally brought under control. King Dhammazedi, himself a *zawgyi*, has gone down in Burmese history as the "master of the runes". Next to the eastern entrance of the terrace is the **U Nyo Tazaung**, which has woodcarved panels that recount events in the life

Wooden souvenirs outside the Shwedagon Pagoda.

The Legend of Shwedagon

Myanmar's most famous sight has a long history, with its origins shrouded in legend.

The legend of the Shwedagon Pagoda goes back 2,500 years and centres on Okkalapa, King of Suvannabhumi, who lived near Singuttara Hill in Lower Burma during the time when Siddhartha

The Rakhaing Tazaung Buddha, Shwedagon.

Gautama was still a young man in northern India. The hill is considered holy because of the relics of three Buddhas enshrined on its summit. Local belief asserts that a new Buddha comes into existence every 5,000 years. As nearly 5,000 years have elapsed since the time of the last Buddha, it was thought that the hill would lose its blessedness unless a new incarnation offered a gift to be enshrined as a relic for the next five millennia. To this end Okkalapa spent many hours on the hill meditating and praying.

In India, meanwhile, Gautama was close to achieving enlightenment under the Bodhi tree in Bodhgaya. Buddhist chronicles assert that he appeared before Okkalapa and promised that the king's wish would be granted. Gautama meditated under the Bodhi tree for 49 days before he accepted his first gift from his disciples: a honey cake offered by Tapussa and Bhallika, two Burmese merchant brothers who had come from the village of Okkala. To express his gratitude, Gautama plucked eight hairs from his head and gave them to the brothers, who then set off on a return journey that proved difficult. First, they were robbed of two of the Buddha's hairs by the King of Ajetta. Then, while crossing the Bay of Bengal, another couple of hairs were taken by the seabed-dwelling King of the Nagas. Despite the losses, the brothers were welcomed by Okkalapa who held a great feast attended by all the native gods and *nat,* who decided a grand stupa should be built to house the relics.

When Okkalapa opened the casket containing the Buddha's hairs, lo and behold, he saw eight hairs in place. As he looked on in astonishment, the strands emitted a brilliant light that rose high above the trees, radiating to all corners of the world. Suddenly, the blind everywhere could see, the deaf could hear, the dumb could speak and the lame could walk. As this miracle took place, the earth shook and bolts of lightning flashed. The trees blossomed and a shower of precious stones rained onto the ground.

As a result of the legend of the hairs, the site chosen to enshrine the Buddha's hairs – Singuttara Hill – is considered one of the country's most sacred places, and the golden Shwedagon Pagoda is regarded as the holiest of the country's pagodas. "*Shwe*" is the Burmese word for "gold", and "*dagon*", a derivative of "*trihakumba*" (contracted to "*trikumba*", "*tikun*" and then "*dagon*"), means "three hills".

The Shwedagon Pagoda was later built over the shrine containing the Buddha's relics. Smaller pagodas, constructed with silver, tin, copper, lead, marble and iron brick, were built, one on top of the other, in the golden pagoda to enshrine the relics.

Night descends on the Shwedagon's main stupa.

of the Gautama Buddha. Close to the southeast corner of the platform is a **Hamsa Tagundaing**  or prayer pillar. Such columns are said to guarantee the health, prosperity and success of their founders.

At the far southeastern corner of the terrace is a **Bodhi Tree** which, like its cousin in the northwest corner, is said to be descended from the original at Bodhgaya. On the octagonal base which surrounds it is a huge Buddha statue. A **Curio Museum** (open daily; charge) is situated to the east of the pagoda's south entrance. It contains a collection of small pagodas, statues and other objects.

Part of the way down the Southern Stairway you will find a **Pigeon Feeding Square**. Pagoda pilgrims can buy food here to feed the dozens of pigeons, thereby earning merit for a future existence.

AROUND THE SHWEDAGON PAGODA

Numerous sites of religious and cultural interest lie dotted around the Shwedagon Pagoda, an area which

after Independence became the spiritual nerve centre of the fledgling Burmese nation.

Maha Wizaya Pagoda

A short distance southeast of the Pagoda, on the opposite side of U Htaung Bo Road, **Maha Wizaya Pagoda** ⓫ was built in 1980 using public donations to commemorate the unification of all Theravada orders in Burma. Its central image, housed in a circular shrine whose interior is festooned with painted stucco scenes of Buddha's life and Enlightenment, was a gift from the King and Queen of Nepal.

Dargah of Bahadur Shah

One of Yangon's rare Muslim monuments lies on an inconspicuous side street just south of the Shwedagon Pagoda. The **Dargah of Bahadur Zafar Shah** ⓬, at 6 Zi Wa Ka Road, is the final resting place of India's last Mughal emperor, who spent the final four years of his life at a house on the spot. An erudite, religiously tolerant and sensitive polymath with a talent

Souvenirs for sale outside the Shwedagon compound.

Maha Wizaya Pagoda, next to the Shwedagon.

TIP

The best way to nip
between sights uptown
is to wave down a cab
as and when you need
one, rather than book a
car and driver for the
day. Taxis are cheap and
plentiful across the city.

for Islamic calligraphy and poetry, Zafar somewhat reluctantly became a rallying point for the mutinous sepoys in the ill-fated Delhi Uprising of 1857 – and paid dearly for backing the wrong side. After the rebellion had been crushed, the British all but destroyed his former capital and palace, executing thousands and dispatching the king and the few surviving members of his family into permanent exile in Burma, where he died in 1862.

The exact whereabouts of the grave, which the colonial authorities kept secret for fear that it would become a martyr's shrine, was revealed in 1991 when workmen digging foundations for a mausoleum near the site of Zafar's former house came across a brick-covered structure 1.1 metres (3.5ft) beneath the surface. It turned out to be the grave of the last Mughal, alongside that of his wife and grandson. Since his death, the former ruler has come to be regarded as a latter-day saint and his modern tomb is now a place of pilgrimage for Indian Muslims. The three silk-covered tombs on the ground floor are for show; the real ones lie hidden in a tiled crypt below, which the caretaker can unlock on request.

Martyrs' Mausoleum

Also worth a visit in this area is the **Martyrs' Mausoleum** ⑬, which crowns a low hill to the north of the Shwedagon Pagoda, beyond Arzarni Road. This essentially secular, patriotic monument contains the tombs of Aung San, father of Aung San Suu Kyi and leader of the Burmese independence movement, as well as six of his ministers who were assassinated during a cabinet meeting in 1947. Aung San was only 32 at the time. The pre-World War II prime minister, U Saw, was subsequently found to be the instigator of the plot, and was executed the following year, together with the hired assassins. The mausoleum is also notorious as the site of the bombing of October 1983 which killed 21 people, including three South Korean ministers who were accompanying their President on a state

*Meditating inside
Botataung pagoda*

MEDITATION COURSES

As a profoundly Buddhist nation, Myanmar naturally attracts individuals from all over the world who wish to study the techniques of meditation. Residential courses, which typically last for a week, are offered by several monasteries in and around Yangon. Longer courses, lasting four weeks or more, are also available, but these require a special Meditation visa. The best-known venue is the Mahasi Meditation Centre (www.mahasi.org), established by the esteemed Mahasi Sayadaw in 1947. The programme is definitely only suitable for those with a high level of commitment: the day's meditation and rituals typically begin at 3am and end at 11pm, and on some courses students are required to remain completely silent for the duration of their stay.

visit. Members of the North Korean army were later found to have carried out the attack.

Nga Htat Gyi Pagoda and Kyauk Htat Gyi Pagoda

From the mausoleum, if you take the northern exit on to Shwegondaing Road, turn right and follow the main road northwest for ten minutes, you'll reach the spectacular **Nga Htat Gyi Pagoda** ⓮, in which a huge sitting Buddha, dating from 1558, resides in an early 20th-century shrine. Sometimes called the "five-storey Buddha" because of its size, the figure is unique for the huge, flame-like pieces of gilded armour, or "magites", protruding from his giant head and shoulders.

On the opposite side of Shwegondaing Road, **Kyauk Htat Gyi Pagoda** ⓯ (aka the "Chaukhtatgyi Temple"), the other beautiful temple in this area, lies only five minutes' walk away. Not really a pagoda in the traditional sense, the Kyaukhtatgyi is actually a *tazaung* (pavilion) housing a colossal, 70-metre (230-ft)

reclining Buddha. Although the sculpture is bigger than the reclining Shwethalyaung Buddha of Bago, it is not as well-known or as highly venerated. Elsewhere in the pagoda enclosure is a centre devoted to the study of sacred Buddhist manuscripts. The 600 monks who live in the monastery annex spend their days meditating and studying the old Pali texts.

Koe Htat Gyi

You'll need to jump in a cab to visit the last of the major religious sites in the Shwegadon area. The **Koe Htat Gyi** ⓰ (literally "Nine Storey") **Pagoda** lies a 10–15-minute drive west on Bargayar Road, a stone's throw from the river. Its centrepiece is a 20-metre (65ft) -high sitting Buddha, with eerily life-like eyes made from blown glass. Inside the figure, a small casket is said to contain relics of the historical Buddha, as well as those of some of his disciples. In the area surrounding the complex are a great many kyaung (monasteries), where early birds can watch the monks emerging onto the

On the boat leaving for Dalah (Delta Region).

Reclining Buddha at Kyauk Htat Gyi Pagoda.

streets to fill their alms bowls just after sunrise.

PARKS AND LAKES

Yangon boasts more than a dozen public parks and gardens, and locals take great pleasure in spending the hot hours of the day resting in them, preferably beside a lake, in the shade of mature trees. Just east of the Shwedagon Pagoda, the northern shore of **Kandawgyi** ("Royal") **Lake** is given over to **Bogyoke Aung San Park** ⑰, dedicated to the country's most famous martyr, and whose children's playgrounds and picnic areas are popular attractions with young families.

The park's best-known sight is the surreal **Karaweik Restaurant** ⑱, on the eastern shore. Constructed in the early 1970s, the floating structure replicates a *pyi-gyi-mun*, or royal barge, such as those Burma's kings and queens would traditionally have used on ceremonial occasions. With its double bow depicting the mythological *karaweik*, a water bird from Indian prehistory, and a multi-tiered

pagoda on top, the restaurant is made of brick and concrete (wood was not considered because it has a relatively short life span) and anchored to the lake bottom. Its equally sumptuous interior contains some striking lacquerwork embellished with mosaics in glass, marble and mother-of-pearl. In the evenings, starting at 6.30pm, popular buffet dinners (K20,000/US$25 per head) feature a three-hour culture show including music, classical dance and puppetry.

Inya Lake and around

Continuing through the winding residential streets north of the Shwedagon, past the "Yangon modern" stucco houses built for Westerners in the colonial era, you'll arrive at enormous **Inya Lake** ⑲. As well as the Yangon University campus, the lush area surrounding it holds some of the city's most prized real estate and exclusive neighbourhoods, including the British-era home of NLD leader, Aung San Suu Kyi, whose tall, barbed-wire-covered gates are invariably patrolled

Ornate Karawik restaurant, on Kandawgyi Lake.

by a gaggle of photographers and journalists. Next to the university, the 15-hectare (37-acre) lakeside park is the most popular place in the city for romantic trysts – images of amorous couples schmoozing on the grassy verges are a cliché of Burmese movies and popular song videos.

The southwest corner of the lake, by contrast, is tainted with much darker associations. During the civil unrest of 1988, an estimated 283 students were beaten to death or drowned by military police on the shore – an event dubbed "the White Bridge Massacre". A further 3,000 people are thought to have lost their lives in the brutal crackdown that ensued.

With its prize exhibits now moved to a display in the new Burmese capital, Naypyidaw, the government-run **Gems Museum**, at 66 Kaba Aye Pagoda Road (Tues–Sun 9am–5pm; charge), just north of Inya Lake, is a lucklustre affair despite some impressive sapphires and star rubies, as well as a whole floor of jewellery emporia where you can purchase objects fashioned from Burmese jade and precious stones.

The Kaba Aye Pagoda and Mahapasana Cave

Immediately northeast of Inya Lake is the **Kaba Aye Pagoda** ⓴, which the first prime minister of independent Burma, U Nu, built in the early 1950s. Legend has it that an old man dressed in white appeared before the monk Saya Htay while the latter was meditating near the town of Pakokku on the Ayeyarwady River, handing him a bamboo pole covered with writing. He then asked Saya Htay to pass the pole on to U Nu, accompanied by a demand that the prime minister actively do more for Buddhism.

U Nu was as well versed in religious affairs as in politics, and not only received the bamboo pole but amazingly complied with the old man's demand. The country's leader built the Kaba Aye Pagoda about 12km (8 miles) north of downtown Yangon in preparation for the Sixth Buddhist Synod of 1954 to 1956, and dedicated it to the cause of world peace.

Although lacking some of the aesthetic appeal that distinguishes the other Yangon pagodas, the Kaba Aye is interesting. It is circular in shape,

Performing the Aung Mingalar dance.

A walkway filled with souvenirs at the Kaba Aye Pagoda.

TIP

If you're in the area in late January, it's worth trying to coincide your visit with the Thaipusam festival, in which local Tamil devotees of the Hindu God Murugan stick skewers through their cheeks and walk on hot coals.

Lawka Chantha Abhaya Labha Muni (or Kyauk Daw Kyi Pagoda).

and contains relics of the two most important disciples of the Buddha, discovered in 1851 by an English general; they were only returned to their rightful place in the Kaba Aye Pagoda after spending many years at the British Museum in London. Opposite each of the five pagoda entrances stand 2.4-metre (8ft) -high Buddha statues. A platform holds another 28 small gold-plated statues that represent previous Buddhas. Some 500kg (1,100lbs) of silver were required to cast the central Buddha figure in the inner temple.

In the grounds of the Kaba Aye Pagoda is the **Maha Pasana Guha**, or "great cave", which U Nu also had specially built for the Sixth Buddhist Synod. It is supposed to resemble India's Satta Panni Cave, where the First Buddhist Synod took place shortly after the death of Gautama. Devout Buddhist volunteers completed the project only three days before the start of the Synod in 1954. The cave has an assembly hall that can accommodate up to 10,000 people. When the Synod ended, the Institute for Advanced Buddhist Studies was founded with its headquarters in the Kaba Aye Pagoda compound. Funds from the Ford Foundation contributed to the construction of its handsome main building, which successfully blends elements of modern architecture with traditional symbolism.

In December 1996, during a ritual when pilgrims were streaming through to see a tooth relic of the Buddha, the complex was the scene of a bomb attack that killed five people and injured dozens more. The atrocity is thought to have been mounted by the military regime as part of a campaign to provide justification for a crackdown on political opposition.

THE NORTHERN OUTSKIRTS

A couple of sights on Yangon's northern outskirts may tempt you to break a journey to or from the city's international airport.

The **Mai La Mu Pagoda ㉑**, in the suburb of Okkalapa, is named after the mother of King Okkalapa, founder of Dagon and original donor of the Shwedagon. According to legend, Mai La Mu – said to have been born from a mango *(me-lu)* tree and raised by a

AN AUSPICIOUS MOVE

One of the ways in which the kings of ancient Burma expressed their wealth and power – and acquired cosmic merit at the same time – was by creating huge stone Buddhas. In 2000, the country's military generals revived the tradition with the arrival at a purpose-built hilltop temple on the outskirts of Yangon of a giant Buddha carved from a single block of flawless white marble.

The boulder used to make it had been discovered the previous year by master sculptor, U Taw Taw, at the famous quarry of Sangyin, near Mandalay. It took him and his sons twelve months to carve. Recognising the PR potential of sponsoring the project, the generals spared no expense to bring the 600-tonne colossus to Yangon, constructing a special 8-rail train line to transport it to the Ayeyarwady, and a huge golden barge to ship it downriver. The 12-day trip, featuring a flotilla of vessels, was cheered from the banks by vast crowds. Another specially laid rail line conveyed the statue to its new home atop Mindhamma Hill, where the 11-metre (37ft) image – christened Lawka Chantha Abhaya Labha Muni – was enshrined inside a giant glass case. Attracting constant streams of devotees, the mighty white Buddha is today one of Yangon's most popular religious attractions.

hermit – had this pagoda built to alleviate her grief after the untimely death of her young grandson. Her statue can still be seen on the southwestern flank of the Shwedagon Pagoda. The complex, a wonderland of gilded spires and vibrantly painted statues, is of particular interest because it contains numerous illustrations and figures from the *Jataka* tales, depicting the Buddha in earlier lives and fashioned in a singularly Burmese style. The pagoda also holds a large reclining Buddha.

West of the airport, in the township of Insein, stands the **Ah Lain Nga Sint Pagoda** ㉒ – a centre of worship for adherents of the branch of Burmese Buddhism that places great emphasis on the occult and supernatural phenomena. The grounds contain a five-storey tower, a hall with statues of all kinds of occult figures, and a *kyaung* which serves as a residence for monks.

Lawka Chantha Abhaya Labha Muni and Elephant Park

A popular visitor destination in the northern suburbs of Yangon is the temple housing the enormous **Lawka Chantha Abhaya Labha Muni** ㉓ statue. Carved from a single block of white marble, the 11-metre (37ft) -tall image was sculpted in 1999–2000 and installed in a lavish new shrine paid for by the military government. See box below.

Less than five minutes from the new temple, on Mindhamma Road in Inthein Township, is the site of another prestige-winning initiative by the Burmese junta. The leafy **Elephant Park** ㉔ (daily 9am–6pm) is where the government houses a trio of rare white elephants. Such creatures are traditionally regarded as conferring good luck on a country's rulers and have been much sought after by the infamously superstitious military regime. One thing you'll discover if you venture up here is that the elephants aren't so much white as reddish-brown (or pink when they're wet). They're actually albinos, hence the importance of shade to keep their fragile skin out of the sun. Pampered they may be with nutritious food

Old jeeps, Downtown Yangon.

and regular baths in a specially built waterfall, but the spectacle of such dignified creatures hobbled with chains in a cramped concrete pagoda is one unlikely to inspire animal-lovers.

AROUND YANGON

In addition to the pottery town of Twante on the Ayeyarwady Delta (see page 143), a couple of other destinations across the Bago River offer escape from the crowds and noise of Yangon. Foremost among them is the port of **Thanlyin**, overlooked by a particularly wonderful hilltop pagoda. Half an hour further south, **Kyauktan** is the site of another pretty Buddhist shrine, this time marooned on an islet. Finally, heading northwest towards Bago and the Sittaung Valley, a recommended stop for anyone interested in the events of World War II is the **Taukkyan War Cemetery**, where thousands of graves and memorial plaques commemorate the fallen of Allied and Commonwealth countries.

Making a call on the public phones, Downtown Yangon

Thanlyin and Kyauktan

The city of **Thanlyin** ㉕ (formerly "Syriam"), on the opposite side of the Bago River from Yangon, has served for centuries as Burma's principal harbour – a role it continues to play thanks to the modern deep-water container port of Thilawa installed on its waterfront. Most of the country's trade passes through here, making this something of an industrial boom city, with a population that quadrupled in the 1980s following the construction of an iron road bridge connecting it with Yangon. The main incentive to make the traverse is to visit the wonderful hilltop pagoda of Kyaik-Khauk, on Thanlyin's southern outskirts, and to hop on a ferry to the atmospheric Yele Paya temple at nearby Kyauktan – both of which provide a welcome change of scene from the hectic streets, fumes and traffic of the metropolis.

The seeming absence of ancient monuments in the city belies the fact that it has played a seminal role in Burmese history. A major port since the time of the Hindu Andhran dynasty in the 2nd century BC, it rose to national

prominence after being captured by the Kingdom of Arakan in the late 16th century. The invading army was led by the maverick Portuguese soldier of fortune Felipe de Brito y Nicote, who'd left Lisbon decades earlier as a cabin boy (see page 36).

Aside from a weed-choked Catholic church on the roadside, precious little has survived from the Portuguese interlude. The main focus for day-trippers is the much more ancient Kayaik-Khauk Pagoda (charge), rising from a low hill on the southern fringes of Thanlyin. Inscriptions suggest a stupa may have been erected on the site as long ago as the third century AD, but the present structure, said to hold hairs of the historical Buddha, is around 700–800 years old. A smaller version of the Shwedagon, it is exquisitely gilded and affords grandiose views across the city and surrounding countryside.

At **Kyauktan** ㉖, about 20km (13 miles) south of Thanlyin on a tributary of the Yangon River, the **Ye Le Paya** (charge) is famous for its unusual situation – on an islet in the river.

Foreign visitors have to travel to it in a special launch.

At the jetty on the far bank, join the queue to buy food for the huge catfish writhing in the water. With its gilded upturned eaves, seven-tiered roofs and frame of swaying palm trees, the temple itself is an architectural gem, though one somewhat diminished by its ugly backdrop of telephone masts.

Taukkyan War Cemetery

Just off the main Yangon–Bago highway, 35km (21miles) north of the city, **Taukkyan** ㉗ (Htauk Kyant) is the largest of Burma's major war cemeteries. It holds the graves of 6,374 Allied and Commonwealth servicemen killed in World War II, as well as memorial plaques listing the names of 27,000 more whose bodies were never found or identified. A large proportion of them were from India and Africa. Maintained by the Commonwealth War Graves Commission, the site is impeccably well kept and a moving tribute to the mainly young men who lost their lives fighting the Japanese in the early 1940s.

Taukkyan Allied and Commonwealth war cemetery.

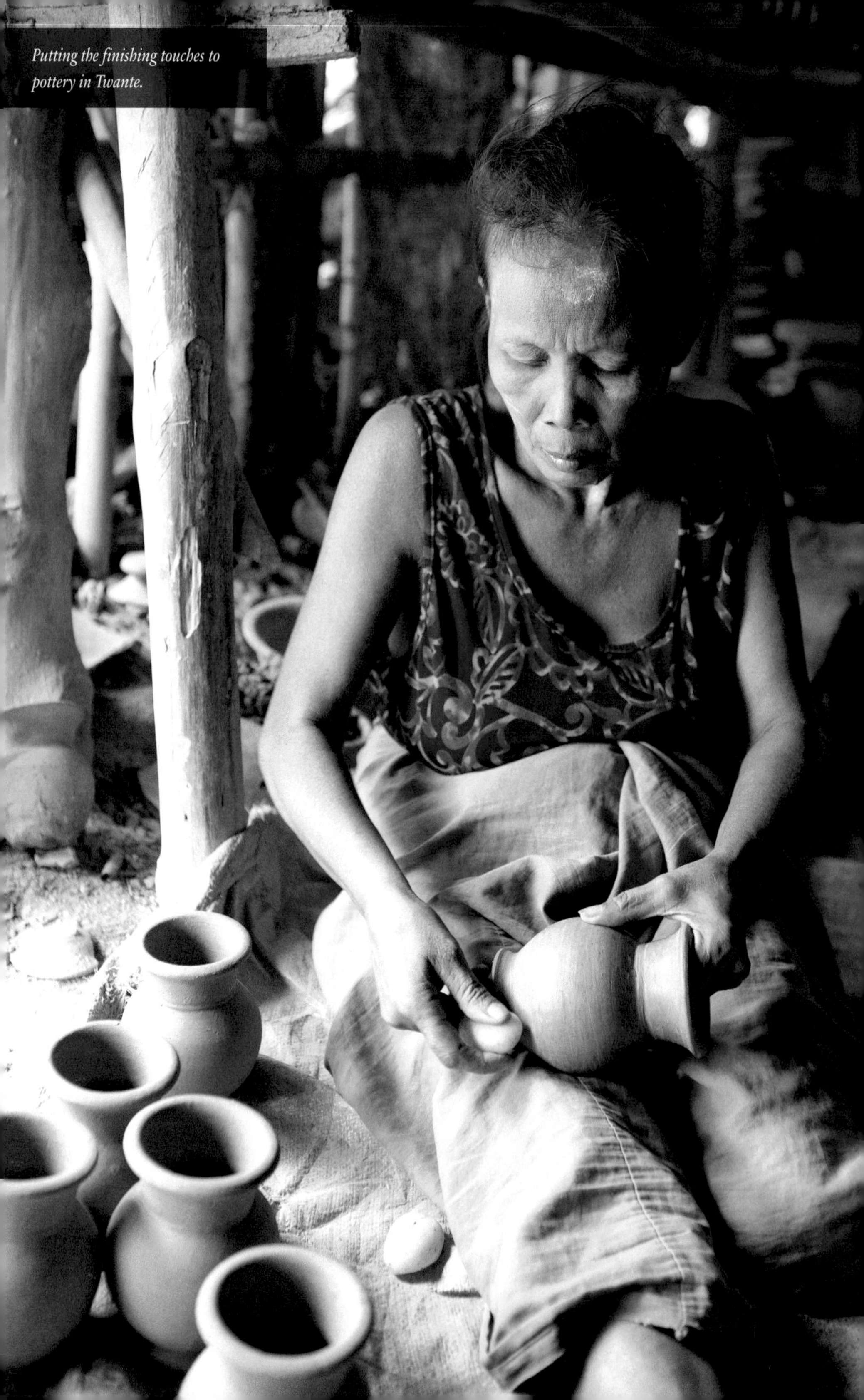

Putting the finishing touches to pottery in Twante.

THE DELTA REGION

The fertile, green Ayeyarwady Delta – one of
Southeast Asia's prime rice-growing regions – offers
one of the most beautiful journeys in Myanmar.

A giant patchwork of lime-green paddy and twisting waterways, the **Delta Region** west of Yangon is the rice bowl of Myanmar. Its famed fertility derives from the silt deposited by the Ayeyarwady as it reaches the end of its 1,200km (750-mile) journey from Upper Myanmar to the Andaman Sea, fraying like the end of an old rope into hundreds of narrow, sinuous channels.

Although rice cultivation is the mainstay here, the Delta also supports numerous fish farms producing carp, threadfin and giant sea perch, as well as prawns and other shellfish for export. The resulting prosperity has spurred a sharp rise in population since Independence, yet little government money has been invested in sea defences, despite the fact that most of the area lies at only 3 metres (10ft) above the high-tide mark.

Just how vulnerable the densely populated towns and villages of the Delta are to the elements became tragically apparent on 2 May 2008, when Cyclone Nargis swept ashore from the Bay of Bengal. One of the most powerful tropical storms ever to hit the country, the cyclone left an estimated 77,000 dead and 56,000 missing, as well as 2.5 million people homeless – the overwhelming majority of them from the Delta. Confronted with a disaster on this unprecedented scale, the Burmese regime failed to mount an effective relief effort, and was strongly criticised by many foreign governments for hampering the efforts of international NGOs attempting to reach the region's worst-hit areas.

A cause of concern for the future was the damage to the mangroves that fringe many of the Delta's saltwater creeks. These help protect the low-lying land behind them from flooding, but many were wiped out by the cyclone, leaving the alluvial plain behind them more exposed than ever.

Main Attractions
Twante
Pathein
Chaungtha Beach

At work in the rice fields.

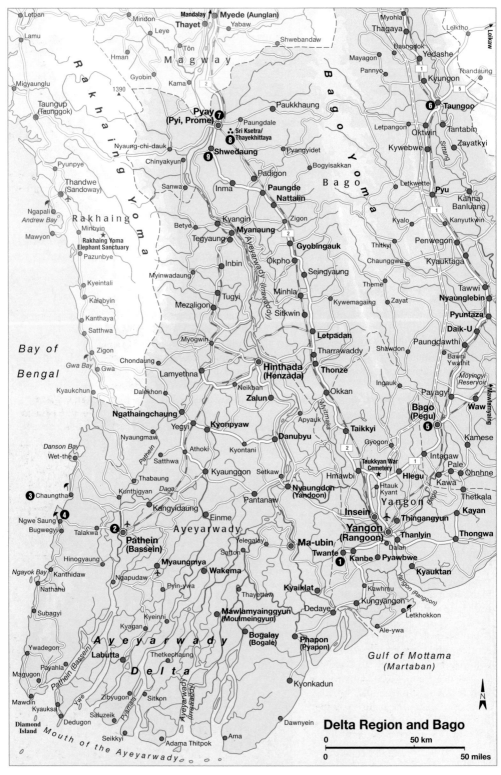

Delta Region and Bago

Much of the Delta can, with time and determination, be explored by government ferries and other small boats, but in practice, travellers tend to head from Yangon to its largest city, **Pathein**, via the main road skirting the north of the region, and from there proceed to one or both of the beach resorts on the west coast: **Chaungtha** and **Ngwe Saung**. More conveniently covered in a day trip from Yangon, **Twante** is a pottery town renowned for its gilded pagoda, the Shwesandaw, though note that to reach it you'll need to obtain a permit (see below).

Twante

The day trip west to the pottery town of **Twante** ❶, on the Ayeyarwady Delta, is deservedly among the most popular from Yangon, not least because of the enjoyable (if short) ferry trip over the river at the journey's start. The crossing only takes five minutes. Once at **Dalah**, on the opposite bank, jeeps are on hand for the remaining 45 minutes by road.

Twante has one significant pagoda, the spectacular, 76-metre (250ft)

Shwesandaw, which was built in 1057 to enshrine hairs of the historical Buddha, Gautama. The canal banks around the town are lined with pottery in all shapes and sizes. Visitors can see potters at work and completed pieces being fired in old-fashioned kilns.

Pathein

With a population of around 237,000, **Pathein** ❷ (also known as "Bassein") is the capital of the Delta and Myanmar's fourth-largest city. It has a noticeably more upbeat and well-heeled feel than many Burmese cities of comparable size, thanks largely to its port, which handles the bulk of the region's lucrative rice trade. Pathein's other claim to fame is its traditional parasol workshops which, along with a handful of impressive Buddhist monuments, entice a steady stream of travellers to pause here en route to or from the beach resorts further west. Transport connections from Yangon, 190km (118 miles) east, are frequent, with daily trains and buses, as well as an overnight ferry that's one of

Making offerings outside Shwesandaw Pagoda, Twante.

Pick-up trucks wait to take people home.

Myanmar's great river journeys.

The name "Bassein" was an anglicised version of Pathein, which itself is said to derive from the local word for Muslims: "Pathi". In past centuries, communities of Muslim merchants from India and the east African coast settled here, reflecting the town's importance as a clearing house for goods travelling across the Andaman Sea. Today's inhabitants include Kayin, Rakhaing, and a small minority of Mon, most of whom are Christian.

Pathein's resplendently gilded centrepiece is the **Shwemokhtaw Pagoda** ("Stupa of the Half Foot Gold Bar") **Ⓐ**, whose shimmering, bell-shaped profile soars in spectacular fashion above the city centre, market area and riverside. According to legend, a Muslim princess named Onmadandi was responsible for its construction, along with two others which she commanded

her lovers build in her name. Burmese chronicles, however, identify the 12th- and 13th-century kings Alaungsithu and Samodagossa as the true creators of the 47-metre (132ft) paya, which may have been erected on top of considerably more ancient ruins dating from the time of the Mauryan emperor, Ashok. Its crowning glory is a priceless hti umbrella finial made from more than 6kg (14lbs) of gold, with lower layers of solid silver and bronze, encrusted with hundreds of diamonds, rubies and semi-precious stones.

The pagoda's presiding image, housed in a hall on the south side of the complex, is the Thiho-shin Phondaw-pyi sitting Buddha, believed to have been one of four sculpted in ancient times in Sri Lanka and floated to the Ayeyarwady Delta on a raft.

Spread over the slopes of a low, wooded hill on the northeastern edge of town is Pathein's second main temple, the **Settayaw Pagoda Ⓑ**. An elegant arched, red-and-white-painted bridge leads to the complex, which was built around a footprint said to have been left by the Buddha during

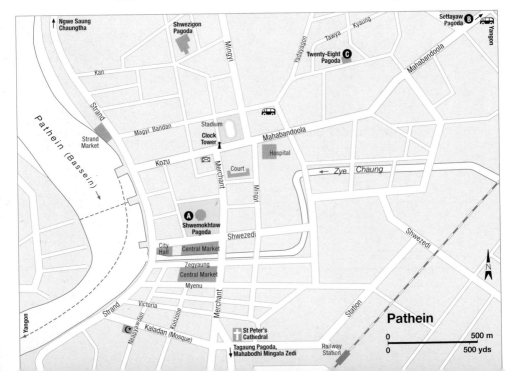

Pathein

| 0 | 500 m |
| 0 | 500 yds |

his peregrinations around southeast Asia. A Mandalay-style Buddha image in bronze stands guard over the revered impression.

Also on the northeast edge of the city centre is the **Twenty-Eight Pagoda** **C**, so named because it houses 28 sitting and 28 standing images of the Buddha.

Around a couple of dozen traditional **parasol workshops** are dotted around Pathein, several of them in the vicinity of the Twenty-Eight Pagoda, making pleasant detours from the temple trail. They're all unfailingly welcoming, often serving visitors snacks and tea. You can observe the various stages involved in the manufacturing process, from making the bamboo spokes and handles, to covering and painting the cotton canopy with pigments derived from various natural resins – a painstaking procedure that can take as long as five days. The workshops produce burgundy-coloured parasols for monks, and hand-painted "summer" versions with flower motifs for lay people. They come in a range of sizes, from child-friendly to extra-large.

Delta beaches: Chaungtha and Ngwe Saung

A five-hour drive from Yangon, **Chaungtha Beach** **3** is the area's only fully fledged resort, albeit a very low-key one by the standards of Southeast Asia. Yangonites descend here in droves on weekends to paddle, take bullock cart rides and pony treks along the sand, and dine out on fresh crab at sunset time. If you visit during the week you'll find the place much more peaceful. There's a good choice of reasonably priced accommodation, most of it in simple tiled bungalows right behind the beach, and plenty of seafood restaurants. Should you tire of lazing around, local boatmen are on hand to ferry visitors out to nearby **White Sand Island**, just off the southern end of the beach, where the water

is clearer. Alternatively, turn right at the beachfront and keep walking for a kilometre or so past the sandy outcrop until you reach a stretch that's almost always deserted.

A short hop down the coast, **Ngwe Saung** ("Silver Beach") **4** is the Delta's other beach destination. It's a notch more tranquil and exclusive, attracting a mix of affluent Yangonites on the one hand, and intrepid foreign backpackers on the other: while the former stick to the swanky resorts at the north end of the bay, the latter press on to the more isolated south side, where a handful of small guesthouses provide budget rooms. Comprising 14km (9 miles) of gently shelving, golden sand backed by casuarina and palm trees, the beach remains gloriously unspoilt, though new high-end resorts are springing up each year, equipped with pools, spas and water-sports facilities. A short wade at low tide takes you to Lovers' Island, just off the centre of the bay, which is surrounded by translucent turquoise water.

TIP

The best way to explore Pathein is by trishaw. Try to get one with a rider who speaks some English and who can take you to the main sights and umbrella workshops, which are tucked away along small lanes.

School children on the road to Twante.

Shwemawdaw Pagoda, Bago.

BAGO DIVISION

The provincial capital of this rice-growing region was once a great sea port. Today, its many monuments are a reminder of its glittering past.

The borders of **Bago Division**, the administrative region immediately north of Yangon, encompass a geography as varied as any in the country. To the east, the 420km (260-mile) -long, comparatively infertile Sittaung Valley; to the west, the broader, more lush and traditionally prosperous Ayeyarwady Valley, fed by annual deluges of silt from the Himalayas; and between the two, the eroded slopes and depleted teak forests of the Bago Yoma Range. From the 12th century onwards, this vast expanse of jungle and alluvial plain formed the hinterland of Burma's wealthiest and most powerful city, the port of Pegu, today known as Bago.

Lynchpin of a trade network extending across the Indian Ocean and beyond, Pegu and its rulers, the Mon Kings, amassed wealth that attracted traders from all over the world but inspired murderous envy among its poorer Burmese neighbours at their capital, Taungoo, further north up the Sittaung Valley. Wars between the two erupted repeatedly between the 16th and 18th centuries, resulting in the eventual destruction of Pegu and the dispersal of the Mon across southern Burma.

Nowadays comprehensively overshadowed by Yangon, Bago is little more than a provincial market town on the highway north, though it does retain a hoard of superb Buddhist monuments whose scale and splendour

evoke the glory days of the Mon Kingdom. Lying only an hour-and-a-half by road from Yangon, it can easily be visited as a day trip, or as a stopover on the longer haul north to Mandalay via Taungoo, the old Burmese capital, with its splendid pagodas.

To the west, across the Bago Yoma hills, the town of Pyay (formerly "Prome") on the Ayeyarwady River is the springboard for the ancient capital of Sri Ksetra, near the village of Hmawza, whose outlandish conical stupas, rising from the surrounding

Main Attractions
Bago
Taungoo
Pyay
Sri Ksetra
Shwedaung

The Shwethalyaung reclining Buddha.

fields like the helmets of buried giants, are the last vestiges of a civilisation that thrived here between the 5th and 7th centuries.

BAGO

Bago ❺ – or "Pegu" as it was formerly known – retains an amazing concentration of temples, pagodas and giant Buddha statues for a town of its size – a legacy of its former prominence as a regional capital and port city of Burma's Second Empire. Most have been painstakingly maintained or restored, often with coats of vibrant gold leaf and modern paints that make them seem considerably less ancient than they actually are, but the monuments are no less impressive for that. As the majority lie in, or within easy reach of, the centre, you can comfortably get around them by trishaw or rented cycle. Note that foreigners are obliged to buy passes, on sale at the Shwemawdaw Pagoda, covering all of the sights in a single ticket ($10) – though you have to pay extra for cameras and videos.

Situated around an hour-and-a-half by road (92km/57 miles) from Yangon,

Bago makes an easy day trip, but its low-density feel also makes it an ideal first stop if you're heading north.

History

Local lore suggests Bago dates back to AD 573, but most historians believe the city was founded in 825 by two brothers from Thaton, the Mon capital. In 1057, King Anawrahta of Bagan conquered Thaton and the whole of southern Burma fell under Bamar sovereignty, a situation that continued for the next 250 years. This king's successor, Byinnya-U, transferred the capital to Bago (Hamsawaddy, named for its symbol, the *hamsa*, a mythological duck whose mate had to perch on his back) in 1365. Thus began the city's golden era, a time of considerable prosperity that lasted until 1635, when the capital was transferred to Inwa (Ava), not far from Mandalay. By that time, the harbour at Bago had become very shallow as a result of silt deposits, preventing trading vessels from docking there.

A feature of Bago's golden era, which endured for nearly three centuries, was the emergence of the

Buddha statues and planetary prayer posts, Shwemawdaw Pagoda.

Hamsawaddy dynasty's great rulers – such as King Razadarit (1385–1425), Queen Shinsawpu (1453–72) and King Dhammazedi (1472–92) – who are commemorated through the dynasty's legacy of sacred monuments and still respected by the Burmese people today.

In 1541, the Taungoo dynasty's King Tabinshweti, founder of the Second Burmese Empire, peacefully annexed Bago and made it the capital of his empire. His successor was the bellicose Bayinnaung, who extended the empire's boundaries but drained the treasury with his military campaigns. He twice conquered Ayutthaya, capital of Siam, but was unable to leave a stable government in the subjugated region. Thus while Bago was probably the most splendid city in the whole continent during this period, the country itself was reduced to poverty. In 1599, the finishing touches to the country's decline were applied when Anaukhpetlun, ruler of Taungoo, conquered Lower Burma and razed both Bago and Thanlyin.

In 1740, Bago became the capital of a short-lived Mon Empire. In 1757, however, the city had to suffer the agony of total destruction again. Alaungpaya, founder of the Konbaung dynasty, was ruthless in suppressing the upstart empire, sieging and sacking Bago in a particularly bloody manner. The city was taken at moonrise and the assembled Burmese population of starved men, women and children massacred "without distinction". Alaungpaya then rode in to the city on elephant back, and razed to the ground its walls and twenty gates.

Bago's Mon inhabitants either fled to Thailand or intermarried with the victorious Bamar. Though King Bodawpaya (1782–1819) attempted to rebuild the city, partly due to the changing course of the Bago River, it never again approached its former greatness. Today, only Bago's many monuments serve as reminders of its glorious past.

Shwemawdaw Pagoda and Hintha Gon

The most outstanding of Bago's attractions is the **Shwemawdaw Pagoda** **Ⓐ** (Great Golden God Pagoda; daily; charge), which is to Bago what the

A trishaw waiting outside Shwemawdaw Pagoda.

Shwedagon is to Yangon. Its stupa can be seen from about 10km (6 miles) outside the city. Richly gilded from base to tip, the pagoda has many similarities to the Shwedagon, and is in fact even taller than its more famous cousin, standing at 114 metres (374ft) in height.

Legend has it that two merchant brothers, Mahasala and Kullasala, returned from India with two hairs personally given to them by Gautama Buddha. They built a small stupa over the relics, and in the following years, this shrine was enlarged several times, with sacred teeth added to the collection of relics in 982 and 1385. King Dhammazedi installed a bell on the pagoda's main platform, which he had inscribed with runes that can still be seen, indecipherable though they are.

In the 16th century, King Bayinnaung gave the jewels from his crown to make a *hti* (jewelled umbrella) for the pagoda, and in 1796, King Bodawpaya donated a new umbrella and raised the height of the pagoda to 90 metres (295ft). In the 20th century, the Shwemawdaw was hit by three serious

Admiring Shwemawdaw Pagoda.

earthquakes, the last of which, in 1930, almost completely destroyed it. After World War II, however, the pagoda was rebuilt by unpaid volunteers with the proceeds of popular donations to stand higher than ever. In 1954, it got a new diamond-studded *hti*.

Like Yangon's Shwedagon, the Shwemawdaw's main terrace can be approached from four directions by covered stairways. There are not as many brightly coloured *tazaung* (pavilions) or *zayat* (resting places) here, but there is a small museum containing some ancient wooden and bronze Buddha figures salvaged from the ruins of the 1930 earthquake. The terrace also features the pagoda's eight planetary prayer posts, as well as a number of statues honouring certain *nat* – the heroes of Bago's history. The stairways leading to the pagoda are like bazaars, with everything from medicinal herbs to monastic offerings for sale, and are guarded by huge white *chinthe* (half-lion, half-griffin beast), each containing a sitting Buddha in its mouth. Faded murals along the main entrance steps recall

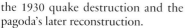

the 1930 quake destruction and the pagoda's later reconstruction.

On a hilltop just to the east, reached via a flight of steps beginning opposite the main entrance to the Shwemawdaw Pagoda, lie the ruins of a more ancient stupa – the **Hintha Gon**. In front of it is a statue of a pair of *hamsa*, the mythological birds associated with the Mon princes' foundation of Bago. Geologists suspect that the hill was at one time an island in the Gulf of Mottama, and may thus have been the spot where the *hamsa* were believed to have landed. A high-roofed platform atop the hill provides a good view of the surrounding countryside.

Kanbawzathadi Palace

The area to the south of the Shwemawdaw Pagoda and Hintha Gon is believed to have been the site of the original Mon city of Hanthawady, where Bayinnaung subsequently erected his palace in 1553. Destroyed only fifty years later, the lavish complex of 76 buildings lay forgotten until 1990, when archaeologists uncovered a series of huge post holes and teak pillars beneath half a dozen mounds of brick and soil. Together with 16th-century drawings, these provided the blueprint for a massive restoration programme initiated by the Burmese military government. Its centrepiece is a shoddily built "replica" of Bayinnaung's **Kanbawzathadi Palace** Ⓑ (daily 9am–5pm), featuring a gilded Lion Throne Room, Settaw Saung and Queen's Bee Hall, complete with spray-stencilled decor. Quite how closely they resemble the originals is anyone's guess, but the buildings hint at the extraordinary wealth and sophistication of the Second Burmese Empire. A small museum on the site houses the huge pillars and other artefacts discovered by archaeologists during the excavations of the 1990s.

The Snake Monastery

A couple of blocks southwest of the Kanbawzathadi Palace is Bago's quirkiest sight, a **Snake Monastery** Ⓒ devoted to a Buddhist abbot from Hsipaw who was reborn in the form of a giant Burmese python. Pilgrims and tourists file through year round to pay their respects to the snake, which measures a whopping 9 metres (29ft) from head to tail and is now thought to be well over a century old.

The Shwethalyaung Buddha

The rest of Bago's monuments lie on the opposite, western side of town. Foremost among them is the **Shwethalyaung Buddha** Ⓓ, which is said to depict Gautama on the eve of his entering *nibbana* (nirvana). Revered throughout Myanmar as the country's most beautiful reclining Buddha, the statue measures 55 metres (180ft) in length and 16 metres (52ft) in height. It is not quite as large as Yangon's more recent Kyaukhtatgyi (built in the 1960s) but, as a result of its quality and long history, is much the better-known and loved of the two.

It was left to decay for nearly 500 years until it was restored during

TIP

As most of Taungoo's attractions are concentrated in the city centre, they can be visited easily by hiring a trishaw for a couple of hours.

The main stupa and pavilion at Shwemawdaw Pagoda.

Detail of the feet of the giant reclining Buddha, Shwethalyaung.

Dhammazedi's reign. In the centuries that followed, Bago was destroyed twice, and by the 18th century the Shwethalyaung Buddha had become lost beneath countless layers of tropical vegetation. It was only in 1881 that a group of contractors who were building a railway for the British administrative station stumbled across it. In 1906, after the undergrowth had been cleared away, an iron *tazaung* was erected over the Buddha, which protects it from the elements, although it does somewhat detract from the view of the statue inside. The Buddha was most recently renovated in 1948, when it was re-gilded and painted.

Kalyani Sima

To the south of the Shwethalyaung Buddha stands the **Kalyani Sima E**, or ordination hall, built by King Dhammazedi in 1476, with the idea of rejuvenating the Burmese *sangha* (monkhood). When the unity of Buddhism in Burma was threatened by schisms following the downfall of the

First Burmese Empire, Dhammazedi dispatched 22 monks to Ceylon (now Sri Lanka), in those days regarded as the stronghold of Theravada. The monks were ordained at the island's Mahavihara Monastery, founded in 251 BC on the banks of the Kalyani River. Upon their return to Burma after surviving a shipwreck, Dhammazedi built the Kalyani Sima, which he named after the Ceylonese river.

To the west of the hall, 10 tablets provide a detailed history of Buddhism in the region and of the country's 15th-century trade with Ceylon and south India. Three of the stones are inscribed in Pali, seven in Mon. Although some of the tablets are shattered and others are illegible in places, the complete text has been preserved on palm-leaf copies.

The Kalyani Sima, which served as a model for nearly 400 other *sima* built by Dhammazedi, did not escape the ravages of the Mon's aggressive politics – or indeed the hostility of other ambitious imperialists. The Portuguese adventurer de Brito destroyed it in 1599, and Alaungpaya razed the reconstructed hall when he sacked Bago in 1757. The structure collapsed following the earthquake of 1930, but, once rebuilt 24 years later, it was rededicated to its original purpose at a ceremony attended by U Nu. Today, the monks live in lodgings around the *sima*, set today amid peaceful, leafy grounds.

The Mahazedi Pagoda and around

Mahazedi Pagoda F, to the west of the Shwethalyaung Buddha, is famous in Myanmar as the place where King Bayinnaung enshrined a gold- and jewel-encrusted tooth of the Buddha to confirm the divine appointment of his reign. He had bought it from the King of Colombo on the understanding that it was the original, and much revered, Tooth of Kandy, but the relic turned out to be nothing of the kind.

Undeterred, Bayinnaung locked the tooth away in the Mahazedi Pagoda, where it remained until 1599, when

Kanbawza Thadi Palace.

Anaukhpetlun transferred it to his capital, Taungoo. A short time later, King Thalun built the Kaunghmudaw Pagoda in nearby Sagaing to house the relic, where it can still be seen today. The Mahazedi Pagoda was destroyed during Alaungpaya's time, and levelled again by the 1930 earthquake. With the reconstruction work recently completed, the uppermost walkway around the stupa affords a marvellous view of the surrounding plain.

A short distance west of the Mahazedi, on the outskirts of town, stands the **Shwegugale Pagoda** ⑤, in which 64 Buddha figures sit in a circle in a gloomy vault around the central stupa. About 1.5km (1 mile) further south, you'll find the **Kyaik Pun Pagoda**. Built by Dhammazedi in 1476, it consists of four Buddha figures, each 30 metres (98ft) tall, seated back to back against a square pillar facing the four cardinal points.

TAUNGOO

Until the construction of Naypyidaw in 2005, **Taungoo** ⑥ was the largest city in the Sittaung Valley and remains the stop of preference for travellers heading between Yangon and Mandalay on the new expressway. In the 15th and 16th centuries it was the capital of a powerful dynasty whose rule spanned 150 years and seven kings, including that of the infamous Bayinnaung, scourge of the Mons and their port city of Bago. Much of the booty obtained in Bayinnaung's audacious military campaigns was lavished on Taungoo, though few monuments survive from this era today, the royal palace having fallen prey to Japanese bombers during World War II.

The one outstanding historic sight that the town retains is the Shwesandaw Pagoda, which attracts streams of Buddhist pilgrims year-round. Foreign visitors also use Taungoo as a springboard for trips into the jungle-covered Bago Yoma Range, to the northwest. Teak and other hardwoods harvested in these ancient forests have formed

the mainstay of the local economy for decades; elephants are still extensively used to extract timber. With a little forward planning, it's possible to see tuskers at work at logging camps around Karen villages – a trip that's all the more tempting if you press on across the Bago Yoma hills to Pyay in the Ayeyarwady Valley.

Taungoo's pagodas

The iconic focal point of Taungoo's **Shwesandaw Pagoda**, in the centre of the town, is its gilded bell-shaped stupa, built in 1597 on the site of a much more ancient one that was believed to have contained sacred relics of the Buddha. Sculptures of the seven Taungoo kings stand in the precinct surrounding the monument; one of its shrine buildings (*tazaung*) houses a reclining Buddha attended by various devas, while another shelters a sitting Buddha 3.6 metres (11ft) tall. This latter icon was donated by a devotee in 1912, who gave the equivalent of his weight in bronze and silver to cast the statue, and whose ashes have been interred behind it.

Frieze behind the Shwethalyaung reclining Buddha depicting King Migadippa and the making of the statue.

*Stairway detail,
Mahazedi Pagoda.*

A two-minute stroll south of the Shwesandaw Pagoda takes you to Taungoo's second pagoda, the Myasigon, a modern structure centered on a gilded stupa. Facing it are two Chinese images of goddesses, one seated on an elephant, the other on a Fu dog, which were gifts from a visiting German Buddhist in 1901. The adjacent museum features a three-headed bronze elephant, the Erawan, believed to have been Indra's mount and rubbed to a brilliant sheen by worshippers, as well as a standing Buddha taken from the Siamese by King Bayinnaung and two 19th-century British cannons. A moat, earth ramparts from a former palace and the royal lake of Lay Kyaung Kandawgyi, on which a few islands are crowned by pavilions, are all reminders of Taungoo's past glory. You can stroll across the picturesque lake on wooden walkways that link the pavilions.

Elephants and forest camps

*The four seated
Buddha statues of
Kyaikpun Pagoda.*

A fascinating trip that can be arranged through hotels in Taungoo is the three- to four-hour drive over rutted timber trails into the Bago Yoma hills to watch elephants at work in one of the area's logging or forest camps. You can travel there and back in a day, or choose to spend a night at a Karen village deep in the forest en route.

Most of the tours revolve around the **Sein Ye Camp**, 55km (35 miles) northwest of Taungoo, where 16 rustic chalets and a dining hall are set in 40 hectares (100 acres) on the edge of a sprawling teak plantation established in the 1920s by the British. From Sein Ye, visitors take short rides on elephant back, explore the forest on guided soft treks, watch trained elephants shifting timber and visit nearby Karen villages. Bamboo rafting and mountain biking are other optional extras offered by many local travel agents and tour operators.

The Oktwin–Pakkhaung road

An unsurfaced logging track connects the town of Oktwin, 9km (5.5 miles) south of Taungoo, with Pyay in the Ayeyarwady Valley, via the Ye Sein Camp and a string of Karen villages. Passing through 62km (38.5 miles) of wild country (that was until recently in the grip of a long-running insurgency), the route is not open to independent travellers, although foreigners may follow it on pre-arranged tours in 4-wheel-drive vehicles. Aside from the beauty of the scenery, the great thing about this road is that it cuts across the Bago Yoma range separating the Sittaung and Ayeyarwady valleys, enabling travellers to make a time-saving short cut to Sri Ksetra (Thayekhittaya) and Pyay.

PYAY

Headquarters of the former Burma Irrawaddy Flotilla Company, **Pyay ❼** – or "Prome" as it was known to the British – sprang up in the late 19th century as a transhipment port for river traffic travelling between Mandalay and Yangon. The magnificent Shwesandaw Pagoda rising from its midst, however, points to the town's much older roots. Even before the rise of Bagan, it dominated

trade along the Ayeyarwady – then the key link between southwest China and the Indian Ocean. The imposing ruins of ancient Sri Ksetra, scattered just to the east of town, attest to the wealth this commerce must once have brought to the region, and to the sophistication of the Pyu Kings who sited their capital here between the 5th and 9th centuries AD.

While the great gilded pagoda and archaeological site on the outskirts are undeniably Pyu's stand-out attractions, the town itself makes a very pleasant place to break the long trek between Yangon and Mandalay, with lively market squares and a waterfront full of Burmese atmosphere.

Shwesandaw Pagoda

Crowning a low hill to the southeast of the town centre, Pyay's Shwesandaw Pagoda is one of Myanmar's largest gilded stupas, topping out at a full metre taller than the Shwedagon in Yangon. Its mesmerising form, soaring like a giant rocket above the tin-rooftops and palms below, is reason enough to take time out of the trip to

or from Bagan. Come at sunset, when the rich evening light turns the gold leaf a magical colour and the river to the west glows molten orange, for the full effect.

Although its origins are believed to date from 589 BC, the Shwesandaw was enlarged and rebuilt several times by conquering kings, notably Kyanzittha of Bagan in AD 1083, who also commissioned a series of stone inscriptions detailing the pagoda's history. These are now housed in a brick building on the northeast side of the precinct. It was Alaungpaya, however, who gilded the stupa in 1754, and who added a second *hti* to the finial – a feature unique to this *paya*, and which – somewhat ironically – the king hoped would symbolise the "unity of the Burmese people" after his brutal sack of the town.

Looking east from the Shwesandaw, it's impossible to miss the mighty seated Buddha, or Sehtatgyi Paya, whose head rises to almost the same height as the great pagoda. Most visitors content themselves with this view of the giant, but the terrace encircling the statue

The seated Buddha statues of Kyaikpun Pagoda – close-up of fingers.

A dusty road in Pyay.

Statue of Aung San on horseback on the central square in Pyay.

Shwesandaw Temple complex, Pyay.

makes a dramatic spot from which to view the Shwesandaw at sunrise.

Sri Ksetra (Thayekhittaya)

The remains of ancient **Sri Ksetra** ❽ – a site better known as Thayekhittaya – are dotted around the village of Hmawza, 8km (5 miles) east of Pyay. Between the 4th and 9th centuries, this was the largest of four walled city states founded by the Pyu people, whose kings controlled river-borne trade up and down the Ayeyarwady and out to the open sea to India, from where they drew much of their religious and cultural inspiration.

Three distinct dynasties ruled at Sri Ksetra (from the Sanskrit for "City of Splendour") before their capital fell under the sway of Bagan in the 10th century. Absorbing influences from southwest as well as southeast India, its rulers erected an impressive array of brick-built stupas, palaces and monasteries, encircled by moats and walls whose vestiges are still clearly visible. At its peak twelve centuries ago, the city was the largest and grandest fortified settlement in Asia: 46 sq km (18 sq

miles) of land lay behind its ramparts, with most of the buildings grouped on the south side of the site, and fields to the north (ensuring food supplies were protected in times of siege).

Contemporary Chinese chronicles talked of Sri Ksetra's brilliance: "The city wall, faced with green-glazed brick, is 600 lines in circumference and has 12 gates and pagodas at each of the four corners. Within are more than 1,000 monks, all resplendent with gold, silver and cinnabar. The women wear their hair in a top knot ornamented with flowers, pearls and precious stones, and are trained in music and dance."

Whether invasions by the Mons or the silting up of the Ayeyarwady Delta were responsible for Sri Ksetra's gradual decline, no one is absolutely sure, but by the 10th century the capital proved easy pickings for Bagan's army. Today, only the chocolate-brown brick stupas survive, forming a surreal vision as they erupt from the flat rice and mustard fields of Hmawza village. None approaches the scale and drama of those at Bagan, but their great antiquity and the site's sleepy, rural

feel make for a memorable half day's exploration.

You're permitted to walk around the site, but there's precious little shade and the heat can be infernal. Cycles are forbidden. Foreigners have to purchase a $5 entry ticket; the warden will also encourage you to buy another $5 ticket for the site museum, but its poorly displayed, desultory collection of votive terracottas, funerary urns and coins doesn't merit the expense, most of the prize finds dug up here having been taken to London (where many remain on show at the Victoria & Albert Museum) or the National Museum in Yangon.

Approaching via the main road in the north, the first of the large pagodas you pass is the helmet-shaped Payagyi. Dating from the 4th century AD, it's Myanmar's oldest intact stupa – though renovation work has been carried out to its exterior and a golden hti added on top. Further west, just beyond the turning to the site, the equally striking Payamar Pagoda is an exact contemporary of the Payagyi, which local tradition holds enshrines a finger, collar bone and toenail of the Buddha.

Heading further south still from here, through Hmawza village and past its tiny train station, cart drivers make for the vestiges of the Old Palace, scattered over a rectangular enclosure, before striking out across the fields towards the main concentration of monuments beyond the Rahanta Gate. Once clear of the earthworks where the city's southwestern entrance would once have stood, you approach Rahanta Pagoda, a hollow stupa housing seven sitting Buddhas (there would originally have been eight). Skirting Yahan Tar Lake, you'll then come to the site's most famous monument, the 46-metre (150ft) -tall Baw Baw Gi Pagoda, which dates from the 5th century and served as the prototype for most of Myanmar's ancient payas. A couple of hundred metres to its east, the Bei Bei Pagoda is a square structure surmounted by three terraces from which an undecorated, round-topped tower rises. Inside it, statues of the Buddha and two of his great disciples peer out of the gloom; look for the ancient Pyu inscriptions on their bases.

Shwedaung

A popular stop on the Ayeyarwady Valley's pilgrimage trail is the **Shwemyetman Pagoda** at **Shwedaung** ❾, 14km (9 miles) south of Pyay on the main Yangon highway, whose central shrine encloses a laquerware Buddha famous as the only one in Myanmar to wear gold-rimmed spectacles (*myetman*). Local legend asserts that the original pair were a gift of King Duttabaung in the 4th century AD after the monarch lost his sight. The unconventional donation brought about a dramatic recovery, and once news of his miraculous cure spread across the country, worshippers began to pour in. However, thieves have repeatedly stolen the famous specs, and replacement pairs have had to be made on several occasions, including once in the colonial era when the local deputy commissioner, a Mr Hurtno, donated a set of gold-rimmed glasses to the temple to cure his wife's blindness.

TIP

The easiest way to get around the sandy tracks threading through the ruins (daily 8am–5pm; charge) is by ox-cart; local drivers appear on arrival at the entrance.

The spectacled Buddha at Shwemyetman Pagoda in Shwedaung.

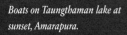
Boats on Taungthaman lake at sunset, Amarapura.

GETTING AROUND THE COUNTRY

Travel in Myanmar is seldom boring. The calendar may refer to the 21st century but some modes of transport are straight out of the 19th century.

Visitors to Myanmar are often amazed at the out-moded and archaic forms of transport in the country. Nevertheless, the clanking old buses, trains and ferries still work, even though they can be frustratingly slow and, in some cases, very polluting. One thing is for sure, however – they add to the fun and charm of travel around the country. With Myanmar largely isolated from the outside world for much of its recent history, practical solutions to getting around had to be found and people had to make do with whatever they had to hand – hence the reliance on animal power and farm equipment such as tractors. So bullock- or ox-carts and horse-drawn carriages – long abandoned in many countries – continue to be seen on the streets today.

Recycling culture

The lack of replacement parts also means that where vehicles are available, owners have to be inventive to keep whatever they have on the road. No fuel tank? No problem. Just feed petrol off a plastic tube from a jerry can next to the driver's seat. Vintage cars, including American Jeeps from World War II, and motorbikes are treasured by their owners and no vehicle is considered too old to be of use. With the country opening up to trade, newer forms of transport are now available in the cities, but it will be some time yet before ox-carts, horse-drawn carriages and trishaws disappear completely.

Cycle rickshaws are ubiquitous in Myanmar's towns and cities.

A typically overloaded pick-up truck provides a welcome lift to Mount Popa.

Ox and cart, Inwa, near Mandalay. Some aspects of rural life in Myanmar are have barely changed over the centuries.

Catching the ferry to Dalah from downtown Yangon.

THE EVOLUTION OF RIVER BOATS

The classic form of travel in Myanmar is by river. The ancient Burmese kings travelled in resplendent royal barges powered by 30 to 40 oarsmen. Ordinary folk sailed on steamers operated by the Irrawaddy Flotilla Company which started operations in 1865. In its heyday in the 1930s, 602 vessels were ferrying 9 million passengers and tonnes of goods along the river from as far north as Bhamo to Yangon. The barges and steamers are long gone (many were scuttled into the Ayeyarwady during World War II to prevent them from falling into Japanese hands), replaced by double-decker diesel-powered riverboats. Until recently, tourists could only travel on these boats, sitting on bare floors, crammed in with other passengers and their goods. Despite the lack of comfort, this is still a great way to see the unfolding scenes on the banks of the river. Today, newer vessels and cruise ships are available to foreign visitors (for more on travelling on Myanmar's rivers, see page 305).

Pre-war, rickety, smoke-spewing buses chug along in the major cities replete with wooden gear-sticks and planks for floors.

ough-and-ready transport in rural Myanmar.

'orse and carriage transport gives a clue to Pyin U-Lwin's 'sort status.

A tree-lined road offers welcome shade on the way to Inwa.

MANDALAY AND ENVIRONS

Mandalay is not only Myanmar's cultural heartland, it is also the spiritual hub of Buddhism in the country.

Teak carving, Shwe In bin Kyaung, Mandalay.

The next major destination on travellers' itineraries after Yangon is Mandalay. The country's second city and a major commercial centre, Mandalay also represents the cultural heartland of Myanmar. It was originally established by King Mindon as a new focal point for the teaching of Buddhism, as well as his capital.

Mandalay did not survive long as the "Golden City" of Buddhist teachings, but it remains an important cultural hub, with numerous splendid pagodas. Today, despite the pre-eminence of Yangon, the city has not lost its position among the Burmese as a religious centre. It is said that two-thirds of the country's monks still make their home in the Mandalay area.

As a result of its proximity to China, Mandalay has benefited from an influx of investment and development. The city is now home to a whole array of new hotels and commercial buildings. Taking it even further along the road of progress is the upgraded airport, constructed with technical assistance from an Italian–Thai joint venture company, and designed to handle 45,000 aircraft movements a year.

In the city environs, there are several places worth visiting – all reminders of its glorious past. The three ancient capitals of Amarapura, Inwa (Ava) and Sagaing, as well as the town of Mingun, all lie within a stone's throw of Mandalay. Among the ruins of palaces, pagodas and *kyaung*, the visitor can find abundant evidence of the political and religious power that belonged to Upper Burma between the 14th and 19th centuries, between the fall of Bagan and the British occupation.

U Min Thonze Pagoda, Sagaing.

Sagaing was the capital of the Shan-dominated Upper Burma for a brief period beginning in 1315. The seat of government was shifted to Inwa in 1364, and there it remained for almost 400 years.

Shwebo (Moksobo) was the royal capital from 1760 to 1764, but the government returned to Inwa, before King Bodawpaya moved the capital to his newly built Amarapura. Kings often moved their headquarters at this time; Inwa (Ava) was again the capital of Upper Burma from 1823 to 1841, then Amarapura regained the distinction for 20 more years until King Mindon moved his court to Mandalay.

To the east – in the foothills of the vast Shan Plateau – is the town of Pyin U-Lwin (Maymyo), a former British hill station. A mild climate, pleasant gardens, quaint atmosphere and colonial trappings make the resort a popular tourist destination. Beyond lie the wild Shan State and the Kachin country of the north, parts of which have been off limits to visitors due to the insurgency and to opium trading.

Visitors at Kuthodaw pagoda in Mandalay

MANDALAY

Romantic-sounding Mandalay is a centre of Burmese tradition. The city centre is dominated by monument-strewn Mandalay Hill; the grid of dusty streets below lack charm, but there are plenty of hidden gems.

Since its creation as a royal capital midway through the 19th century, **Mandalay** has been a byword for everything that's most exotic about Myanmar – from gilded pagodas to secretive walled palaces filled with precious stones and courtiers dressed in outlandish, heavily bejewelled costumes. The modern reality is somewhat more prosaic, with traffic, dust, fumes and bleak concrete architecture dominating most arrivals' first impressions. But give Myanmar's second city some time and its leafier fringes, in particular, can yield up fascinating vestiges of the elaborate courtly culture and arcane religious rituals that all but disappeared following the British invasion of 1885.

The city was founded in 1857 by King Mindon in fulfilment of an ancient Buddhist prophecy. It is said that Gautama Buddha had once visited Mandalay Hill with his disciple, Ananda, proclaiming that on the 2,400th anniversary of his death a metropolis of Buddhist teaching would be founded at its foot. The vision came true when Mindon deposed his half-brother Pagan Min as the Konbaung ruler and moved his capital – with 150,000 people and most of the palace – from Amarapura, 20km (12 miles) away, to establish the fabled "Golden City" foreseen in the Buddhist scriptures.

Mindon's vision, however, was short-lived. On his death in 1878, he was succeeded by King Thibaw and his imperious wife, Supalayat – Myanmar's own Lady Macbeth. During a reign of terror, the pair had many of their friends and relatives killed to deter a royal rebellion. Their excesses, along with the king's courting of the French, provided just the excuse the British needed to sail up the Ayeyarwady from Rangoon with a fleet of gunboats and army of Indian sepoys to annexe

Main Attractions
Mandalay Hill
Shwe Nandaw Kyaung
The Royal Palace
Maha Muni Pagoda
Gold Leaf Workshops
Boat to Bagan

Shwe In bin Kyaung.

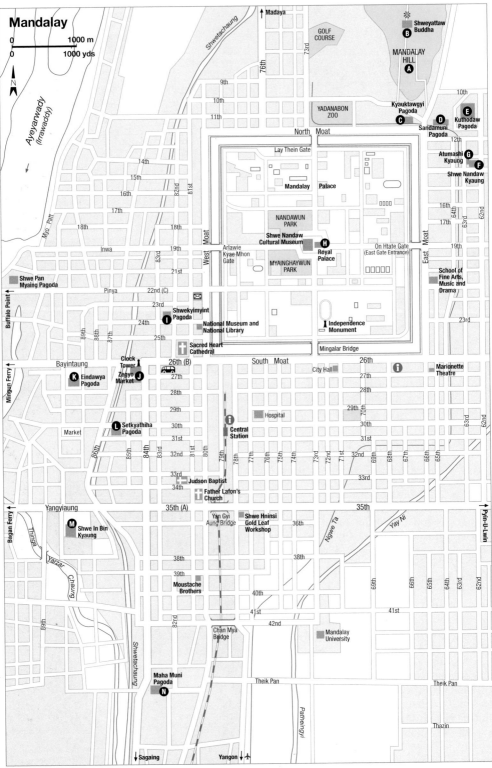

Upper Burma in 1885. Unprepared for the showdown, King Thibaw handed the town over to General Prendergast without a shot being fired and meekly went into exile with his queen. The surrounding countryside descended into anarchy, and Mandalay became just another outpost of British colonialism, now renamed "Fort Dufferin".

Although its treasures were looted by Prendergast's men, the palace's carved teak buildings survived largely intact – only to be destroyed by Allied bombers in 1945, after the Japanese had commandeered the complex as a supplies store. Mindon's resplendent "Golden City", the last of Asia's great wooden palace complexes, was reduced to ashes by the raid; only its walls and moat, and a couple of minor structures, remained intact.

Another series of devastating fires ripped through the heart of Mandalay in the 1980s. More than 23,000 people were left homeless in the wake of the infernos, and whole districts razed. Many of these newly created urban wastelands were snapped up by Chinese immigrants from Yunnan, heralding a huge influx from across the border. Between 30 and 40 percent of Mandalay's million-strong population are now of Chinese origin. Although a source of controversy among native Burmese, their presence has revitalised the local economy. High-rise buildings and shopping malls erected by Chinese entrepreneurs these days punctuate the largely low-rise skyline downtown.

In most respects, though, Mandalay remains, first and foremost, a centre of Burmese tradition. Although Mindon's plan to make his capital a centre of Buddhist teaching was thwarted, more than 700 monasteries survive here, while the city is a bastion of Burmese classical music and dance, as well as other traditional arts and crafts.

The way to get your bearings on arrival is with a barefoot ascent of Mandalay Hill, the sacred, stupa-encrusted hillock overlooking the northeast corner of the royal palace, from where a mesmerising panorama extends over the city and its flat

WHERE

Mandalay's grid plan makes the city easy to navigate. Streets are numbered up to 49th from north to south, and from 50th east to west. Thus an address listed as "39th St, 80/81" means the place in question is on 39th St between 81st and 82nd. Some of the major thoroughfares, however, also have names.

Small stupas line the way up Mandalay hill.

TIP

Entry for foreigners to Mandalay's principal sights is by means of a $10 combo ticket, valid for a week from its first use. Proceeds go to the Burmese government.

environs of riverine rice fields. Visible immediately below is the giant square of the royal enclosure, with its vast moats and walls. Mandalay's most illustrious pagodas and monasteries are clustered outside the palace's northeast corner. The rest of the sights, including the markets and craftsmen's quarters, lie further south and west towards to river.

NORTH MANDALAY

The area to the north and east of downtown is dominated by the palace and hill overlooking it, around whose base are dotted some of Mandalay's most revered pagodas and monasteries. It's a district best explored on foot, in the relatively cool hours of morning or early evening. Mandalay Hill itself is reached via covered walkways that take around 45 minutes to ascend: the most popular is the southern one, flanked by a pair of colossal, white-painted *chinthe* (half-lion, half-dog leogryphs). Alternatively, you can take a taxi up a long, looping road that climbs to the foot of an escalator.

Mandalay Hill

Rising 240 metres (790ft) above the city and its surrounding plains, **Mandalay Hill** Ⓐ (daily 8am–5pm; charge) has been an important pilgrimage site for Burmese Buddhists since King Mindon sited his palace around its foot in the mid-19th century. Aside from the meritorious ascent of its sacred stairways to reach the hilltop's richly decorated shrines, the main reason to make the climb is for the spellbinding views from the summit, which extend for many kilometres in every direction.

Remember to take off your shoes at the bottom. The most frequented southern route comprises 1,729 steps, shaded by a roof that keeps the stone cool and protects visitors from the sun while still allowing fresh air to circulate. Along the way, astrologers and souvenir peddlers ply their trades, while monks, nuns and Burmese pilgrims (often smoking huge *cheroots*) scale the steps. About halfway up you'll encounter the first large temple, which contains three bones of the Buddha

Su-Taung-Pyi Pagoda, Mandalay Hill.

originally unearthed in Peshawar, Pakistan.

The four different stairways converge two-thirds of the way up the hill on the gold-plated **Shweyattaw Buddha** **B**, his outstretched hand pointing to the spot where the Royal Palace was built. This stance is unique in the Theravada world, symbolising Gautama Buddha's prophecy which King Mindon realised in 1857 when he moved his capital to Mandalay.

Further up the steps rests another unusual statue – that of a woman kneeling in front of the Buddha, offering him her two severed breasts. According to legend, Sanda Moke Khit was an ogress who was so overwhelmed by the Master's teachings that she decided to devote the rest of her life to following him. As a sign of humility, she cut off her breasts. When the ogress's brother asked the Buddha why he smiled as he accepted the gift, he replied that Sanda Moke Khit had collected so many merits that in a future life she would be reborn Min Done (Mindon), the King of Mandalay.

The view from the summit, reached after 40–45 minutes, is phenomenal. To the west lies the Ayeyarwady and beyond that, crowned with pagodas and temples, the Sagaing and Mingun hills. To the north, the Ayeyarwady rice country extends into the distance. The purple Shan Plateau can be seen in the east. To the south, in the midst of this vast plain, lies the city of Mandalay and the palace complex.

British and Commonwealth troops suffered heavy casualties here in 1945 when they stormed the hill to oust its Japanese defenders, resorting to bitter hand-to-hand fighting that lasted for days. A British regimental insignia is the only visible remains of the battle.

Kyauktawgyi Pagoda

Diagonally opposite the South Stairway, with its giant *chinthe*, is the **Kyauktawgyi Pagoda** **C** (charge). Work on the temple began in 1853, to a plan modelled on the Ananda Paya at Bagan. Completed in 1878, its focal point is a huge Buddha figure carved from a single block of marble from

Chinthe at the foot of Mandalay hill.

Kuthodaw Paya.

Buddha seated next to Shweyattaw Buddha statue, Mandalay Hill.

the Sagyin quarry – an undertaking of Herculean proportions. An estimated 10,000 men took 13 days to transport the rock from the Ayeyarwady to the pagoda site. The 20 figures on each side of the image represent the Buddha's disciples. A painting of King Mindon hangs inside the pagoda.

Sandamuni Pagoda

To the east of the Kyauktawgyi temple, the **Sandamuni Pagoda** ❶ (daily 8am–5pm; charge) was built on the site of King Mindon's temporary palace where he resided while the main walled complex was under construction. It was erected over the burial place of Mindon's younger brother, Crown Prince Kanaung, who was assassinated in an unsuccessful palace revolution in 1866. Commentaries on the *Tipitaka* (Buddhist scripture) have been chiselled into 1,774 stone tablets housed in the pagoda, a work credited to the monk U Khanti.

Kuthodaw Pagoda

Further to the east, at the base of Mandalay Hill's southeast stairway

Downtown Mandalay.

and surrounded by a high wall, is Mindon's **Kuthodaw Pagoda** ❺ (daily 8am–5pm; charge). Its central structure, the 30-metre (100ft) -high Maha Lawka Marazein stupa, built in 1857, was modelled on the Shwezigon Paya in Nyaung U, near Bagan. The 729 whitewashed pagodas that surround it were erected in 1872 during the Fifth Buddhist Synod to individually house the marble tablets upon which, for the first time, the entire *Tipitaka* was recorded in Pali script, veneered with gold leaf. When first unveiled, it took 2,400 monks six months to recite the text, which is often dubbed "the world's largest book".

The Kuthodaw Pagoda was comprehensively plundered during the annexation of 1885. British looters stripped the *hti* of its precious stones, peeled the gold leaf from the pagoda, carried off 6,570 brass bells from the subsidiary stupas, disfigured statues and used the stone *zayat* tablets of the *Tipitaka* to build a military road. It took over a decade to repair the damage.

Shwe Nandaw Kyaung

At one time part of the royal palace, the **Shwe Nandaw Kyaung** F (daily 8am–5pm; charge) is the only building from Mindon's "Golden City" to have come through bombing of World War II intact. It was dismantled and moved, piece by piece, to its present site by Thibaw after his father died inside it. The king then used the building for private meditation, but he later gave it to the monks as a monastery. Its survival was miraculous, allowing future generations a glimpse how sumptuous Asia's last great teak palace complex must have been before the British invasion. Intricate woodcarvings of ornamental figures or flowers adorn most of its surfaces. Although the monastery was once gold-plated and adorned with glass mosaic, both inside and out, all that's left of the gold today is layered on the imposing ceiling. Thibaw's couch and a replica of the royal throne are displayed inside.

Atumashi Kyaung

Next to the Shwe Nandaw stands the yellow-ochre and white-painted

Atumashi Kyaung G (daily 8am–5pm; charge) or the "Incomparable Monastery". A structure of extraordinary splendour, routinely described by European visitors in the 19th century as "one of the most beautiful buildings in all of Mandalay", it burnt down in 1890, but has since been extensively restored and is said to approximate its former glory. A famous Buddha image – clothed in silk, coated with lacquer and with an enormous diamond set in its forehead – was once the pride of the shrine, but it was stolen during the British seizure of Mandalay in 1885 and never returned.

The Royal Palace

Mindon's **Royal Palace** H (daily 7.30am–4.30pm; charge) was the last in a long line of fortified royal citadels erected on the banks of the Ayeyarwady by successive Burmese rulers. All followed an almost identical ancient Brahmin-Buddhist blueprint,

Inscribed slabs of marble, Kuthodaw Paya.

Shwe Nandaw Kyaung Monastery.

TIP

Mandalay Marionettes, on 66th St, 26/27, is the home of a nationally famous puppet theatre where you can catch a traditional show and buy souvenir marionettes. See page 86.

conceived in the form of a giant "mandala", or sacred diagram, representing the Cosmos with sacred Mt Meru – here symbolised by the royal Throne Room – at its heart. Divided into 16 portions by straight roads, the square was enclosed by 8km (5 miles) of outer walls and a 64-metre (210ft) -wide moat. Twelve gates pierced this formidable perimeter, corresponding to the signs of the zodiac. Each is said to have been inaugurated with a human sacrifice: a total of 52 men, women and children (plucked at random from unfortunate passers-by) were buried under teak posts at each of the entrances to protect the palace's most vulnerable points in the event of attack.

Dismantled, like most of the palace, at Amarapura and re-assembled block by block *in situ*, the centrepiece of the complex was the **Lion Room**, where Burma's last two rulers held court on a sumptuously carved and gilded throne (now displayed in Yangon's National Museum). From its roof rose a seven-tiered, 78-metre (250ft) -high *pyathat* (tower), embellished with jewels and gold leaf. With its forest of gleaming finials, upswept eaves and staggeringly elaborate carvings, the teak-built complex must have been an astonishing sight. Sadly, however, most of its treasures, including the famous library and hoard of rubies and other precious stones kept in the royal treasury, were looted by Prendergast's army in 1885, after which the royal apartments, shrine rooms and assembly halls were commandeered for use as a barracks. Finally, in 1945, during the battle to retake the city from the Japanese, Allied bombers razed all but a few fragments of Mandalay Palace.

Most of what you see today inside the walls dates from the 1990s, the fruit of a major restoration project by the Burmese government. However, rather than employing traditional artisans and materials to replicate the "Golden City" of King Mindon and his son, corrugated iron and concrete were extensively used by the military's architects and the results bear little resemblance to the originals, though they do succeed in conveying the scale of the 19th-century campus.

Mandalay Palace.

The visitors' entrance is via the **East Gate**, from where a broad central avenue leads to the core of the former palace – the only part open to the public. Of the 40 or so reconstructed buildings, the most impressive are the **Throne Room** and adjacent **Glass Palace**, where Thibaw lived amid great pomp and luxury until the British occupation. His crystal-pillared four-poster is one of the exhibits of an otherwise disappointing **Culture Museum**, on the western side of the campus, which formerly served as the Queen's Audience Hall. You can also scale the curious, spiral-shaped **Watchtower** from which Queen Supalayat is said to have followed the progress of the invading British Expeditionary Force up the Ayeyarwady in 1885.

CENTRAL MANDALAY

The hectic traffic and lacklustre concrete architecture of the district immediately south and west of the palace enclosure prove a disincentive for many visitors, but the downtown area holds a handful of special temples worth taking in if you have time, as well as a bustling market quarter, while the cooling breezes and intriguing sights of the riverfront area lie only a short ride west.

On 24th Road between 82nd and 83rd streets, the **Shwekyimyint Pagoda ❶** is the oldest Buddhist shrine in Mandalay. Erected in 1167 by Prince Minshinsaw, the exiled son of King Alaungsithu of Bagan, it houses a Buddha image consecrated by the prince himself, as well as a collection of gold and silver Buddha figures adorned with precious stones. The images, which were removed from the Royal Palace during the British occupation and previously worshipped by Burmese kings, are brought out for public veneration on religious occasions. In a pavilion at the back of the pagoda precinct is an unusual reclining Buddha depicted on a long throne with an upright torso. Shimmering glass mosaics encrust the walls of the shrine chamber in which the image rests, separated from the remainder of the room by a delicately carved wooden screen.

Details of teak carvings at Shwenandaw Kyaung Monastery.

Jade traders at the Jade Market.

TIP

One waterside spot that's especially picturesque at sunset time is **Buffalo Point**, at the far west end of 22nd Street/Pinya Road (aka C Road), where you can watch water buffalo hauling hardwood logs floated down the Shweli and the Ayeyarwady rivers from the north.

A couple of blocks southwest, **Zegyo Market** ❶, on 84th Street between 26th and 28th roads, is Mandalay's most important market area and a great zone for aimless wandering and people-watching, as well as souvenir hunting. The colonial-era buildings that originally stood here burned down long ago, to be replaced by more modern, Chinese-style precincts. As well as fresh produce and flowers, you'll find local handicrafts, clothes, jewellery and furniture shops crammed into the narrow back lanes.

The **Eindawya Pagoda** ❷, at the western edge of the market district on 27th Road and 89th Street, enshrines an ancient chalcedony Buddha figure carried to Burma in 1839 from Bodhgaya in India, where Gautama achieved Buddhahood. Covered all over in gold leaf, the elegantly proportioned stupa, with classic bell-shaped dome and octagonal base, was built in 1847 by King Pagan Min.

At 31st Road and 85th Street, four blocks south of the Eindawya, stands the **Setkyathiha Pagoda** ❸, which was rebuilt after being badly damaged

One of the Moustache Brothers trio.

in World War II. The richly gilded stupa contains a 5-metre (16ft) -high bronze Buddha, cast at Inwa (Ava) by King Bagyidaw in 1823. Overlooking the terrace is a "Golden Rock" similar to the one at Kaikhthiyo, and a Bodhi tree planted by U Nu, the country's first prime minister.

For a break from the mayhem of downtown, the quickest route is via 26th Street (Bayintaung Road), which cuts due west to the **riverfront**, where you can while away an hour or two watching the cargo boats unloading at the jetties. A marvellous view extends across the Ayeyarwady to Sagaing and the Mingun hills, on the river's west bank, which is studded with pagodas and *kyaung*.

SOUTH MANDALAY

The trip out to Amarapura and Sagaing leads through the densely packed districts of south Mandalay, where it's worth pausing to admire the city's most important religious complex, the Maha Muni Pagoda, and the fascinating craftworkers' quarter surrounding it. While you're in the area,

THE MOUSTACHE BROTHERS

An essential part of Mandalay's tourist scene these days is an offbeat, slightly surreal comedy show held in a cramped garage off 39th Street. Rooted in a Burmese brand of vaudeville known as an *yeint*, combining clowning with traditional dance, puppetry and satire, it's staged by a trio of resplendently moustachioed locals who made international headlines in 1996 after they poked fun at Myanmar's ruling generals in a performance at Aung San Suu Kyi's Yangon home. The jokes landed them in dire trouble and two of the brothers were sentenced to seven years in a hard labour camp.

Thanks to a high-profile campaign by Amnesty International, they were released after five-and-a-half years on the condition they would never do their act in Burmese again. So, at 8.30pm most evenings, you can watch their routine in front of an exclusively foreign audience, to a commentary in broken, heavily accented English – an unlikely but entertaining way to spend an idle evening in Mandalay.

Apart from earning them a living wage, the Moustache Brothers' international notoriety seems to have brought them some protection from political persecution – though just how fragile this situation may be was shown following the 2007 unrest, when one brother, U Par Par Lay, was imprisoned again for 36 days. Since then, however, the government's police have kept a low profile, and T-shirt and ticket sales have boomed.

make time for the splendidly atmospheric Shwe In Bin monastery, on 35th Street – one of Mandalay's few surviving antique wooden buildings.

Shwe In Bin Kyaung

The beautiful **Shwe In Bin Kyaung** , situated just south of 35th Road in the heart of the city's monastery district, was donated by a pair of wealthy Chinese jade merchants at the end of the 19th century. Richly carved with decorative motifs and scenes from the Buddha's life, it retains a delightfully tranquil, off-track feel. Come early in the morning and you'll catch hundreds of monks streaming through its precinct and through the surrounding tree-lined lanes on their way to prayers.

Maha Muni Pagoda

The **Maha Muni Pagoda** (charge), 3km (2 miles) south of the city centre on the road to Amarapura, is the most revered Buddhist shrine in Mandalay (and second, in national terms, only to the Shwedagon), thanks to the presence in its central chamber of a magnificent gold Buddha image – the eponymous "Maha Muni", or "Great Sage" – which Bodawpaya's troops took as booty from the Rakhaing (Arakan) campaign of 1784. Revered by pilgrims from all over the world, it is believed to have been one of only five likenesses of the Enlightened One made during his lifetime, although historical evidence suggests the statue was probably cast in AD 146, five or more centuries after the Buddha's death.

A striking feature of the image's body, rising to 3.8 metres (12ft 8ins) in height, is its covering of pounded gold. So many leaves have been pressed on to it as offerings that they now form a 15cm (6in) -thick, lumpy carapace extending all the way around the back. The Buddha's face, however, remains gleaming, as it is lovingly polished twice each day at 4.30am and 4pm by the monks.

the other two Moustache Brothers

Maha Muni Pagoda entrance.

The present temple complex is largely modern and undistinguished, its predecessor having been destroyed by fire during Thibaw's reign in the late 19th century. In its northern corner, a cement structure houses six magnificent bronze statues brought as plunder with the Maha Muni from the Arakan capital, Mrauk-U. Representing Hindu deities, they are of Khymer origin and once stood in the great temple of Angkor Wat. Pilgrims believe them to possess healing powers, and rub the body parts of the statues corresponding to their own afflictions, which have left them with burnished patches. A total of 30 statues were originally carried off from Mrauk-U, but many were melted down for use as bronze cannonballs by King Thibaw in the 1880s.

Craftsmen's quarter

The streets around the Maha Muni Pagoda are home to Mandalay's craftsmen's quarter. Using the same skills and methods as their forefathers, the main focus of their work is of course religious sculptures – Buddha images in all positions, Buddha footprints,

Bashing gold with a hammer in the Gold Pounders' district.

lotus-blossom pedestals and even an occasional statue of the Virgin Mary, as a throwback to colonial days and the early missionaries. You can observe Buddha figures being hewn from alabaster and marble by stonemasons on a street near the Maha Muni Pagoda.

West of the Maha Muni are the makers of pagoda crafts, a booming trade given the Burmese propensity to seek merit through the building and renovation of pagodas. Not far away, woodcarvers create more Buddhas, as well as altars for worship at home and in pagodas. Foundry workers cast replicas of ancient Buddha images and musical instruments.

Gold leaf is produced in a large number of workshops in the southeastern section of Mandalay. This venerable craft is extremely old, and even in the 21st century, the manufacturing process is carried out according to a time-honoured tradition. When travelling in the neighbourhoods in and around Mandalay, you should make a point of visiting other artisans, among the most interesting of which are the skilled silk and cotton weavers of Amarapura.

GOLD LEAF MAKING

The making of gold leaves is one of the country's typical cottage industries. To the devout, the application of gold leaves on to Buddhist statues is a sign of reverence. Indeed, when a Burmese family makes a pilgrimage to a pagoda, its members usually buy a packet of gold leaves at one of the pagoda bazaars and, once at the pagoda, paste their offerings to a stupa or Buddhist image. Mandalay has several workshops engaged solely in the production of these gold leaves.

Typically, a worker begins with a 2.5cm x 1cm (1in x 0.4in) gold leaf. To get an idea of their delicacy, 200 of these leaves weigh just 12 grams (0.4oz). The leaf is pounded with a wooden mallet for half an hour, resized, then pounded again for about one hour, resized and then again pounded for another five hours.

Workers then take the ultra-thin pieces with which they manufacture individual 2.5 sq cm (0.4 sq inch) gold leaves before packaging them in multiples of 10. The original piece is enough to make about one packet of leaves, which normally sells for K400.

Visitors are welcome to drop in at Shwe Hninsi Gold Leaf at 108, 36th Street between 77th and 78th streets to witness the leaf-making process.

By Boat from Mandalay to Bagan

The classic way to travel south to the ruins of Bagan is via the Ayeyarwady, the "Road to Mandalay" as the British dubbed Myanmar's greatest river.

The rail journey from Pyin U-Lwin to Lashio is a picturesque one, taking in the magnificence of the Gokteik Viaduct.

Several tour operators offer luxury cruises as part of their packaged holidays. These vary in price and quality, depending on the vessel used, and can last one to three nights, with stops along the route.

Market leaders include the London-based Pandaw company (www.pandaw.com), whose boats are replicas of the old "double-decker" Irrawaddy Flotilla Company steamers, and the German-run Amara Cruise (www.myanmar-discovery.de), who operate boutique-style, 7-cabin teak cruisers. The other main firm is Orient Express, which runs an upscale 43-berth liner, complete with swimming pool and on-board spa.

Travellers on more modest budgets, meanwhile, take rather less ritzy ferries from Mandalay to Bagan. Two types of boat are on offer: slow government ones, which cover the distance in 12–14 hours (depart Wednesdays and Sundays at 5.30am); and a more expensive fast service on board the *Malikha 2*, run by Malikha Travels (departs 7am, no fixed schedule; www.malikha-rivercruise.com), which takes only nine hours.

River sights

After leaving the environs of Mandalay, this 36-km (20-mile) stretch of river passes through one of the most cultured places in the world. Modern civilisation has largely bypassed this region, where the spiritual wealth is felt in the kyaungs of the Sagaing valleys, which have been preserved over centuries.

Between Inwa and Sagaing, the river flows west for a short while before turning south again. The **Ava** (Inwa) bridge and another at Pyay are the only bridges to cross the Ayeyarwady along its 2,170-km (1,350-mile) length. Shortly after navigating this part of the river's treacherous shoals, boats pass the confluence with the Mu river.

Boats travel on to **Yandabo**, where the treaty that ceded Assam, Rakhaing and Tanintharyi to the British was signed in 1825. Yandabo, which can only be accessed by river, is well known for its terracotta pottery, which is made with the yellow mud from the river bank. Further south is a shallow stretch along the confluence with the Chindwin and its many shifting sandbanks. If travelling on a local slowboat at low water, this is where the boat has the most chance of running aground. It can take hours before the boat is ready to be refloated.

Once the boat has turned south again, the heartland of the Bamar people lies to the left. This land south of Mandalay, irrigated for more than 2,000 years, was the breadbasket of the various Burmese kingdoms. Its surplus permitted the development of the advanced civilisation that started with the First Burmese Empire in the 11th century.

Passing **Myingyan** during the dry season, one can feel the dust and heat that bakes this part of the country where rain is scarce. Eventually, boats reach **Pakokku** – the gateway to western Myanmar. Pakokku is worth visiting for its bustling market and workshops producing handwoven cloth and cigars. From here you can reach **Mount Victoria,** which, at more than 3,000 metres (10,000ft), is the highest peak of the Rakhaing Yoma. Once past Pakokku, the jetty at **Nyaung-U**, the jump-off point for Bagan, is only a few kilometres away.

Deck view from the Road to Mandalay boat (Orient Express).

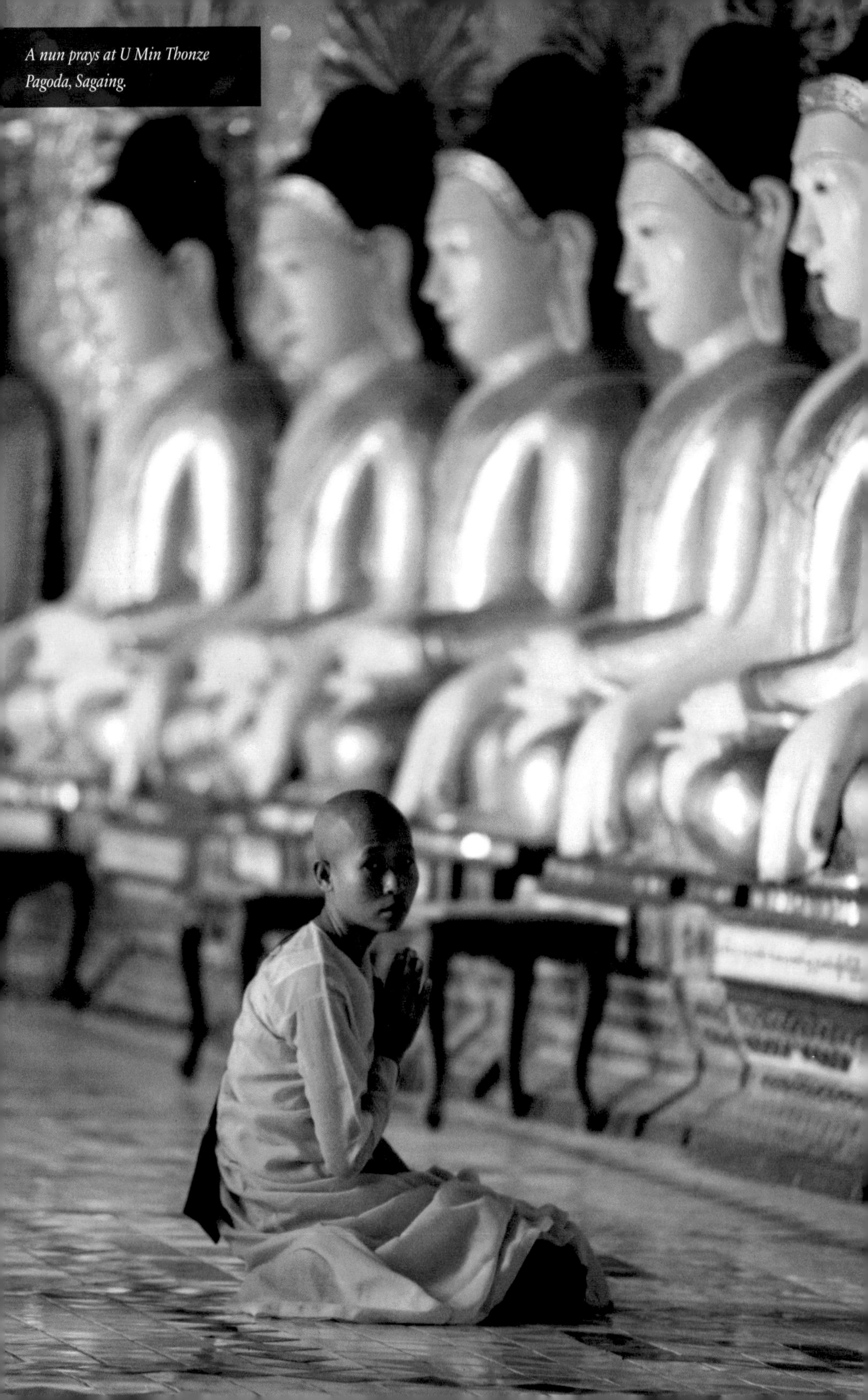

A nun prays at U Min Thonze Pagoda, Sagaing.

AROUND MANDALAY

From the ancient city of Amarapura to the sacred shrines of Sagaing and further afield to the hill station of Pyin U-Lwin and beyond, the environs of Mandalay have much to interest the traveller.

For the majority of visitors to Mandalay **❶**, the attractions of the modern city pale next to the wonders hidden in the surrounding countryside. Clustered along the banks of the Ayeyarwady, amid the vestiges of former capitals and ancient pilgrimage places, are some of Myanmar's most iconic sights: the famous U Bein's Bridge, the teak causeway along which streams of villagers and red-robed monks file each morning and evening, against the unfeasibly exotic backdrop of Sagaing Hill's gilded and white-washed stupas; the exquisitely carved wooden monastery at Inwa; and the vast, red-brick cube of Bodawpaya's unfinished stupa at Mingun.

These alone hold enough interest to fill two or three days of sightseeing. But with a little more time you could make a foray west to the market town of Monywa, springboard for another crop of amazing Theravada sites: the ornate Thanboddhay temple, where more than half a million Buddha images are enshrined amid a forest of multicoloured stupas; a medieval cave complex hewn from solid rock at Hpo Win Tang; and a pair of gargantuan Buddha images – one standing, one reclining – rising from a hilltop at Bodhi Tataung.

After touring the bumpy back roads and rivers of Mandalay's hinterland, you'll be more than ready for a respite

from the heat, and the hill station of Pyin U-Lwin, on the fringes of the Shan Plateau a day's journey northeast of the city, provides the perfect setting for a recuperative spell away from the plains, just as it did for the British burrasahibs who founded the town in the 19th century.

Finally, travellers heading south down the Sittaung Valley to Yangon will encounter further hightlights en route, namely the pleasant lakeside town of Meiktila, where Aung San Suu Kyi and Michael Aris spent

Main Attractions

Amarapura
Inwa
Sagaing
Mingun
Taungbyon Nat Pwe
Bodhi Tataung
Pyin U-Lwin

On Taungthaman lake, Amarapura.

TIP

You can travel across Lake Taungthaman one way by oar-powered gondola to the Kyauktawgyi Pagoda, then return by walking over U Bein's Bridge to get a perspective of the lake's size. Sunset is a good time to cross the bridge for the views.

their honeymoon, and the rather more imposing modern capital of Naypyidaw – a bizarre monument to the megalomania and bombast of the country's ruling generals.

AMARAPURA

Founded by Bodawpaya in 1782, **Amarapura ②** – "City of Immortality" – is the youngest of the royal capitals near Mandalay. It replaced Inwa (Ava), an hour's walk southwest, on the advice of royal astrologers, who were concerned about the bloody way in which the king ascended to the throne. In May 1783, the court and entire population duly packed up their belongings and shifted to land allocated to them around a newly built palace, surrounded by a wall 1.6km (1 mile) in circumference, with a pagoda standing at each of its four corners. The site, however, would only be occupied for less than 70 years. In 1857, King Mindon dismantled the royal enclave and transported it to a completely new location, 11km (7 miles) further north at the foot of Mandalay Hill.

Today a town of 10,000 inhabitants, the former capital has almost merged with the southern fringes of Mandalay's metropolis to its north, but it has a markedly different feel to the big city, its streets draped around the leafy shores of a shallow lake. Many of Amarapura's families are engaged in the silk industry, weaving exquisite *acheik htamein* (ceremonial *longyis*) that are worn on special occasions by Burmese women. Every second house seems to hold a weaver's workshop, and the clickety-clack of looms forms a constant soundtrack as you stroll around. Amarapura's other traditional industry is bronze casting: cymbals, gongs and images of the Buddha are made here out of a special alloy of bronze and lead.

With U Bein's Bridge at the far southern end of town and most of the other points of interest grouped around the north, you'll need a taxi or bicycle to get around the sights if you're travelling independently. Come early in the morning or late in the afternoon to avoid the large tour groups: Amarapura and its teak bridge get swamped in peak season.

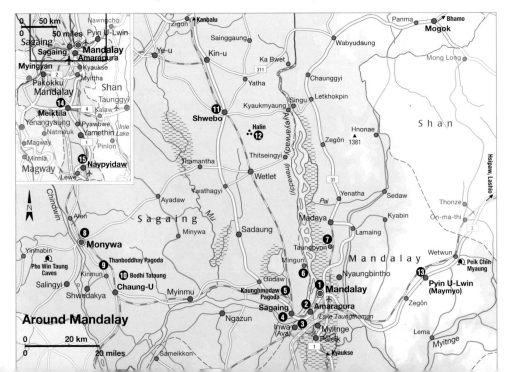

Amarapura's main sights

Today, virtually nothing remains of the former **Royal Palace**, situated to the east of Amarapura's centre (between a military base and timber yard). Some of the wooden buildings were reconstructed in Mandalay by Mindon, while the walls that were left standing were used by the British as a source of cheap material for roads and railways. The four pagodas which once marked the corners of the city wall, however, can still be seen, as can two stone buildings – the treasury and the old watchtower. The graves of Bodawpaya and Bagyidaw also survive.

In the southern part of town sits the well-preserved **Patodawgyi Pagoda**, built by King Bagyidaw in 1820. A bell-shaped stupa, it stands on five terraces which are covered with *Jataka* reliefs. An inscription stone nearby tells the story of the construction of the pagoda.

Amarapura also hold one of the largest monasteries in Myanmar. The presence of up to 1,200 monks (during the Buddhist Lent) in the **Mahagandhayon Monastery** contributes to the religious atmosphere of the city. Visitors are welcome and it is a spectacular sight to witness the hundreds of monks lining up for their one daily meal every morning at 11am – though don't expect to be alone. Bus loads of foreigners descend on the refectory to photograph the spectacle.

U Bein's Bridge

To the south of Amarapura lies Lake Taungthaman, a seasonal body of water which dries up in the winter and leaves fertile, arable land in its wake. It is spanned by the 1.2km (0.7-mile) -long **U Bein's Bridge**, constructed from the teak planks of Inwa by King Bodawpaya's mayor (U Bein) following the move to Amarapura. Little altered in two centuries, it takes 15 minutes to cross on foot. The best time to view the bridge is early in the morning, when hundreds of locals – from farmers and market stallholders to groups of monks – plod over it, to the delight of the bus parties of foreign tourists who turn up in droves at the little boat jetty on the far western side, where they're met by crowds of gee-gaw and postcard sellers. You can,

Crossing Taungthaman lake by boat, U Bein bridge in background.

however, bypass the crowds by starting your visit from the far, eastern side. Tea stalls dotted along the bridge provide much-needed shade and sustenance.

Kyauktawgyi Pagoda

In the middle of a widely scattered village on the east side of U Bein's Bridge is the **Kyauktawgyi Pagoda**, built by King Pagan in 1847. Like the Kyauktawgyi in Mandalay, it was intended to be a replica of Bagan's Ananda Temple. Inside, an enormous Buddha made of pale-green Sagyin marble dominates the central shrine.

In the same chamber stand 88 statues of the Buddha's disciples, as well as 12 *manushia*, mythical half-man/half-beast beings. The temple's east and west entrances are decorated with murals depicting the daily life of the Burmese at the time of the pagoda's construction. If you look carefully you may be able to make out European faces among the paintings.

The area surrounding the Kyauktawgyi Pagoda is full of smaller pagodas in various stages of decay. These temples have been systematically

plundered ever since the prices of ancient Burmese artefacts reached astronomical levels in the antique shops of Bangkok. On Amarapura's Ayeyarwady bank, 30 minutes' walk away from Amarapura's main street, stand two white pagodas – the **Shwe-kyet-yet Pagoda** and the **Shwe-kyet-kya Pagoda** – fronted by a pair of carved lions. Both date from the 12th century. A short distance downriver, King Mindon's **Thanbyedan Fort** was designed in European style by French and Italian advisors. The bastion was intended to stop hostile armies from attacking with warships from the Ayeyarwady. Yet when the British invaded Mandalay in 1885 in exactly this way, not a shot was fired – the Burmese, lacking strong armed forces, had already given up.

INWA (AVA)

The city of **Inwa ❸**, known in British times as "Ava" but by its former inhabitants as "Ratnapura" ("City of Gems"), was founded in 1364 by King Thadominbya, and later served as the capital of the Konbaung dynasty.

Walking back over U Bein bridge

Numerous vestiges of its former prominence survive, including a magnificent teak monastery, marooned amid empty fields and grassy expanses on the banks of the Ayeyarwady. You can drive there overland, but most visitors, including nearly all tour groups, opt to arrive by boat via a short crossing of the Myitnge River bounding the east of the site, where you transfer to a horse-cart for the leisurely tour of the ruins. It's a great way to see the monuments, and makes a relaxing change after the frenzy of central Mandalay.

Unlike most of Myanmar's other royal cities, Inwa's city wall was not square, but shaped like a sitting lion, such as those found in front of large pagodas. Only a part of the wall still stands; the most complete section is at the north gate (near the horse-cart rank and jetty), known as **Gaung Say Daga**, or "gate of the hair-washing ceremony". Every April during the Thingyan Festival, this ritual hair-washing takes place as a purification rite to welcome the king of the *nat*. Today, the ritual is performed only in homes, but in imperial times even the king washed his hair at this spot.

Near the north gate are the ruins of the **Nanmyin Watchtower**, the so-called "leaning tower of Inwa". All that remains of Bagyidaw's palace, this erstwhile 27-metre (89ft) lookout was damaged so heavily by an 1838 earthquake that its upper portion collapsed. Shortly afterwards, the construction began to lean to one side due to the earth sinking beneath it.

Not far from the "leaning tower" is the best preserved of all buildings in Inwa, the **Maha Aungmye Bonzan Monastery**. Also known as the Ok Kyaung, the tall, stucco-decorated brick structure dates from 1818 and was conceived in the same style as that of more common teak *kyaung*; yet its masonry guaranteed that it would survive longer than its wooden cousins. In the middle of the monastery is a statue of the Buddha, placed on a pedestal trimmed with glass mosaic. Beside the entrance archway stands an old marble plaque which tells, in English, the story of an American missionary's Burmese wife who was a staunch convert to

Maha Gandayon Monastery, Amarapura.

Kyauktawgyi Pagoda, Amarapura.

In the vicinity of the Maha Aungmye Bonzan Monastery is the Adoniram Judson Memorial. Judson, an American missionary who compiled the first Anglo-Burmese dictionary, was jailed during the First Anglo-Burmese War and endured severe torture during his imprisonment. He had mistakenly assumed that the Burmese would distinguish between the British colonialists and the American missionaries.

Treelined road on the way to Inwa

Christianity until her death during the First Anglo-Burmese War. Next door to the *kyaung* is a seven-tiered prayer hall, which suffered heavy damage in the 1838 earthquake, but was repaired in 1873 by Hsinbyumashin, the daughter of Nanmadaw Me Nu.

Numerous pagodas are scattered around the outlying areas of the site. Among the most interesting is the **Htilaingshin Paya**, built by King Kyanzittha during the Bagan era. Other important shrines include the four-storey **Le-Htat-Gyi Pagoda** and the **Lawkatharaphy Pagoda**, both in the southern part of the former city. Some 1.5km (1 mile) south of the site stands **Inwa Fort**, once considered part of the "unconquerable triangle", which included the Thanbyedan and Sagaing citadels.

Bagaya Kyaung

Inwa's single most impressive building, however, is the beautiful **Bagaya Kyaung**, a cavernous, ornately carved teak monastery which, despite its relatively well-preserved appearance, is considerably older than its masonry counterpart to the northeast. It dates from 1593 and once formed the far southern corner of the royal enclave, close to the confluence of the Ayeyarwady and Myitinge rivers. The *kyaung* is famous, above all, for its traditional woodcarving. Doorways, window surrounds, partitions and pillar bases are all richly carved in high Burmese style, combining floral arabesques with reliefs of birds, animals and figures from Buddhist mythology. Enlivening the gloomy and dusty interior, the only splashes of colour are a sumptuously glass-inlaid, lacquered trunk, and the presiding Buddha image itself, which sports a coat of gold leaf. A total of 267 massive pillars support the building, whose seven storeys denote its former royal status. Next door stands a working monastery that was totally rebuilt recently after being destroyed by fire.

The Inwa bridges

North of Inwa loom the parallel **bridges** over the Ayeyarwady. Erected by the British in 1934, the older of the pair has 16 spans and supports

a railway; to forestall the Japanese advance, it was partly demolished by the Allies and not resurrected until the 1950s. The modern one next to it, completed in 2005, is crossed by a highway. Both connect Inwa with Sagaing, although the traverse can also be made by ferry. There are military posts at each end of the bridges, where a small toll is collected.

SAGAING

One of the most serene spectacles Southeast Asia has to offer is the vision of **Sagaing Hill** ❹ at sunrise, its countless stupas, spires and temple towers glowing gold and pale-crimson above the dark, silty water of the Ayeywarwady. Although invisible from the far banks, a maze of stepped walkways and colonnades threads around these otherworldly monuments, swathed in palms, frangipani, tamarind and mango bushes.

Around 5,000 monks live amid Sagaing's Arcadian landscape, in 600 monasteries and a township of private homes scattered over a tangle of valleys and ridgetops. For Burmese Buddhists,

this is sacred ground: "the foothill of Mount Meeru". Refugees from the city retreat here – for a day or a lifetime – to meditate; devout families bring their young sons to undergo the *shin pyu* ceremony, consigning their loved ones to a period of monastic life. From before dawn until well after dusk, rows of monks file around the lanes, and cymbals, gongs and pagoda bells echo between the whitewashed buildings, as they have for centuries.

Sagaing's unique atmosphere ensures it features prominently on Myanmar's tourist trail, as well as the Buddhist pilgrimage circuit. You can get there by ferry from Inwa, or via the road bridge. Jeep taxis and horse-carts are on hand to shuttle visitors from the flat town centre to the monastery-studded hilltop behind, or you can walk, improvising a route up the stepped paths.

Sagaing's pagodas

Whatever your means of transport, you'll probably be dropped in the hilltop outside Sagaing's most famous landmark, the **Sun U Ponya Shin**

Nanmyin Watchtower, the so-called "leaning tower of Inwa".

Guide at Tojang Paya, Inwa

Pagoda, a favourite viewpoint for photographers and an important religious site centred on a huge gilded stupa. The monument dates from the early 14th century when the city was first established as the seat of the Sagaing kings, one of the dynasties to emerge after the demise of Bagan. After their decline, Sagaing became a fiefdom of the princes of Ava, but rose to be a capital once again in the three-year reign of King Naundawgyi, beginning in 1760. A terrace to the rear of the pagoda affords superb views across the river to Mandalay.

Sagaing's other monuments are scattered over a wide area and, if you're not on a pre-arranged tour, you'll need a horse-cart or taxi to get around the highlights.

At the far, south end of town not far from the old Ava Bridge, the **Htupayon Pagoda** – built by King Barapati in 1444 – was destroyed by the 1838 earthquake, and King Pagan, who wanted to have it rebuilt, was dethroned before repairs were completed. The 30-metre (98ft) -high base is still standing, however, and

represents a rare style of temple architecture in Myanmar.

The **Aungmyelawka Pagoda**, built by King Bodawpaya in 1783 on the Ayeyarwady riverfront near the Htupayon Pagoda, is a cylindrical sandstone replica of the Shwezigon Pagoda in Nyaung U. Bodawpaya had it built to balance the "necessary cruelties" of his reign and improve his merit for future incarnations.

The nearby **Ngadatgyi Pagoda** features an enormous seated Buddha image, installed in 1657 by King Pindale, the ill-fated successor to King Thalun. Pindale was dethroned by his brother in 1661, and a few weeks later was drowned, together with his entire family (this was a common means of putting royalty to death as no blood was spilled on the soil).

Of rather more recent vintage is the **Datpaungzu Pagoda**, which was built only upon completion of the Myitkyina Railway. The monument provided a repository for relics from a number of other stupas which had to be demolished or relocated while clearing the way for the train line across the

Teaching novice monks at Bagaya Kyaung, Inwa.

Ava Bridge. The relics are much venerated by the people of the region.

Probably the most famous of all Sagaing's temples, however, is the **Kaunghmudaw Pagoda** ❺, 10km (6 miles) northwest of the city on the far side of the Sagaing Hills. Built by King Thalun in 1636 to house relics formerly kept in the Mahazedi Pagoda in Bago (Pegu), it is said to contain the Buddha's "Tooth of Kandy" and King Dhammapala's miracle-working alms bowl. The Kaunghmudaw's perfectly hemispherical shape is, according to legend, a copy of the breasts of Thalun's favourite wife. Recently gilded, its huge egg-shaped dome, 46 metres (151ft) high and 274 metres (900ft) in circumference, rises above three rounded terraces. The lowest is decorated with 120 *nat* and *deva*, each of which can be found in a separate niche. A ring of 812 moulded stone pillars, 1.5 metres (5ft) high, surrounds the dome; each one has a hollowed-out head in which an oil lamp is placed during the Thadingyut Light Festival on the occasion of the October full moon. Burmese Buddhists come to the Kaunghmudaw Pagoda from far and wide to celebrate the end of Buddhist Lent at this annual event.

En route to the Kaunghmudaw, it's worth stopping at the **U Min Thonze Pagoda**, just north of the Sun U Ponya Shin, where 45 Buddha images gaze from a crescent-shaped grotto, against a backdrop of superbly elaborate red and turquoise glass mosaic. Among the traditional handicraft stalls at the bottom of the steps leading to it, look out for ones specialising in bags made from stitched watermelon seeds.

Pagodas dot the hilltops of Sagaing.

MINGUN

The trip up the Ayeyarwady to **Mingun** ❻, 10km (6miles) northwest of the city, deservedly ranks among the most popular half-day excursions from Mandalay, as much for the pleasure of the boat ride as the spectacle of King Bodawpaya's immense, unfinished pagoda looming in surreal fashion above the river bank. In addition to the superb panoramic view from the top of the monument, the site also holds a couple of other photogenic buildings, as well as Myanmar's

Forty-five Buddhas line the crescent-shaped grotto at U Min Thonze Pagoda, Sagaing.

Mingun Paya.

The view across the Ayeyarwady from Sun U Ponya Shin Pagoda, Sagaing.

largest bell, and is set amid some bucolic countryside.

A government-run boat service departs from Mandalay at 9am daily, returning at 1pm. The fact that most visitors use the service to get to Mingun means the site suffers from intense congestion from around 10am, and you may prefer to side-step the crowds by travelling there by road earlier in the day (when the heat is less oppressive and the light more photogenic). Alternatively, wait until the afternoon, by which time all but a few stragglers will have headed homewards.

Mandalay "Combo" tickets cover admission to the site; otherwise, a small fee is levied at the foot of the steps leading to the pagoda. Refreshments and souvenirs are sold at the tea shops and stalls lining the road from the jetty.

The Mantara Gyi Pagoda

From a distance, **the Mingun** (**Mantara Gyi**) **Pagoda**'s appearance is just that of a large mound. Yet it has played an extremely important role in Burmese history during the last century. The pagoda was built between 1790 and 1797 by Bodawpaya, fourth son of Alaungpaya and the founder of the Konbaung dynasty. Bodawpaya was lord of Taninthayi (Tenasserim), the Mon lands, and Rakhaing, as well as central Burma. He had underscored his invincibility by carrying the Maha Muni from Rakhaing to Amarapura and was at the peak of his power, wanting the world to see it.

In 1790, a Chinese delegation visited Bodawpaya's court, carrying a tooth of the Buddha as a gift. Bodawpaya had the pagoda built to house the tooth – the same one that both Anawrahta and Alaungpaya coveted but had failed to obtain. He then moved his residence to an island in the Ayeyarwady for the next seven years while he supervised the construction work on the pagoda. Bodawpaya intended to make his Mantara Gyi Pagoda ascend a full 152 metres (500ft) in height. In order to achieve this, he imported thousands of slaves from his newly

conquered southern territories to work on the pagoda.

The lack of available labour in central Burma was irritating to Bodawpaya. Worrying rumours, which had circulated some 500 years earlier during the construction of the Minglazedi Pagoda, had resurfaced, and concerned voices were saying, "When the pagoda is finished, the great country will be ruined." But Bodawpaya, convinced of his destiny as a future Buddha, was not to be dissuaded. He had the pagoda's shrine rooms lined with lead and filled with 1,500 gold figurines, 2,434 silver images and nearly 37,000 other objects and materials, including a soda-water machine – just invented in England, according to the British envoy to Bodawpaya's court, Hiram Cox. Only then were the shrine rooms sealed.

However, the economic ruin which raged at the turn of the 19th century persuaded Bodawpaya to halt construction work on the pagoda. The king died in 1819, aged 75, having ruled for 38 years. He left 122 children and 208 grandchildren – but none of them continued his work on the great pagoda.

Even though it was never completed, the ruins of the Mingun Pagoda are impressive. The upper sections of the pagoda collapsed into the hollow shrine rooms during the 1838 earthquake, but the base of the structure still towers nearly 50 metres (162ft) over the Ayeyarwady. An enormous pair of *chinthe* (leographs), also damaged in the quake, guard the riverfront view. The lowest terrace of the pagoda measures 137 sq metres (450 sq ft) in size and arches project from each of its four sides.

The Mingun Bell

The famous **Mingun Bell** stands in an enclosure a short walk north of the main pagoda, just off the main street through the village. Weighing 87 tonnes and standing at 3.7 metres (12ft) high and 5 metres (16.5ft) wide, it is the largest functioning bell in the world. King Bodawpaya had it cast in 1790 with the intention of dedicating it to his huge Mingun Pagoda, also intended to be the world's largest.

Sun U Ponya Shin Pagoda, Sagaing.

Stairs leading to the top of Mingun Paya.

By imagining how painstaking the moulding and casting procedures must have been in the 18th century, one can appreciate what a fine work of art this bell really is. Bodawpaya recognised this fact, and to prevent the feat from being repeated elsewhere, he ordered the creator of the bell to be executed.

During the terrible earthquake of 1838, the Mingun Bell and its supports collapsed. Fortunately, there was no damage. Today, the bell is held up by heavy iron rods beneath a shelter. Small Burmese boys who frequent the site encourage visitors to crawl inside it while they strike the metal with a wooden mallet.

Mingun's other pagodas

Standing on the riverbank at the south side of the souvenir and tea stalls, the **Pondaw Pagoda** is a small replica of the original Mantara Gyi, yielding a clear idea of what the great stupa would have looked like had it been completed. A stone's throw to the north, the white-washed **Settawya Pagoda** was built by Bodawpaya in 1811 to hold a marble footprint of the Buddha.

The Mingun Bell.

Mingun's prettiest stupa, however, stands at the far north of the village. The Hsinbyume or **Myatheindan Pagoda** was built by Bodawpaya's grandson, Bagyidaw, in 1816, three years before he ascended the throne, as a memorial to his favourite wife, Princess Hsinbyume. Severely damaged in the 1838 earthquake, it was rebuilt by King Mindon in 1874. The building's design is a rendition of the Sulamani Pagoda, believed to rest atop Mount Meru in the centre of the universe. The king of the gods (known as Indra Sakka, or Thagyamin) is depicted here on the summit, surrounded by seven additional mountain chains, represented by seven wave-like railings leading to the central stupa. Five kinds of mythical monsters stand guard in niches around the terraces, though most have been defaced or beheaded by temple robbers. In the highest part of the stupa, reachable only by a steep stairway, is the *cella*, containing a single Buddha figure.

The nearby village of **Taungbyon** ❼, 20km (13 miles) north of Mandalay,

is the focus of Myanmar's largest and most intense *nat* festival *(see page 192)*.

FURTHER AFIELD

The town of **Monywa** ❽, 136km (84 miles) west of Mandalay, sits on the banks of the Chindwin River, a tributary of the Ayeyarwady. A bustling, hot, flat market hub, it's visited primarily as a base from which to take in the trio of monuments hidden in its rocky hinterland, as well as by a trickle of adventurous travellers ferry-hopping their way south to Bagan.

Monywa's sights

The closest sight to town is the flamboyant **Thanboddhay Pagoda** ❾, built in 1939 by the much venerated Burmese abbot, Moe-hnyin Sayadaw. Guarded by a pair of huge white elephants, the complex, found 10km (6.2 miles) northeast of town, consists of a central stupa surrounded by a forest of 845 smaller ones, all painted in a blaze of rainbow colours and encrusted with glass mosaic. The prayer hall inside (daily 6am–5pm; charge) is no less astonishing for

its wealth of stucco figures. Among the myriad Buddha statues, look out for the finely dressed ladies with their parasols, the tigers and playful monks. The locals will tell you there are 582,357 images enshrined here altogether.

While Thanbodday may be famous for its host of tiny Buddhas, **Bodhi Tataung** ❿, 8km (5 miles) further east, is renowned with two extremely large ones. The first is a vast, 116-metre (424ft) standing Buddha – the **Laykyun Setkyar** – said to be the second biggest of its kind in the world (it's just outstripped by China's Spring Garden Buddha, though still nearly three times the height of New York's Statue of Liberty). Stairways twist through sixteen storeys inside the colossus, enabling visitors to climb through a series of galleries depicting lurid scenes of demons torturing human souls, hammering stakes through hearts and cooking up stews of sinners in big pots. The corridors lead to various windows from which you can survey the site.

TIP

If you're travelling to Monywa by car from Mandalay, note that Bodhi Tataung and the Thanboddhay Paya may be visited en route as they lie to the south and east of town.

The Bodhi Tataung giant statues, near Monywa,

Detail of a pavilion at Thanbhodday temple donated by the Aw brothers – from a Chinese family who made their fortune producing Tiger Balm.

Mediums dance in one of the numerous shrines dedicated to the nats (spirits) during the Taungbyon Nat festival.

At the foot the standing giant sprawls an equally huge reclining Buddha, measuring 95 metres (312ft) from head to toe. This was the first statue to be completed on the site by its founding father, the Most Venerable Sayadaw Bhaddanta Narada, a local abbot who spent the last years of his life touring the world to raise funds for the project. Sadly, he died shortly before the mighty Laykyn Setkyar was finished.

Tens of thousands of smaller Buddha statues rest in neat rows under Bodhi trees radiating from the 131-metre (430ft) **Aung Setykar Pagoda**, on flat ground at the bottom of the complex, which was officially inaugurated in 2008 and looks set to become one of the country's most popular Buddhist pilgrimage sites.

Pho Win Taung caves

A considerably more ancient, neglected feel hangs over the **Pho Win Taung** cave complex, a cluster of 492 prayer chambers hewn from three sandstone outcrops 23km (14 miles) west of Monywa. Most were excavated between the 14th and 18th centuries, but with their peeling plaster murals and time-worn Buddha images they feel much older, like an apparition from the Central Asian silk route.

You'll need a decent torch to admire the decoration of the caves' interiors. Some were elaborately painted in geometric designs rendered in earthy reds, browns and blues. Others lead to colonnaded walkways lined with meditating or reclining Buddhas.

The fact that the site lies completely off the beaten track adds to its allure; come prepared for a complete absence of facilities – as well as troupes of pilfering monkeys. Getting there under your own steam from Monywa can require some determination. You have to take an open-top ferry across the Chindwin and pick up a jeep from the far side for the remaining 22km (14 miles). Travelling by car, your driver will detour north to cross the Chindwin via the newly built river bridge, which takes you past the **Shwetaung-U Pagoda** (worth visiting for its panoramic views) and rather more unsightly Ivanhoe open-cast copper mine.

BROTHER LORDS FESTIVAL (NAT PWE)

Each year for eight days before the full moon in August, the village of Taungbyon plays host to a major festival (there are smaller festivals in December and March). Tens of thousands attend the event, held since the 11th century in honour of a pair of *nats* (spirit heroes), known as the "Brother Lords". Thought to have been the sons of a Muslim warrior, who recovered the Mon's Buddhist scriptures during Anawrahta's conquest of Thaton, they became part of the labour force coerced by the king into building a pagoda in Taungbyon village, but collapsed from exhaustion and were executed for their frailty.

For reasons that have been lost in the mists of time, the Burmese mourned these two young men's untimely demise with great passion. Their spirits soon became so powerful that a remorseful Anawrahta proclaimed them *nat*, ordering that a shrine be built in their honour in Taungbyon and a summer festival be held to venerate them annually.

The eight-day event, in which the brothers are represented by gilded wooden effigies that are ceremonially washed and paraded through crowds, now ranks among the most fervent displays of Burmese animism in the religious calendar. It features ritual floral offerings, wild *hasaing* music, spirit possession rituals and consultations with transvestite shamans, as well as an enormous bazaar, and lots of eating, gambling and carousing.

Shwebo

About 100km (60 miles) north of Mandalay, **Shwebo** ⑪ was the 18th-century capital of the warring King Alaungpaya, founder of the Konbaung dynasty; it was from here that the reconquest of Burma began after the Mon had seized Inwa in 1752. Alaungpaya didn't much care for its original name – "Moksovo", meaning "the hunter chief" – and changed it instead to Shwebo, the "Golden Chief", after which his home village of 300 houses grew to become a prosperous city. "Shwebo-tha!" ("Sons of Shwebo!") was the battle cry of his marauding army, heard across the length and breadth of what is now modern Myanmar during the mid-18th century, in the course of which Alaungpaya's Burmese forces ousted the Mon from Syriam (Thanlyin) and Pegu (Bago) to become the region's pre-eminent power.

Precious little remains from Alaungpaya's illustrious era, his palace having long since burned to the ground, although the government recently erected replicas of the splendid throne halls, the **Shwebdon Yadana** (daily 7.30am–5.30pm; charge), whose multi-tiered towers rise from lawned grounds in the centre of the city, over-looking remnants of the old moat. A memorial to the great king marks the spot where his body was cremated in 1760.

Also worth a visit, five minutes' walk south of the old palace grounds, is the **Shwe Daza Pagoda**, which is thought to be five centuries old.

Halin

A millennium and a half before the rise of Alaungpaya and the Konbaung Dynasty, these same sun-scorched plains between the Ayeywarwady and Mu rivers gave rise to another important regional capital, the Pyu city of **Halin** (Halingyi). Hardly any visitors cover the 18km (11miles) of unsurfaced tracks and back roads separating Shwebo from the **Halin Archaeological Zone** ⑫ (no set hours; charge, admission with same ticket as Shwebdon Yadana), but the site has a beguilingly forlorn atmosphere, while the adjacent village is dotted

Market outside Shwebon Yadana (gilded thrown room), Shwebo

The Naga Hills

Remote and unknown, the Naga Hills comprise a formidable geographical barrier along the Indian border in far northwestern Myanmar.

The Naga Hills of Myanmar, in the far north of Sagaing State a short distance west from the Kachin border, are as isolated as anywhere in Asia. Centred on the mountainous Angpawng Bum range, Burmese Nagaland comprises the eastern third of the Naga-inhabited hills straddling the Myanmar–India frontier

The term "Naga" is loosely applied to a group of more than 20 tribes inhabiting the border area. The many Naga languages belong to the Tibeto-Burman group of the Sino-Tibetan language family. Almost every village has its own dialect; different groups of Naga communicate in broken Burmese, Assamese, or sometimes in English and Hindi.

Most Naga live in villages strategically placed on hillsides near to water. Shifting cultivation (*jhum*) is commonly practised, although some tribes farm

Farmland in Naga Hills.

terraces where rice and millet are the staples. Weaving and woodcarving are also highly developed art forms, while Naga fishermen are noted for the use of intoxicants to kill or incapacitate fish.

Tribal organisation ranges from autocracy to democracy, and power may reside in a council of elders or tribal council. Descent is through the paternal line; clan and kindred are fundamental to social organisation. Due to missionary efforts in the 19th century, a sizeable majority of Indian Naga became Christians, although in Myanmar, animism remains predominant.

In the 1970s, Burmese Nagaland became a base for rebels fighting for independence in neighbouring Indian Nagaland. The National Socialist Council of Nagaland (NSCN), led by Indian Naga Isak Chishi Swu and Thuingaleng Muivah, together with the Burmese-born Naga S.S. Khaplang, who ruled the Burmese Naga Hills, preached a strange blend of nationalism and born-again Christianity under the slogan "Nagaland for Christ".

In 1988, Khaplang rebelled against the Indian leadership of the NSCN and took over the rebel movement on the Burmese side of the border. He maintained a base in a remote area north of the town of Hkamti, on the Chindwin River, but in 2011, after securing autonomous status for the Nagas in Myanmar as well as top cabinet jobs for Naga leaders in the National Assembly, he signed a bilateral cease-fire.

One of the consequences of the truce is that foreigners can now undertake trips to the Naga homeland to experience the tribe's flamboyant New Year celebrations, held in mid-January. Government-accredited tour operators can arrange the necessary permits for the trip, which take in the colourful, two-day Pole Erection ceremony, where Naga men don their finest traditional headdresses and jewellery, as well as soft treks to Naga villages.

A Naga tribesman in Leshi village takes a rest during the New Year festival, which comes after the mid-January harvest.

with dozens of ancient, crumbling monuments.

Reduced almost to dust and barely visible today, the Pyu settlement was surrounded by rectangular brick walls enclosing an area of roughly 500 hectares (1,250 acres). This appears to have been pierced by 12 fortified gateways, whose remains have been radiocarbon dated to between the 2nd and 6th centuries AD. Excavations, conducted in three main waves during the 20th century and still ongoing, pockmark the site and its surrounding area, where numerous graves have been uncovered containing gold ornaments, bronze figures, seals and decorated weapons. Recently, local farmers also came across a skeleton with gold-inlaid teeth, which they were in the process of scraping clean when an archaeologist intervened and bought it off them.

Pyin U-Lwin

For anyone with a weak spot for the atmosphere of British colonial times, and others just seeking to escape the dusty misery of Mandalay's hot season, a visit to **Pyin U-Lwin (Maymyo)** ⑬,

in the foothills of the Shan Plateau, is a must. A two-and-a-half-hour drive by jeep takes the traveller to an elevation of 1,070 metres (3,510ft), from where there are breathtaking views of the Mandalay plain.

Pyin U-Lwin – originally "Maymyo", or "May Town" – was named after one Colonel May, an officer in the Bengal Infantry who was posted to this hill station in 1887 in order to suppress a rebellion that flared up after the annexation of Upper Burma. At a strategically important point on the road from Mandalay to Hsipaw, the town, blessed with a temperate climate, served as the summer capital for the British administration until the end of the colonial era in 1948.

Pleasant temperatures predominate in Pyin U-Lwin even during the hot season, and in the cold season there is no frost. It's no wonder the British felt at home here. A number of Indian Sikhs and Nepalese gurkhas, whose forebears entered the country with the Indian army, have settled here, retaining many of the old colonial traditions in their work as hoteliers, carriage

Gilded pagoda on Kandawgyi Lake, National Kandawgyi Gardens.

The National Kandawgyi Gardens, Pyin U-Lwin.

TIP

For a panoramic view of Pyin U-Lwin, climb to the hilltop Naung Kan Gyi Pagoda, north of the railway station.

drivers and gardeners. They also run many of the tea shops in the hill resort.

Pyin U-Lwin also retains a bumper crop of former British country houses, many of which have been converted for use as small hotels. The best known is the former **Candacraig** (now called "Thiri Myaing"), to which servants of the Bombay Burma Trading Company used to repair for a spot of R&R. Built in 1905 in the style of an English country home, it still offers many of the traditional British comforts which once made the lives of the company's clerks so pleasurable – freshly cooked English food, early-morning tea and a great big fireplace.

Pyin U-Lwin also has a 175-hectare (430-acre) **Botanical Garden** (daily 7am–5.30pm; charge) where you can take a relaxing stroll or picnic by a lake. There is an 18-hole golf course and three waterfalls in the vicinity for swimming and picnics. Horse-drawn carriages resembling Wells-Fargo stage coaches are the chief mode of transport.

The resort's cool weather has allowed many flowers and fruits commonly found in milder climes to thrive, including magnolias, chrysanthemums, cherry trees, peaches, strawberries and plums.

Twenty-seven km (15 miles) east of Pyin U-Lwin are the **Peik Chin Myaung** caves (also known as Maha Nandamu), depicting scenes of Buddha's life in fairy-tale surroundings. Most of the images have been donated by the leaders and family members of the present government to atone for sins previously committed.

Beyond Pyin U-Lwin, Myanmar's northern and eastern frontiers are now accessible to foreigners. The rail line which passes through Pyin U-Lwin from Mandalay continues as far as the northern Shan administrative centre of Lashio. Further north, the road from Singu along the Ayeyarwady, opposite Kyaukmyaung, leads to the town of **Mogok**, famous for its ruby mines. Independent tourists are barred from visiting the area, although accompanied tours to the city are readily available through local travel agencies in Yangon and Mandalay.

White elephant at the Hsin Hpyu Daw park.

WHITE ELEPHANTS

A party was thrown in the Burmese capital, Naypyidaw, in November 2011 to welcome a pair of white elephants into captivity after they had been captured in the jungles of Rakhaing State. Highly revered symbols of power and good fortune, these albino elephants, with their pale hides, toenails and eyelashes, are regarded as auspicious in Myanmar.

So seriously do Myanmar's generals take the old dictum that these rare animals confer blessings on heads of state that they even name their personal aircrafts after them, hence "White Elephant 1" and "White Elephant 2".

Myanmar today possesses a total of six white animals, with three of them housed on the northern outskirts of Yangon, in a park close to the airport.

Meiktila

Straddling a major crossroads at the head of the Sittaung Valley, the lakeside town of **Meiktila** ⑭ is infamous as the site of one of the Burma campaign's fiercest battles in World War II. In late February 1944, Allied forces took the town from its poorly equipped Japanese defenders, only to find themselves under siege soon after. The ensuing fight dragged on for two months, until the fall of Rangoon sealed defeat for the Japanese. A legacy of these events, and of Meiktila's strategic position in the country's heartland, is that today the town serves as the home of Myanmar's largest airforce base.

As a tourist destination, however, Meiktila has little to offer, most of its historic buildings having burned down in a major fire in 1991. That said, if you've time to kill while overnighting here en route between Bagan and Inle Lake, take a cycle around the lakeside, on the west flank of town, where the **Phaung Daw U Pagoda**, a floating temple built in the shape of a golden Karaweik bird, is the principal landmark. A scattering of stately old wooden mansions on the opposite, western shore, recalls the colonial era. Aung San Suu Kyi and her British husband, Michael Aris, spent their honeymoon in one of the largest of them.

A colonial house in Pyin U-Lwin.

Naypyidaw

There can be few capital cities in the world visited by virtually no tourists, but **Naypyidaw** ⑮ – also spelt "Nay Pyi Taw" or "Naypyitaw", literally "Abode of Kings" – is one of them. Built from scratch, at vast expense and with considerable haste, the project was the brainchild of Senior General Than Shwe. No one is quite sure why, in 2002, the former Commander-in-Chief of the Myanmar armed forces decided to move the Burmese seat of government 320km (200 miles) north up the Sittaung Valley from Yangon: the official reason was "lack of space". It was, however, widely rumoured at the time that Than Shwe's personal astrologer had foreseen some kind of foreign invasion by sea, and that the general

A horse-drawn carriage speeds through Pyin U-Lwin.

preferred this much more easily defensible site in the centre of the country.

Whatever its inspiration, Naypyidaw, 252km (157 miles) south of Mandalay, is here to stay. A sprawling, soulless, white-elephant city of empty 8-lane highways and giant concrete buildings, it cost an estimated $4-billion to create and required the relocation of hundreds of thousands of government employees (most of whose families still reside in Yangon).

Much of the new construction, still very much in progress, consists of tower blocks whose roofs are colour-coded to denote the rank or job of their inhabitants. Widely spaced so as to minimise the potential impact of air raids, these are already showing signs of age, with peeling plaster and mildew-streaks staining their walls. The top brass, meanwhile, live in swanky mansions and Orange-County-style villas in the suburbs and surrounding hills, complete with secret bunkers and tunnels.

Naypyidaw is decidedly not somewhere you come for sightseeing, so much as for its strange, slightly sinister, atmosphere. But the city does boast one

stand-out monument: the huge, gold-covered **Uppatasanti Pagoda**. An almost exact replica of Yangon's Shwedagon Pagoda, the giant stupa was donated by General Than Shwe and his wife and is hollow, containing dioramas illustrating scenes from the life of the Buddha. On the east side of the stupa, look out for the shelter where the general's much-prized **white elephants** are housed.

Visits to the government enclave, with its 31-building Parliament complex, are not allowed. Also off limits is the military zone in **Pyinmana** to the east, which is a pity as the latter holds the most outlandish of all the follies erected in the new capital by the regime – a vast square overlooked by three colossal statues of Burma's great kings: Anawrahta, Bayinnaung and Alaungpaya. The space serves mainly as a venue for displays of military might.

The only other sight of note in Naypyidaw is the city's showpiece **Zoological Gardens and Safari Park** (Tue–Sun 8.30am–8pm; charge), a forty-minute taxi ride northeast of the centre, where you can see everything from alpacas to zebras.

The parliament building in Naypyidaw.

From Pyin U-Lwin to Lashio by Train

Buying food for the journey.

The rail journey from Pyin U-Lwin to Lashio is a picturesque one, taking in the magnificence of the Gokteik Viaduct.

Although the train from Pyin U-Lwin originates in Mandalay, many travellers prefer to board it at the hill station, something which saves time as the 45-minute road journey is more than three hours shorter. Departures are also later in Pyin U-Lwin (in Mandalay, it starts at an uncomfortable 4.45am); and besides, the most interesting part of the journey is from Pyin U-Lwin to Lashio.

Pyin U-Lwin to the viaduct

The rail journey starts in Mandalay Division, but most of the towns it passes through are in northern Shan State.

Until 1995, these towns were unexplored, as the route from Mandalay to Lashio was considered a haven for bandits. When this problem was eliminated, restrictions on train travel by foreigners were

The mighty steel girders of the Gokteik Viaduct.

also lifted. Although it is possible to go by road, the train provides a more comfortable ride, albeit in carriages that have seen better days. The journey covering the 220km (146 miles) between Pyin U-Lwin and Lashio takes about 11 hours and is a great way to glimpse northern Shan State.

After Pyin U-Lwin, the train passes gardens full of cabbages and strawberries which soon open out into broad valleys dotted with hamlets. Mist-covered mountains loom in the distance as **Wetwun**, the first stop 90 minutes later, approaches. As soon as the train stops, vendors hop on board to sell snacks.

The highlight of the journey is the **Gokteik Viaduct**, which is a magnificent steel bridge spanning a 300-metre (990ft) -deep river gorge, which the train passes after Wetwun. The approach is stunning – the giant steel girders stand out from the dense jungle like silver latticework, set against a craggy, ochre mountain face. The steel viaduct was something of an engineering marvel when it was completed in 1903. In his book, *The Great Railway Bazaar*, Paul Theroux, who travelled this way in 1973, described it as "a monster of silver geometry in all the ragged rock and jungle... Its presence there was bizarre, this man-made thing in so remote a place, competing with the grandeur of the enormous gorge and yet seemingly more grand than its surroundings, which were hardly negligible – the water rushing through the girder legs and falling on the tops of trees, the flight of birds through the swirling clouds and the blackness of the tunnels beyond the viaduct."

Beyond the viaduct

After crossing the viaduct, the train passes through lush valleys surrounded by green mountains. The following stop, **Kyaukme**, is deep in Shan territory and dotted with Shan hill-tribe villages. Green valleys soon give way to rice fields, banana plantations, bamboo groves and orange orchards on the approach to the next station, **Hsipaw**. The train then snakes through jungle-clad valleys cut through by the rapid-strewn, emerald-coloured Namby River, which flows all the way to **Lashio**. By twilight, the panorama fades and darkness envelopes the rest of the ride until Lashio is reached at about 8pm.

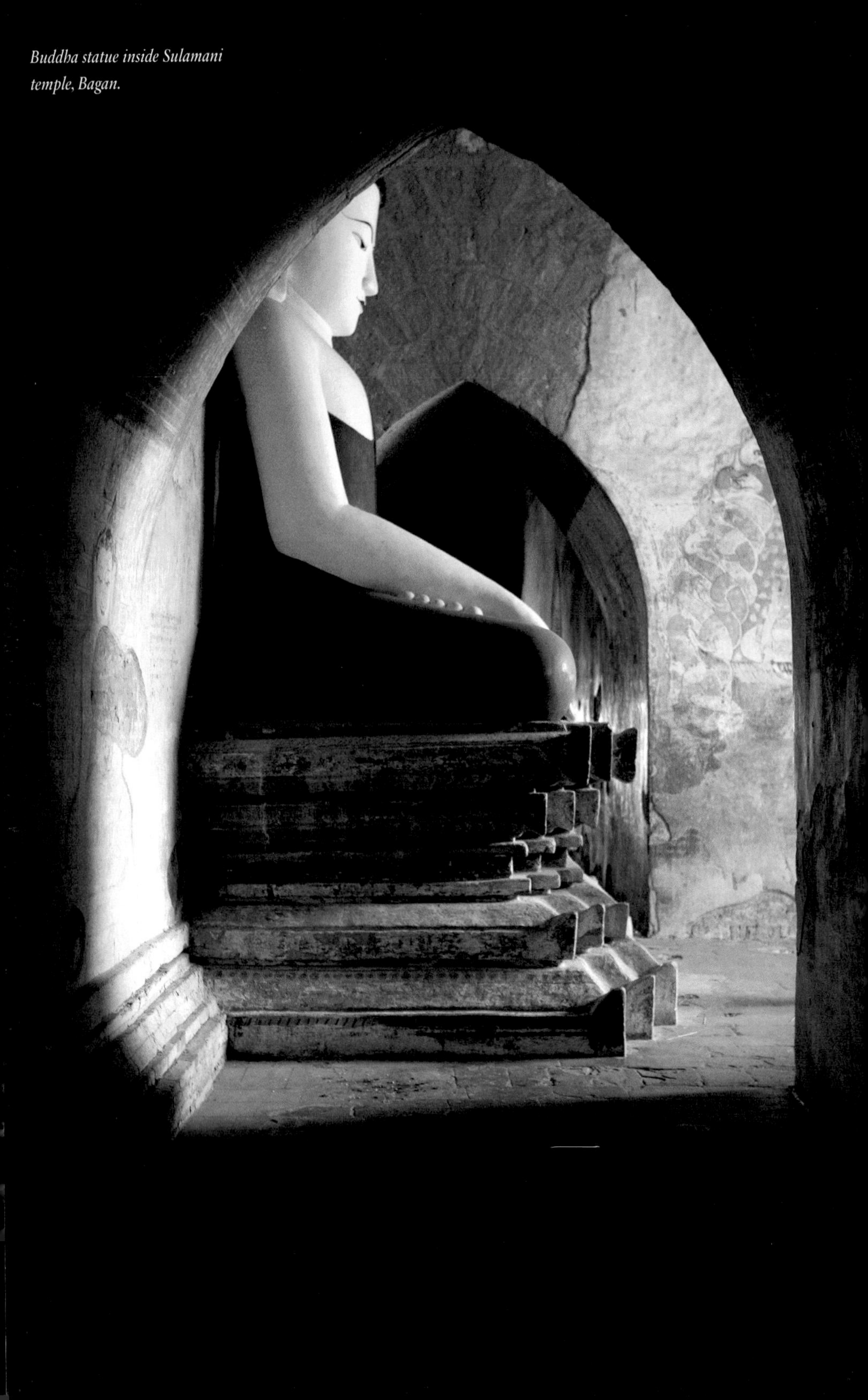

Buddha statue inside Sulamani temple, Bagan.

THE PLAINS OF BAGAN

Bagan's glory days are over, but what remains is the
most beautiful collection of ruined stupas and
temples in Myanmar.

Sulamani temple, stupa detail.

Providing a direct trade corridor between southwest China and the Indian Ocean, the Ayeyarwady River always offered rich pickings for any dynasty powerful enough to control traffic along it. Not until the early 11th century, however, did one emerge with sufficient strength to unify the warring regions of lowland Burma: the Bamas. The result was vast wealth and a capital of unparalleled splendour, founded on a flat, arid bend in the river roughly midway along its course. In classical Pali, the city was known as "Arimaddanapura", "City That Tramples on Enemies", and in Old Burmese as "Pukam" or "Bagan".

Over a period of around 250 years, a succession of rulers erected an astonishing crop of religious monuments on the site to glorify their reign and assure merit for the afterlife. Travellers and pilgrims from across the Buddhist world were amazed by the brilliance of the capital at its zenith, recording with wonder the spectacle of 13,000 temples, monasteries and gilded stupas that rose from Bagan's dusty plains.

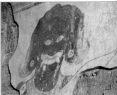

A Sulamani temple fresco.

Among them was a young Marco Polo, who came to the city in 1277. "The towers," he recalled in his account of the journey, "are built of fine stone, and one has been covered with gold a finger thick, so that the tower appears to be of solid gold. Another is covered with silver in a similar manner and appears to be made of solid silver... They make one of the finest sights in the world...When illuminated by the sun they are especially brilliant and can be seen from a great distance".

The decline of the Bamar Empire's fortunes, coupled with the unforgiving Burmese climate and frequent earthquakes, has taken its toll. All of the secular buildings have long since disappeared, being made of easily degradable wood, bamboo and thatch. However, more than 2,000 religious monuments survive, forming a spectacle no less mesmerising for modern eyes than it must have been for medieval pilgrims 700 or more years ago, when the crumbling brick and stucco towers which these days soar above the scrub and red dirt were smothered in gold and silver.

Bagan today is far and away Myanmar's most important visitor attraction. As a result of some heavy-handed restoration work carried out by the military government over the past decade, the site has been denied coveted Unesco World Heritage status. But with the tourism boycott now lifted, the wider world is fast rediscovering these amazing ruins, whose impressive scale and exquisite setting in the rain shadow of the Rakhine-Yoma mountains assure it a place alongside the likes of Angkor Wat, Sigiriya and the Taj Mahal as one of the undisputed wonders of medieval Asia.

Horse drawn carriages riding down a dusty road in Bagan

BAGAN ARCHAEOLOGICAL ZONE

The great plain of Bagan is the site of thousands of ancient Buddhist pagodas, temples and monasteries.

The ruins of medieval **Bagan** – nowadays officially known as the "**Bagan Archaeological Zone**" – are scattered over an area of roughly 50 sq km (26 sq miles), 290km (180 miles) southwest of Mandalay on the east bank of the Ayeyarwady River. Formerly inhabited by between 50,000 and 200,000 people, the lost city is now largely deserted, with most of the local population and tourist-related businesses confined to settlements on the peripheries, leaving the monuments rising in a state of charismatic isolation inland.

An estimated 2,200 temples, pagodas, *kyaung* and other religious structures rise above the plains here – survivors from the crop of around 13,000 erected between Anawrahta's conquest of Thaton in 1057 and Kublai Khan's invasion of the Bamar Empire in 1287. The spectacle of their towers and finials bristling from the table of flat scrubland is hypnotic at any time of year, but especially so on mid-winter mornings, when river mist and cooking-fire smoke often enfolds the brick and stucco structures, glowing red in the first rays of daylight.

At the height of the tourist season, between mid-December and late January, droves of visitors converge via a maze of dusty footpaths and cart tracks on the more famous viewpoints to savour this exotic spectacle. But you can easily sidestep the crowds by venturing a short way off-piste. Indeed, aimless explorations of Bagan's fringes are just as likely to yield memorable visions as the dozen or so "must-sees" that dominate tourists' tick lists. Wherever you wander, though, glimpses of exquisitely proportioned stupas and temple towers are guaranteed, along with swirling *Jataka* murals in beautiful earthy red hues, and meditating Buddhas in dimly lit shrine chambers.

Main Attractions
Balloon Flights
Ananda Temple
Shwezigon Pagoda
Abeyadana Temple
Dhammayangyi Temple
Upali Thein
Shwesandaw Pagoda

Sulamani Temple.

Balloon over Bagan.

The majority of visitors spend at least two days and three nights at Bagan, but you could conceivably spend double that here without retracing your own footsteps. Begin at Old Bagan, the walled city enclosing the largest concentration of monuments, and work your way clockwise around the Zone from there through highlights picked out in our account. Unmissable locations include the enigmatic **Dhammayangyi Temple**, the best-preserved monument on the site, the delicately shaped Ananda Temple, with its four teak Buddhas, and the frescoes in the **Upali Thein** and **Abeyadana Temple**. Due to a ban on climbing inside the temples, it's no longer possible to scale most of them for sunset views; the main exception is the Shwesandaw Pagoda (see margin tip).

The riverside villages dotted around the Archaeological Zone, where most of the hotels, restaurants and shops are located, are where you're most likely to kill time between temple tours. A handful of waterfront cafés offer breezy spots from which to admire views of the distant Rakhine-Yoma hills, while sunset cruises on the river provide a relaxing perspective on the site and its environs. The ultimate way to see Bagan, however, has to be from the air, from one of the hot-air balloons that drift over the ruins each morning and evening.

Site practicalities

The Burmese government levy a $10 admission fee, collected on arrival at the airport or boat jetty and valid for one week. You'll be issued with an individually numbered ticket card, normally retained by your tour operator if you're on a pre-booked holiday.

Guides and transport around the **monuments** (daily Tue–Sun 9.30am–3.30pm) are also taken care of by holiday companies, but independent travellers will have to organise their own horse-carts and drivers. These charge by the day, or half day, and are a leisurely, if rather uncomfortable, way of getting around the Archaeological Zone. The cart drivers, most of whom speak rudimentary English, know the ground well, and where to find the key

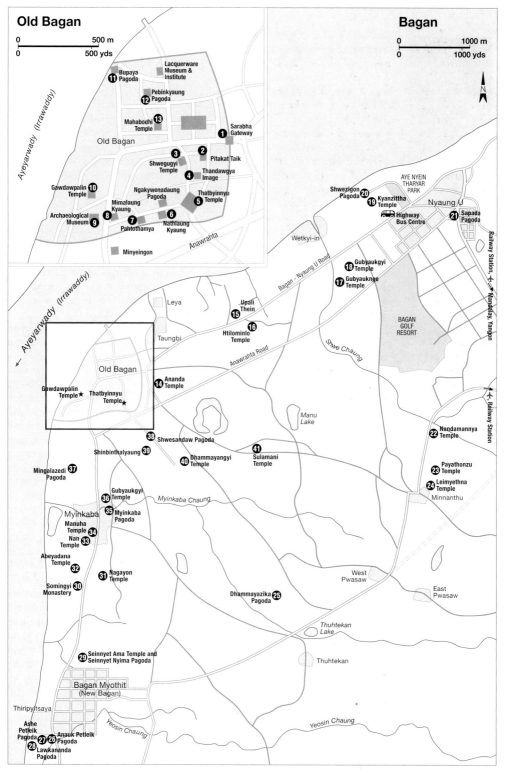

Old Bagan

0 — 500 m
0 — 500 yds

Old Bagan

11 Bupaya Pagoda
Lacquerware Museum & Institute
12 Pebinkyaung Pagoda
13 Mahabodhi Temple
1 Sarabha Gateway
3 Shwegugyi Temple
2 Pitakat Taik
4 Thandawgya Image
10 Gawdawpalin Temple
5 Thatbyinnyu Temple
Ngakywenadaung Pagoda
8 Mimalaung Kyaung
9 Archaeological Museum
7 Pahtothamya
6 Nathlaung Kyaung
Minyeingon
Anawrahta

Ayeyarwady (Irrawaddy)

Bagan

0 — 1000 m
0 — 1000 yds

N

AYE NYEIN THARYAR PARK
Nyaung U
20 Shwezigon Pagoda
19 Kyanzittha Temple
21 Sapada Pagoda
Highway Bus Centre
Railway Station, Mandalay, Yangon
Wetkyi-in
18 Gubyaukgyi Temple
17 Gubyauknge Temple
BAGAN GOLF RESORT
Bagan - Nyaung U Road
Leya
Taungbi
15 Upali Thein
16 Htilominlo Temple
Anawrahta Road
Shwe Chaung
Railway Station
Old Bagan
Gawdawpalin Temple ★
Thatbyinnyu Temple ★
14 Ananda Temple
Manu Lake
22 Nandamannya Temple
38 Shwesandaw Pagoda
39 Shinbinthalyaung
41 Sulamani Temple
40 Dhammayangyi Temple
23 Payathonzu Temple
24 Leimyethna Temple
Minnanthu
37 Mingalazedi Pagoda
36 Gubyaukgyi Temple
Myinkaba Chaung
35 Myinkaba Pagoda
Myinkaba
34 Manuha Temple
33 Nan Temple
32 Abeyadana Temple
31 Nagayon Temple
30 Somingyi Monastery
West Pwasaw
East Pwasaw
25 Dhammayazika Pagoda
Thuhtekan Lake
Thuhtekan
29 Seinnyet Ama Temple and Seinnyet Nyima Pagoda
Bagan Myothit (New Bagan)
Thiripyitsaya
Ashe Petleik Pagoda
27 Anauk Petleik Pagoda
26
28 Lawkananda Pagoda
Yeosin Chaung
Yeosin Chaung

Ayeyarwady (Irrawaddy)

The "Golden face" nat shrine at Sarabha gate, Old Bagan.

The "Mr Handsome" nat shrine at Sarabha gate, Old Bagan.

warden for a monument if it is locked (a precaution for those temples whose wall paintings or *Jataka* panels are at risk from vandals). Although admission to the locked temples is technically covered by your entrance ticket, the warden generally collects a small gratuity for his trouble.

In the evenings, **sunset boat trips** from the jetty at Old Bagan are a popular way to experience the atmosphere of the river. Most of the boats tend to be booked by holiday companies in high season, but you can usually find one with a spare space or two by asking around.

Pressure for tickets is even more intense for the **balloon flights** over the site run by an entrepreneurial Australian-Burmese outfit called Eastern Safaris (www.easternsafaris.com). The 45-minute–1-hour trips offer a truly magical perspective on the ruins. The experience begins with a pre-dawn hotel pick-up in a vintage teak Chevrolet bus, which takes you to the river bank to watch the balloon being inflated over a light champagne breakfast. After the flight, horse-carts collect you from wherever the balloon lands. Tickets cost a hefty $330–360 if they're pre-booked, or $300–330 for a late availability (maximum 48hrs before departure) – and they're like gold dust over the Christmas–New Year period. The firm flies five balloons each morning and evening between October and March (sunrise is best because the cooler temperatures allow the pilots to descend closer to the monuments).

History

There has been a settlement in the region of Bagan since early in the 2nd century AD, when Thamuddarit, a Pyu king, led his followers here. The city walls were erected by King Pyinbya in 849, but it was left to King Anawrahta, 42nd ruler of the Bagan dynasty, to usher in the city's age of glory.

Anawrahta ascended to the Bagan throne in 1044, and his victory over the Mon through the conquest of their capital of Thaton in 1057 marked the turning point in Bagan's history. Theravada Buddhism had not yet permeated Upper Burma at the time. A young monk from Thaton, a Brahman priest's son named Shin Arahan, was so successful in converting Anawrahta to the Theravada school that the king became consumed with spreading the doctrine.

Following Anawrahta's death in 1077, his son Sawlu succeeded to the throne only to be faced with major rebellions among the Mon to the south. Under the rule of his half-brother Kyanzittha, Bagan became known as "city of the four million pagodas". Hundreds of monuments were erected during his 28-year reign. Kyanzittha established the Mon Buddhist culture as paramount. It was not difficult to do so; the 30,000 Mon captives who had been brought north after the conquest of Thaton had already significantly altered the lifestyle of the Pyu and Bamar (Burman).

Kyanzittha's grandson Alaungsithu succeeded him as ruler of Bagan, and held the throne for another 45 years in the 12th century. A highly developed irrigation system supported the production of rice and provided the economic backbone of the empire.

But Bagan's power slowly weakened in the 13th century under the threat of growing Shan influence and the menacing Mongol army of Kublai Khan, which had already overwhelmed China. When King Narathihapate refused to pay a tribute to the Khan, his armies were defeated on the battlefield, and the Mongols took control.

Following the empire's decline, Bagan slipped into relative obscurity, hastened by the numerous earthquakes that devastated the area in the 19th and 20th centuries – the largest of them, measuring 6.2 on the Richter scale, in 1975.

This tremor reduced many of the monuments to rubble, prompting Unesco to launch a multi-million-dollar renovation project. Their efforts were, however, subsequently eclipsed by those of the Burmese government which, using funds donated by merit-seeking religious sponsors from at home and abroad, embarked on its own ambitious reconstruction programme,

heavily criticised by Unesco, which claimed the restoration work was at best "speculative" and refused to confer on the site World-Heritage status (though it has since been restored to the Tentative List). The government, meanwhile, continues its work undeterred by international criticism, erecting a wholly new ersatz Bamar palace and viewing tower inside the Archaeological Zone. Further controversy attended the government's decision in 1990 to forcibly re-locate villagers from Old Bagan, the walled area on the riverside, to a peanut field 4km (2.5 miles) further south at New Bagan.

OLD BAGAN

The walled enclave overlooking the bend in the river, known as **Old Bagan**, formed the centre of the medieval city and still boasts the greatest density of monuments. They can be covered on foot, though an early start, sun hat and plenty of drinking water are recommended. Beginning at the main east entrance, the route outlined below proceeds in a clockwise direction.

TIP

Bagan is huge. Don't underestimate the size of the site or the heat of the central plains. It's better to see some temples in detail and slowly than to rush through too many and exhaust yourself.

Thatbyinnya temple.

Shin Arahan: the Great Reformer

King Kyanzittha and Monk Shin Arahan statues in Ananda.

Legendary in the annals of medieval Burma, Shin Arahan is the missionary monk who consolidated Buddhism's hold in the country.

Through his influence over four successive kings of Bagan in the 11th and early 12th centuries, Shin Arahan ensured Theravada Buddhism became the state religion of Myanmar at a time when it was fast declining elsewhere in Asia.

He was born in AD 1034, in the southeastern Mon Kingdom of Thaton. The local rulers had long since embraced Buddhism, but its beliefs and practices were increasingly under threat from Hinduism, which is why Shin Arahan, then a monk in his early 20s, fled north up the Ayeyarwady to meditate in a forest near the capital of Bagan.

Bagan was the most powerful, prosperous city in central Burma in the mid-11th century, but its religious life was a wild mix of *nat* nature spirit worship, Tantricism and Tibetan-influenced Mahayana

The south-facing standing Buddha – Kassapa – at Ananda.

Buddhism, promulgated by an order of forest monks known as the Ari, who were rumoured to engage in debauched rituals strongly disapproved of by Bagan's King Anawrahta.

Shin Arahan's rise

According to the Burmese chronicles, when reports reached Anawrahta that a yellow-robed monk "of pure heart and mind" was living alone in woods near his palace, he summoned the young ascetic to his court. But rather than perform the usual prostrations, Shin Arahan simply sat on the King's throne – an act normally punishable with summary execution. The monk, however, claimed merely to be demonstrating his belief that "the only True Law was the teachings of the Buddha".

The ruse worked. Anawrahta appointed the 22-year-old monk as his chief spiritual adviser, and Shin Arahan became the vanguard in Bagan's battle with *nat* worship and the Ari order. At his behest, an army was dispatched south in 1057 to conquer Thaton, his homeland, whose king owned a coveted set of Buddhist scriptures known as the *Tipitaka*, setting out the Buddha's Three Sermons.

Bagan triumphed and its forces returned with thousands of Mon prisoners, among them architects, skilled craftsmen and scholars learned in Pali texts whose talents would be deployed over the coming decades building magnificent pagodas, temples and libraries – the splendid ruins of which still litter the Bagan Plains to this day. Their ranks were swollen by many eminent monks from the big Buddhist universities of northern India, at that time suffering repeated incursions by Muslim raiders.

Espoused by four generations of Bagan kings, Shin Arahan's brand of traditional, pure Theravada Buddhism quickly spread across the kingdom, and by the time of the great reformer's death at the age of 81, had taken root in the neighbouring states of Siam (Thailand), Laos and Cambodia, where it remains the predominant school.

The monastery built for Shin Arahan by his first royal patron, Anawrahta, where the sage gave his first sermons in Bagan, is the principal memorial to the much venerated monk. It stands to the west of Hnget Pyit Taung Compound on the outskirts of Nyaung U.

Sarabha Gateway

The principal entrance to Old Bagan is via the **Sarabha** (aka "Tharabar") **Gateway ❶** the only section of King Pyinbya's 9th-century city wall still intact. Bagan's guardian spirits – the Mahagiri *nat* – have their prayer niches in this eastern gateway. The two *nat*, Nga Tin De ("Mr Handsome") and his sister Shwemyethna ("Golden Face"), are called "Lords of the Great Mountain" because it is believed they made their home on sacred Mount Popa. After Thagyamin, king of the *nat*, they are the most important spirit beings in Burma.

Pitakat Taik

One of the few surviving secular buildings in Bagan is **Pitakat Taik ❷**, King Anawrahta's **library**, reached by taking the first left turn immediately after passing through the Sarabha Gate. Anawrahta had it built not far within the city's east gate to house the 30 elephant-loads of scriptures he brought back to Bagan after his conquest of Thaton. From this structure, it is possible to get an idea of what the wooden buildings might have looked like during the city's golden age. Its original appearance, however, was altered in 1783, when King Bodawpaya had finials added to the corners of the five multiple roofs.

Shwegugyi Temple

The oldest of the Bamar-style temples, the **Shwegugyi ❸** ("Great Golden Cave") stands a block west of the old library. It was built by King Alaungsithu in 1131 and took just seven months to erect, according to an inscription set on stone slabs within. Unlike most Buddhist monuments, which face east, the Shwegugyi stands on a high platform facing north, towards the royal palace. Its hall and inner corridor are well lit by large windows and doorways, one of the main features distinguishing Bamar architectural style from the older Mon style. King Alaungsithu

died in the Shwegugyi Temple at the age of 81.

Thandawgya Image

In a small brick temple just down the lane from the Shwegugyi sits the **Thandawgya Image ❹** – a great seated Buddha figure measuring six metres (19.7ft) in height. It was erected by Narathihapate in 1284 and shows the Master with hands in *bhumisparsa mudra*, signifying the moment of Enlightenment. The plaster has crumbled away over the centuries, leaving only greenish sandstone blocks, which give the statue an entrancing, mystical appearance.

Thatbyinnyu Temple

The centre of Bagan is dominated by the **Thatbyinnyu** ("Omniscience") **Temple ❺**, a block south of the Thandawgya image, just inside the old walls. At 61 metres (201ft), this is the tallest building in Bagan, and it is regarded as the archetype of the Bamar architectural style.

Built by Alaungsithu in the mid-12th century during one of the

TIP

It's much cheaper to hire a taxi in Nyaung U than New Bagan ($30 per day as against $80 or more).

Gawdawpalin temple.

*Stupa near
Shwesandaw temple.*

high points of the dynasty's political power, the Thatbyinnyu is similar in shape to the Ananda, although it does not form a symmetrical cross – the eastern vestibule projects out of the main structure. The construction of this temple introduced the idea of placing a smaller "hollow" cube on top of a larger Bamar-style structure, whereas the previous Mon-style shrines were of one storey. The centre of the lower cube is solid, serving as a foundation for the upper temple, which houses an eastward-looking Buddha figure.

There are two tiers of windows in each storey of the Thatbyinnyu, as well as huge arches inlaid with flamboyant pediments, making the interior bright and allowing a breeze to flow through. The first two storeys were once the residence of monks. The third level housed images, and the fourth, a library. At the top was a stupa containing holy relics. The upper storey can be reached by

Bupaya Pagoda.

climbing interior stairs to the intermediate terraces, then taking an exterior staircase to the *cella*. From here, a narrow flight of internal steps leads to the three upper-most terraces, which are crowned by a *sikhara* and a stupa. The view from this platform is marvellous: the temple dominating the mid-ground to the east is the Ananda.

Ngakywenadaung Pagoda and Nathlaung Kyaung

Immediately west of the Thatbyinnyu, on the right (north) side of the lane, stands the bulbous-shaped **Ngakywenadaung Pagoda**, a stupa on a circular base. Measuring 13 metres (43ft) from top to bottom, it dates from the 13th century.

Diagonally opposite, the **Nathlaung Kyaung ❻** is the last surviving Hindu temple at Bagan and a perfect example of the religious tolerance that prevailed here in the early 10th century. It is thought to have been constructed by Taungthugyi in 931 – well before Theravada Buddhism was introduced from Thaton – and was dedicated

to Vishnu. The Nathlaung Kyaung remained Bagan's greatest Hindu temple throughout its golden age, a time when Theravada and Mahayana Buddhism, and *nat* and *naga* worship, were followed, and the Tantric practices of the Ari monks were tolerated.

The main hall and superstructure of the Nathlaung Kyaung still stand today, although the entrance hall and outer structures have crumbled and disappeared. The 10 *avatar* (past and future incarnations) of Vishnu were once housed in niches on the outer walls of the main hall. Seven can still be seen today. Remains of the Nathlaung Kyaung's central relic sanctuary indicate that it once contained a large Vishnu figure, which sat on the mythical Garuda with spread wings. Stolen by a German oil engineer in in late 1800s, this now resides in the Dahlem Museum, Berlin.

Pahtothamya Temple

Dating from the 11th century, when Theravada Buddhism was in the ascendant at Bagan, the **Pahtothamya Temple ❼**, on the left (south) side of the lane just beyond the Nathlaung Kyaung, is said to have been built to look like those at Thaton, even though no similar shrines have ever been discovered there. Mural paintings decorating the interior ambulatory are some of the most ancient in the whole site.

Mimalaung Kyaung

A stone's throw west of the Pahtothamya, the **Mimalaung Kyaung ❽**, near the old city's south gate, was erected in 1174. The small, square temple is characterised by multiple roofs and a tall spiral pagoda standing on a 4-metre (13ft) -high plinth, intended to protect it from destruction by fire and floods.

The temple's creator, Narapatisithu, is noted in Bagan's history for the way in which he became king in 1173: his brother, King Naratheinka, had stolen his wife and made her queen while Narapatisithu was on a foreign campaign. The wronged sibling returned to Bagan with 80 trusted men, murdered his brother and re-took the throne. His wife, Veluvati, remained queen.

Buddha statues around Mahabodhi temple.

Bupaya Pagoda is used as a navigation aid by boats due to its prominent location.

Ananda temple and surrounding temples.

Archaeological Museum

Opposite the Mimalaung Kyaung stands the government-run **Archaeological Museum ➒** containing displays of Bagan's varied architecture, iconography and religious history. Its prize exhibits are the **Myazedi Inscriptions** (AD 1113) - Myanmar's own Rosetta Stones, which tell the story of King Kyangsittha and Prince Yazakumar in four ancient languages. The translations enabled scholars to decipher the script of ancient Pyu, the first civilisation of the Ayeyarwady Valley.

Gawdawpalin Temple

One of the most majestic buildings in Bagan, the 12th-century **Gawdawpalin Temple ➓** rests on the opposite side of the lane from the museum. It was built by King Narapatisithu in late Bamar style to resemble the Thatbyinnyu Temple, but suffered more damage than any other monument in the 1975 earthquake. The *sikhara* and stupa, which previously reached a height of 60 metres (200ft), collapsed during the quake, and a wide crack opened through the middle of the two-storey cube of the central structure. Renovation work since, however, has remedied most of the damage. Square in plan with porticoes on all four sides, the shrine is one of the largest in Bagan, featuring a vaulted corridor inside which reside four gilded Buddhas.

Bupaya Pagoda

From the Gawdawpalin, turn left on to the main lane running north and follow it to the far, northern perimeter of the old walled city, where the **Bupaya Pagoda ⓫** enjoys a prime site overlooking the river. According to tradition, the stupa was built by the third king of Bagan, Pyusawti (AD 162–243), who found a way to get rid of a gourd-like climbing plant *(bu)* that infested the river banks. As a reward, Thamuddarit, the founder-king of Bagan, gave him the hand of his daughter in marriage – and the Bamar throne. Pyusawti had the Bupaya Pagoda built to commemorate his stroke of good luck. As the first and prototypical stupa in the city, this

edifice became the basic model for all those built after it. The structure has a bulbous shape, similar in some ways to the Tibetan *chorte*, and is built on rows of crenellated walls. Because of its prominent position on the river bank, it is used as a navigation aid by boats. On the pagoda grounds, beneath a pavilion with a nine-gabled roof, is an altar to Mondaing, *nat* of storms.

Pebinkyaung Pagoda

The **Pebinkyaung Pagoda** ⑫, a five-minute stroll southeast of the Bupaya, is notable for its conical Sinhalese-style stupa, which contains relics mounted on top of the bell-shaped main structure in a square-based relic chamber. The construction of this brick stupa in the 12th century confirms that close ties existed between Burma and Ceylon (now Sri Lanka), a consequence of King Anawrahta's sponsorship of Theravada Buddhism. Although Theravada had been introduced to Thaton by the Sinhalese monk Buddhaghosa in AD 403, it was not until 1076, when Anawrahta was in power, that the bond between Burma and Ceylon was strengthened.

Mahabodhi Temple

Across the road from the Pebhink-yaung stands the **Mahabodhi Temple** ⑬, a replica of a 6th-century structure of the same name built at Bodhgaya in India, where the Buddha achieved Enlightenment. The pyramidal shape of the temple tower is of a kind favoured during India's Gupta Period, and is quite different from the bell-shaped monuments common elsewhere in Burma.

Constructed during the reign of Nantaungmya (1210–34), it followed a long-standing fascination among Bagan's kings for Indian architecture. More than a century earlier, Kyanzittha had sent men and materials to India to carry out some renovation work on the Bodhgaya Temple, and in the mid-12th century, Alaungsithu made the king of Rakhaing (Arakan) do the same.

The lower section of the Mahabodhi is a quadrangular block supporting the pyramidal structure, which in turn is crowned by a small stupa. The pyramid is completely covered with niches containing seated Buddha figures. Apart from a copy that was erected on the terrace of the Shwedagon in Yangon, the Mahabodhi is the only temple in Burma built with such profuse exterior decoration.

Stupa detail, Mahabodhi temple.

NORTHERN PLAIN

Half a dozen noteworthy monuments lie on the plain dividing Old Bagan from Nyaung U. Though relatively close to the site's tourist amenities, you'll need some form of transport to reach them. The following account works from west to east, starting at the area's most distinctive landmark, the whitewashed Ananda Temple.

Ananda Temple

Just to the east of the old city walls, the **Ananda Temple** ⑭ is considered the masterpiece of Bagan's surviving Mon architecture. Completed in 1091, it was, according to *The Glass*

Fresco at Upali Thein temple.

Palace Chronicle, inspired by a visit to Kyanzittha's palace by eight Indian monks, who arrived one day begging for alms. They told the king they had once lived in a legendary Himalayan cave temple and, using meditative powers, made the mythical mountain landscape appear before Kyanzittha's eyes. Overwhelmed by the beauty of the vision, the king immediately decided to build a replica of this snowy abode at Bagan and is said to have been so awe-struck by the result that he personally executed the architect to ensure the temple could not be duplicated.

The structure of the building is that of a simple corridor temple. Four large vestibules, each opening out symmetrically into entrance halls, surround the central superstructure, which itself is inlaid with four huge niches. The entire enclosure, 53 metres (174ft) on each side, is in the shape of a perfect Greek cross. In the alcoves facing the four cardinal points are four 9.5-metre (31ft) –tall teak Buddha images, dimly lit from the slits in the sanctuary roof. The

Htilominio temple.

north- and south-facing statues are originals, but those facing east and west are later copies.

The roof above the central superstructure consists of five terraces, covered with 389 terracotta-glazed tiles illustrating *Jataka* tales. Together with those inside the temple and at its base, they represent the largest collection of such tiles in Bagan.

Capped by a golden stupa that reaches 51 metres (168ft) above the ground, Ananda's beehive sanctuary tower *(sikhara)* rises from the tiered roof. Smaller pagodas, copies of the central spire, stand at each of its four corners, creating the impression of a mountainous Himalayan landscape.

Proof of this temple's purpose as a place of meditation and learning can be found within Ananda's labyrinthine corridors. Each of the four main halls contains the same 16 Buddha images as the other three, enabling four groups of Buddhist students to undergo their instruction simultaneously.

From these halls, facing the vestibules containing the large Buddhas, continue into the central corridor where 80 reliefs depict the life of the Buddha from birth through to enlightenment. On the west-facing porch are two Buddha footprints, each one divided into 108. Nearby are two statues of particular interest. One represents Kyanzittha, the Ananda Temple's founding father, and the other, Shin Arahan.

Upali Thein

About 1.5km (1 mile) down the main road from the Ananda Temple towards Nyaung U, the 13th-century **Upali Thein** , or hall of ordination, was named after the monk Upali. Although of brick construction, it is said to resemble many of the wooden buildings of the Bagan Era which have long since disappeared. The roof has two rows of battlements and a pagoda at its centre. The Konbaung dynasty undertook extensive renovations at the end of the 18th century, re-painting the beautiful frescoes of Buddhas and *Jataka* stories that adorn the walls.

Htilominlo Temple

Across the road from the Upali Thein stands the last Bamar-style temple built in Bagan, the **Htilominlo** ⑯. The building was constructed in 1211 under the orders of King Nantaungmya who, according to *The Glass Palace Chronicle*, was the son of one of King Narapatisithu's concubines. He chose this spot to site the shrine because it was where the white umbrella used to identify future rulers tilted in his direction.

The Htilominlo Temple is 46 metres (150ft) high and 43 metres (140ft) long on each side at its base. Four Buddha figures placed on the ground and four more figures on the first floor face the cardinal points. Some of the old murals can still be discerned, as can a number of the friezes. Several old horoscopes, painted to protect the building from damage, survive on the walls.

Gubyauknge and Gubyaukgyi

Half a kilometre further up the main road towards Nyaung U, near the village of Wetkyi-in, the **Gubyauknge** ⑰ is notable for the fine stucco work on its exterior walls. Standing next to it is the **Gubyaukgyi** ⑱, which dates from the early 13th century and has a pyramidal spire similar to that of the Mahabodhi. Inside are some of Bagan's finest *Jataka* murals. Unfortunately, many of these were collected by a German enthusiast in the late 19th century and apparently spirited out of the country.

NYAUNG U

The principal hub for the Archaeological Zone is **Nyaung U**, a busy little riverside market town, 5km (3 miles) north of the walled village of Old Bagan. This is where you'll find the largest concentrations of budget hotels, restaurants, markets and souvenir shops, as well as transport connections. The town also holds its own small collection of historic monuments, notably the huge and

Feeding pigeons outside Shwezigon Pagoda, Nyaung U.

Buddha statue at Upali Thein temple.

Dhammayazika Pagoda aglow at sunset.

resplendently gilded Shwezigon Pagoda, one of Bagan's most iconic landmarks.

Kyanzittha Cave

On the southwestern outskirts of Nyaung U, close to the Shwezigon Pagoda, is the **Kyanzittha Temple** , a cave shrine that also once served as a place of lodging for monks. Although its name would seem to indicate Kyanzittha as its creator, in all probability it dates from Anawrahta's reign. The long, dark corridors are embellished with frescoes from the 11th, 12th and 13th centuries; some of the later paintings even depict the Mongols who occupied Bagan after 1287. Visitors are advised to carry their own torches as the attendant family has only candles.

Shwezigon Pagoda

The **Shwezigon Pagoda** ❷⓿, a short walk north of the cave temple, ranks among Myanmar's most revered Buddhist shrines. The prototype for all Burmese stupas, it was built after the rule of Anawrahta at a spot designated by a

while elephant to house the empire's most sacred relics: a replica of the Tooth of Kandy; frontal and collar bones of the Master; and an emerald Buddha image from China. Only three terraces of the pagoda had been finished when Anawrahta was killed by a rampaging buffalo in 1077. His son, Kyanzittha, completed the structure in 1089.

The bell of the Shwezigon surmounts the three terraces, reached by stairways from the cardinal directions. The pagoda spire, crowned by a *hti*, rises above the bell in a series of concentric mouldings. Smaller stupas can be seen at the corners of the terraces, each one decorated with glazed plaques illustrating the *Jataka* tales. Small square temples on each side of the central stupa contain standing Buddhas in the Indian Gupta style. To the left and right of the eastern entrance are two stone pillars, each inscribed on all four sides, recording the establishment of the pagoda during Kyanzittha's reign.

During the second week of the Burmese month of *Nadaw* (November and December), Buddhist pilgrims

from throughout the country converge on the Shwezigon for the temple's annual festival. The event is one of the nation's most popular, largely because it was at the Shwezigon that *nat* worship was first allowed to combine with Buddhism. Anawrahta had the images of the traditional 37 *nat* carved in wood and erected on the lower terraces, believing that "men will not come for the sake of the new faith. Let them come for their old gods and gradually they will be won over." The *nat* are no longer on the terraces, but they are housed in a small hall to the southeast of the pagoda, where they are still venerated today.

Sapada Pagoda

An example of a stricter adherence to orthodox Theravada Buddhism can be seen at the **Sapada Pagoda** ㉑, at the eastern end of Nyaung U on the airport road. Built in the 12th century by the monk Sapada, it is similar to the Pebinkyaung Pagoda, but bears witness to a great schism in the Theravada school. Sapada was one of the monks sent to Ceylon in the latter part of the 12th century, and who returned to Burma a decade later expounding a very orthodox version of Buddhism. It differed markedly from the school absorbed from the Mon, who predominated in Bagan at the time. And it was distinctly different from the courtly religion of Mahayana Buddhism, as well as the Vashnava and Shaivite cults of Hinduism. But Sapada's interpretation was accepted by King Narapatisithu and embraced by Bagan's people.

SOUTHERN PLAIN

The tract of plain immediately south of Nyaung U holds a huge number of temple ruins that can most easily be reached via the main road running from the airport to New Bagan, past the villages of **Minnanthu** and **Pwasaw** – though the majority of horse-cart drivers prefer to reach it via the sandy tracks of the central belt. Being so far from Old Bagan and the tourist enclave, this is among the least frequented corners of the Archaeological Zone, and one that's received less attention from the restorers over the past couple of decades, which makes it all the more atmospheric.

Nandamannya Temple

The **Nandamannya Temple** ㉒, 500 metres (1,640ft) north of Minnanthu village, is among the few monuments in this far-flung southern group to attract much attention – a fact attributable to the erotic murals adorning its interior walls. Unusual for the normally austere Theravada tradition, these depict a scene known as the "Temptation of Mara" in which the demon Mara tempted Buddha with visions of beautiful maidens – a myth personifying the dangers posed to the seeker of Enlightenment by the mundane or alluring side of life.

Originally called Ananta Panna ("endless wisdom"), the temple's name was changed to Nandamannya to avoid confusion with the Ananda

Dhammayazika Pagoda detail.

Crafting lacquerware in Myinkaba village.

Temple. It dates from the 13th century, and holds a seated Buddha image in a state of advanced decay.

Payathonzu Temple

The **Payathonzu Temple** ㉓, the next but one temple south, contains more fine frescoes which archaeologists think were probably painted by the same artist responsible for those of the nearby Nandamannya, although they're somewhat less sensuous. Unusually, the structure consists of three interconnected buildings – the name means "Three Shrines" – joined by narrow vaulted passages and crowned with a *sikhara*. Three empty pedestals stand inside, their Buddha images having long since disappeared. The frescoes fascinate art historians for showing both Mahayanic and Tantric influences. As the Payathonzu was erected in the late 13th century, this suggests that some form of Mahayana Buddhism, albeit as a minority faith, was practised in Bagan throughout the Era of the Temple Builders. It has also been suggested that the triple nature of this *paya* harks back to the *trimurti* of Indian religion, the Hindu holy trinity of Vishnu, Shiva and Brahma – though Buddhists might argue that the triple nature of Buddha, *sangha* and *dhamma* would provide an equally valid interpretation. This temple is often locked (except for group tours), so make enquiries beforehand at the museum in Old Bagan.

Leimyethna Temple

On the northern fringes of Minnanthu village, just beyond the Payathonzu, is the whitewashed **Leimyethna Temple** ㉔. Topped by a gilded spire in the same style as that of the Ananda, it was built in 1222 by Ananthasuriya, Naratheinhka's minister-in-chief, in commemoration of a verse written by his predecessor and close namesake, Ananthathurya. Sentenced to death by King Narapatisithu, this man penned a poem that is still regarded as a Burmese literary treasure. "If... I were to be released and freed from execution I would not escape Death," he wrote. "Inseparable am I from Karma." The king was reportedly so moved he reconsidered and decided to pardon the poet, but was too late – the unfortunate minister had already been executed. The temple, which faces east, contains some still vibrant murals.

Dhammayazika Pagoda

Located midway between Minnanthu and Myinkaba is the circular **Dhammayazika Pagoda** ㉕, which was built in 1196 by King Narapatisithu. The partly gilded stupa rises from three five-sided terraces ringed by small temples, each containing a Buddha image; some also hold Konbaung Dynasty murals. The outer wall also has five gateways, leading to speculation that the figure five was of special significance to the temple builder. It has been suggested that this fifth aspect (added to the more usual four) represents the Maitreya Buddha or the Buddha to come. The Dhammayazika rests in its own grounds about 500 metres (1,640ft)

Abeyadana temple details.

west of Pwasaw village and commands fine views over the central plains.

NEW BAGAN AND THIRIPYITSAYA

If you're travelling on a pre-arranged tour, chances are you'll be based in the settlement of **Bagan Myothit** or **New Bagan** at the southwest corner of the Archaeological Zone, where most of the mid-range and upscale hotels and restaurants are to be found, in and around a grid of streets that were laid out in the 1990s to accommodate people forcibly re-located by the government from the walled city of Old Bagan. With trees and shrubs planted by the locals now well established, Bagan Myothit is no longer the unreservedly barren place it was a decade ago and makes a relaxing base.

On its southwest corner, tiny **Thiripyitsaya Village**, where King Thinlikyaung's 4th-century palace was situated, was a mooring place in the time of Bagan's Golden Era, where foreign ships plying the Ayeyarwady from lands as far away as Sri Lanka dropped anchor. Today, the chief attractions are a trio of well-preserved pagodas. Two of them, known as the **Anauk** or **Eastern Petleik** ㉖ and **Ashe** or **Western Petleik** ㉗ were built in the 11th century, but collapsed in 1905. The unglazed terracotta plaques originally housed in the vaulted corridors are now preserved under replicas of the original roofs. Of the two *paya*, the Anauk is the better preserved. The numbered plaques depict 550 *Jataka* tales; they include the only known representations of three Buddha lifecycle stories, as only 547 *Jataka* are officially recognised by the Theravada Buddhist *sangha*.

At the south end of Thiripyitsaya is the **Lawkananda Pagoda** ㉘, raised in 1059 as one of only three stupas known to have been built by Anawrahta in the Bagan area (the other two are the Shwesandaw and the Myinkaba). It has a cylindrical bell, and stands on three octagonal terraces, the lower two with stairways on each side. This *paya* still functions as an everyday place of worship and houses what is believed to be a replica of the Buddha's tooth.

The **Seinnyet Ama Temple** and Seinnyet Nyima Pagoda ㉙ are a short distance down the road. Tradition attributes these sanctuaries to Queen Seinnyet, who lived during the 11th century, although the style is more typical of the 13th. The pagoda in particular is notable for its design, incorporating Buddhas in niches at each of the cardinal points on the bell-shaped dome, and lions guarding miniature stupas in the corners of the second terrace.

MYINKABA

When King Anawrahta returned to Bagan in 1057 with the Mon royalty in tow, he exiled King Manuha and his family to Myinkaba (Myinpagan), 2km (1.2 miles) south of the city walls. With royalty present, the settlement became the site of the most splendid Mon-style architecture on the Bagan plain. Many of these monuments still stand.

Scratching a pattern into lacquerware calls for meticulous attention to detail.

Reclining Buddha inside the Manuha temple shrine.

Somingyi Monastery

Almost halfway between Myinkaba and New Bagan is the **Somingyi Monastery** ㉚, one of the few brick *kyaung* on the Bagan plain. It is an example of the myriad monasteries that once dotted this arid tableland; most of them, then as now, were built of wood and over the intervening centuries have disappeared without trace. A lobby surrounds the raised platform of the *kyaung* to the east, monks' cells to the north and south, and a two-storey chapel, which houses an image of the Buddha, to the west. It is thought to have been built around 1204 and is named after the woman who sponsored its construction.

Nagayon Temple

The **Nagayon Temple** ㉛, where Kyanzittha is said to have hidden during his flight from Anawrahta, stands on the opposite side of the road from the Somingyi. Legend has it that a *naga* offered the fugitive protection here, much as the Naga Muchalinda shielded the meditating Buddha from a storm. Like all temples built by Kyanzittha, this one has a characteristic Mon style, although it also shows influences from India's Orissa region – a major trading partner.

In the interior of the Nagayon are stone reliefs depicting scenes from the life of the Buddha. A standing Buddha, flanked by two smaller seated figures, is housed within the shrine.

Abeyadana Temple

A short distance north of the Somingyi, on the river-side of the road, the **Abeyadana Temple** ㉜ was named after Kyanzittha's first wife, whom he married as a young warrior. Local legend insists it is situated at the place where she waited for him during his flight from Anawrahta. Abeyadana, originally from Bengal, was probably a follower of Mahayana Buddhism: the frescoes on the outer walls of the corridor represent Bodhisattva, or future Buddhas, and on the inner walls are images of Brahma, Vishnu, Shiva, Indra, and other gods of the Hindu pantheon paying homage to the Master, along with 550 wonderful *Jataka* murals.

A scaffolding-covered Mingalazedi.

Nan Temple

The **Nan Paya Temple** ㉝, just north of the Abeyadana, is said to have once been Manuha's residence. Its interior, which holds some of Bagan's most accomplished sculptural detail, is evidence of the Brahman influence affecting the Theravadin Mon kings. Four pillars are decorated with friezes and bas-reliefs, the one of the god Brahma holding a lotus being particularly striking. On the outside of the temple are friezes of the mythological *hamsa* bird, which, besides being the heraldic crest of Mon royalty, was also the vehicle on which Brahma was usually depicted riding. The temple is kept locked most of the time – ask for the key at the nearby Manuha Temple.

Manuha Temple

A short stroll further north, the **Manuha Temple** ㉞ was built by the captive king of Thaton just south of Myinkaba village in 1059. Because he feared he would be made a temple slave, Manuha sought to improve his *karma* for future incarnations – and so sold some of his jewels in order to finance the construction of this shrine. One reclining and three seated Buddha images cramped within the narrow confines of the building are said to symbolise the distressed soul of the defeated king.

In contrast to most other Mon-style temples, the Manuha has an upper storey. This collapsed during the 1975 earthquake and buried the Buddhas beneath it, but renovation work was completed in 1981. A corner of the temple compound is dedicated to the *nat* of Mount Popa.

Myinkaba Pagoda

On the banks of a small stream at the north side of the village is the **Myinkaba Pagoda** ㉟, which allegedly marks the spot where Anawrahta slew his predecessor and half-brother, Sokkate, in a duel for the kingship in 1044. Sokkate and his elder brother Kyiso had wrested the Bagan throne from Anawrahta's father, Kunhsaw Kyaunghpyu, himself a usurper, in AD 986; but Anawrahta's victory over Sokkate with his mythical spear "Areindama" put an end to over

View of Shwesandaw temple.

Decorative detail at Sulamani temple.

a century of court intrigues. This shrine's bulbous form and round terraces mark it clearly as predating the establishment of Mon Buddhist influence in the Bagan region.

Gubyaukgyi Temple

Close to the roadside at the northern edge of Myinkaba village, the **Gubyaukgyi Temple** ❸❻ is famous above all for the **Myazedi Stones** originally found inside it. The tablets, discovered in 1887, helped philologists decipher the ancient Pyu language, and are now housed inside the Archaeological Museum at Old Bagan (see page 214). The many visitors who seek out this single-storey shrine today, however, do so for a glimpse of the well- preserved murals inside its main prayer hall where, illuminated by light filtering from some fine pierced-stone windows, the 547 *Jataka* tales adorn the walls. They're believed to date from 1113, when Rajakumar built the temple upon the death of his father, Kyanzittha. The east-facing vestibule contains a representation

On the way to Dhammayangyi temple.

of a 10-armed Bodhisattva typical of Mahayana Buddhism.

CENTRAL PLAIN

The belt of central plain running east from Myinkaba in parallel with the road to Nyaung U features some of Bagan's largest and most visited temples, among them the mighty Shwesandaw Pagoda.

Mingalazedi Pagoda

Close to the left bank of the Ayeyarwady, between Myinkaba and Old Bagan, the **Mingalazedi Pagoda** ❸❼ was the last of the great stupas erected during the Era of the Temple Builders, and represents the pinnacle of Bamar stupa architecture. Six years in the making, it was completed in 1287 by Narathihapate, the last of the Bagan kings to reign over the entire Burmese Empire, only ten years before the Mongol invasion.

Steep flights of steps lead up to the main platform from the middle of each side. Miniature stupas in the shape of Indian *kalasa* (nectar pots) stand at the corners of each of the

terraces, whose walls are adorned with large glazed plaques depicting scenes from the *Jataka*. These were considered great luxuries in their time, and the fact that a full set of 1061 was commissioned is indicative of the wealth and extravagance that prevailed in the twilight of the empire. Many have been stolen, but 561 survive *in situ*.

The central tower of the stupa soars 40m (131ft) above ground level. Its pinnacle was destroyed in the 1975 earthquake but has since been repaired and now forms a striking sight.

Shwesandaw Pagoda

The **Shwesandaw Pagoda** ❸❽ and adjacent **Shinbinthalyaung** ❸❾, with its reclining Buddha, comprise one of only three religious sites Anawrahta built in Bagan. Erected in 1057 upon his victorious return from Thaton to enshrine hairs of the Buddha (sent by the king of Bago as a token of thanks for the Burmese military support against the Khymers), the Shwesandaw is sometimes called the Ganesh Temple, after the elephant-headed Hindu god whose image once stood

at the corners of its five successively diminishing terraces. The cylindrical stupa, nowadays sporting a spectacular coat of gold leaf, stands on an octagonal platform atop these terraces, which, like the nearby Mingalazedi, was originally adorned with glazed ceramic *Jataka* plaques. The original *hti*, which collapsed along with the rest of the central spire in the 1975 earthquake, can still be seen lying near the pagoda. Affording spectacular panoramic views across the Bagan plains, it's the most popular sunset-viewing spot on the site and attracts crowds of visitors and postcard sellers towards the end of the day.

The long flat building within the walls of the Shwesandaw enclosure contains the **Shinbinthalyaung Reclining Buddha**. Over 18 metres (60ft) in length, this 11th-century image lies with its head facing south and therefore depicts the sleeping Buddha (only the dying Buddha faces north).

Dhammayangyi Temple

Despite occupying the throne for only a short time, Narathu is remembered as

There are dozens of temples in the Bagan Archaeological Zone.

ARCHITECTURAL STRUCTURES

The spread of Theravada Buddhism in Burma was responsible for the great number of wondrous pagodas and temples that we still see today in Bagan.

While the wooden structures have disappeared and most of the sandstone ones too, the majority of the remaining structures were made of brick, and therefore more durable. Stupas are a solid mass, almost pyramidal in silhouette, finely detailed and usually taking the form of a bell-shaped dome atop receding terraces, and crowned with a finial.

However, the temple type is the more usual form of religious architecture in Bagan, its components clearly articulated, the main entrance and windows plainly indicating their purpose, with the corners properly defined. The entrance arch-pediment protruding from the vestibule gives an impression of space and extends a welcome to the spiritual world within.

In the temple type of structure, there are two sub-types, one of which has a single entrance, with a main hall or vestibule and a central inner sanctum for the Buddha image. The other sub-type has four identical entrances, although in some rarer temples there is a main entrance – usually on the eastern side – with a bigger vestibule than the other three.

A sign reminds visitors to remove their shoes at Dhammayangyi temple.

leaving Dhammayangyi temple.

the founder of Bagan's largest shrine, the **Dhammayangyi Temple** , which rises from the scrub a short stroll southeast of the Shwesandaw. Deeply concerned about his karma for future lives after having murdered his father and brother, Narathu built the Dhammayangyi intending to atone for his misdeeds. It is today the best-preserved temple in Bagan, with a layout similar to that of the Ananda but lacking the delicate, harmonious touch of its prototype. The brickwork and masonry, however, are without equal.

Local legend asserts that Narathu oversaw the construction himself and that masons were executed if a needle could be pushed between the bricks they had laid. The building, however, was never completed. Before work could be finished, Narathu himself was assassinated by an Indian suicide squad dispatched by the father of one of his wives, whom he'd had executed because he disliked her Hindu rituals. Disguised as Brahmin priests, the assassins drew swords as soon as they'd been received by the king, then slew one another.

Sulamani

Marooned in the middle of Bagan's central plain, well off the site's surfaced roads, the **Sulamani Temple** ⑪ is considered one of the former city's great two-storey monuments. It resembles the Thatbyinnyu in plan, and was built by Narapatisithu in 1183. The building takes its name from the legendary palace of the god Indra, crowning the peak of Mount Meru high above the plain on which ordinary mortals reside. A paragon of the fully developed Bamar architectural style, the Sulamani's upper storey rests on a huge central pillar that occupies the middle of the ground floor. The lower level has seated Buddha images on all four sides. Porches face the four cardinal points on each storey, with those oriented eastwards being larger than the others. The remains of some 18th-century murals can be seen inside the temple.

Responsible Tourism

After more than two decades, foreign visitors are no longer being asked to boycott visiting Myanmar on ethical grounds, but challenges still exist.

In 2010, after the military government embarked on a process of democratic reform in Myanmar, Aung San Suu Kyi's National League for Democracy (the NLD) declared an end to the longstanding tourism boycott of the country. Foreigners had long been discouraged from visiting the country on the grounds that their presence legitimised and generated income for the repressive regime of Myanmar and its cronies – while thousands of political prisoners languished in jail, and ethnic minorities such as the Karen, Kachin and Chin were subject to torture, forced labour and other forms of abuse perpetrated by the Burmese army (Tatmadaw).

Things have moved on rapidly since the NLD's announcement. Peace accords have been signed with most of the rebel groups, tourism is booming as never before and the country is well on the way to becoming a democracy, with its own fully elected parliament.

However, the NLD has remained somewhat ambivalent about tourism, maintaining a stance against large tour groups, and advising visitors to avoid hotels owned by or connected to high-ranking members of the junta – even though tax revenue from such enterprises is nowadays benefiting a government of which the NLD is a part.

Ethical practice

So is it now really ethical to visit Myanmar? The answer is "more so than in previous decades", but with some caveats.

Basically, it's impossible to make sure none of your cash ends up in the back pockets of unscrupulous middle men and entrepreneurs with contacts to the shadier corridors of power. But you can, by following some simple principles, ensure your presence in the country is as much of a force for good as possible. The following are based on recommendations formulated by the British NGO, Tourism Concern (tourismconcern.org).

Travel independently rather than as part of a large organised tour, using locally owned accommodation wherever possible.

If you do book a tour, avoid large foreign-owned operators in favour of smaller, independently run ones

with a clear policy on benefiting local economies.

Quiz your holiday company on its stance regarding ownership of the hotels they use. In compiling accommodation recommendations, we consulted the most up-to-date blacklist compiled by the Paris-based pressure group, Info Birmanie (info-birmanie.org), an organisation with close connections to Aung San Suu Kyi and the NLD. Blacklisted hotels have been excluded from our listings, except where they are the only options in any given place, in which case their connection with the junta or its associates is flagged.

Spread your money around as widely as possible. Patronise different taxi drivers, eat in family-run restaurants and buy souvenirs from local shops rather than the boutiques back at your hotel.

Interact at every opportunity with Burmese people you meet – though avoid at all costs discussing politics or any subject likely to incriminate them in the eyes of the government.

Don't take photographs of people without first seeking their permission.

Wear appropriate clothing and behave respectfully when visiting religious sites.

Rather than giving money to individuals, make donations to social projects such as schools, orphanages and clinics, where your gift may contribute to ongoing work.

Selling sand paintings outside Abeyadana temple.

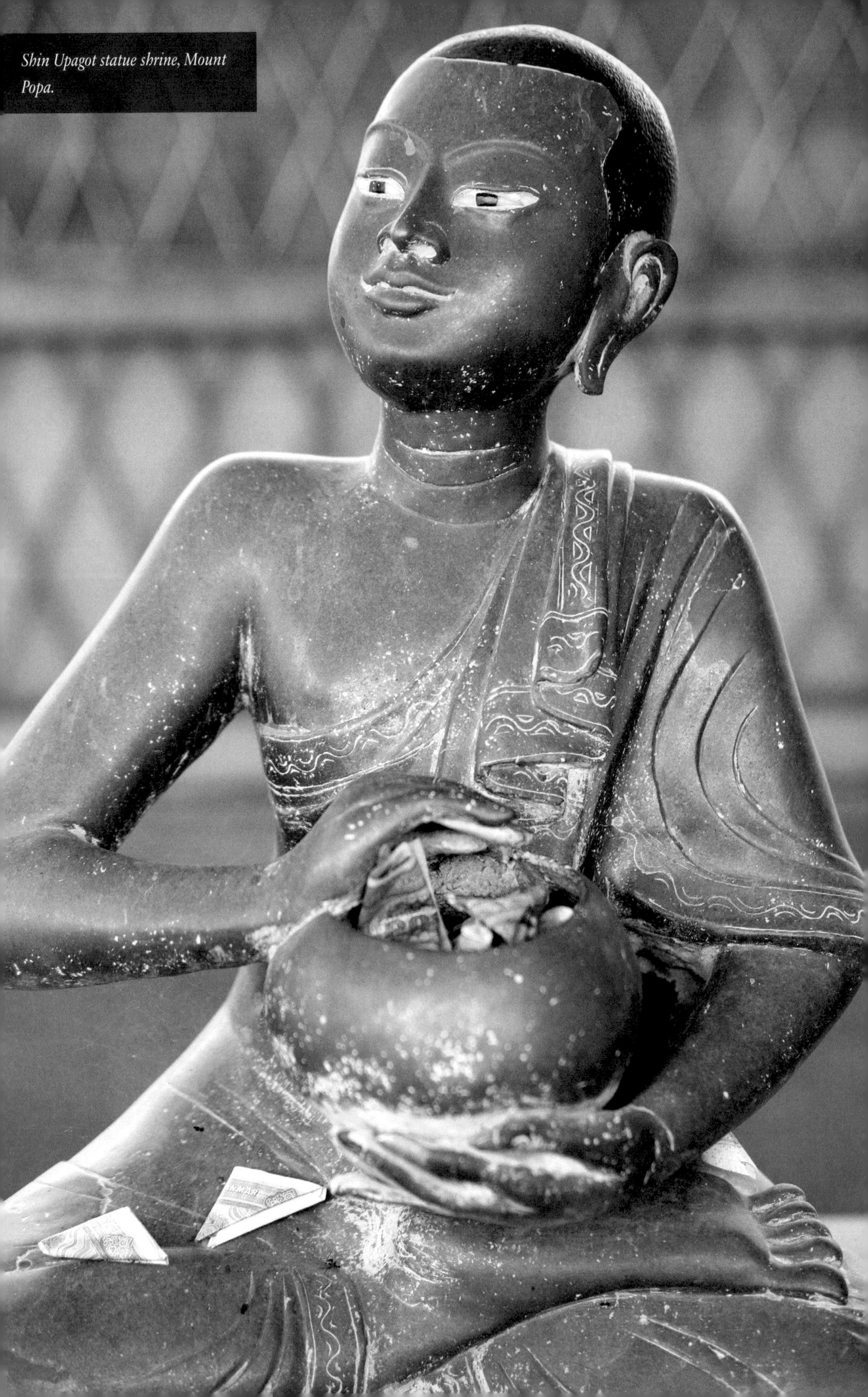

Shin Upagot statue shrine, Mount Popa.

AROUND BAGAN

Dominated by the magnificent Mount Popa, the otherwise flat plains around Bagan are scattered with ancient temples and bustling market towns.

Bagan

Yangon

The arid plains around Bagan hold several options for day trips should you feel like a break from the ruins. An hour-and-a-half's drive southeast, **Mount Popa** is an extinct volcano whose dramatic profile can be seen on the horizon in clear weather, and where a geological curiosity – a craggy basalt plug – has become the country's principal centre for *nat* worship. It's worth making the trip just for the views to be had from the top of the hill, which surveys an awesome sweep of mountainous landscape. The village, visited in huge numbers during two annual temple festivals, even boasts a decent hotel should you be tempted to stay the night for the trek up to the nearby volcano early the following morning.

Closer to **Bagan** ❶, a cluster of off-track ancient temples lies upriver, reachable by boat from the jetty at Nyaung U, while the region's market towns provide a splash of local atmosphere.

Temples upriver from Nyaung U

Boats leave throughout the day from Nyaung U's little jetty for a trio of small temples upstream – a trip that takes around three or four hours including stops at the monuments.

This wood will be used as fuel to heat palm sugar and turn it into jaggery.

The first site you come to, 1km (0.6 mile) north, is the 13th-century **Thatkyamuni Temple** ❷, in which panels of murals depicting Ashoka, the great Mauryan Emperor who ruled in India during the 3rd century BC, adorn the walls. Other scenes record the introduction of the Buddhist faith to Sri Lanka. On a low hill close by, the **Kondawgyi Temple** was a contemporary of the Thatkyamuni, and also holds some paintings, this time of *Jataka* scenes and floral patterns.

Main Attractions

Boat trips from Bagan
Pakhangyi
Popa Taung Kalat
Mount Popa

Nuns collecting alms.

The boats continue for 3km (2 miles) until they reach a clay escarpment overlooking the Ayeyarwady, from which the **Kyaukgu Temple** ❸ surveys the river. A maze of passages leads into the caves behind: the stone-and-brick-built chamber is in fact an enlargement of the natural hollow. A large Buddha sits opposite the entrance, and the walls are embellished with stone reliefs. The Kyaukgu's ground storey dates from the 11th century; the upper two storeys have been ascribed to the reign of Narapatisithu (1174–1211).

Pakokku

Further afield, but still within the general Bagan area, the town of **Pakokku** ❹, on the right bank of the Ayeyarwady, made international headlines in the so-called "Saffron Revolution" of 2007, when local monks spearheaded a protest against petrol prices. The protest subsequently went national and led to a massive military clampdown on pro-democracy campaigners.

There's little to see in the town beyond the local market, which specialises in tobacco and *thanaka* wood. But with a little time on your hands a commendable side trip would be the 20km (12-mile) foray northeast to visit the 19th-century ruins of **Pakhangyi** ❺, comprising old city walls, an archaeological museum and a great wooden temple – one of the oldest in Myanmar – supported by a forest of more than 250 teak pillars.

Myingyan and the Chindwin River

About equidistant between Mandalay and Bagan, on the left bank of the Ayeyarwady, the Bamar market town of **Myingyan** ❻ is both a river port and an important cotton-trading centre, forming a junction between a branch railway to Thazi and the main line between Yangon and Mandalay. There isn't much of historical interest on offer, but the central market is thriving, and food and accommodation are readily available, making Myingyan a convenient overnight stop for

A local scoops her kid goat into her arms.

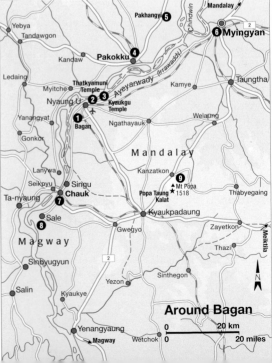

Around Bagan

travellers by road between Mandalay and Bagan.

Myingyan is located just downstream from the mighty **Chindwin River**, the main tributary of the Ayeyarwady.The Chindwin is formed in the Patkai and Kumon ranges of the Indo-Myanmar border by a network of headstreams including the Tanai, Tawan and Taron. It drains northwest through the Hukawng valley and then begins its 840km (520-mile) main course. The Chindwin flows south through the Naga Hills and past the towns of Singkaling Hkamti, Homalin, Thaungdut, Mawlaik, Kalewa and Monywa. Below the jade-rich Hukawng valley, falls and reefs interrupt it at several places. At Haka, goods must be transferred from large boats to canoes.

The Uyu and the Myittha are the main tributaries of the system, which drains around 114,000 sq km (44,000 sq miles) of northwestern Myanmar. During part of the rainy season (June–November), the Chindwin is navigable by river steamer for more than 640km (400 miles) upstream to Singkaling Hkamti. The Chindwin's outlets into the Ayeyarwady are interrupted by a succession of long, low, partially populated islands. According to tradition, the most southerly of these outlets is an artificial channel cut by one of the kings of Pagan. Choked up for many centuries, it was reopened by an exceptional flood in 1824.

Chauk, Sale and Kyaukpadaung

About 30km (19 miles) south of Bagan, **Chauk** ❼ is a small town and petroleum port for the Singu-Chauk oil fields. Traditionally, people of the Mon minority gathered asphalt in the area to weatherproof houses. In 1902, the British discovered a sizeable oil field, and later crude from the area was pumped through a 563km (350-mile) pipeline to Thanlyin for refining. Insurgent sabotage of the artery confined marketing of Chauk's oil to

northern Burma after World War II, when tankers began operation on the Ayeyarwady as an alternative means of transport to the damaged pipeline. The Chauk refinery was renovated in 1954, and the pipeline repaired.

Just 8km (5 miles) south of Chauk, the small riverside settlement of **Sale** ❽ (also spelt Salay) developed as an adjunct of Bagan during the 12th and 13th centuries. It's well off the beaten track, and a more active Buddhist centre than the Archaeological Zone, with fascinating colonial architecture, a strong Bamar flavour, and little-visited ruins.

Kyaukpadaung, a small junction town about 40km (25 miles) southeast of Bagan, is the railhead and bus station for nearby Mount Popa, about 10km (6 miles) to the south. There's nothing of historical interest to see, but basic accommodation and food are available *in extremis*.

POPA

The most popular excursion from Bagan is to the *nat* temple of **Popa Taung Kalat**, 50km (30 miles)

Collecting palm sugar, destined for the manufacture of jaggery.

The Pandaw 3 takes to the water.

Enjoying the views from Mount Popa, monkeys and all.

southeast. Confusingly, this spectacular pilgrimage place, which centres on an eerie outcrop of rock rising sheer from the plains, is often referred to as "**Mount Popa**", strictly speaking the name of a much larger mountain to the east. While the former can be reached in an easy day trip from Bagan, the latter massif requires a dawn start and a full day of leg work to ascend, for which you'll need to stay in the area.

The name "*popa*", Sanskrit for "flower", is believed to derive from the profusion of blooms nourished by the famously fertile soil of the mountain. Local legend asserts that the volcano first appeared in 442 BC after a great earthquake forced out of the Myingyan plains. Volcanic ash gradually coalesced into rich soil, and the great peak was soon festooned with flowers. For the inhabitants of the surrounding regions this seemed a true miracle and Popa soon became legendary as a home of the gods

Mount Popa.

– the "Mount Olympus" of Burma. Alchemists and occultists settled on its slopes, and people generally became convinced that mythical beings, the *nat*, inhabited its woods.

Popa Taung Kalat

The plug of an extinct volcano, the weirdly shaped hill of **Popa Taung Kalat** is in Burmese mythology closely associated with the 37 *Mahagiri Nat*, or "Great Spirit Heroes", of local tradition, for whom this is the country's most powerful centre. Worshippers from all over Burma come here to propitiate the deities installed in the ancient temple complex at its base, whose focal point is a gallery containing images of the 37 principal *nat*, as well as various ogresses and other guardian spirits of water, trees and households.

From the *nat* temple, a covered walkway lined with stalls selling religious souvenirs winds steeply up the hill itself, culminating in a small, 737-metre (2,417ft) plateau. The walk up takes around 20 minutes and ends at a gleaming complex of Buddhist shrines and gilded stupas from whose terrace a magnificent 360-degree panorama extends across the plains to the Rakhine-Yoma mountains, rising from the dust haze on the horizon. Look out for the voracious macaques that patrol the steps and are not averse to snatching titbits from pilgrims' hands.

Mount Popa

Technically a spur of the **Bago Yoma** range, **Mount Popa** ❾ is an extinct volcano rising due east of Taung Kalat to a height of 1,518m (4,981ft). Numerous trails lead through the lush forests wrapped around the mountain's flanks to the spectacular, 610-metre (2000ft) caldera marking its summit. Far-reaching views are guaranteed from the very start of the strenuous four-hour trek, for which guides can be arranged through the *Popa Mountain Resort* (see page 314). Bird-spotters will find plenty to get excited about flitting through Popa's pristine jungle, home 176 species, including two endemics (the Burmese bushlark and hooded treepie), as well as 65 different kinds of orchid.

The legend of the Mahagiri Nat

A trip to the shrine of the **Mahagiri Nat**, situated about halfway up the mountain, is an essential part of a visit to Mount Popa. For seven centuries preceding the reign of Anawrahta, all kings of central Burma were required to make a pilgrimage here to consult with the two powerful *nat* about their reign.

The legend begins with a young blacksmith, Nga Tin De, and his beautiful sister who lived outside the northern city of Tagaung in the mid-4th century, when King Thinlikyaung ruled in the Bagan area. Perceived by the king as a threat, he was forced to flee into the woods. The king then became enchanted with the blacksmith's sister, and married her. He then convinced his wife that Nga Tin De was no longer his rival and he asked her to call her brother back from the forest. But when Nga Tin De emerged, he was seized by the king's guards, tied to a tree and set alight.

As the fire lapped at her brother's body, Shwemyethna broke free from her escorts and threw herself into the blaze. Their physical bodies gone, the siblings became mischievous *nat* living in the saga tree. To stop them from causing him harm, the king had the tree chopped down and thrown into the Ayeyarwady. The story of their deaths spread rapidly throughout Burma. Thinlikyaung, who had wanted to unite the country in *nat* worship, learned that the tree was floating downstream through his kingdom. He ordered the tree fished out of the river and had two figures carved from it. The *nat* images were then carried to the top of Mount Popa and given a shrine where they reside to this day. Every king crowned in Bagan between the 4th and 11th centuries would make a pilgrimage to the brother and sister *nat*, who would supposedly appear before the ruler to counsel him.

TIP

Come prepared if you plan to climb Popa Taung Kalat. The ascent takes less than half an hour but is very thirsty work. Bring a hat or parasol, and ensure that you have plenty of water with you.

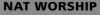

Nat deities inside the "Mother Spirit of Popa" nat shrine at the base of Mount Popa.

NAT WORSHIP

The veneration of spirit heroes known as *nat* is peculiar to Myanmar, where it runs in parallel and seeming harmony with the rituals of Theravada Buddhism. *Nat* shrines often appear next to, and frequently inside, Buddhist temples, and Burmese worshippers tend to see no contradiction in this, even though numerous kings tried to stamp out the tradition. After failing spectacularly in the 11th century, King Anawrahta chose to incorporate *nat* into local Buddhist mythology – albeit in an inferior position to the Buddha himself.

It was Anawrahta who first fixed the *nat* pantheon and established the 37 *Mahagiri* or "Great Nat" that dominate ritual life today. Numerous temples are dedicated to these flamboyant gods, which all have their own peculiar origin myths and proclivities. They all died violent deaths – all, that is, except Thagyamin, the King of the *Nat*, usually portrayed riding a three-headed white elephant and carrying a conch shell.

Believers propitiate different *nat* depending on what they need; an offering will be made at a local shrine or, perhaps, a visit will be made to a temple of national importance. However, *nat* worship is practised in its most fervent form at *nat pwes*, annual festivals where special oracles called *natkadaws* dominate proceedings. After a serious drinking session, the *natkadaws* enter trances during which they're possessed by the presiding *nat* and appeased with offerings by worshippers.

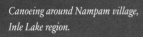
Canoeing around Nampam village, Inle Lake region.

THANAKA AND LONGYI: BURMESE TRADITIONS

Longyi, the national costume, is worn every day by both men and women, while *thanaka* is the cosmetic of choice for Burmese women.

A Burmese, it is often said, never feels comfortable in anything but a *longyi*. Since the 19th century, when it was introduced by families from southern India, this simple panel of cloth wrapped around the waist has been the mode of dress for all Burmese, from commoners to members of the royal court.

Traditional *longyis* comprise rectangular lengths of cloth, around 2 metres (6ft) long, which are sewn into a tube shape. When worn by men it is known as a *pasoe*; or as a *htamein* if worn by a woman.

Both look similar but are wrapped differently: men tie a knot in front, while women tie one to the side, with the knot tucked into a black waistband called a *htet sint*, sewn to the top of the *longyi*.

Simple, checked or striped patterns in subdued colours are used for men; ladies don flowery designs and bright hues. Men complete the ensemble with a Western-style shirt, women with a short blouse.

For special occasions more elegant silk *longyis* – or *acheiks* – are usually worn, with jackets and turbans for men, and for women, a tailored top and velvet-thong slippers.

The Burmese Premier, General Than Shwe, and other members of the *junta* caused a stir in February 2011 when they appeared on national television wearing women's *acheiks* and *longbon* headscarves – an act widely perceived as superstition. Fortune-tellers have repeatedly predicted that a woman will one day rule Myanmar, and so the generals' cross-dressing was seen as an attempt to forestall the rise of Aung San Suu Kyi.

Turning thanaka wood into a paste for applying as sunscreen.

A young souvenir-seller in Inwa sporting thanaka on her cheeks.

A woman protects her face with thanaka as she chops bamboo destined to be used in the making of mats and as the walls of houses.

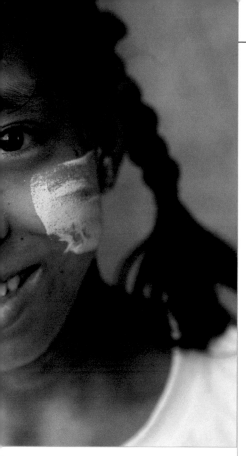

Men and women alike wearing longyi for some shopping at Nampam market.

THANAKA – THE FACE OF MYANMAR

Thanaka is the yellowish-white paste that most Burmese women and girls daub over their faces and arms. The cream is made from the ground bark of several trees, and is worn to protect fragile complexions from the darkening, dehydrating effects of strong sunlight. With a fragrance close to that of sandalwood, the cream has been used for at least 2,000 years. Styles vary, ranging from a simple circular patch on each cheek to more complicated patterns painted using intricate leaf stencils.

Apart from its cosmetic and sun-blocking properties, *thanaka* is believed to cure acne and act as an antiseptic, which perhaps goes some way to explaining why this most Burmese of traditions has so resolutely stood the test of time.

A thanaka-daubed aubergine-seller on the platform at Aungban train station.

n army of sweepers at Shwedagon Pagoda esents a colourful array of longyi.

extiles for sale in Bogyoke market, the flowery designs and right shades aimed at female customers.

Statue detail, Indein Paya, Inle Lake region.

NORTHEASTERN MYANMAR

The hills of Shan State extend north to China, east to Thailand and Laos, and south to Kayah. In the far north, Kachin State reaches into the Himalayas. For visitors, these far-flung regions are some of the most rewarding in Myanmar.

A novice monk cradles a kitten at Shweyan Pyay Monastery.

The image of an Intha fisherman standing at the stern of a flat-bottomed canoe, rowing with one leg past a backdrop of mist-shrouded mountains over the shimmering waters of Inle Lake is one of Myanmar's most iconic. With its idyllic stilted villages, ancient *stupa* complexes and fabulous backdrop of green hills, Inle is the top attraction of Shan State, in the country's hilly northeast. But the region holds plenty of other compelling destinations, many of them in areas newly opened to tourists.

In the forest hills due west of Inle, Kalaw, a former British hill station, is visited primarily by travellers wishing to make treks into the tribal areas surrounding it. The most popular routes wind east to the lake, through pine forests and a fertile belt that's intensively farmed by a variety of colourfully dressed minority groups. Another popular trail works its way 110km (70 miles) northwest to the fabulous Pindaya Cave, with its thousands of carved Buddha images. An alternative trekking hub is the market town of Hsipaw in the Nam Tu Valley, to the northeast of Pyin U-Lwin. The choice of accommodation is more limited here, but the tribal villages nestled in the surrounding countryside see correspondingly fewer visitors.

Eyes down over the goods at Nampam market.

Shan is Myanmar's largest state, extending west as well as east from its administrative capital, Taunggyi, for 350km (220 miles) to Laos and the notorious "Golden Triangle" of the opium trade; nearly as far north to the Burma Road and the Chinese border; and south a lesser distance to the tribal states of the Kayah and Kayin (Karen). This is largely a region of high, roadless peaks, of rugged river gorges and fiercely independent tribes-people who until recently were locked in a war with the Burmese government.

North of Shan and Kayah states is Kachin State, which has slowly opened to foreigners. Foremost among its attractions is the week-long trip down the Ayeyarwady from the towns of Myitkyina or Bhamo, which can be covered on a government ferry or on one of the handful of luxury cruises that operate on this relatively unfrequented stretch. Home to colourful tribal groups, Kachin State's Indawgyi Lake, the largest in Myanmar, is breathtaking, as are its snowcapped mountain ranges in the far north around the town of Putao, near to the border with India.

The state is also an important source of Burmese jade, which has long enthralled gem merchants far and wide.

Young residents of the stilt houses of Nampam village.

SHAN AND KAYAH STATES

The former lands of the Shan princes are home to gilded Buddhas and hot sulphur springs, as well as serene Inle Lake, heartland of the Intha people.

Shan State, in eastern Burma, encompasses a beautiful plateau of rolling highlands, lakes and forests that extend all the way from the central plains to the borders of China, Laos and Thailand. This vast hill tract, which accounts for around a quarter of the country's total surface area, has always been something of a land apart – geographically remote, difficult to govern and perennially vulnerable to invasion. For most of the past four decades armed conflicts of one kind or another have rendered much of it off limits to foreign tourists. However, a recent accord signed by the Burmese government with more than a dozen insurgent groups seems to be holding fast. Visitor numbers have increased accordingly – not just in the popular destination of Inle Lake, in the west of Shan, but also the much less explored frontier districts of the state's far east – heartland of the so-called "Golden Triangle".

History

The present-day population of Shan State is mostly descended from Mongol soldiers who accompanied Kublai Khan in the late 13th century and never left. Since then, the region has been dominated by a mosaic of petty princedoms ruled by *saopha* or *sawbwa*, chiefs who were allowed to retain their regalia and privileges after

the Konbaung Dynasty annexed the area in the 18th century. In return, the chiefs paid tribute to Mandalay and provided troops for the Burmese army. Shan soldiers were at the forefront of the Konbaung's wars of conquest in the south of Burma and played a seminal role in the First Anglo-Burmese War of 1824–26.

In order to ensure the good behaviour of the Shan Chiefs, the Burmese kings kept their sons as de facto hostages at court. The British did something similar after they took the region

Main Attractions
Boat trips, Inle Lake
Hill-tribe trekking from Kalaw
Five-day markets
Kakku
Pindaya Caves
Kengtung
Trekking from Hsipaw

Sampling the goods in Kalaw market.

in the late 1880s, only instead of holding the Shan boys in the capital, they sent them to public schools in the hill town of Taunggyi, and later to universities in Great Britain. The result was a generation of anglophile local rulers who were more sympathetic to British rule than that of their former Burmese overlords. When the latter came to dominate the nation's political life following independence, many of the Shan chiefs began agitating for self-rule, leading to the formation of an embryonic insurgent army on the Thai border.

The political situation became even more unstable in 1950, after 20,000 troops of the Chinese People's Liberation Army swarmed across the frontier to oust Kuomintang (KMT) forces that had settled in the area. While the Chinese communists fought from the east, the Burmese battled from the west. In the end, the KMT were defeated and the People's Liberation Army headed home triumphant, but large numbers of Chinese troops chose to stay behind in Shan – the first of several waves of immigration from neighbouring China that has totally changed the ethnic complexion of the state's eastern flank.

A full-blown Shan insurgency erupted in 1964 after General Ne Win's military coup. Fuelled by income from the Golden Triangle's booming opium trade and illegally mined rubies, this rumbled on for nearly four decades until the government and various strands of the Shan State Army (SSA) signed a cease-fire agreement in 2011.

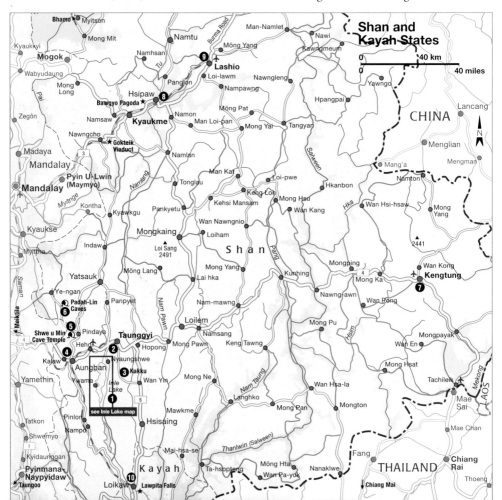

Armed rebellion has also dogged neighbouring Kayah State, homeland of the Karen people, which has seen some of the worst atrocities committed by the Burmese government and their insurgent adversaries in the modern era. Although the situation in Kayah looks more peaceful now than it has for many years, the region can only be visited on government-sanctioned tours.

What to see

The strife of the recent civil wars feels a world away from serene Inle Lake, this region's main visitor attraction, whose glassy waters are cradled by verdant hills on the placid, western rim of the Shan plateau. While you're in the area it's well worth making a detour up to the former British hill station of Kalaw, a genteel Raj-era town whose colonial architecture and mild climate make it an ideal springboard for treks into the neighbouring hills, home to a colourful array of ethnic minority groups.

East of Shan's administrative capital and main market town, Taunggyi,

the landscape grows more rugged as you approach the so-called "Golden Triangle", where the Burmese border bisects those of Thailand, Laos and China. Fought over for much of the 20th century by rival states and drug lords, this backwater region is nowadays stable and accessible again. A strong Thai influence pervades the streets of its attractively old-fashioned capital, Kengtung, which can be reached by air from Mandalay, Yangon and Heho (Inle Lake), or via a tortuous road journey across the mountains from Taunggyi. More than its traditional Buddhist monasteries and temples, the main incentive to make the trip is the chance to trek in Kengtung's hilly hinterland, populated by minority groups whose way of life has changed little since the Konbaung Dynasty ruled more than a century ago.

INLE LAKE

Thanks to its cooler climate and picturesque setting in the lap of the Shan Hills, **Inle Lake ❶** these days attracts serious numbers of visitors during

One legged rowing technique and floating gardens, Inle lake

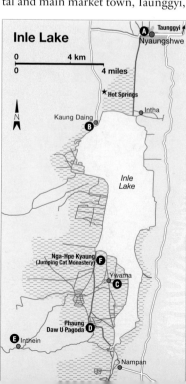

Inle Lake

0   4 km
0   4 miles

N

Ⓐ Taunggyi
Nyaungshwe

★ Hot Springs

● Intha

Kaung Daing
Ⓑ

Inle Lake

Nga-Hpe Kyaung
(Jumping Cat Monastery) Ⓕ

Ywama
Ⓒ

Phaung
Daw U Pagoda Ⓓ

Ⓔ Inthein

Nampan

the winter tourist season. In between leisurely sojourns gazing from their hotel verandahs across the water, travellers while away days taking boat trips to ruined *stupas*, hot springs and the stilted villages of the local Intha people. The Intha are responsible for Inle's defining image – that of the local "leg-rowing" fishermen, who propel themselves across the lake's surface by wrapping one leg around oars fixed to the stern of flat-bottomed canoes.

Around 70,000 Intha live in the towns and scattered villages clustered on the shores of the lake, which is approximately 21km (13 miles) long and 11km (7 miles) wide. As well as their distinctive rowing technique, the minority are known for their "floating gardens", or *kyunpaw*, which they create by collecting weeds from the surface and lashing them together to form metre-thick strips. These are then anchored to the bed of the lake with bamboo poles, and heaped with mud scooped from the bottom. One advantage of the method is that it can be used regardless of fluctuating water levels. Crops – including cauliflower,

tomatoes, cucumbers, cabbage, peas, beans and aubergine – are grown year-round.

Surplus produce is taken by boat to the local markets, hosted in a five-day rotation by the settlements that ring the lake. These also provide a popular daytrip destination for visitors, attracting minority people dressed in their finest traditional garb, and are a great source of authentic souvenirs, such as locally handwoven Shan shoulder bags and *longyis* made from lotus silk.

An immigrant tribe from Dawei (Tavoy) on the southeast coast who left their former homeland in the 18th century to escape the perpetual conflicts between the Burmese and Thais, the Intha are also skilled metalworkers, carpenters and, above all, fishermen. A regular sight on the lake is local men using long conical traps, which are used to catch Inle's metre-long carp, giant catfish and eels.

With regular connections to Heho airport (40km/25 miles northwest) from Yangon, Mandalay and Bagan, getting to Inle is straightforward if you fly. Overland it's a tougher

Canoeing around Nampam village on Inle Lake.

undertaking by bus or taxi along mountain roads via the junction town of **Shwenyaung**, or highland capital Taunggyi to the lake's principal town and transport hub, **Nyaungshwe**.

Nyaungshwe

Nyaungshwe Ⓐ, the oldest of about 200 Intha settlements around Inle Lake, stands on a 5km (3-mile) -wide belt of silt and tangled water hyacinth on the north side of Inle Lake. Since the tourism revival, the town has grown considerably and now holds the lion's share of the area's accommodation, restaurants and other visitor facilities. Lake trips by motorised boat, canoe or bicycle are the main focus here, but you could spend an enjoyable morning looking around the **Yadana Man Taung Pagoda**, the town's principal Buddhist shrine, whose centrepiece is a towering, gilded *stupa* made to a unique seven-stepped design.

The largest monastery in Nyaung-shwe is the **Kan Gyi Kyaung**, a couple of blocks east of the Yadana Man Taung on Myawady Road, which boasts a resident population of around 250 monks. Photographers, however, tend to make a beeline for the **Shwe Yaunghwe Kyaung**, a couple of kilometres north of the centre, whose teak-built ordination hall is lined with picturesque oval windows – the young novices know the drill and pose cheerfully in them for visitors as soon as any turn up.

Kaung Daing

Kaung Daing Ⓑ, to the southwest of Nyaungshwe on the lakeshore, is the site of a couple of large upscale resort hotels. The village also has hot sulphur springs and is a popular destination for day-tripping tourists wishing to see the "long-necked" Padaung tribes-women who wear brass coils to lower their collar bones. The small community, who live on a reserve near the hotel, are originally from Loikaw in Kayah State.

Ywama

About 12km (7.5 miles) from Kaung Daing on the southwest side of Inle, the village of **Ywama Ⓒ** is about as

Frying snacks at a roadside teashop in Nyaungshwe, Inle Lake region.

The floating gardens on Inle Lake

touristy as the lake gets, with a clutch of hotels, restaurants and lanes lined with souvenir stalls, as well as a fleet of water-borne trinket sellers hassling any visitors who venture out on boats. Every tour group in the region comes here once every five days for the village's famous "floating market", which started out as a purely authentic local veg bazaar but has been overwhelmed in recent seasons.

Ywama serves as a springboard for boat trips to the nearby **Phaung Daw U Pagoda** ⓓ, venue of one of the country's most important festivals. The event centres around the procession of four sacred images which are enshrined with a fifth in the temple. These were carried back to Burma by the widely travelled 12th-century King Alaungsithu upon his return from the Malay Peninsula, and then deposited in a cave near the lake. They were not rediscovered until centuries later, since when they've been covered with so many layers of gold leaf that they're unrecognizable as Buddha figures.

Inthein

Among the most popular day-trip destinations on Inle Lake is the village of **Inthein** ⓔ, which sits at the end of two long, winding rivulets running inland just southwest of Ywama and the Phaung Daw U Pagoda. Lined by reed beds and open fields, the channels narrow as they approach the village, which is famous for its collection of crumbling Shan *stupas*. The most accessible of these is **Nyaung Ohak**, a short stroll south across a footbridge from the village proper. While some have been restored with fresh coats of limewash and gold leaf, many more are half-collapsed and overgrown with weeds. Stucco reliefs of guardian deities and mythical creatures flank the ornately carved fronts of the older monuments. From Nyaung Ohak, you can follow a long covered walkway lined with souvenir stalls uphill to the **Shwe Inthein Pagoda**, a much larger complex of 17th-century *stupas* arranged around a central shrine. The views over the lake from here are magnificent.

The largest numbers of visitors descend on Inthein when it hosts one

Performance of a show held in Heho which features jumping cats.

of the lake's famous five-day markets, which fills a dusty market square in the centre of the village. To escape the melee, follow the lane running from the northwest corner of the square and take the footpath striking left off it shortly after to the *stupa* crowning the hilltop above, from whose base extends another stupendous panorama over Inle and its mountain backdrop.

Nga Hpe Kyaung (Jumping Cat Monastery)

One of Myanmar's wackier visitor attractions is Inle's **Nga Hpe Kyaung** **F**, better known on the tourist circuit as the "**Jumping Cat Monastery**", where the resident felines have been trained to leap through hoops in exchange for titbits. Every day during the winter season, a steady stream of inquisitive foreigners files through to photograph the curious spectacle and most leave nonplussed: the cats tend to be less than enthusiastic performers, and the whole event can feel like a rather cynical way to relieve visitors of their cash. Of more interest is the superb collection of antique Buddhas

housed in the carved wood meditation hall.

TAUNGGYI

The administrative centre and main market hub for the Inle Lake region is **Taunggyi** **2**, seat of the Shan Council of Chiefs during the British colonial period. The town was founded by Sir James George Scott, one of the most respected colonial officers in the history of British Burma. A devoted student of Burmese history and culture, Scott, under the pseudonym Shway Yoe, wrote the book *The Burman, His Life and Notions* – generally regarded as the 19th century's finest work on Burma and one which remains a frequently consulted source.

Despite its altitude, Taunggyi no longer enjoys as mild a climate as it did in the past, and lacks the traditional atmosphere of settlements around the lake itself. If you come here at all it will probably be to visit the five-day market, visited in large numbers by the region's hill tribes who flock here to buy and sell home-grown fruit and vegetables,

TIP

Find out the name of the village where the Phaung Daw U festival will take place on the day that you wish to see it and hire a boat the night before. Be sure to start out early (preferably before 5am) as festivities kick off before dawn.

A barge carrying the Buddha images of Phaung Daw U Pagoda during the festival of the same name.

THE PHAUNG DAW U FESTIVAL

The Phaung Daw U Pagoda's annual festival, celebrated in October to mark the beginning of Buddhist Lent, is Shan State's principal religious celebration, attracting devotees from across the region and beyond. Its focal point is the parade of the temple's amorphous Buddha statues around Inle's 18 largest settlements aboard a re-created royal barge with a huge gilded *karaweik* bird at its prow. The procession, which lasts two weeks, is a reminder of the pomp that once attended the Buddhist courts.

Only four of the five sacred images are used in the parade. Legend has it that all five were at first employed in the procession, but that in 1965, a storm capsized the barge carrying the images, and it sank to the bottom of the lake. Only four images were recovered and these were taken back to the Phaung Daw U Pagoda, where, lo and behold, the fifth one was also found, still covered with weeds. Since then, this fifth image has never left the pagoda. Today, the spot on the lake where the barge capsized is marked by a pole crowned by the sacred mythological *hintha* bird. The Phaung Daw U festival draws crowds from all over Myanmar, arriving in boatloads carrying elaborate offerings. They come not only for the "royal" procession, but also for the famed leg-rowing competitions, where crews of Inle oarsmen race each other in sprints around the lake.

and to stock up on household essentials imported from China.

In the city centre, close to a monument to Bogyoke Aung San, stands the Taunggyi Museum (also known as Shan State Museum, Mon–Fri, 9am–4pm; charge). It is small, but worth a look if you're interested in the region's hill tribes, with displays of 30 or so costumes from Shan minorities.

Kakku

The archaeological site of **Kakku** ❸ (also spelt "Katku"), 42km (26 miles) south of Taunggyi, comprises a forest of ancient *stupas* rising in spectacular fashion from a valley on the far side of the mountains from Inle Lake. There are said to be 5,257 individual pagodas here, arrayed in rows. Some date from the Bagan period (11th to 13th centuries), but others may even have their origins in the distant Mauryan Empire of the Indian ruler, Ashoka (304–232 BC). Little else is known about them but closer examination reveals a remarkable wealth of decorative detail.

Kakku lies on Pa-O land, so in addition to the entry charge you have to employ a local Pa-O guide to show you around. Book ahead at the tourist office in Taunggyi if you're not on a pre-arranged tour.

KALAW

Perched on the western rim of the Shan Plateau, **Kalaw** ❹, 70km (44 miles) west of Taunggyi, was once a favourite hill-station retreat for British officials and their families during the hot season – little wonder, considering its beautiful setting amid bamboo groves, orange orchards and pine woods. In common with mountain retreats in the Himalayan foothills of India, the town retains a faded colonial atmosphere, and a noticeably cosmopolitan mix of people descended from the Sikhs, Tamils, Nepalis and Indian Muslims who were drafted in as a labour force in the late 19th century. In addition to this cultural legacy, the British left behind some attractive gardens and Victorian buildings, but most visitors come here to trek in the surroundings hills. Kalaw also hosts one of the region's most vibrant five-day markets, for which minority people descend en

Crumbling stupas at Indein Paya.

masse from the hills dressed in traditional costume.

Trekking from Kalaw

Innumerable trails thread through the green, forested hills around Kalaw, but the ones most commonly followed by foreign visitors are those leading to Inle Lake. Passing numerous Buddhist pagodas and villages of the Palaung, Danu, Pa-O and Taungyo tribes, the routes take between two and four days to cover, and usually wind up at the ruined *stupa* complexes of Inthein, from where you'll be transferred back to your hotel by motorboat. The trails are not all that physically demanding, but standards of comfort vary greatly in the village houses and monasteries where you'll overnight along the way. Bring a flashlight and plenty of insect repellent. Treks can follow stretches of surfaced road, winding over ridges into lush valleys, across patchworks of tea plantations, *tanaq-hpeq* bushes (whose leaves are used for rolling cheroots), orange groves and rice paddies, so you'll need footwear that can cope with a variety of terrain, as well as warm clothes for those chilly evenings in the hills.

Green Elephant Camp

A worthwhile excursion from Kalaw, especially if you're travelling with children, is the delightful **Green Elephant Camp**. The privately run centre, set in a beautiful conservation area a 45-minute drive out of town, cares for sick and retired forestry elephants, using profits from tourist visits to protect traditional local lifestyles and some 60 hectares (150 acres) of woodland. Visitors may undertake treks of varying lengths on elephant back through the surrounding countryside, as well as feed and bathe the resident pachyderms under the watchful eye of their mahouts. Guides also lead walks to a nearby waterfall, and you can do your bit for local conservation by joining tree-planting programmes.

Hill-tribe etiquette

Trekkers should follow certain guidelines to protect hill-tribe sensibilities and promote good relations. Use common sense, accompanied by a friendly smile. Always ask permission before entering any building or before taking a photo. Avoid photographing old people, pregnant women and babies. Avoid touching, photographing or sitting beneath village shrines. Avoid stepping or sitting on doorsills as, according to custom, this brings bad luck. Avoid changing clothes in public and always dress modestly. Avoid public displays of overt affection and excessive wealth. Always try to speak calmly and quietly.

PINDAYA

Pindaya, a three- to four-hour drive northwest of Nyaungshwe (Inle Lake), is famous across Myanmar as the site of the extraordinary **Shwe U Min Cave Temple ❺**, a huge, convoluted complex of limestone grottoes crammed with around 9,000 Buddha images. Varying in size and style, the figures were mostly installed between the 16th and 18th centuries, and are made

Pa-O buddha image and Pa-O deities, Kakku pagoda,

Pa-O guide at Kakku Pagoda.

TIP

You can hire a car through your hotel or guesthouse for the trip from Nyaungshwe to Kakku. The round-trip fare costs about US$80 and the vehicle can comfortably seat six people.

of gold, silver, marble, lacquer, teak and ivory.

The caves honeycomb a steep hillside rising above **Pone Taloke Lake**. They are accessed via a network of covered stairways and lifts leading to ornately gilded and decorated entrance pavilions. It's obvious from the start that the Buddha statues are very much objects of active veneration: worshippers young and old bow before them, offering flowers and incense in clasped hands to honour the principles of kindness, compassion and tolerance which the images embody.

The most revered cave is the **Antique Pagoda**, built by King Sridama Sawka more than 2,000 years ago, comprising a myriad of golden Buddhas sitting in red niches stacked one above the another.

Padah-Lin Caves

Situated near the village of Ye-ngan, northwest of Pindaya, are the **Padah-Lin Caves ❻** (open daily), Myanmar's most important Neolithic site. Countless chips created by the hacking away of stone axes have been found here, leading archaeologists to believe the caves were a site of tool- and weapon-making in prehistoric times. In one of the caves, traces of early wall paintings can still be seen. Images of a human hand, a bison, part of an elephant, a huge fish, and a sunset are clearly visible.

EASTERN SHAN: KENGTUNG AND BEYOND

The far east of Shan State is one of the most remote corners of Myanmar open to foreigners. Separated from the rest of the country by a convoluted mountain range, it has retained strong cultural affinities with neighbouring Thailand and Laos, from where its original settlers migrated with the Chiangmai Dynasty in the 13th century. Opium has long been the region's principal cash crop, and protracted armed struggles for control of the narcotics trade have until recent years kept much of the so-called "Golden Triangle" off limits to outsiders.

Tourists, however, can nowadays travel the rough but scenic **Highway 4** across the endless green ridges and

Kalaw street scene.

river gorges separating Taunggyi from the capital of eastern Shan, Kengtung. Between the 14th and mid-20th centuries, this route served as the major trade artery from China. Mule trains were used as transport; today, trucks have taken over but the link remains as vital as ever. The wares have changed over the centuries, however, so now instead of carrying tea, silk, camphor and walnuts from Yunnan and, on the return journey, lacquerware, silver and cotton, the modern commerce consists mainly of electronic goods and gemstones.

Kengtung

Kengtung ❼, the "Walled City of Tung", can seem an anticlimax after the epic overland journey to reach it, but improves rapidly on closer inspection. Laid out around **Nawng Tung Lake**, its medieval centre preserves a taste of old Asia, with a wealth of striking Tai Khün temples and markets frequented by the many hill tribes who inhabit the town's rugged hinterland, including the Akha, Palaung, Kachin, Lahu, Pa-O, Shan and Wa.

In the centre is clustered a group of impressive 19th-century Buddhist sites. The **Maha Myat Muni** ("Wat Phra Jao Lung" in Shan/Tai) boasts an interior richly decorated with gold paintings on a red background; the even more spectacular **Zom Kham** (**Wat Jom Kham**) is a tall, gilded *stupa* topped by a golden *hti* that's inlaid with precious stones. The monument is believed to date from the 13th-century migration from Chiang Mai's Lanna Kingdom.

If you're in Kengtung on its weekly market day, you'll be treated to a feast of traditional costume. The Kung, who make up around 80 percent of the town's population, wear horizontally striped green *longyi*, while women of the Lahu tribe wear black dresses with wavy patterns. The Lu are noted for their silver elbow and wrist bangles, but the most colourful are the Shan-gyi (Big Shan) women, in their yellow blouses, *longyi*, and green-striped headdresses. Local specialities on sale

at the market include dried frogs and gingered quail eggs.

NORTHERN SHAN

While Inle Lake and its environs in the southwest are the main lure for travellers to Shan State, its northern region has attractions, too. The most frequented route is by rail from Pyin U-Lwin to Lashio(see page 199) via the **Gokteik Viaduct,** but you can also travel northeast by bus or car. **Kyaukme** is the first town of significance on the Pyin U-Lwin–Lashio road. Located 85km (56 miles) from the ruby, sapphire and jade mines of restricted **Mogok** in the northwest and the silver mines of **Namtu** in the northeast, Kyaukme is an active trading town for gem stones and jewellery and is a good place to shop for them.

Hsipaw

Hsipaw ❽, an old mountain valley town on the sinuous Tu River, was once the administrative centre for the state of the same name, one of nine formerly ruled by Shan princes. The town is noted for its *haw*, or European-style

Ingredients for paan (a stimulating betel leaf preparation that is chewed) in Kalaw market.

Washing off water buffalo near Kalaw.

TIP

Outside town, on the twin-peak summit of Taungkwe, is the Taungkwe Zedi, which offers great views of Loikaw. You can also visit the Lawpita Falls, which drive a large hydroelectric power plant.

palace, where the last *sawbwa*, Sao Kya Seng, and his Austrian-born wife, Inge Sargent, lived until the military coup of 1962, when the chief disappeared. He was later found to have been murdered by the regime – events described in vivid detail in Sargent's bestselling biography, *Twilight Over Burma*. The old palace is now occupied by Sao Kya Seng's nephew, the affable Mr Donald, who, until he was arrested by the government for showing foreigners around the building, used to act as an unofficial tour guide. Mr Donald has since been released from prison but no longer welcomes callers.

The majority of travellers who make it as far northeast as Hsipaw tend to come in order to trek to **hill-tribe villages** in the area, which are far less frequented and accustomed to foreigners than the country around Kalaw. For those travelling independently, trips of varying lengths, from day hikes to full-on expeditions lasting a week or more, may be arranged through local hotels and guesthouses.

Hsipaw's main pagoda is the **Mahamyatmuni Paya** on Namtu Road, a much more modest complex than its namesakes further south but

which is worth a visit for its immaculately painted *stupas* and gleaming brass Buddha statue, backed by a halo of flashing red and purple UV lights. Of more traditional interest is the old quarter just north of the centre where, among numerous antique wooden buildings, stands the **Maha Nanda Kantha Kyaung**, home to a Buddha made entirely from strips of woven bamboo.

For a great panoramic view over the town, head 1km (0.6 miles) south to Five Buddha Hill, where the terrace fronting the **Thein Daung Pagoda** offers a popular spot for a late-afternoon stroll, whence its local nickname, "Sunset Hill".

Bawgyo Pagoda

A good time to be in Hsipaw is the full moon in March when the **Bawgyo Pagoda**, 8km (5miles) west of town, hosts its annual festival. Focus of the event is a spectacular *stupa* encased in a pavilion whose pillars, walls and domes are adorned in elaborate, multi-coloured mirror mosaic – an amazing spectacle at night, when the complex is brightly lit.

Posing for a group photo at the entrance to Pindaya caves.

During the festival, the temple's four Buddha images are paraded around the precinct for pilgrims to make offerings of gold leaves. Members of the tea-growing Palaung minority people attend the Bawgyo festival in great numbers. Ox-carts trundle in with pottery, lacquerware, baskets and other handicrafts to sell, while vendors set up stalls offering food and games of chance. Lively *pwe* (shows) are held in the evening.

Lashio

The end of the Mandalay rail line is **Lashio ❾**, 100km (66 miles) away from the Yunnan border. The last large town before the start of the historic **Burma Road** to China, which supplied the nationalist Kuomintang forces in World War II, it retains a frontier atmosphere, with a mostly Han-Chinese population. Devastated by a fire in 1988 and largely rebuilt in concrete and corrugated iron, the town is far from the prettiest in Myanmar. If you come here at all it will probably be en route to or from the airport – the nearest to Hsipaw. With time to kill, the most worthwhile option is the ornately

gilded **Thatana 2500-Year Pagoda**, nestling amid the forest on a ridge top overlooking the centre. Also deserving of a visit is the **Kwanyin Shang** temple, on the southern fringe of town, where Lashio's Chinese Buddhists worship in a multicoloured modern shrine with traditional upswept eaves.

KAYAH STATE

Southwest of Shan is the small, diamond-shaped state of **Kayah**, which until recently was off limits to foreigners but can now be visited on government-sponsored tours. Its capital is **Loikaw ❿**, linked by a new railway line to Aungban, which supplements the old road. Eight ethnic groups comprise the state's inhabitants, among which the Padaung are the best known. Padaung women wear brass coils (often mistaken for rings) to make their necks appear elongated. In reality the heavy coils depress their collarbones, creating the illusion of a longer neck.

The best place to see the Padaung and other tribal groups such as the Bre, Yinbaw, Taungthu and Kayah, is at Loikaw's Thirimingala market.

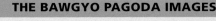
A parasol workshop's dainty output, Pandaya.

Buddha statues in the Pindaya caves.

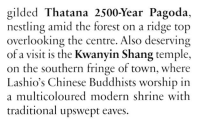
THE BAWGYO PAGODA IMAGES

According to local legend, a celestial being gave the 11th-century King Narapatisithu of the Bagan Dynasty a piece of wood out of which four Buddha images were carved. The king built the Bawgyo Pagoda to house the images for his people to worship. The rest of the wood was planted in the courtyard and it miraculously took root. The tree is thriving to this day and is considered sacred by the Burmese.

The four Buddha images are enshrined in the inner sanctum of the Bawgyo Pagoda and brought out only once a year during the March pagoda festival to allow devotees to venerate them and gild them with gold leaves.

For many years in the past, due to fears of robbery, the images were kept in the *haw* in Hsipaw for safekeeping. When it was time to take out the images for display, there would be a grand ceremonial procession, including a parade of elephants, to accompany the images back to the Bawgyo Pagoda.

During the reign of the *sawbwa*, the festival was the only time when gambling was allowed; it was also considered an important social event that brought together disparate peoples: the Shan, as well as ethnic minorities from all over the country, gathered to display and sell their goods.

At Namti, a passenger leans out of the window of the train to Myitkyina to buy some food.

KACHIN STATE AND THE UPPER AYEYARWADY

In the far north of the country, gold mines spread out along the banks of the Ayeyarwady, while Myanmar's largest lake, Indawgyi, rests among high hills and teak forests.

Yangon

Main Attractions
Indawgyi Lake
Cruising the Ayeyarwady
Welatha Cliff (Second Defile)
Kyundaw Island
Hkakabo Razi

Comparatively few travellers venture beyond Mandalay into Myanmar's northernmost state, Kachin. The handful that do nearly all stick closely to the Ayeyarwady, flying first to the capital, Myitkyina, or the market town of Bhamo, a couple of days' journey downstream, and make the trip in a southwards direction, following the flow of the river. Whether you're chugging on an old government ferry or being pampered in a luxury cruiser, traversing this stretch yields an experience of Myanmar in the raw. Don't expect to encounter many other tourists along the way. Development in the region has been painfully slow since Independence, frustrated by repeated outbreaks of civil war between the Burmese government and Kachin rebel armies, who have since the 1960s maintained control of the region's trade in jade, precious stones, narcotics and smuggled goods. Although they account for only 2 percent of the country's total population, the predominantly Christian Kachin form the majority in their homeland, and beyond the main train lines, trading posts and towns, the regime holds only token power.

The rule of the state weakens the further north you travel, which explains why overland trips to Myanmar's northernmost town, Putao, are forbidden to foreigners. If you want to explore the rugged hills and jungles of the border valleys, where the frontiers of China, India and Myanmar intersect, and where the country's highest peak, Hkakabo Razi (5,889m/19,321ft), brings the country to a suitably spectacular climax, you'll have to fly there and travel as part of a pre-arranged tour.

At the time of writing, in late 2012, Kachin was the only state in Myanmar still experiencing a major insurgency. After a 17-year-long cease-fire, fighting between the Kachin Independence

Spinning a potter's wheel with the foot at a pottery workshop in Kyaukmyaung.

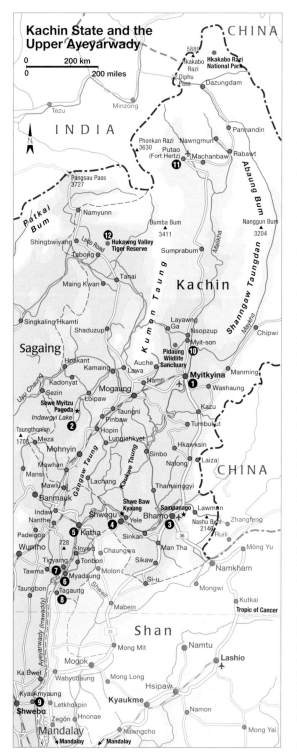

Kachin State and the Upper Ayeyarwady

0 — 200 km
0 — 200 miles

Army (KIA) and government forces erupted in June 2011 around the town of Laiza, the KIA's headquarters on the Chinese border between the capital, Myitkyina, and Bhamo. International NGOs estimate that somewhere between 50,000 and 75,000 people have been displaced by the conflict and are living in refugee camps along the frontier. This accounts for the current ban on overland travel between Myitkyina and Bhamo, which includes the river route. Access to the capital is only permitted by air – though the situation may well improve in the near future if negotiations resolve the conflict.

Myitkyina

Myitkyina ❶ the state capital, is located 144 metres (476ft) above sea level below the foothills of the Himalayas. Following the completion of the Yangon–Mandalay–Myitkyina rail link in 1898, the town became the commercial hub of the north and is today the largest settlement in the region.

Myitkyina was levelled during World War II in fierce fighting between the Allies and Japanese, in which it changed hands several times. Today, the landing strip on its outskirts is still a place of pilgrimage for the few surviving British "Marauders" and "Chindits". Veterans of the Japanese army, who lost 3,200 soldiers in the battle for Myitkyina, paid for the renovation of the town's principal Buddhist shrine, the gilded **Hsu Taung Pye Pagoda**, near the riverfront at the north end of Strand Road, which also holds a huge reclining Buddha.

Fighting between the Kachin Independence Army (KIA) and Burmese government forces along the Chinese border to the southeast has raised ethnic tensions in a city where Christian churches, Buddhist *kyaung* and Chinese Confucian temples stand cheek by jowl. In November 2011, ten people were killed when a terrorist bomb tore apart a hostel for Kachin students.

Due to the proximity of the jade mines, there has been an influx of

Chinese money, which has helped to modernise the town. Myitkyina holds little in the way of sights, but its early morning fresh produce market is a particularly picturesque one thanks to the stalls piled with mandarin oranges, apples, grapefruit and kumquats, all of which grow abundantly in the north.

Indawgyi Lake

One of the principal attractions of Kachin State is **Indawgyi Lake ②**, the largest body of fresh water in Myanmar. Around 24km (16 miles) from north to south and 12km (8 miles) across, it is sustained by a dozen streams feeding into a depression. Large gold deposits are held in the surrounding hills, as well as extensive teak forests worked by three major logging camps.

A chain of picturesque Shan villages dots the lake shore, comprising clusters of wooden stilted houses. From an island in the middle of the lake rises the dazzling white and gilt **Shwe Myitzu Pagoda** where relics of the Buddha are said to be enshrined. It sits on a two-tier platform consisting of a central golden

stupa surrounded by scores of smaller white *stupas*. Panels depicting scenes from the Buddha's life decorate the ceilings covering the lower tier of the platform, which is also adorned by statues of *nat*, said to still roam the Indawgyi area. Access is via a narrow sand causeway that gets partially submerged in the wet season. Visitors can take in the various villages, wooden monasteries, Kachin churches and *manaotaing* (decorative totem poles used for festive occasions), or drop in at one of the three logging camps to see elephants at work. The jade mines of Hpakant, to the north of Indawgyi, are strictly off limits to tourists.

Travelling to the lake from Myikyinta by train, the jump-off point is **Hopin**, a sleepy town with a large ethnic Chinese population, reached after five hours. Pick-up trucks are available to ferry travellers from the station over the remaining 45km (28 miles) of bumpy, sinuous mountain roads. A couple of basic guesthouses offer accommodation for visitors. Note that if you visit this region by car you need to obtain a permit.

Monks from Shwe Daza Paya collecting alms, Shwebo.

THE MANAO FESTIVAL

If you're anywhere near Myitkyina around 10 January, don't miss the colourful Manao Festival. Celebrated in the town stadium, the event brings together all seven Kachin tribal groups in dance, fun and games centred around four totem poles. Some of the headgear on display includes tassels, beads, horns, feathers and even stuffed birds. The rhythms of the drums and chants resemble the Pow Wow gatherings of Native American Indians. Since most Kachin have converted to Christianity, this originally animist festival has now become a mixture of religion and culture.

A *manao* is one of many dances at a thanksgiving feast hosted by the tribal chieftains honouring various *nat* (spirits) to ensure a bumper harvest or to celebrate good fortune. Meaning "centre" or "summit", it was referred to by the ancient Kachin as a "meeting of gods" and was formerly hosted by rich and noble chieftains.

Today, the *manao* has come to mean a traditional dance performed as part of a festival of offerings to the Kachin *nat*. Such dances are generally held among the Kachin to celebrate a special occasion (the Ninghtan Manao is a wedding feast, for instance, and the Hting Hkring Manao is performed when moving to a new house). The whole neighbourhood is often invited and the celebrations may last for days.

TIP

Train tickets to Hopin should be booked on the eve of departure. Arrive at the Myitkyina railway station early as there is almost always a long queue.

BHAMO AND BEYOND

The largest town on the Ayeyarwady between Myitkyina and Mandalay, **Bhamo** ❸ is the closest and most accessible point on the river to China (the border is only 65km/40 miles west). This was always a site of huge strategic and commercial importance, attracting Western colonialists since the 16th century – the British may not have admitted it at the time, but control of the land route running north into Yunnan was one of the principal goals of the Anglo-Burmese Wars in the 19th century. Although not yet surfaced, the old caravan route up the Daying Jiang Valley, which Marco Polo followed in the 13th century, is still in use.

Remnants of the Shan capital of Sampanago, comprising an overgrown wall and gateway, lie on Bhamo's outskirts, 5km (3 miles) north of the centre (ask your driver to take you to "Bhamo Myo Haung", or "Old Bhamo"). The only vestiges of the ancient city not in a state of terminal decay here are the Eikkhawtaw and the Shwekyaynar payas – two gold-tipped *stupas* thought to date from the 5th century.

Having been destroyed by fire, the centre of Bhamo was recently rebuilt and no longer holds many historic buildings, though the spacious new **marketplace**, frequented by minority people from the surrounding hills, deserves an early morning browse. Also in the town centre, the Thai-style **Theindawgyi Paya**, which contains a tooth relic and is supposed to have been built by King Ashoka in the 3rd century BC, recently received a new precious ruby-encrusted *seinbu* (golden orb).

Photographers shouldn't miss the pretty **ceramics market**, at the south end of the riverfront area, where each morning hundreds of pots in a bewildering range of sizes are set on the banks of the Ayeyarwady for sale – a delightful scene against the comings and goings of freighters and other boats on the water behind.

Second Defile

After leaving Bhamo, the Ayeyarwady crosses a fertile plain as it approaches the **Second Defile**. Flanked by steep cliffs cloaked in dense vegetation, the 13.5km (7.5-mile) passage is the most

Monks from Shwe Daza Paya collecting alms, Shwebo.

scenic along the entire length of the river. During the rainy season the water's depth can reach an amazing 61 metres (180ft), and when the water is low, elephants haul huge teak logs from the jungle to the river's shore.

At the narrowest point of the defile rises a spectacular 300-metre (985ft) cliff, the **Nat-Myet-Hna-Taung** ("Face of the Nat Mountain"), also called the **Welatha cliff**. Not far away is the famous **Parrot's Beak**, a painted rock that acts as a marker for river traffic: if the water reaches the parrot's red beak, the current is deemed too strong for boats to pass.

Shwegu

The first stop after the defile, where the river widens again and flows through a series of sun-bleached sand banks, is **Shwegu ❹**. Elephants still roam the jungle in the hills behind the town, but the main reason you might wish to jump ship here is to explore the island of **Kyundaw**, in the river opposite, where 7,000 or more *stupas* are dotted around the monastery of **Shwe Baw Kyaung**. The monuments range from crumbling 10th-century piles choked in creepers and weeds to immaculately whitewashed and gilded modern *zedis*.

Katha

On a bluff overlooking the west bank of the Ayeyarwady, **Katha ❺** stands in in the shadow of the Gangaw Taung hills, presiding over a fertile plain where kidney beans are the principal cash crop. This quiet provincial town, shaded by ranks of beautiful trees, is the main administrative hub of the district, and an obligatory stop if you're travelling by riverboat. A branch of the mainline railway also serves the town, allowing you a fast option to Mandalay if the slow ferry is starting to lose its allure.

Katha's one and only claim to fame is that it served as the inspiration for George Orwell's fictional town of Kyauktada in his novel *Burmese Days*. Orwell, or Eric Blair as he was christened, was stationed here as a police officer in 1926. A handful of colonial-era buildings featured in the book survive, including the town jail and British Club. For more on Katha's Orwell connection, track down a copy

The natural causeway to Shwe Myitzu Pagoda, which appears at festival time.

THE LEGEND OF INDAWGYI LAKE

According to local legend, Indawgyi was once the capital of the Htamanthy tribe. Two dragon brothers were looking for a place to call home and chanced upon Indawgyi. They found the people there living wicked lives and, as punishment, flooded the city and turned it into a lake for themselves.

Until about 240 years ago, Indawgyi Lake remained uninhabited as it was believed to be guarded by fierce spirits. It was only when the Shwe Myitzu Pagoda was built by a monk, U Thawbita, during the reign of King Mindon, that people's fears were sufficiently allayed and they started to settle in the area.

The pagoda has since been built over three times until it gained its current height of 15 metres (50ft). Shwe Myitzu is the most important pagoda in Kachin State and is the focus of a 10-day festival held each year in March.

Apparently, just before the start of the festival, two sandbanks emerge. One of these stretches all the way from the shore to the Shwe Myitzu Pagoda, allowing pilgrims to walk the entire distance. The other is broken in parts and is believed to be a passage for the gods.

Somewhat mysteriously, both sandbanks disappear into the water after the festival is over.

TIP

The Ayeyarwady boats usually have tiny cabins better suited to single than double occupancy. If you are travelling with a companion, you may prefer separate cabins as the fare is per person, not per cabin.

of Emma Larkin's entertaining trave-logue, *Finding Orwell in Burma*.

Shweli sandbars

South of Katha the boat passes the estuary of the **Shweli**, Myanmar's main logging river, which enters the country from China after crossing the jungles of the Northern Shan State. As well as cascades of teak and other hardwoods, its waters also sweep along vast quantities of silt which has, over the years, coalesced into a sandbar off **Inywa**, at the mouth of the estuary. This prohibits the entry of larger boats from the main channel, and as a con-sequence, the large government ferries have to anchor midstream off Inywa until daylight, since even local pilots cannot steer boats safely through the shifting sandbars in the dark.

Myadaung and Tigyaing

The next port of call south on the Ayeyarwady is **Myadaung** ❻, a market town facing the southern end of the beautiful **Gangaw Taung**, the densely forested ridge stretching south from Myitkyina. The range has a mystical

A market street in Bhamo.

quality, especially when the white pagodas on the hilltop above the town appear through the early morning fog. Wide landscapes and high river banks form the typical setting of the fertile Upper Burma plain. Each of the dock-ing stations is fairly similar to the one just passed, with locals getting on and off with huge sacks, cartons and bas-kets on their heads.

From Myadaung the boat crosses the river to call at **Tigyaing** ❼, another atmospheric thatched town with an old pagoda on its hilltop. A stroll through this little community provides a real window on everyday life in Upper Myanmar. Small stalls and tea shops line the narrow lanes, which are for the most part calm and peaceful. Only when the Ayeyarwady boat arrives does the town erupt into a frenzy of activity. Regardless of the time of day, the entire population assembles on the steep shore, joined by those from regions further inland for whom Tigyaing is the vital gateway to the rest of the world.

Both the *stupas* at Myadaung and Tigyaing are said to have been built

by King Alaungsithu back in the 12th century.

Tagaung and the Third Defile

Tagaung ❽, the next major stop on the river route to Mandalay, is believed to have been one of Burma's ancient capitals. There is some debate as to whether or not it was established as long ago as 850 BC by an Indian dynasty, the Satkyas, but the town was definitely a major Pyu settlement between the 6th and 9th centuries. The ruins of at least two lost cities have been discovered in the vicinity by archaeologists, though the remnants are none too impressive. The only surviving monument to speak of today is a huge golden *nat* shrine said to represent the founder of the ancient centre.

Beyond Tagaung, the river runs in a straight north–south direction to enter the **Third Defile** 45km (26 miles) before reaching Kyaukmyaung. During the low-water season, hundreds of boats can be seen panning for gold in the river sand at **Ka Bwet**, midway along the passage.

Kyaukmyaung

The town of **Kyaukmyaung** ❾, at the southern end of the Third Defile, lies 17km (10 miles) east of Shwebo and 46km (28 miles) north of Mandalay. Long a minor port of call on the Ayeyarwady, it is famous today principally for its pottery industry, centred on the clay-rich river bank known as Ngwe Ngein to the south of town, where you can see scores of ceramic items drying picturesquely in the sun. Most striking among them are the massive 50-gallon vessels known since early colonial times as "Martaban jars" or "Ali Baba pots". They were first made here in the mid-18th century by captive potters from Pegu (Bago), brought to the town by the Bamar king, Alaungpaya, after his defeat of the Mons. The jars, which could hold two hogshead of palm liquor, *ngapi* fish paste, *ngapy-ayei* fish sauce or peanut oil, were the main vessel used in the Mons' international maritime trade. Shards of them have been found across China and the Middle East. This is now one of the few places in Myanmar where they are still made according to the traditional

A cheerful resident of Shwebo.

Cruising the Ayeyarwady: Myitkyina/Bhamo to Mandalay

One of the most enjoyable activities for visitors to Myanmar, a cruise along the mighty Ayeyarwady is not to be missed.

Myanmar's greatest river, the Ayeyarwady, has its source in Kachin State, just north of the capital, Myitkyina, from where it flows south in a sweeping "S" bend through the Kawkwe Taung Hills and out on to the plains at Bhamo. A mighty slick of yellow-brown, silty water, it makes another arc before plunging definitively south towards Mandalay

This northern stretch sees far fewer foreign tourists than the one between Mandalay and Bagan – not least because of recent travel restrictions resulting from the civil war being waged in the region. The conflict threatens the operation of luxury cruise companies which, until the breakdown of the KIA cease-fire in 2011, offered cruises once or twice

Passengers ride on the roof of this boat on the Ayeyarwady River at Bhamo.

each season. However, a resolution to the conflict is widely expected in the near future, which will enable travellers to experience this unspoilt region again.

Assuming the Kachin insurgency comes to an end, the cheapest way to enjoy a cruise – referred to for obvious reasons as "the slow boat" – is on the double-decker IWT ferries that chug three times per week between Bhamo and Mandalay. These take the best part of a week to cover the distance, depending on water levels and the state of the vessel's engine. A few cabins are available, but most passengers sleep on deck, eating and drinking whatever the itinerant vendors happen to be hawking.

Quicker, smaller, private boats, carrying between 40 and 80 people, operate all the way from Myitkyina. They're faster and depart much more regularly, but don't run at night, so you have to break the journey at towns en route. The fast boats also tend to be more uncomfortable, with passengers wedged tightly together on wooden seats for the duration of the journey.

As the landscape is largely flat and monotonous for most of the route, life on the river itself, and on board the ferry, provides the main interest. Calling at 47 different stops along the way, the ferry boats are a lifeline to communities in the Upper Ayeyarwady, carrying farm produce and essential supplies as well as people. During the harvest season, huge drums of molasses and sacks filled with sesame seeds, fruit, beans or rice are regularly hauled on board, while vendors line up on the deck to sell fruits, cookies, shashlik kebabs and a variety of other small luxuries, from flowers and cheroots to candles, tobacco leaves, Mandalay beer, rum and soft drinks. You'll even come across towers of woven cane hats and live chickens in cane cages for sale.

Karom is a popular pastime among the male passengers, and crowds form around the best players. Monks have their own platform on which they sit in full lotus position, puffing one cheroot after another while running their prayer beads through their fingers. In the rear of the upper deck is the kitchen where, on an open fire, tea, coffee and a variety of foods are prepared.

The sunsets on the Ayeyarwady are glorious and are best seen from the bridge. Often, during the night, the boat docks somewhere along the high, sandy embankment and the air is filled with the shouting of villagers carrying barrel after barrel of goods on board. Just remember to bring plenty of insect repellent – the Ayeyarwady's bugs can be voracious.

process. The shape and ochre-glazed rosette motifs adorning the upper portion of the jars has altered little in centuries, but the rich earthy red-brown colour is an innovation, achieved by using a mix of clay from Shan State and battery acid powder. The potters are happy for you to browse and photograph, and will show you the massive brick-and-earth-floor kilns where their work is fired for a week.

Kyaukmyaung is also the epicentre of a recently established Protection Zone set up to protect the rare Irrawaddy dolphin, for whom this stretch of the river is something of a stronghold.

THE FAR NORTH

Sandwiched between Arunachal Pradesh in India and the Chinese province of Yunnan, the far north of Myanmar contains some of the last true wilderness in Southeast Asia – a spectacular amphitheatre of jungle-covered foothills ringed by the eternal snows of the Himalayas. Unfortunately, access to this formidable cul-de-sac remains problematic. The KIA maintains control of all but a few outposts, and although conflict with the

Burmese government has ceased, infrastructure of any kind is minimal outside the region's main hub, **Putao** (**Fort Hertz**). Overland travel via the dilapidated Myitkyina–Putao road is strictly forbidden. With the necessary permits, tourists can, however, fly into the region, but only as part of a pre-arranged tour with an accredited operator – and even then, route options are limited.

That said, given sufficient time, money and determination, it is possible to penetrate the leech-infested rainforest north of Putao and press on through wild, beautiful mountain valleys inhabited by minority people for a close encounter with Southeast Asia's highest peak, **Hkakabo Razi**, which rises to 5,889 metres (19,320 ft).

Myit-son

The official source of the Ayeyarwady is the confluence of the Maykha and Malikha rivers, near the town of **Myit-son ⑩**, 42km (21 miles) north of Myitkyina. In the 1990s, the Burmese government attempted to develop the area around the spot where the rivers merge as a visitor attraction, but what

An Irrawaddy dolphin in the river at Kampi village, Kratie province.

A FISHERMAN'S BEST FRIEND

In many countries of the world, dolphins are regarded by fishermen as competitors, but at several places along the Ayeyarwady in central Myanmar, a unique bond has evolved between local cast-net fishers and pods of Irrawaddy dolphins – a rare species of cetacean distinguished by its beluga-like high, round forehead. When attracted by the knocking of oars against the side of a wooden canoe, the dolphins round up shoals of fish and drive them into the waiting nets – a service for which they're rewarded with a share of the catch.

This form of cooperative fishing has been handed down from father to son for generations on the river, but in recent decades has come under threat as dolphin populations have plummeted. Gill net fishing and mercury poisoning from gold-mine run-off are thought to be the main culprits; the spread of dams in the region has also contributed to the decline. Only around 60–70 dolphins now survive on the river.

However, efforts have recently been made to revive populations along a 74km (46-mile) stretch of the Ayeyarwady between the pottery town of Kyaukmyaung and Mingun, just north of Mandalay, which has been designated as a Protection Zone. Sightings in this area, where long gill nets are banned, are common from ferry and cruise boats.

natural splendour there may have been is these days comprehensively eclipsed by the mud slicks and dirt scars of the open-cast gold mining fields lining the riverbanks. An environmental disaster potentially even more devastating than this, however, threatens to engulf the entire valley if work on Myit-son's controversial **mega dam** is ever completed. Funded by the Chinese, the $3.6bn project will see the construction of a 140-metre (466ft) -high, 1,310-metre (4,297ft) -long barrage across the river. Some 770 sq km (300 sq miles) of agricultural land is scheduled to be flooded – an area the size of Singapore – which will force the relocation of 13,000 people from 47 villages. This, along with fact that the electricity generated will go to China, has proved a lightning rod for anti-Chinese sentiment in Kachin. Popular opposition, however, has for once made some impact on the normally recalcitrant ruling generals. Bowing to public pressure in late 2011, President Then Sein ordered that work on the dam be stopped – though whether or not the bulldozer ban can hold out against mounting political

Oxen and cart on the road to Kyaukmyaung.

opposition to the halt from the Chinese remains to be seen.

Putao

Myanmar's northernmost town, **Putao**  (population: 10,000), was known by its original Shan inhabitants as "Hkamti Long" – "Great Place of Gold", but later renamed **Fort Hertz** by the British after the district commissioner William Axel Hertz, who first explored and mapped this remote corner of the country in 1888. Some 354km (220 miles) north of Myitkyina, the outpost became legendary in the annals of the Burma campaign of World War II for remaining out of Japanese hands throughout the conflict. For most of 1942, until the parachute regiment dropped in with fresh supplies, the airfield also remained out of radio contact with Allied command. But once the runway had been upgraded, it served as an emergency landing strip for planes making the notorious flight over the "Hump" of the eastern Himalayas to re-supply Chinese forces.

Although the road from Myitkyina is these days open during the dry season,

sporadic flights from Yangon are the only way foreign nationals are permitted to travel to Putao, which sits in a valley encircled on all sides by mountains, with the snowcapped ridges of Hkakabo Razi dominating the northern horizon. The few visitors who come here each winter generally do so on three- or four-day tour extensions, staying at the luxurious and beautifully sited Malikha Lodge on the outskirts of town, from where guests make day trips to Putao's Myoma market, local picnic sites, suspension bridges, tribal villages and logging camps in the area, or else recuperate after treks into the nearby ranges.

A popular route is the ten-day round trip to the summit of **Mount Phonkan Razi** (3,630m/11,909ft), a superb vantage point on the valley.

Hkakabo Razi

Foreigners are also permitted to trek to the base camp of **Hkakabo Razi** (5,889m/19,321ft), a ten-day round route from Putao. First climbed by a Japanese expedition in 1996, the mountain lies within the Hkakabo National Park, a 2,414 sq km (1,500 sq mile) tract of protected rainforest and high valleys whose flora and fauna were first surveyed by the American conservationist Alan Rabinowitz in 1996. As well as rare stone martens, blue sheep and an endemic species of deer, Rabinowitz came across a community of indigenous forest-dwelling pygmy people in his reconnaissance work. Known as the Taron, they had for generations been enslaved by the local Kachins and were fast approaching the point of extinction. Frail from inbreeding, the twelve surviving individuals had apparently made a pact not to have children.

Hukawng Valley Tiger Reserve

Alan Rabinowitz also played a leading role in the creation of another national park in Myanmar's far-flung north: the **Hukawng Valley Tiger Reserve** ⑫. The sanctuary, which can be reached

by road from Myitkyina via the market town of Tanai, extends over a sprawling 13,602 sq km (8,452 sq miles) of swampy jungle to the southwest of Putao, cradled by the hills lining the Indian border. Around one hundred tigers were estimated to be present in the park in 2003, though only fifty to sixty have survived the past decade of poaching and habitat erosion through gold mining, illegal logging and slash-and-burn cultivation. Critics argue that the creation of the park was merely a ruse to wrest control of the region from the Kachin Independence Army (KIA), citing the increase in government-sponsored logging, and the granting of oil exploration and uranium mining rights to foreign companies by the Burmese government.

Any tourists wishing to visit the Hukawng Valley have to travel on a packaged tour arranged by a government-accredited agency, though at the time of writing permits were not being issued by the government due to ongoing armed conflict in the area between KIA guerrillas and government forces.

A pottery workshop's wares in Kyaukmyaung.

A potter stops for a smoke.

View of the plain of temples at dawn, Mrauk-U.

Ngapali Beach, Myanmar's best-known resort.

WESTERN MYANMAR

Isolated from the Bamar heartland, the western
coastal region of Myanmar has a distinctly South
Asian feel.

A fisherman with his nets.

O nly open to visitors since the 1990s, western
Myanmar is still very much off the beaten track. It's
an extensive region of placid, sandy beaches, slow-
moving broad rivers, jungle and impenetrable hills. From
the beaches of Rakhaing in the south, to the Indian border
in the north, it is isolated from central Myanmar by a series
of hardy mountain ranges – the Rakhaing Yoma, the Chin Hills and the
Letha Taung. To the southwest, the region is washed by the Indian Ocean,
then the land frontier marches north by Bangladesh's Chittagong Hill
Tracts and the Indian states of Mizoram and Manipur.

In historical terms, western Myanmar is a peripheral land, neither
Burmese nor Indian, though it becomes more integrated into
Burmese culture by the year. Rakhaing is where the historically
independent Kingdom of Arakan once flourished, a Buddhist state
where the kings traditionally also carried a Muslim title, and where
Southeast Asian Buddhism met and intermingled with Bengali
Islam. Even today the area holds a distinctively south Asian feel in
its cuisine, dress, and the facial characteristics of its people.

*At the Mrauk-U temples, the
massive Ratanabon Paya is
ringed by 24 smaller stupas.*

North of Rakhaing the unexplored hill tracts of Chin State
remain one of the least-known parts of Myanmar – not just unvis-
ited by foreigners, but unfamiliar to all but a handful of Bamar,
most of them military men or frontier police. The most traditional part of Chin State is in the south, where unmarried Chin
women still wear traditional dress. Further north, the Chin have been
Christianised and have, in large part, adopted Western dress.

Western Myanmar is not the easiest part of the country to visit. While
access by sea or by road is certainly possible, these are slow and unreliable options. Most people choose to fly in from Yangon or Mandalay,
the great majority landing at the Rakhaing capital of Sittwe. Once in
Rakhaing – Chin State remains, for the moment, off the tourist itiner-
ary unless by special invitation or arrangement – the best way of getting
about is by boat, often an old, overcrowded river steamer. Despite these
discomforts, it is well worth making the trip. Rakhaing offers some of
the finest beaches in Southeast Asia, and while the facilities are still rudimentary, the waters are clear, the sand pristine, and there are almost no
other visitors – for the present, that is. Moreover, beyond the beaches, up
the rolling Kaladan River, lies the mystical and all-but-forgotten city of
Mrauk-U, the temple-studded capital of Old Arakan.

MRAUK-U AND CHIN STATE

On an isolated plateau in western Myanmar stand the charismatic ruins of an ancient royal city, while further south, Ngapali Beach is fast blossoming as an international resort.

Screened from the Ayeyarwady Valley by a long wall of jungle-covered mountains, Rakhaing (aka "Arakan") State in the west of Myanmar is today one of the most remote, under-developed parts of the country. Yet 350 years ago, its coastal strip formed the heartland of a powerful, prosperous kingdom presided over by the most cosmopolitan court in the history of Southeast Asia.

Its capital was Mrauk-U, a port founded in 1430 by King Man Co Mwan (aka "Naramithla"), who had spent 25 years in exile fleeing attacks from his Burmese enemies in the Bengali city of Gaur. Although himself a Buddhist, Naramithla was seduced by the hybrid, Indo-Muslim sophistication of Bengali high culture, and on his return encouraged a similarly inclusive ethos in his own court. The result was a highly advanced brand of royalty, with a monumental architecture to match. At the empire's height in the mid-16th century, when Arakan territory extended all the way from Dhaka to the mouth of the Ayeyarwady, the splendour of Mrauk-U's temples, monasteries, palaces and libraries was legendary across Asia.

The glory days, however, were short-lived. In 1784, after Arakan lost Chittagong to the Mughals and descended into a bloody civil war, the Burmese army of King Bodawpaya invaded, leaving in its wake devastation from which Mrauk-U never recovered. Today, the ruins of Man Co Mwan's great city stand smothered in creepers and weeds, its brickwork crumbling into the fields and forests, priceless Buddhas peering from the undergrowth.

Although nowhere near as extensive as the remains of Bagan, Mrauk-U is all the more atmospheric for its neglected state. Moreover, getting to the site is a real adventure. With the road over the Rakhaing Yoma range closed to

Ngapali Beach.

foreigners, most visitors fly to the coastal town of Sittwe, and from there proceed 65km (40 miles) upriver by boat.

Government ferries also provide an inexpensive way to reach the far south of Rakhaing State, where the fledgling beach resort of Ngapali is attracting ever greater numbers of foreign visitors. With daily flights to and from Yangon, the resort is easily accessible, yet relatively unspoilt for the time being, its pristine white sands and turquoise water backed by low-rise luxury hotels.

At the diametric opposite end of Myanmar's economic and cultural spectrum, landlocked Chin State, to the northeast of Rakhaing, is the country's most disadvantaged region. Members of the persecuted Chin minority group, who live from hunting, fishing and shifting cultivation in remote jungles and hills, comprise the majority of its population. A long-standing insurgency, coupled with the virtual absence of infrastructure, ensures that this far-flung corner of Myanmar remains off limits to tourists, although foreigners are granted permission to scale its

The ferry to Mrauk U.

highest peak, Nat Ma Taung (aka "Mt Victoria"; 3,053m/10,016ft), reached from the Bagan-Ayeyarwady Valley side of the Rakhaing Yoma range.

Sittwe (Akyab)

Occupying a breezy site at the mouth of the estuary where the Kaladan, Mayu and Lemro rivers converge, **Sittwe ❶** capital of Rakhaing State, was founded in 1826 by the British, who moved their barracks from Mrauk-U to escape the inland humidity during the First Anglo-Burmese War. Daily steamers from Calcutta (Kolkata) used to dock here in the hey-day of the Raj, whose Anglo-Indian legacy can still be traced in the architecture of the grid-planned centre. These days, however, Sittwe – formerly known by its Bengali name, "Akyab" – remains somewhat remote from the mainstream of Burmese life and looks a little down on its luck, though the city's fortunes may well improve when the new $120 million harbour, funded jointly by the Burmese and Indian governments, is completed.

With the new railway line still under construction (at the time of writing), visitors bound for Mrauk-U are obliged to pass through Sittwe, from where boats leave early in the morning for the five- to six-hour trip upriver to the archaeological site. Most spend at least a night here, as the boats nearly all leave at the crack of dawn.

Conventional sights are thin on the ground, but if you've time to kill between transport connections, the main **market** district, on the riverfront at the northeastern edge of the centre, is lively and colourful throughout the day. A 3km (1-mile) trishaw ride south, the locals' favourite spot for a stroll is the so-called **View Point** ("Point" for short), where a spit of land jutting into the estuary is crowned by an old lighthouse that's been converted into a lookout tower. Beer stations and cafés offer relaxing vantage points from which to admire the sunset vistas over the water on both sides. Also worth a visit is the huge **Lokananda Pagoda**, 2km (1.2 miles) northwest of the Point near the airport, where a massive gilded *stupa* donated by General Than

Shwe dominates the city's fringes. In a building next to it, reached via a doorway on the precinct's west side, rests a correspondingly massive, bronze Shakyamuni, its surface teeming with thousands of mini Buddhas. Finally, as a primer for a visit to Mrauk-U, it's worth having a look around the **Rakhaing State Cultural Museum** on Main Road (Tue–Sat 10am–4pm; charge), for its collection of stone inscriptions, carvings and Buddha images. An exhibition devoted to Arakanese culture occupies the upper floor.

Next to the museum, between Strand Road and Main Road No. 1, is the South Asian style **Jama' Masjid**, which marks the centre of Sittwe's predominantly Bengali-Muslim Bodawma Quarter.

MRAUK-U

The ruins of the Arakan Dynasty's former capital, **Mrauk-U** ❷ (**Myohaung**), are strewn over a plateau between the Kaladan and the Lomro rivers, 65km (40 miles) upriver from Sittwe. Comparisons with Bagan are inevitable: the houses and other

Within the walls of Koethaung Pagoda, one of the Mrauk-U highlights.

Evening mist and smoke from village cooking fires swirl around Ratanabon Paya, Mrauk U.

secular buildings that would once have lined the city's streets have long since disappeared, leaving in their wake dozens of religious structures marooned amid the bleached grass, tropical foliage and fields. Yet the site doesn't nearly approach the scale or grandeur of its older counterpart on the Ayeyarwady; many of the monuments languish in a lamentably tumbledown state, often literally in cultivated land where buffalo graze and villagers tend their radish patches – all of which, of course, add considerably to Mrauk-U's allure. Choked with weeds and creepers, the brick *stupas* and temple complexes exude a feeling of tantalising remoteness that more than repays the time and trouble required to reach the site.

Pending the completion of a controversial new rail line being bulldozed through the edges of Mrauk-U, the only way foreigners can access the ruins is by catching a plane to Sittwe, and picking up a boat for the remaining leg – a delightful river journey that heightens the overall sense of anticipation. If you're on a pre-arranged tour

you'll be transported in a comfortable, fast motorboat. Independent travellers have three options: a slow, double-decker ITW ferry (depart Tue and Fri, return Wed and Sat), which takes around 7 hours to cover the route; a faster, more expensive private boat (5–6 hours; $150 for six or seven passengers); or, the speediest option of all, the express **Shwe Pyi Tan** (depart Mon and Wed at 3pm), which is frequently booked by groups but only takes two to three hours. Either way, after following a broad river and then narrower tributaries, you'll be dropped at Mrauk-U's jetty, a bumpy five-minute jeep ride from most of the hotels.

"City of the Monkey Egg"

At the peak of its power in the mid-17th century, Mrauk-U – literally "Monkey Egg" – harboured a population of around 160,000. The city's prosperity – founded on the export of rice and slaves to the Dutch colony of Batavia, and by tax income from its Bengali possession, Chittagong – attracted not only settlers from the Burmese hinterland, but Bengalis,

Stone Buddha statues seated in rows, Mrauk-U.

A 17TH-CENTURY METROPOLIS

Father Sebastiao Manrique, writing in the 17th century, left a vivid description of Mrauk-U's formidable appearance. Surrounded on all sides by high rocky mountains, its thoroughfares were waterways navigable by large and small vessels alike. "The greater number of houses in the city are made of bamboo... much ingenuity and labour are spent on making the houses' mats of the finest material and of many colours, which are very neat and handsome."

His description of Mrauk-U's market at the time of the king's coronation is a portrait of a true metropolis: "So numerous were the different classes of dress and language, such the varied customs at that capital, that the eye was kept busy trying to distinguish the different nationalities by their apparel."

The town also had a rich and flourishing trading community, dealing in a huge variety of commodities: "In the shops were being sold in abundance, diamonds, rubies, sapphires, emeralds, topazes, gold and silver in plates and bars, tin and zinc. Besides these articles, there was much copper, fine brass ambergris, musk, civet scent, fragrant resin, essence of almonds, incense, camphor, red lead, indigo, borax, quicksilver, saltpeter, opium, tobacco..."

Afghans, Persians, Thais, Abyssinians, Japanese Christians and Portuguese freebooters. The king even boasted a personal bodyguard of Samurai warriors. Art and literature – both Arakanese and Bengali – received passionate royal patronage.

The accommodating spirit of the Arakan court, however, would prove its downfall. In 1660, the Mughal prince Sha Shuja, son of the recently deceased Emperor Shah Jahan and a former governor of Bengal, took refuge in Mrauk-U after a failed bid to seize his father's throne. The royal fugitive and his entourage were at first generously received by Sanda Thumadha, the Arakan king. But after a year of effective house arrest, it became increasingly clear to the prince that the Arakanese were intent on killing him in order to seize the treasure he'd brought with him. Shah Shuja duly fled to the countryside, while some of his Bengali followers mounted a rebellion among the local Bengali population, which ended with the burning of Mrauk-U. Shah Shuja managed to escape to neighbouring Tripura in the

ensuing melee, but his sons were captured and beheaded by a furious Sanda Thumadha, and their wives incorporated into the royal harem.

The executions enraged Shah Shuja's brother, the new Mughal Emperor Aurangzeb, who promptly dispatched a punitive army to annexe Chittagong and the eastern portions of Bengal occupied by the Arakans, effectively cutting them off from their main source of prosperity.

The loss was the beginning of the end of Mrauk-U. Soon, the state sank into civil war and the countryside into poverty and disorder, encouraging the Kingdom of Ava to invade in 1784. Hundreds of thousands of Arakanese men, women and children were massacred or taken prisoner by the Burmese, and the very symbol of their sovereignty, the majestic, gold-covered Maha Muni image, was carried off across the hills to the Ayeyarwady plains, leaving the former capital to be reclaimed by the jungle.

Today, more than two centuries after the conquests of Bodawpaya, the Arakanese still regard themselves

Sakyamanaung Paya, Mrauk-U temples.

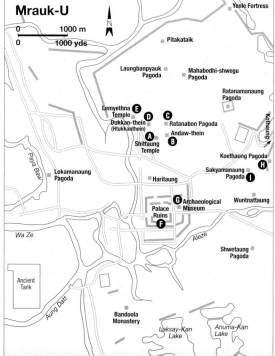

Mrauk-U

0   1000 m
0   1000 yds

Yenle Fortress

Pitakataik

Laungbanpyauk Pagoda

Mahabodhi-shwegu Pagoda

Ratanamanaung Pagoda

Lemyethna Temple
Dukkan-thein (Htukkanthein)

Ratanabon Pagoda
Andaw-thein

Shittaung Temple

Kothaung

Koethaung Pagoda

Sakyamanaung Pagoda

Lokamanaung Pagoda

Haritaung

Wuntnattaung

Archaeological Museum
Palace Ruins

Aleze

Wa Ze

Shwetaung Pagoda

Ancient Tank

Aung Datt

Bandoola Monastery

Laksay-Kan Lake

Anuma-Kan Lake

TIP

En route to or returning from Mrauk-U, especially near dusk, watch out for mosquitoes – wear long-sleeved tops and trousers and always carry a spray repellent to apply liberally.

Leymyathna Temple, Mrauk U.

as a separate entity. In particular, the Muslim minority, the Rohingya, along the border of Bangladesh, feel estranged from and hostile to the current Bamar-Buddhist regime dominated by the Burmese military. Thousands try to flee every year to Bangladesh, Malaysia and other countries in the region each year, in an attempt to escape persecution that human rights groups claim includes forced labour, violence against Rohingya women and restrictions on movement, marriage and reproduction. Communal tensions remain high throughout the region, occasionally erupting into riots and periods of martial law.

Visiting Mrauk-U

Encircled by fragments of a 30km (19-mile) fortified wall, Mrauk-U's surviving monuments are spread over a 5 sq km (3 sq mile) area, extending north and east from the village centre and the remains of the former royal palace. A $5 entry fee is charged on arrival at the jetty. Transport is generally in a mixture of jeeps and horse-carts,

depending on how long you have and how much you wish to see: a couple of full days is sufficient to take in the highlights, although you could profitably spend two or three times as long pottering around more remote locations by bicycle. Come armed with a strong torch – essential for viewing carved reliefs and murals in dimly lit corridors.

The Northern Group

The cluster of pagodas lying to the north of the village includes some of the most spectacular on the entire site; most stand within easy walking distance of each other.

Begin at the **Shittaung Temple** Ⓐ erected by the most formidable of all the Arakan rulers, King Minbin, to celebrate his conquest of Bengal in 1535. It centres on a large bell-shaped *stupa* surrounded by a myriad of smaller ones and is regarded as the grandest of all Mrauk-U's monuments. Next to the entranceway on the northern side, the 3-metre (10ft) **Shittaung Pillar** enumerates in eroded Sanskrit script the history of

the Arakan dynasties from the 5th until the 8th centuries. On entering the central **prayer hall** inside, you'll see why the shrine was dubbed as the "Temple of 80,000 Images". Encircling the central chamber and its presiding Buddha statue are two inner passageways containing scores of meditating Buddhas and superb bas-reliefs of *Jataka* scenes, many of them revealing vivid glimpses into life in 16th-century Arakan. The stone corridors are well lit: notice the clumsy grey cement work liberally applied by Archaeology Department workers to stop water from leaching inside the building and spoiling its treasures.

Numerous sitting Buddha figures are also found in the early 16th-century **Andaw-thein** ❸ ordination hall, the next structure northeast of the Shittaung Temple. The name means "Tooth Shrine", and the temple is believed to encase yet another of the Master's molars, originally encased here in the 8th century. It's similar to the Shittaung in layout, though much smaller, and with sixteen *stupas* rising from an octagonal base. Two concentric passages surround the central hall inside, where a brick-built Buddha provides the centrepiece.

Dating from 1612, the **Ratanabon Pagoda** ❸, just to the north of the Andaw-thein, is as elegant an example of a brick-built *stupa* as you'll see in Myanmar. Its central, bell-shaped *zedi*, which received a direct hit from Japanese bombers in World War II but has since been substantially restored, looks like a piece of exquisitely lathe-turned wood and is encircled by 24 smaller *stupas*.

Standing on a hillock to the west, the **Dukkan-thein** (**Htukkanthein**) ❹ ordination hall consists of another large, bell-shaped *stupa*, only this time surmounting two raised terraces. A stepped entrance on the east side leads to vaulted passageways that spiral to a central chamber. These are lined

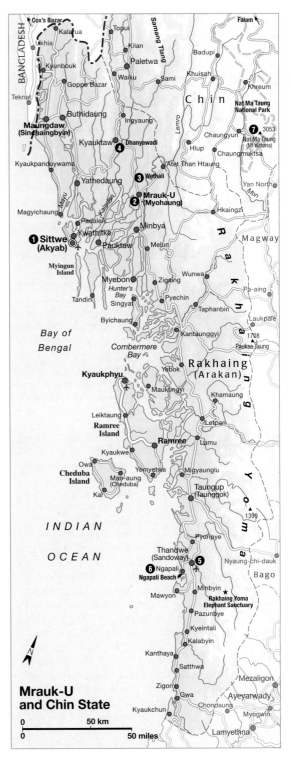

Mrauk-U
and Chin State

0   50 km
0   50 miles

A red-robed Buddha statue in one of the temples at Mrauk-U.

with stone images, including some of Mrauk-U's best-known sculptures, showing seated ladies (thought to be the wives of Arakan noblemen) offering lotus buds to the Master. Each of the 64 figures sports a different hairstyle. Niches in the side walls contain more Buddha statues.

Immediately northwest of the Dukkan-thein, the **Lemyethna Temple ❺** is renowned for the eight seated Buddhas placed with their backs against an octagonal central column. The shrine's early 12th-century donor left behind an evocative inscription, describing the monument's sacred contents: *"we encased (in the Lemyethna) holy relics in a sandalwood casket, placed it in a crystal casket, then a red sandalwood casket, then a gold casket, then a silver casket, and lastly into a miniature stone pagoda, the spire of which was made of gold and the golden umbrella of which was hung with pearls and coral. In the chamber of the temple we made four images of the Lord placed back to back and facing the cardinal points, and made them shine wondrously with gems".*

The Maha Muni image.

Royal Palace

Looming above the centre of the city like a Southeast Asian Acropolis, the Arakan kings' **Palace ❻** was Mrauk-U's nerve centre and most splendid building. Sadly, little remains to hint at its former glory other than the old sandstone walls – the outermost of three concentric ramparts that once surrounded the royal abode. A stone platform on the site of the former reception rooms and private chambers provides a vantage point from which to view the surrounding monuments and their backdrop of wooded hills.

The **Palace Archaeological Museum ❼** (Mon–Fri 9am–4pm; charge), just inside the palace's western wall, gathers together artefacts found around the site, including stone inscriptions, ceramics, gold and silver ware, weapons, coins and numerous Buddha statues, along with a scale model of Mrauk-U.

The best viewpoint for admiring the palace area itself is the **Haridaung Pagoda**, a diminutive whitewashed temple crowning a hilltop just to the north of the old palace walls.

MAURICE COLLIS ON THE MAHA MUNI IMAGE

"The Yattara bell was not sounded as a warning, but as an occult offensive. The notes, provided the particularities of the tables were complied with, would operate to put the invaders to flight by deranging their astrological chart and so placing them in jeopardy. In the exact centre of the top of this enclosure was the shrine (of the Maha Muni image). The original had been destroyed at the time of the Mongolian or Arakanese invasion of 957 and… rebuilt during the period when the country was a feudatory of the Pagan kings of Burma. In Manrique's time it must have resembled a small pagoda of the Pagan Dynasty type, a structure with massive brick or stone walls enclosing a chamber and surmounted by a spire. In the chamber was the famous image, a bronze over 10 feet high representing the Buddha… seated on a throne, his legs folded under him, his left hand opened on his lap, the right touching the earth with the tips of his fingers, a symbolic gesture denoting active compassion for mankind. The image was removed in 1784 to Mandalay… it has been plastered so thickly with gold leaf that its antique beauty has been smothered… you would never guess that it belonged to the first centuries of Indian colonisation eastwards, a classical bronze perhaps 1,800 years old."

Eastern Group

Scattered over flat paddy fields and marshland to the east of the Palace is another significant group of monuments, dominated by the profile of the splendid **Koethaung Pagoda** , Mrauk-U's largest surviving temple. The building was said to have been intended by its creator, King Minbin's son, Mintaikkha, as an attempt to trump the Shittaung erected by his father – whence its superior number of Buddha images and name ("Koethaung" means "90,000"). For a perfect view of the complex, climb up to the **Peisidaung Pagoda** which crowns a hilltop immediately to the south.

The other outstanding monument in this area is the graceful **Sakyamanaung Pagoda** ❶, a kilometre northeast of the palace walls, whose *hti* soars to an impressive 82 metres (280ft).

AROUND MRAUK-U

The lush rice fields that patchwork the alluvial land dividing the Kaladan and Lemro rivers underpinned the rise not merely of Mrauk-U, but a succession of much older city-states, the scant remains of which litter the countryside north of the archaeological site. At Wethali, a half-hour jeep ride north, you can see the vestiges of ancient walls and a palace dating from the 4th century AD. Further north at **Dhanyawadi** is the Buddhist temple from where the famous **Maha Muni Buddha** image was stolen by Bodawpaya's army in 1784. By far the most popular excursion from Mrauk-U, however, is the trip up the Lemro River to visit villages of the Chin minority, where older women have their faces tattooed in traditional style.

Wethali

Founded in AD 327 by King Dvan Sandra, the ancient city of **Wethali** ❸ lies 8km (5 miles) north of Mrauk-U, on the road to Dhanyawadi. Fragments of the old walls can still be traced, along with the ground plans of Buddhist temples and ordination halls excavated in the 1980s, but the site's principal vestige is the **Great Wethali Payagyi**, a 5-metre (17ft) Buddha image carved from a single boulder during the reign of Dvan Sandra. It's one of the oldest Buddha images found in Myanmar, though its original features have been lost to more recent renovation work.

Occupation of the walled site, also known as Vesali, spanned from the 4th until the mid-11th century AD, a period coinciding with Pyu townships such as Sri Kshetra in the Ayeyarwady Valley, whose overall shape and plan this settlement closely resembles. The inscribed pillar now displayed in Mrauk-U's Shittaung Temple was originally found here and recalls the names of the twenty kings who ruled ancient Wethali. The rest of the coins, sculptural pieces and other artefacts unearthed on the site are displayed at Mrauk-U's palace museum.

Dhanyawadi (Maha Muni)

Arakanese chronicles assert that Lord Buddha himself visited the city of **Dhanyawadi** ❹ ("Grain Blessed"),

Koethaung Pagoda, one of the Mrauk-U temples.

TIP

Visitors unhappy with the human zoo aspect of tribal tourism may admire a selection of Chin facial tattoos online, at the website of German photographer Jens Uwe Parkitny (www. bloodfaces.com), who has been visiting Rakhaing to record this dying tradition since the 1990s.

40km (25 miles) northwest of Mrauk-U, in 554 BC – an event commemorated by the casting of Myanmar's most revered Buddha image, which was made from precious metals donated by the local nobility. Worshipped for centuries by the Arakan kings, Maha Muni was the country's most powerful protector deity and attracted streams of devotees until King Bodawpaya took the statue home as war booty in 1784. It's now enshrined in Mandalay, but the temple survives, albeit in a heavily modernised form, and its three presiding stone images, housed on the topmost level, still command great adoration among the Buddhist population of Arakan and beyond. A small museum adjacent to the shrine (free) houses a modest array of sculpture fragments and Sanskrit inscriptions.

The temple is the most visible remnant of a city that thrived here between the 4th and 6th centuries AD. Encircled by a 10km (6-mile) oval of perimeter walls, remains of a square palace compound and other stone structures can be discerned in the fields immediately south of the Maha Muni shrine

Selling fruit.

and adjacent village, though you get a much more vivid sense of the site's scale from satellite imagery.

Chin villages

Mrauk-U is the starting point for boat rides up the bucolic Lemro River to visit villages inhabited by Chin subsistence farmers and fishing communities. One of Myanmar's most marginalised and poorest minorities, the Chin are famous above all for the facial tattoos traditionally worn by their women. The practice, however, was banned by the socialist regime in the 1960s and discouraged by the American missionaries who evangelised most of the Chin population during the colonial era. Only older women in more remote settlements today sport the inky, blue-green spider's-web patterns on their faces, and those in a couple of villages two hours' upriver from Mrauk-U are cashing in on their tattoos to supplement their families' meagre incomes. The skin art was not, as is often claimed, done to protect them from the unwanted attentions of local noblemen, but to beautify their faces. All-inclusive trips are arranged by local travel agents in Mrauk-U for around $100, including transport and meals. Expect an early start.

SOUTHERN RAKHAING

The southern coastal strip of Rakhaing State, home to Myanmar's principal beach resort, **Ngapali**, is unreachable overland from Sittwe and the north of the state. To get there, most people fly from Mandalay or Yangon to the town of **Thandwe**, a short taxi ride north of Ngapali. Flights also operate between **Sittwe** and **Thandwe**, and government ferries ply the coast between Sittwe and Taungup (Tuanggok) (an hour's drive north of Thandwe).

Thandwe

Thandwe ❺ is southern Rakhaing's largest town and the springboard for visits to nearby Ngapali Beach. In

ancient times, when it was known as Dvaravati, the harbour served as a port of call for Indian seafarers en route to or from the Malay Peninsula. The Buddha is said to have lived three of his 547 previous lives here. Local pagodas enshrine various animal relics from the era: the tooth of a cobra in the Andaw Pagoda, just across the river; the rib of a partridge in the Nandaw Pagoda, 1.6km (1 mile) west of the centre; and a yak hair in the Sandaw Pagoda, west of the centre. Other than the temples, there's little to see in this former garrison town, known in British times as "Sandoway". If you've time to kill, the local market (housed in a Raj-era prison) is full of intense local sights and smells, and well worth a browse.

Ngapali

Myanmar's only fully fledged beach resort, **Ngapali** ❻ 10km (6 miles) southwest of Thandwe, centres on a tranquil, palm-lined bay in the south of Rakhaing. Its soft, white shell sand, translucent water and wonderful seafood offer a welcome respite from the dust and humidity of travel inland. Visitors on luxury tours comprise the majority of the clientele here, served by a string of small-scale hotels dotted around the bay. For the time being the atmosphere is peaceful, with oodles of space on the sand. Fishermen from the nearby villages well outnumber tourists, and their boats bob around offshore unmolested by jet-skis and powerboats. All that looks set to change, however. Plans are afoot to extend the runway of nearby Thandwe airport to accommodate long-haul flights from Bangkok and Singapore, and a batch of ultra-swish five-stars is already taking shape in the surrounding palm forest in expectation of the coming bonanza.

Snorkelling and fishing trips offer alternatives to lounging on the sand in one of the string of breezy bars dotted along the bay. Most of the hotels are clustered at the north end of the beach, but it's worth taking a walk south around the headland to the picturesque fishing village of **Gyeiktaw**, strewn behind a south-facing cove.

Chin woman with facial spider-web tattoo.

Myanmar's Elephants

Myanmar is richly endowed with teak forests, and the lucrative industry that they supply still relies on elephant power.

Elephants are most readily found in upcountry logging camps, but they also exist in the wild – roaming the slopes of remote mountain ranges from the borders of Shan and Kachin State in the east, to the Rakhaing Yoma in the west. Estimates put the total number at around 8,000–10,000, or about one-third of all those in Asia; of these, 4,755 are thought to be engaged in timber extraction, making Myanmar home to by far the largest herd of working pachyderms in the world.

The Burmese authorities have now established a sanctuary for wild elephants in the southern Rakhaing Yoma, not far from Minbyin on the upper waters of the Thandwe River. Encompassing 175,000 hectares (432,400 acres) of forested hills to the southeast of Ngapali, the Rakhaing Yoma Elephant Sanctuary is currently closed to tourists,

Preparing an elephant for work with Burmese Arakan drover.

but as development gathers pace on the nearby coast, it may well open up.

Working elephants extract over a million tonnes of fine teakwood and other hardwoods from the Burmese forests each year. The trees are cut by forestry workers and sawn into sections, after which powerful bull elephants begin hauling with harness and drag trains to the encouragement of shouts from their *uzi* or handlers, also known as *mahouts*. Trained elephants are amazingly adept. Using their heads, trunks, tusks and feet, they push, pull and otherwise manoeuvre logs of up to five tonnes to the banks of Myanmar's fast-flowing rivers. From here, the timber can be floated out of the forests and down to the sawmills.

Properly managed – as in Myanmar and in India's Andaman Islands – teak forestry can be a self-sustaining industry in which elephants play a major role. They can haul and manoeuvre without damaging the environment in much smaller spaces than bulldozers or cranes. These skills ensure that today, and for the foreseeable future, Myanmar will remain one of the last places in Asia with a thriving elephant culture.

While many working elephants are bred in captivity, some are captured in the wild and trained. Each year, the Burmese Forestry Department determines how many of such elephants are to be taken from the forest under the Elephant Control Scheme. Capture is a dangerous process involving specially trained elephants called *kunkee*. In times past it was even more risky as elephants had to be lassoed; today, tranquiliser darts are used. A wild calf can usually be trained to basic levels in only a few months using a combination of "carrot" (tasty morsels of food, hypnotic singing and small kindnesses) and "stick" (sleep deprivation, confinement, limited food intake), but it takes around 20 years before an elephant is fully trained.

Mahout and his elephant clearing logs.

CHIN STATE

The shadowy hills visible to the north of Mrauk-U mark the southern limits of Chin State, a region of remote, lush, densely forested valleys and mountains the size of Belgium, which tapers northwards along the frontier of the Indian state of Mizoram. Penetrated by few roads, it is Myanmar's least developed, poorest province, and one visited by few outsiders. Travel permits are rarely issued to foreigners other than those wishing to trek to the state's highest peak, **Nat Ma Taung ❼** (aka "**Mt Victoria**"; 3,053 metres/10,016ft), and even then, only with plenty of advance planning and the services of a government-accredited travel agent.

The overwhelming majority of this state's 500,000-strong population are members of the Chin minority, most of whom live from shifting "slash-and-burn" agriculture in far-flung, roadless valleys. It took the British more than a decade to subdue the infamously fierce Chins at the end of the 19th century, since when a combination of American Christian missionaries and persecution by the Burmese military junta has had a devastating effect on the area's traditional culture.

Attempts to resist the systematic "Burmanisation" of the Chins by the Yangon government coalesced in the late 1980s into a fully-fledged insurgency, spearheaded by the Chin National Front (CNF) and its armed wing, the Chin National Army (CNA). The backlash was predictably brutal. Throughout the 1990s, human rights groups reported the extensive use by the Burmese military of forced labour, arbitrary arrest and religious suppression, as well as widespread rape of Chin women by soldiers.

A wave of mass emigration resulted, mostly into neighbouring Mizoram. Then, in 2007, famine broke out in many parts of the state after the once-in-fifty-year flowering of the Chin bamboo forest – the "Mawta" – which caused a surge in the local rat population, and thus the decimation of grain stocks.

Other reasons the Myanmar government are cagey about allowing foreigners access to Chin is a thriving cross-border narcotics trade, and fears that the Burmese Chin will join forces with their even more rebellious brethren over the frontier in Mizoram.

Nat Ma Taung (Mt Victoria)

The only place in Chin State that registers on Myanmar's tourist map is the mountain soaring majestically above the Ayeyarwady Valley 80km (49 miles) west of Bagan. Rising to 3,053 metres (10,016ft), Nat Ma Taung (Mt Victoria) stands proud of the rest of the Chin Hills range, forming a so-called "sky island" with its own distinct micro-climate, flora and fauna. From Bagan, the round trip to the summit and back takes a minimum of six days (four of trekking and two of jeep travel). Government-accredited tour agents, such as Asterism Travels and Tours in Yangon (www.asterism. info), can help negotiate the necessary permits, but allow at least one month to be sure of getting your paperwork in time.

TIP

Rakhaing, especially in its northern reaches, has a substantial Muslim population. If visiting mosques remember to dress modestly – and behave respectfully. Remember, too, to remove your shoes.

Palm-fringed Ngapali Beach.

Relaxing and swimming in the Thanlwin River at the end of a long day.

A monk walks past a file of life-size statues of monks at Kawtka Thaung cave.

SOUTHEASTERN MYANMAR

Myanmar's lush southeastern strip is the homeland of the Mon and contains the recently opened Kayin State.

A backpacker naps on the bow of a boat travelling upstream on the Thanlwin River.

Tapering down the western side of the Gulf of Mottama (Martaban) to the Isthmus of Kra, Southeastern Myanmar is a long, narrow finger of land extending from Kayin and Mon State, through Tanintharyi (Tenasserim), almost to the Thai island of Phuket. In historical terms, this is a marginal land, until recently peripheral to the Bamar centre, with distinct cultural, ethnic and historical ties to neighbouring Thailand and to the Malay-Indonesian world further to the south.

Age-old antipathies between its predominantly Karen population and the Burmese have for decades ensured that the region has been blighted by one of Asia's longest-running civil wars, and that is has been inaccessible to visitors. However, with a peace accord between the government and insurgent armies now firmly in place and the conflict seemingly at an end, the area is bound to open up over the coming decade.

Foremost among its many unique attractions is the beautiful "Golden Rock" Pagoda of Mount Kyaiktiyo in Mon State, which can be reached in a day from Yangon. Further south, the Mon capital, Mawlamyine (Moulmein), retains a distinct colonial-era charm and serves as the start, or end, point of cruises by old double-decker ferries on the Thanlwin (Salween) River

Kyaiktiyo's Golden Rock.

into neighbouring Kayin State, where the striking limestone hills, caves and mountaintop monasteries around the town of Hpa-an entice increasing numbers of travellers.

Still more isolated is the exquisite coast of Tanintharyi (Tenasserim), in the far south, which is slowly opening up to foreign travellers. At present, the entire region is a delightful tropical backwater, perhaps fifty years removed from the relative affluence and openness of neighbouring Thailand. A more pristine, more beautiful part of mainland Southeast Asia would be hard to find.

With judgement and care, the Tanintharyi Coast, and more especially the totally undeveloped Myeik Archipelago of 800 coral-fringed islets offshore, could become a major source of foreign exchange for Myanmar and its people.

MON AND KAYIN STATES

Myanmar's southeastern regions – long off limits to foreign travellers – are finally opening up to display their considerable riches.

Main Attractions
Kyaiktiyo: "Golden Rock Pagoda"
Mawlamyine (Moulmein)
Mount Zwegabin
Saddar Cave
Hpa-an–Mawlamyine river trip

Bordered along its western flank by the Andaman Sea and on its eastern side by Kayin State, **Mon State** is home to one of the ethnic groups that have traditionally dominated the Burmese lowlands. Squeezed gradually southwards by the Bamars, the Mon were ousted from their capital, Bago, in the mid-18th century by King Alaungpaya, and retreated southwards along the coast to their former heartland, where they survived the turbulence of succeeding centuries thanks to the fertility of the region's rice fields.

The Mon martial tradition, however, weathered defeat by the Bamars to re-surface in World War II, when Mon regiments fought bravely alongside Allied forces, in recognition of which the British promised them their own autonomous state. But self-rule never materialised – even after a decades-long war against the Burmese-dominated government fought by Mon guerrillas in the hills of the Tenghyo range, to the south.

The enduring and sporadic nature of this insurgency explains why, despite its numerous attractions, Mon State remains a tourist backwater. Even though the conflict has subsided, few visitors cross the state border and those that do rarely venture beyond the spell-binding "**Golden Rock Pagoda**", Mon

State's principal attraction, in the far north. Yet only a day's journey further south, **Mawlamyine** (**Moulmein**), the capital, is a superbly atmospheric relic of colonial rule with heaps of old-world atmosphere and a bumper crop of monuments to discover, including the world's largest reclining Buddha at nearby Win Sein Taw Ya.

En route to Mawlamyine, it's worth pausing in neighbouring **Kayin State** to experience the otherworldly karst landscape of **Hpa-an** and its hinterland, where you can hike up

A girl waits for customers outside her family's convenience store.

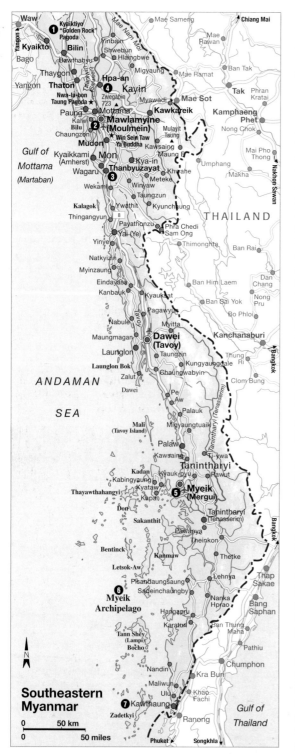

Southeastern Myanmar

0   50 km

0   50 miles

sheer-sided limestone hills swathed in jungle to summits crowned by sacred stupas and monasteries, explore remote Buddhist cave complexes and catch old-style double-decker ferries up the Thanlwin (Salween) River.

MON STATE

Mon State occupies a thin sliver of the Tenasserim coastal belt southwest of Yangon, on the opposite bank of the Gulf of Mottama (Martaban). Backed by the Tenghyo hills, this region was the crucible of the early Mon kingdom. Local historians assert it was the "Suwanabhumi" ("Land of Gold") referred to in ancient Buddhist chronicles, and to which the Mauryan emperor Ashoka dispatched the missionaries Sona and Uttara from India in the 3rd century BC. Recent archaeological and genetic evidence, however, suggests that the Mon, who are of Tibeto-Burman origin, had not even begun their migration across Himalayas by this date. More certain is that they were among the first settlers in lowland Burma to espouse Theravada Buddhism, and that in doing so they absorbed considerable Indian influence.

From their capitals at Bago (Pegu) and Thaton, the Mon dominated lower Burma until the rise of Bagan and military defeat at the hands of King Anawrahta in 1057. Thereafter, their power waned, though Mon influence on Burmese culture has always been considerable. Only after King Alaungpaya's brutal attack on Bago exactly seven centuries later, when the Mon who survived the invasion were either massacred or driven across the border into Siam, did they disappear from the mainstream of Burmese life.

Today, Mon State is emerging from decades of fighting between the military regime and the Mon National Liberation Army (MNLA), which has struggled since the 1970s for greater self-determination. Human rights abuses have been rife in the region, although with the exception of a few remote hill areas, the conflict seems to have subsided since the signing of an accord with the government in 2011. Rice, rubber, fishing and betel nut farming are the mainstays of the local economy, with tourism virtually non-existent beyond the Golden Rock temple at Kyaiktiyo – at least for the time being.

Mount Kyaiktiyo: "Golden Rock Pagoda"

Forming one of the most ethereal spectacles in Southeast Asia, the **Kyaiktiyo "Golden Rock" Pagoda** ❶ crowns a ridge of forested hills in the far north of Mon State, 210km (130 miles) east of Yangon around the Gulf of Mottama. During the pilgrimage season between November and March, tens of thousands of devotees climb daily to the shrine, regarded as the third most sacred in the country after the Shwedagon Pagoda and Maha Muni image in Mandalay, for a glimpse of a modest, 7.3-metre (24ft) stupa mounted atop a lavishly gilded boulder. According to the faithful, only the presence inside the reliquary

spire of a hair of the Buddha prevents the rock from toppling into the sheer-sided ravine below.

The hour-long climb to the hilltop temple can be arduous in the heat, and the journey to and from the starting point of the walk in an open-topped truck is less than comfortable. But the effort is rewarded with the chance to see the magical boulder bathed in the delicate, rose-coloured light of dawn or the afterglow of sunset, when crowds of ecstatic pilgrims and monks illuminate flickering candles and incense sticks as offerings.

Visiting the Kyaiktiyo Pagoda

The turning off the coastal highway for the pagoda is at the town of **Kyaikto**, but the starting point for the pilgrimage proper lies another 10km (6 miles) further northeast at the village of **Kinpun**. While devout Buddhists disembark here to begin the 11km (7-mile) trek to the temple, the majority of locals – and virtually all foreigners – transfer to an open-topped truck fitted with wooden slats

A Burmese man prays beside the Kyaiktiyo Pagoda.

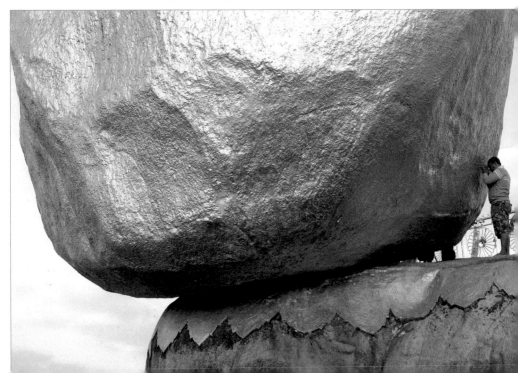

Packaged gold leaf for sale which the devout will stick onto the already heavily gilded Golden Rock Pagoda.

for the bumpy, 45-minute ride to the road end at **Yatetaung**.

From here, a paved path, lined with refreshment and souvenir stalls, zigzags steeply uphill to the main shrine – an hour-long climb that can be tough in the heat. Teams of blue-shirted porters are on hand to carry in sedan chairs those unwilling or unable to make the ascent under their own steam. A government entrance ticket and camera permit have to be paid for at the temple entrance.

Only men are allowed to cross the footbridge over the chasm separating the golden rock from the temple terrace, which devotees do in order to be able to press a propitious gold leaf on to the boulder. To be at the temple for the pre-dawn rituals, pilgrims sleep on the adjacent terrace or in the nearby monastery. Foreign tourists, however, are obliged to spend the night in one the hotels recently

The Pagoda of Kyaiktiyo c. 1900.

built near the top of the hill, or down in Kinpun.

Mawlamyine (Moulmein)

"By the old Moulmein Pagoda
Lookin' lazy to the sea,
There's a Burmese girl a-settin'
And I know she thinks o' me."

Thanks to its fleeting mention in the famous poem *Mandalay* (1890), the former capital of British Burma, Moulmein – or **Mawlamyine ❷** as it's since been re-named – will forever be associated in the foreign imagination with Rudyard Kipling, which is ironic considering the writer only spent a few fleeting hours here. Yet the town, or more accurately the beauty of its women, made a lasting impression on the 24-year-old, who was travelling to England for the first time from Calcutta via the US.

The pagoda in question was one of several encrusting a prominent ridge inland from the city, today home to more than 500,000 people. Strategically sited 28km (18 miles) inland from the mouth of the Thanlwin (Salween) River,

THE LEGEND OF KYAIKTIYO

According to legend, the Kyaiktiyo pagoda was founded in the 11th century by King Tissa to enshrine a hair of the Buddha he had been given by a holy man – with the condition that he install it on a rock the shape of his head. This king was able to do thanks to supernatural powers inherited from his parents – his father was a *zawgyi* (alchemist) and mother a *naga* (serpent) princess – along with the help of Thagyamin, king of the *nat*, who directed him to a suitable rock on the sea bed.

The rock was transferred by boat to the foot of a holy mountain. The legendary boat eventually turned into stone, and can now be found a few hundred metres from Kyaiktiyo. It is simply known as the Kyaukthanban, the "stone boat pagoda".

Moulmein was ceded to the British by the Kingdom of Ava in the Treaty of Yandabo at the end of the First Anglo-Burmese War in 1826, whereupon it was transformed into a thriving teak and rubber port. Few of the once sizeable Anglo-Burmese community that formerly dominated Moulmein remain, the majority having left for more prosperous corners of the Empire after Independence, but plenty of mildewing Raj-era buildings attest to its 19th-century prominence. However, it's the considerably more ancient Buddhist monuments crowning the ridge inland that tend to draw the eye here.

Foremost among them, at the far northern end of the ridgetop, is the **Maha Muni Pagoda Ⓐ** a traditional Mon-style complex whose presiding image is a beautiful replica of Mandalay's Maha Muni. Housed in a shrine that's lined with sparkling precious stones and mirrorwork, the statue was commissioned by a homesick queen, Mibaya-gyi, one of King Mindon's consorts, during her exile following the British annexation of Mandalay in 1885.

For the best views of the city, head further south to the splendid, and much older, **Kyaikthanlan Pagoda Ⓑ**, erected in the late 9th century to house a hair relic, Tripitaka manuscripts and gold images of the Buddha. Successive rulers raised the height of the central stupa, which is now magnificently gilded and the tallest in the area. You can either walk to the upper terrace via a covered staircase, or ascend in an elaborately roofed elevator.

At the southern end of the ridge, **U Zina Pagoda Ⓒ** houses four life-sized statues of the images that inspired young Siddhartha Gautama to take up the life of a wandering ascetic: an old man leaning on a staff; a sick man suffering from a terrible disease; a corpse; and a yellow-robed monk blissfully free of worldly worries.

Around Mawlamyine

Burma's longest bridge, the 7.6km (4.7-mile) **Thanlwin Bridge**, carries the coastal highway and its adjacent

A mosque in Mawlamyine.

Early morning in the capital of Mon State, with the twin minarets of the Soorti Sunni Jamai Mosque visible.

Reclining Buddha statue, one of the largest in the world, at Win Sein Taw Ya.

A much more easily accessible option is the gigantic reclining Buddha at **Win Sein Taw Ya**, 20km (12 miles) south of Mawlamyine just off the main road to Mudon. Measuring 180 metres (600ft) in length, the statue is the largest of its kind in the world and, like the one at Bodhi Tataung near Monywa (see page 191) , holds diorama galleries illustrating the teachings of the Buddha.

While you're in the area, don't miss the striking **Kyauktalon Kyaung**, a peculiar, jungle-draped outcrop of rock rising sheer from the paddy fields a short way further south. Formed from limestone, the flat top of the vertical-sided hillock holds a Buddhist temple, reached via a flight of ancient steps. The Hindu temple at the foot of the rock is patrolled by troops of voracious macaques, so keep any food you may have brought well wrapped up.

rail line north across the river towards Thaton. Crowning the hills overlooking the estuary is a local pilgrimage site, the **Nwa-la-bon Taung**, renowned as the seat of a golden boulder that's far less frequented than the one at Kyaiktiyo. In fact, three separate rocks comprise this natural wonder, balanced precariously on top of each other to create a phantasmagorical monument that perfectly compliments the astounding view over the bamboo forest and jungle-covered valleys below it.

A Burmese woman carries a boy on her back up Mount Kyaiktiyo.

Anyone with a family connection to, or interest in, the history of the infamous **"Death Railway"** (see page 297) will wish to continue

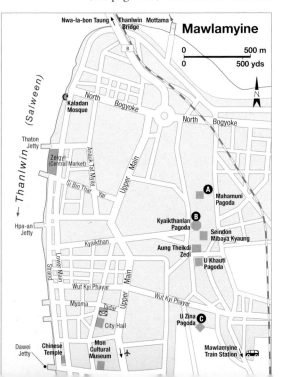

Mawlamyine

0   500 m
0   500 yds

Nwa-la-bon Taung   Thanlwin   Mottama
                   Bridge

North
Kaladan
Mosque
      North   Bogyoke
                  North   Bogyoke

Thaton (Salween)

Thanlwin

Thaton
Jetty

Zeigyi
(Central Market)

Hpa-an
Jetty

Amauk Tai May

Si Bin Thar   Yar

Kyaikthan

Upper   Main

A Mahamuni
       Pagoda

Kyaikthanlan **B**
Pagoda

Seindon
Mibaya Kyaung

Aung Theikdi
Zedi

U Khauti
Pagoda

Lower Main   Strand

Wut Kyi Phayar

Myoma   Tadar

City Hall

Wut Kyi Phayar

U Zina **C**
Pagoda

Dawei
Jetty

Chinese
Temple

Mon
Cultural
Museum

Mawlamyine
Train Station

65km (40 miles) down the highway from Mawlamyine to **Thanbyuzayat ❸**, where the Japanese railway line met the existing British-built one to Rangoon. On the outskirts of town, a large **war cemetery** holds the bodies of 3,617 of the 16,000 or more PoWs who perished during the construction of the Burmese portion of the route. Many more were interred where they expired in camp burial grounds or at remote sites alongside the railway; dog tags removed from thousands of such bodies were incorporated into memorial plaques on the site, which is impeccably maintained by the Commonwealth War Graves Commission.

KAYIN STATE

Kayin State – formerly known as Karen State – comprises one of Myanmar's most perennially troubled regions. Since Independence in 1948, it has seen near-continuous fighting between the Burmese army and various factions of Karen insurgents, the most dominant of them the Karen National Union (KNU) and its armed

Thanlwin Bridge, Mawlamyine.

wing, the KNLA. The conflict, often dubbed the world's longest-running civil war, saw a dramatic escalation in 2010, when the Burmese generals ordered a major offensive in the region. Having wiped out all but a few pockets of Karen resistance, this led in 2011 to the signing of a peace accord with the rebels, guaranteeing representation in parliament in exchange for a cessation of hostilities.

Plans were announced the following year to restore the overgrown **Death Railway** line that formerly

Aung San Suu Kyi talks to the press in April 2012 after meeting with representatives from the Karen National Union (KNU).

ETHNIC CONFLICT

In January 1948, when the British withdrew from Burma, the stage was set for ethnic confrontation. In simple terms, the Bamar Buddhist majority tended to see the Karen, who had fought for the British against the Japanese in World War II, as lackeys of the outgoing Raj. For their part, the Karen were nervous about coming under a Bamar Buddhist-dominated government, and demanded their own state.

As a consequence, the Karen rebelled against Yangon rule, embarking on a vicious, protracted and largely forgotten civil war that would span six decades and force tens of thousands of refugees across the border into Thailand. Its final flurry occurred in the wake of the 2010 elections, when Karen and Burmese forces clashed in the town of Myawaddy. In January 2012, however, a cease-fire accord was signed which seems to have brought a definitive peace to the region.

The Mon were slower to rebel than the Karen. Yet the minority's principal armed faction, the MNLA, still holds out against Yangon in a few scattered and isolated border regions. Both the "forced labour" extension of the southern railway to Ye, in the far south of Mon State, and the construction of a major gas pipeline to Thailand are persistent sores which feed separatist sentiment and arouse international concern.

Nevertheless, both Mon and Kayin states are today increasingly open to international travel, with only a few remote border areas closed to tourists.

TIP

Unfortunately, getting to the Nwa-la-bon Taung temple can be difficult without your own transport as the trucks waiting at the foot of the approach path only leave with a minimum of 45 passengers. The walk takes around three hours.

ran through the interior hills of Kayin to the Thai border at Three Pagodas Pass – a move which, it is hoped, will encourage tourism and trade in this impoverished area. In the meantime, the only part of the state you're likely to want to explore is the capital, **Hpa-an**, with its pretty hinterland of karst hills, sugar-cane and rice fields, where several fascinating Buddhist monuments nestle amid some of the country's most photogenic landscapes. The other worthwhile trip, and a great way to experience backwater Myanmar, is the journey by government ferry from Hpa-an to Mawlamyine via the Thanlwin (Salween) River.

Hpa-an and around

Although holding few sights of note, **Hpa-an ❹** is an easy-going, uncongested state capital with a lively riverfront and market area, and a mostly Karen population of 50,000. The few foreigners that visit the town each year tend to do so for its hotels, which provide the most convenient bases for explorations of the surrounding

countryside, characterised by outcrops of towering, jungle-draped limestone similar to those of Guilin in southern China.

The highest of these spectacular massifs is **Mount Zwegabin** (732 metres/2,373ft), whose unmistakable profile rises 13km (8 miles) south of Hpa-an, soaring out of the paddy fields like a vision from a lost world. If you've the legs for it, consider the hike to the top, via a flight of steep, winding stone and cement steps. The main incentive to brave the two-hour slog, and troupes of aggressive monkeys who patrol the route, is the chance to watch the sunset from the summit of the mountain, where a lonely Buddhist monastery enjoys a fabulous panorama over the beautiful Thanlwin Valley to the distant Andaman Sea. The monks happily accommodate visitors for the night (allow a donation of K2,000–3,000); facilities are limited to a bamboo sleeping mat and basic food, but the privations are worth enduring for the chance to admire the wondrous sunrise the following morning.

Boarding a boat in Mawlamyine for the popular day trip upriver to Hpa-An.

Considerably older Buddha statues lie hidden in the many **caves** riddling the limestone hills around Hpa-an. The largest and most spectacular of these is **Saddar Cave**, 27km (17 miles) southwest of town along the road to Eindu village. Steps lead to an entrance chamber featuring a row of Buddhas and *nats*, followed by a series of gigantic caverns whose walls ooze with amazing rock and crystal formations (bring a good torch). After half an hour underground you emerge on the far side of the hill, where an opening reveals a hidden lake – a truly magical experience.

Another enigmatic sight hereabouts is the **Kyauk Kalap Pagoda**, a small monastery complex centred on a weird finger of rock that juts vertically out of an artificial lake. Reached via a long footbridge (closed noon–2pm), the site is set against a mesmerising backdrop of karst hills and outcrops, best viewed from the summit of the outcrop, which you can climb to via a flight of fifty steps.

By far the most popular excursion from Hpa-an, however, is the

ferry ride to Mawlamyine via the Thanlwin (Salween) River. Services are infrequent, running only twice weekly (the route can be more quickly covered overland these days), and, unlike the ferries plying the northern Ayeyarwady or Chindwin rivers in Upper Myanmar, most of the passengers seem to be foreign backpackers. Nevertheless, the trip is worth making for the rural scenery the ferry chugs through – though be warned that if the boat leaves before sunrise, as is often the case, you'll miss the best of it.

Buddhist monks at the Water Lake Monastery in Hpa-An.

THE DEATH RAILWAY

The Siam–Burma rail line, better known as the "**Death Railway**", was built to supply Japan's advancing army in the run-up to the invasion of India, when Japanese shipping was vulnerable to attack by Allied submarines. It was considered essential to link Burma with Siam (Thailand) and the Malay Peninsula, which was the source of a range of invaluable raw materials required by the armed forces.

A rail line linking Rangoon and Bangkok had been considered before the war, but was abandoned due to prohibitive costs. Japan was able to circumvent this due to the fact that they had a slave labour force of around 180,000 Asian and 60,000 Allied PoWs at their disposal. These unfortunate prisoners, most of whom were captured during the fall of Singapore, were duly forced to carry out the work, which involved the laying of 415km (258 miles) of track, bridges, embankments and cuttings through dense jungle.

Disease, starvation, exhaustion and brutal treatment at the hands of the Japanese cost the lives of an estimated 106,000 men, including 16,000 British,

Commonwealth and European servicemen, over the 14 gruelling months it took to complete the project.

The most notorious stretch, due to its remoteness and extreme terrain, was the one crossing the Tenasserim Hills via the "**Hell Fire Pass**", where 69 labourers were beaten to death or crucified on trees using barbed wire over a period of just six weeks. When the two opposing sections of the line finally met in October 1943, most of the PoWs were transferred to Japan. Those that stayed behind to maintain the railway experienced horrific conditions, as Allied bombing attacks gradually destroyed the line during the final months of the war.

Apart from the war cemetery in **Thanbyuzayat**, and its now-defunct museum, few vestiges of this dreadful chapter in the region's history remain in Myanmar, though in 2012, after signing a peace accord with the Karen rebels who formerly controlled the area, the Burmese government announced plans to reopen the line as far as the Three Pagodas Pass on the Thai border.

A beach on an uninhabited island in the Myeik Archipelago.

MYEIK REGION

The remote, historically fascinating port of Myeik,
with its neighbouring archipelago of unspoilt
islands, is slowly becoming accessible to visitors.

Yangon

he coast of **Tanintharyi (Tenasserim) State**, in the far south of Myanmar, is as spectacularly beautiful as anywhere in Southeast Asia. Yet despite its proximity to neighbouring Thailand, on the opposite, eastern, flank of the Malay Peninsula, it has long been off the beaten track – largely thanks to the decades-old insurgency fought by Karen guerrillas along the mountainous international frontier. This has long been a politically sensitive zone. The main pipeline from the off-shore Yadana petroleum field crosses the area, as does the controversial Yai-Dawei railroad, which opponents of the Yangon military regime claim was constructed by forced labour; both remain sources of considerable Karen indignation.

However, since the signing of the 2011 peace accord, prospects for the far south have improved considerably, not least because of the tourist potential offered by the numerous sand-fringed islets off the coast. At the time of writing, the only places in Tanintharyi technically open to foreigners were three coastal towns served by domestic airports – Dawei, Myeik and Kawthaung – though the situation may well change rapidly if the ceasefire with Karen rebels holds firm.

MYEIK

Although today a provincial backwater, **Myeik** ❺ – or "Mergui" as it was

formerly known – served between 1350 and 1750 as the Thai capital's main sea port for trade between the spice islands and India. Overlooking the mouth of the Tanintharyi River, it was later occupied by the British, and retains the charm of an oriental colonial city. Little has changed since the 1930s, beyond the smuggled goods from Thailand that fill the stands of the market, though the extension of the airport runway on the eastern edge of town promises major development in the coming decades.

Main Attractions
Myeik
Myeik Archipelago

A Moken sea gypsy.

TIP

Wander around the back lanes of Myeik to discover some wonderful old colonial mansions, teak houses and traditional wooden shopfronts.

Foremost among Myeik's Buddhist monuments is the central **Theindawgyi Pagoda**, a classic Mon-style temple lined with well-executed interior mosaic and high-quality bronze Buddha images. On the edge of town, **Kuthein Nayon Kyaung** is another temple built in Mon style with characteristic square shrines. Myeik's real USP, however, is its fine harbour and the views from the waterfront to the nearby twin-peaked barrier island of **Kadan**, whose bulk protects the port from the cyclones of the Andaman Sea and has long ensured the town's viability as a year-round anchorage. Myeik harbour is also the principal embarkation point for ferries and launches bound for the archipelago to the west, an area still off limits to independent travellers.

Myeik (Mergui) Archipelago

Statue of a Chinthe – half lion, half griffin – Myeik.

An atoll of around 800 coral-fringed islands scattered off the coast of Tanintharyi, the **Myeik Archipelago** ❻ is a tropical paradise of the kind that has all but disappeared in Southeast Asia. The ban on independent travel imposed by the government has ensured that the islands remain much as they have for centuries, inhabited by communities of Malay fishermen and semi-nomadic Moken "Sea Gypsies" (see page 300) who, like their contemporaries further south along the Malay Peninsula, spend the dry season on small boats and return to ramshackle villages on land during the monsoons.

The Japanese are engaged in lucrative pearl fishing in the archipelago, while the region's swifts' nests – found in cathedral-like limestone caves accessible only at low tide – are harvested for exotic bird's-nest soup.

Tourism, however, has thus far made negligible impact. While travellers may visit Myeik and Kawthaung – the atoll's two main embarkation ports – they are not allowed to explore the islands; immigration police patrolling the ferry docks will arrest anyone who tries. For the time being, the only option is to check

THE MOKEN SEA GYPSIES

The translucent waters of the Myeik Archipelago, off the coast of Tenasserim in southeastern Burma, are the last stronghold of seaborne nomads who call themselves the 'Morgan' or 'Moken'. Known in Burmese as 'Salone' or 'Selung', and in neighbouring Thailand as Chao Nam ('water people'), the group number between 2,000 and 3,000 and are unique for spending most of their lives at sea. Long-tailed diesel houseboats provide shelter and transport for families who subsist on what they catch and rarely return to dry land except to trade fish or shells for money to buy fuel.

In recent decades, the discovery of petroleum reserves in the region has posed a threat to the survival of the Moken's nomadic lifestyle. Attempts have reportedly been made by the Burmese government to forcibly relocate them in settled villages – a life to which they are ill-suited.

The Moken made headlines in the wake of the tsunami of 2004, which they miraculously survived because they were able to perceive warning signals in the sea and flee to high ground ahead of the tidal wave. Another unusual attribute of the Moken is their ability to see clearly underwater – a faculty they develop in early childhood while diving for shells.

into the incongruous, government-owned and eye-wateringly expensive Andaman Club on Thahtay Kyun Island (see page 317) – a 205-room five-star with its own 18-hole golf course and Vegas-style casino. Alternatively, a handful of Thai scuba crews working out of Phuket run live-aboard cruises to the world-class dive sites in the area.

KAWTHAUNG

Kawthaung ❼, at the southernmost tip of Myanmar, is an unremarkable frontier town dominated by Thai trade. Many locals are bilingual in Burmese and Thai, and the *baht* is welcome everywhere – certainly more so than *kyat*. There's not a lot to see, but if you're coming from Myeik by rust-bucket boats, the town can seem a well-heeled place.

To the south of the harbour lies **Cape Bayinnaung**, a promontory named after the Burmese king of the same name who invaded Thailand several times via this route during the 16th century. A statue of the legendary warrior clad in battle armour

An idyllic corner of the Myeik Archipelago.

and flourishing a sword at the nearby Thai coast serves to remind visitors that Myanmar wasn't always as "down and out" as it is today. Unspectacular accommodation is available at two or three small hotels in Kawthaung, while the offshore Andaman Club resort offers upmarket surroundings for highrollers intent upon golf, duty-free shopping and gambling – casinos are illegal in neighbouring Thailand.

A Moken woman works bamboo at a village on Bada island.

INSIGHT GUIDES TRAVEL TIPS
MYANMAR (BURMA)

TRANSPORT

GETTING THERE AND GETTING AROUND

GETTING THERE

By air

Due to the trade embargo and sanctions imposed on Myanmar's former military government, comparatively few carriers operate to Yangon-Mingaladon, the main international airport. Those that do – listed below – route flights via their home hubs and/or through Bangkok or Kuala Lumpur, which tends to mean painfully long waits in transit. There are no direct flights from Europe or North America, most Yangon-bound passengers change planes at Bangkok or Doha. The only other point of arrival is Mandalay, with flights from Kunming in southwest China.

Air Asia
Ground Floor, Park Royal Hotel.
Tel: 01 251 885; www.airasia.com
Air China
13/23 Shwe Kanayei Housing, Narnattaw Road.
Tel: 01 505 024; www.airchina.com
Air India
127 Sule Pagoda Road.
Tel: 01 253 597; www.airindia.in
Bangkok Airways
3rd Floor, Sakura Tower 339, Bogyoke Aung San Road.
Tel: 01 255 122; www.bangkokair.com
Malaysia Airlines
Central Hotel, 335-357 Bogyoke Aung San Road, Yangon. Tel: 01 2410 0120; www.malaysiaairlines.com
Myanmar Airways International
08-02 Sakura Tower, 339 Bogyoke Aung San Road, Yangon.
Tel: 01 225 440; www.maiair.com
Silk Air
Sakura Tower, 339 Bogyoke Aung San Road, Yangon.
Tel: 01 225 287; www.silkair.com
Thai Airways
Sakura Tower, 339 Bogyoke Aung San Road. Tel: 01 255 499
Vietnam Airlines
1702, Sakura Tower, 339 Bogyoke Aung San Road, Tel: 0125 5066; www.vietnamairlines.com

Overland

Now that the insurgency problems in Myanmar's border areas have abated, it's likely that some of the overland routes into the country will open to foreigners in the next few years. For the time being, however, crossing points are few and far between, and subject to tight restrictions.

In the far south, the port town of Kawthaung opposite the Myeik (Mergui) archipelago can be reached from Ranong in southern Thailand – but only on a short-stay visa. Further north, in Kayin State, the Thai and Burmese governments have also constructed a "Friendship Bridge" across the Moei River between Mae Sot and Myawaddy, but so far travel is still not permitted between the two countries except on a single-day temporary visa (you have to leave your passport with the border guards). Travelling from Kunming in China's Yunnan Province, you may enter Myanmar at the Ruili–Muse border crossing, and continue on to Lashio (5hrs further south) if your transport has been arranged by an accredited tour operator. Finally, from Chiang Rai in Thailand, you can head north into Myanmar's Shan State via the Mai-Sai–Tachilek crossing, though your stay will be limited to 15 days.

Note that these restrictions may well change in the near future and should be checked in advance of travel with a reputable agent in Thailand or China.

GETTING AROUND

Exploring Myanmar on a pre-organised tour, all your travel will of course be booked in advance by your operator, which is just as well as the country's transport infrastructure is rudimentary at best. Travelling independently, you'll be at the whim of ageing vehicles and unreliable timetables. With the exception of those border regions closed due to insurgencies (mainly in the northwest and deep south), foreign travellers can go just about wherever they want, when they want, with no restriction other than the usual practicalities of schedules and route conditions.

Given the parlous state of Myanmar's roads and railways, though, it's no surprise that the majority of travellers make at least a couple of short flights over the course of a standard 28-day visa.

From the airport

On arrival at **Yangon-Mingaladon Airport**, 19km (12 miles) north of the downtown area, expect to be besieged by taxi drivers offering to drive you into the city. The fare is fixed at $8. If you book a room through the hotel desk at the airport, transport into town is usually arranged free of charge. On departure, the fare from Yangon to the airport can usually be paid in local currency, and costs a couple of dollars less.

By air

Travellers to Myanmar often avoid long and potentially uncomfortable road journeys by catching flights between Yangon and Mandalay, or to Nyaung U (for Bagan), Thandwe (Ngapali Beach), Heho (Inle Lake), Sittwe (for Mrauk U), Kengtung (Shan State), Myitkina (on the Upper Ayeyarwady River) and Putao (in the far north). A handful of carriers fly these routes daily (see below), and to 39 other regional airports across the country. However, none enjoys a particularly good reputation for reliability or safety. The worst is the government-run Myanmar Airlines, whose fleet of ageing Fokker F27s and Douglas DC3s has a poor accident record.

It generally works out cheaper to book your tickets through an agent in Myanmar rather than direct with the airline. You'll also be better off going to an agent to obtain Air Mandalay's good-value Discover Myanmar Pass, which buys you four flights between Yangon, Mandalay, Bagan, Heho (Inle) and Thandwe (Ngapali Beach) for $330 (plus taxes).

Domestic airlines

Air Bagan
56 Shwe Taung Gyar Street, Bahan Township.
Tel: 01 513 322; www.airbagan.com
Air Kanbawza
33-49 Corner of Bank Street & Maha Bandoola Garden Street, Kyauktada Township.
Tel: 01 372 977; www.airkbz.com
Air Mandalay
146 Dhammazedi Road, Bahan Township, Yangon.

Ferry across the Ayeyarwady.

Tel: 01 525 488; www.airmandalay.com
Asian Wings
34(A1) Shwe Taung Gyar Street, Bahan Township.
Tel: 0973 135 991; www.asianwingsairways.com
Myanmar Airways
08-02 Sakura Tower, 339 Bogyoke Aung San Road.
Tel: 01 255 260; www.maiair.com
Yangon Airways
No.166, Level 5 MMB Tower, Upper Pansodan Road, Mingalar Taung Nyunt Township.
Tel: 01 652 533; www.yangonair.com.

By river and sea

Myanmar's rivers provide more than 8,000km (5,000 miles) of navigable routes, and as a result, shipping is the most important means of transport for people and goods throughout much of the country.

Rivers

Myanmar has more than 5000km (3000 miles) of navigable river. Even at the height of summer, when water levels are lowest, it's possible to travel all the way from the Delta to Bhamo in the north of the country by ferry along the Ayeyarwady, and in the monsoons you can even reach Myitkyina. Other rivers serving as major transport arteries include the Chindwin, which joins the Ayeyarwady southwest of Mandalay, and the Thandlin (Salween), in the far southeast.

In colonial times, the redoubtable Irrawaddy Flotilla Company, or IFC, plied the country's waterways with its elegant, double-decker river steamers. A handful of these wonderful old tubs survive (some

have been converted into luxury cruisers; see below), but nowadays most of Myanmar's ferry network comes under the jurisdiction of the government-owned Inland Water Transport (www.iwt.gov.mm), whose fleet of 476 boats annually shifts around 25 million passengers along with 4 million tonnes of cargo.

On a package tour, the only kind of boat you're likely to come into contact with is a **luxury cruiser**. These vessels tend to be beautifully restored antique steamers, or else newly built replicas, complete with timber-walled cabins furnished in high colonial style, with sun decks, bars and restaurants. Trips typically last from five to around 13 nights, and include plenty of sightseeing excursions to towns and other places of interest along the way.

Popular river routes

The most travelled river route for tourists is the stretch of the Ayeyarwady between Mandalay and Bagan. A local government slowboat (Mandalay–Myang-U Express; www.iwt.gov.mm) leaves Mandalay at 5.30am, arriving in Bagan at 9.30pm. You can travel deck class on the boat, sharing open quarters with monks, soldiers, nursing mothers, chicken and fruit baskets; alternatively, "first class" gets you a salon in the prow of the upper deck with four wooden benches and a table. Either way, kit yourself out with mosquito netting and repellent, and a blanket or sleeping bag.

Pitched at foreign tourists, a more modern and faster express boat, *Malikha II* (www.malikha-rivercruises.com; tel: 95 1 240 400), sails the same route, leaving at 6am or 7am for the 9-hour journey. The vessel has

Selling wares to train passengers.

an open sun deck and air-con cabin with recliners.

If you have money to burn, book yourself on to one of the **luxury cruises** operating along the Ayeyarwady River. Run by Orient-Express Trains & Cruises, the *Road to Mandalay* sails to Bagan in great splendour. Five- and six-night itineraries spending three and four nights respectively aboard the luxury ship are offered. There are 43 air-conditioned cabins and the ship is fitted with a pool, library and boutique, as well as restaurants and a bar. Guests are pampered with gourmet cuisine and service *par excellence*. An extensive shore excursion programme is included in the fare.

The *Road to Mandalay* cruise season runs late September to April. Contact *Orient-Express Trains & Cruises* in Yangon, tel: 01 296 680, www.orient-express.com.

A smaller cruise boat, the *Irrawaddy Princess II*, runs on a regular basis between Bagan and Mandalay, offering a range of itineraries of between 2 and 7 nights. You can book online or through their Yangon office on Mindhamma, Mayagone Township (tel: 01 655 228).

A third option for the Mandalay-Bagan stretch is on board either the 24-cabin *Pandaw II* or 39-cabin *Pandaw III*, newly built river steamers that recall the experience of river travel during colonial times. Both vessels have comfortable cabins with attached bathrooms. There are overnight as well as 2-night cruises from Mandalay to Bagan and vice versa. All meals and shore excursions to interesting villages and attractions are included in the fare. Stops are also made at schools and monasteries that the IFC help to sponsor.

A longer 4-night cruise (Royal Burma) on board the smaller 16-cabin *Pandaw I* is ideal for those with more time. This option travels north of Mandalay to places like Mingun, Ava and Amarapura before making the journey to Bagan. Travelling on board the charming old-world *Pandaw I* – originally built in 1947 and now completely refurbished – is an experience not to be missed. The *Pandaw I* also operates the 5-night Middle Burma Exploration from Bagan to Pyay (Prome), stopping at little-known towns and villages along the way.

The other luxury option on the Ayeyarwady is the 7-cabin boutique cruiser offered by a German-run company, Amara Cruise (www.myanmar-discovery.de).

A short popular ferry trip for tourists is the one up the Ayeyarwady from Mandalay to Mingun. Boats leave from Mandalay's B Road Jetty at 10am for the one-hour voyage.

A long cruise travels north from Mandalay via the Ayeyarwady's third and second defiles to Bhamo through a constantly changing riverscape. The ultimate river adventure trip, however, is the 20-night cruise up the untamed Chindwin, one of Myanmar's most scenic rivers, to the remote northern outpost of Homalin.

For all the above options, contact the Pandaw Company via its website: www.pandaw.com.

By sea

The **Myanmar Five Star Line** (www.mfsl-shipping.com) manages the country's overseas and coastal routes with a fleet of 21 vessels, only eight of which take passengers. Of interest are the services linking Yangon with Thandwe, Kyaukpyu, Sittwe in Rakhaing and Dawei, Myeik and Kawthaung in Taninthayi. Its Yangon

office is at the corner of Merchant Road and Theinbyu Street (tel: 01 295 279).

By train

Myanmar Railways comprises 5,402km (3,357 miles) of track, with Yangon's Central Railway Station as its hub. While the main Yangon–Mandalay line is reasonably quick, clean and efficient, the same can't be said of the rest of the network. Rolling stock ranges from shabby to decrepit and long delays are frequent. That said, if you're not in a rush, travelling by rail in Myanmar has its pleasures – not least gazing out of the open windows.

There are three classes: Upper (reclining seats); First (wooden slatted seats with padded leatherette bottoms); and Ordinary (bare slatted seats). Some services between Yangon and Mandalay also have sleeper carriages – "standard" and "special"; the latter with compartments instead of benches. Either way, expect a noisy ride, and bring a fleece as it can get cold at night in winter.

Foreigners can purchase their tickets through Myanmar Travels & Tours (see page 335) or direct at the railway station (tel: 01 274 027), advisably 24 hours ahead of departure.

All things considered, you'll nearly always get around more cheaply and quickly by bus – though travelling by train is certainly an adventure, and the views out of the windows of the country's rural hinterland can be delightful.

Yangon to Mandalay

This is the country's premier line, boasting reasonably clean and comfortable rolling stock, though even here journeys can be hot and sticky, schedules erratic and delays frequent. Five services run daily, calling at Bago, Taungoo, Naypyidaw and Thazi; numbers 5 and 3 are the trains to go for as they depart and arrive at more civilised times of day. For the latest timetable info, photos comparing classes and trip reports, check www.seat61.com.

From Mandalay, there are train connections to the hill station of Pyin U-Lwin (Maymyo), 61km (38 miles) east, from where you are now permitted to continue across the famous Gokteik viaduct to Kyaukme and Lashio. Other rail trips of interest to tourists might include the following:

Yangon city bus.

Yangon to Bagan

Bagan can be reached by train, via Naypyidaw-Pyinmana, departing Yangon daily at 4pm. The journey takes about 14 hours.

Mandalay to Myitkyina

The trip between Mandalay and Myitkyina is a bumpy one through rambling countryside that's been heavily logged but remains beautiful. Three to four trains cover the route daily, leaving at 8.30am, 1.50pm, 4.40pm & 5.45pm, arriving 22–24 hours later. En route stops of interest to the traveller are at Naba (for Katha, an Ayeyarwady embarkation point for river trips to Bhamo or Mandalay) and Hopin (for Indawgyi Lake).

By bus and coach

Government buses

Long-distance public bus travel tends to be slow and tedious. Many roads are poor, vehicles are overcrowded, and in the fairly common event of a breakdown, it can be hours before mechanical assistance becomes available.

Private buses

Several companies run comfortable air-conditioned buses from Yangon's Highway Bus Centre, 3km (2 miles) northeast of the airport, just off Highway 3. Services to most destinations (including Mandalay) run overnight, with arrival times more reliable than those of the trains. There are regular stops for food and refreshments.

Air-conditioned coaches and minibuses are the most usual way foreign travellers on group tours get around. Tickets may be booked in advance at the company's offices between Aung San Stadium and Yangon Railway Station on Kun Chan Rd.

Private transport: trishaws and taxis

Bicycle trishaws (*sai-kaa*) or motorised three-wheelers (*thoun bein*) are the most popular means of getting around the streets of the larger cities – less so in Yangon and Mandalay where taxis have taken over. Easily available and cheap, they take their passengers anywhere they want to go in the city for $1 or less per trip. Diesel-powered auto-rickshaws (*thoun bein*) are much handier, though, if you've more ground to cover, and rarely charge more than $1.

Taxis are ubiquitous and inexpensive in all the major cities, where they stand in ranks outside the main hotels and transport hubs. Meters rarely work, but few trips across town cost more than K3000–

Pick-up trucks are a common form of transport.

4000 ($4–5). For longer day trips out of town, expect to pay $50–60, depending on the age and condition of the vehicle.

Pick-up trucks

For longer trips in the vicinity of Yangon, Mandalay and other large population centres, pick-up trucks (*kaa*) – similar to the Thai *songthaew* – carry large numbers of passengers. They don't follow a set schedule; instead, they take off whenever the last seat is taken. For journeys from Yangon to Bago and from Mandalay to Pyin U-Lwin, this is a cheap, fast means of transport.

Car and driver

If you're travelling independently, you'll probably do most of your travelling in a rented car. In Myanmar, these come with a driver (self drive is still virtually unknown). Tourist cars tend to be no more than two or three years old, and are air-conditioned. For a maximum of 12 hours driving per day, including petrol, the driver's fee and expenses, and all toll charges, expect to pay around $100.

ACCOMMODATION

HOTELS, GUESTHOUSES AND RESORTS

PLACES TO STAY

Myanmar now offers a wide choice of accommodation in all its main tourist centres, and the number of beds looks set to soar. In peak season, from mid-November to January, vacancies can be hard to come by.

Budget guesthouses

Costing less than $25 for a double per night, the cheapest accommodation in Myanmar tends to be guesthouses in family homes. At their best, such places offer few comforts (thin mattresses, wood partition walls and shared shower-toilets), but will be clean, sociable and a great way to meet local families. You can expect to the rooms to be well scrubbed, with fans and exterior windows (usually barred). Bring a mosquito net and string to fasten it with, a universal sink plug and a roll of toilet paper.

Mid-range hotels

Basic hotels, costing $30–50 per night, tend to be in the Chinese mould: multi-floored concrete blocks with plain en-suite rooms off galleried walkways. If you spend upwards of $50, you can expect a spacious room with air-con, a proper balcony or verandah, good mattress and tiled bathroom.

Upper mid-range

Things perk up considerably at around the $70 mark, for which you can sleep in great comfort in an air-conditioned room, and expect to have the use of a pool. There'll be private sitting space on a spacious verandah or balcony,

furnished with wicker chairs, and maybe wi-fi (or internet access in the lobby), laundry, room service, a formal restaurant and a travel desk.

Expensive

Set in landscaped gardens, luxury four- or five-star hotels account for the bulk of high-end accommodation in Myanmar. They offer spacious, well-furnished, air-conditioned rooms, and large pools. There'll be a gym, probably a spa, well trained staff and nightly culture shows.

An alternative is the smaller, more stylish boutique hotel, beautifully fitted out in local architectural style, with teak floors, carved railings, hand-made silk throws and brass Buddhas.

Luxury

Only a handful of the finest hotels in Yangon and Mandalay, and the major resorts such as Inle Lake and Ngapali, can command room rates exceeding $200 per night, and they're every bit as ritzy as you'd expect, with international-grade leisure facilities and gourmet restaurants. While some, notably the Strand in Yangon, appeal to customers with their lavish, retro feel, others pile on the regal Burmese style, re-creating the feel of a Konbaung palace.

Politics

When Aung San Suu Kyi announced the end of the tourism boycott in 2010, she did so with the proviso that tourists should stay not in large luxury resorts on pre-arranged tours, but in smaller, independently run places that benefited ordinary, working Burmese people. This is because many of the

larger high-end establishments are owned and run by military generals and their families and cronies.

For this reason, we've avoided listing any hotels in this guide featured on the latest blacklist of properties drawn up by the French NGO, InfoBirmaine (info-birmanie. org), which worked closely with the NLD to establish which places were owned by companies or individuals subject to EU or US sanctions.

In some instances, however, where a blacklisted hotel was the only option, or offered something unique, we've featured it with a note flagging its connection to the former military dictatorship. If you're travelling on a package tour and can choose your hotels, use this list to make an informed decision and, above all, don't be afraid to press your tour operator into using an alternative if you're unhappy with their choice.

Taxes and service charges

There is a mandatory 10 percent tax levied on all hotel bills. Luxury places may add a 10 percent service charge.

Payment

Bills nearly always have to be settled in cash – which in Myanmar means crisp, unblemished dollar notes rather than kyat. Few hotels accept credit or debit cards, and those that do will add a 4 or 5 percent charge.

Booking

With the pressure on beds intense, it's always wise to book a week or more in advance. A phone call or email will suffice; follow up with a call the day before your arrival date.

YANGON

Accommodation in Yangon has been plentiful for years in all brackets, but with the tourism boycott at an end, beds are likely to be hard to come by until supply catches up with the sudden spike in demand. The places listed below represent the pick of a largely unremarkable crop. Apart from the Governor's Residence, Strand and Savoy, few hotels or guesthouses in the city offer much in the way of local or heritage character, most being geared towards visiting business clients. But you should be able to find somewhere clean, comfortable and reasonably priced, even if you travel a little way uptown to find it. Note that even here in Myanmar's biggest city, credit cards are rarely accepted.

Central
335-357 Bogyoke Aung San Road
Tel: 01 241 001; centralhotelyangon.com
An old favourite that's showing signs of wear and tear, but still offers good value in its bracket, with large rooms and welcoming staff. The location close to the market district is hard to beat. **$$$**

Chatrium Royal Lake
40 Natmauk Road, Tamwe Township
Tel: 01 554 500; chatrium.com/chatrium_hotel_yangon
Although it's a bit out of the way, this luxury five-star on the shores of Kandawgyi Lake offers all the comforts you'd expect of its class, including a decent-sized pool and air-conditioned gym. **$$$$**

Classique Inn
No. 53 B, Shwe Taung Kyar Street (Golden Valley Road), Bahan Township
Tel: 01 503 968; classique-inn.com
Buried deep in the smart Golden Valley neighbourhood, the Classique is an impeccably run, friendly B&B offering spacious, attractively furnished rooms with white walls, teak beds and silk throws. The staff couldn't be more attentive, and there's a relaxing garden terrace to lounge on. Well placed for the airport, and within walking distance of Shwedagon, though you'll need a taxi for trips downtown. **$$**

Comfort Inn
4 Shweli Road, Kamaryut Township
Tel: 01 526 865; comfyland.biz
Unassuming budget hotel down a side street off busy Inya Road. The rooms are wood-lined and well aired, and most overlook a leafy garden. Transfers to or from the airport available. Good value. **$$**

East
No. 234-240, (1) Quarter, Sule Pagoda Road, Kyauktada
Tel: 09 7313 3511; www.east.com.mm
Opened in 2011, the East is a dependable mid-scale option right in the city centre, close to the Sule Pagoda and Bogyoke market area. Some of its rooms are on the small side, but they are well furnished and with quality bedding. Patronised mostly by foreign tourists because it's one of the few places you can book online through popular booking websites. **$$**

Governor's Residence
35 Taw Win Road
Tel: 01 229 860; governorsresidence.com
If your budget can stretch to it, this British-owned boutique hotel in the heart of the embassy enclave is the most commendable high-end option in Yangon. Housed in an elegant 1920s mansion, it oozes colonial-era chic. The rooms have polished teak floors and slatted windows opening on to lawned grounds dotted with lotus ponds. Relax on the wrap-around verandah as paddle fans whirl overhead, waited on by staff in traditional *anyi* jackets and longyis. **$$$$$**

Grand Plaza Parkroyal
33 Alan Paya Lan
Tel: 01 250 388; grandplaza.yangon.parkroyalhotels.com
Visiting businessmen comprise the bulk of the Grand Plaza's clientele, though, lying within walking distance of Shwedagon Pagoda and market area, it is well situated for sightseeing too. As with most upscale hotels in the city, the décor could do with an upgrade, but the staff are eager and facilities include quick wi-fi. **$$$$$**

Inya Lake Resort
Kaba Aye Pagoda Road
Tel: 01 662 857; inyalake.dusit.com
Located midway between downtown and the airport, this is one of the city's flagship hotels. It was originally built by Russians in the early 1960s and is now run by the government, so is a little worn around the edges, though the pool is huge and the 15-hectare (37-acre) grounds pleasant. OK for a night or two in transit, but not for longer stays. Generous low-season discounts. **$$$$**

Kandawgyi Lake Palace
Kanyeiktha Road
Tel: 01 249 255; kandawgyipalace.com
Located on the site of the former Rangoon Boat Club and city museum, the government-owned Kandawgyi

Palace Hotel possesses more character than most of the upscale hotels in Yangon, though its prime position looking across the lake to the Shwedagon Pagoda is the real draw. It underwent a major re-fit in 2012. **$$$$**

May Shan
115/117 Sule Pagoda Road
Tel: 01 252 987; mayshan.com
Just a stone's throw away from Sule Pagoda and City Hall, this family-run guesthouse couldn't be more central. The single rooms are pokey and windowless, but the rest are pleasant enough, and the air-con is effective. Free wi-fi in the lobby. Breakfast included in the room rates. **$$**

Panorama
No.294-300, Pansodan Street, Kyauktada Township
Tel: 01 253 077; panoramaygn.com
This aptly named, 10-storey tower block has great views over the downtown district from its comfortably furnished rooms. You don't get much space, but the beds are large and have fabulously thick mattresses, and there's a restaurant on site serving good-value buffet meals. **$$$**

Savoy
129 Dhammazedi (near Shwedagon Pagoda)
Tel: 01 526 289; www.savoy-myanmar.com
Offering all the old-fashioned charm of the Strand but at a fraction of the price, the Savoy occupies a genteel colonial-era building close to the Shwedagon Pagoda, with an airy raised verandah overlooking a small courtyard pool. The furnishings are in-period, the bathrooms sumptuous and staff unfailingly helpful. The most agreeable boutique option in the city. **$$$$–$$$$$**

Sedona Hotel
1 Kaba Aye Pagoda Road (near Inya Lake)
Tel: 01 666 900; www.sedonahotels.com
This anodyne, gigantic, Singaporean-owned chain hotel is popular mainly with visiting businessmen and tour groups. The location's handy for the airport, but less so for the sights. A huge outdoor pool is its greatest asset. **$$$$**

PRICE GUIDE

Prices are for a double room in high season.
$$$$$ = over US$200
$$$$ = US$120-200
$$$ = US$70-120
$$ = US$30-70
$ = under US$30

Strand
92 Strand Road
Tel: 01 243 377; www.ghmhotels.com
Unquestionably the city's premier hotel, often mentioned in the same breath as Raffles of Singapore, though not everyone thinks it lives up to its sky-high room rates. Originally built in 1903 by the Sarkies brothers, the property hosted the likes of Somerset Maugham, Noël Coward and Rudyard Kipling in its heyday, but slipped into disrepair before undergoing a massive overhaul ahead of a gala re-opening in 1995. With its whitewashed, colonnaded facade, polished teakwood, marble floors and antique-filled interiors, it has fin-de-siècle splendour in abundance – though there's no pool. The current owners have close ties to the military and remain subject to EU and Australian sanctions. **$$$$$**

Summit Parkview
350 Ahlone Road
Tel: 01 211 888; www.summityangon.com

One of the first modern hotels in Yangon, and still a popular option with business visitors, as well as tourists in transit. Facilities include a good-sized outdoor pool, health club, coffee shop and a shopping arcade. Ask for a room in the west wing as it has terrific views of the nearby Shwedagon Pagoda. **$$$**

Three Seasons Hotel
83/85 52nd Street
Tel: 01 293 304; Email: phyaung@mptmal.net.mm
Simple, welcoming, family-run B&B located in a quiet suburban street close to the sights. All rooms are air-conditioned and have a fridge. Superb *mohinga* breakfasts served in second-storey dining hall. $10 airport pick-up by arrangement. **$–$$**

Traders
223 Sule Pagoda Road
Tel: 01 242 828; www.shangri-la.com
This towering five-star is a good choice if you want to be in the thick of the action downtown. Fully refurbished in 2012, its rooms boast superb views of

the city skyline and river. Facilities are what you'd expect of an international five-star, including a snazzy curvi-form pool. **$$$$**

YMCA
263 Mahabanoola St, PO 11161, Botataung Township
Tel: 01 380 856
Plainly furnished but impeccably clean, sunny doubles with air-con and well-scrubbed bathrooms, or cheaper non-air-con doubles. Most look over an adjacent park. A great-value budget choice, but you'll need to book well in advance. **$–$$**

Yoma Hotel
146 Bogyoke Aung San Street
Tel: 01 299 243
Popular with local commercial travellers, this small hotel lays on free transfers from the airport – handy if you arrive at an unsociable hour. It's efficiently run and the rooms, though basic, are clean and comfortable, and offer good value for money. **$$**

DELTA REGION

PATHEIN (BASSEIN)

Accommodation options are limited in Pathein, and most travellers only spend the day here in transit, continuing on to the beach resorts further west after a round of the parasol workshops and monuments.

La Paye Wun
30 Mingyi Street
Tel: 042 25151
The best place in town, with five spacious tiled rooms ranged over five floors in a modern white building a couple of blocks east of the river. The slightly pricier options on the upper two floors are larger and worth the extra. **$–$$**

Taan Taan Ta
7 Merchant Street
Tel: 042 24502
The pick of a ropey budget bunch offering mostly windowless cells, with some larger en-suite, air-con doubles. Don't be tempted by the owner's overpriced beach tours and just travel by bus – the journey there is pleasantly brief. **$**

CHAUNGTHA

Belle Resort
Chaungtha
Tel: 042 42113; belleresorts.com
Ritzy new, international-grade resort set right behind the beach, with traditional gable-roofed buildings and a good-sized pool amid manicured lawns and palms. The rooms

are beautifully furnished in Thai boutique style, and open on to breezy verandahs. **$$$**

Shwe Hin Tha
Chaungtha
Tel: 042 42118
Well-run budget travellers' guesthouse at the quiet north end of the beach, offering a choice of standard rooms or funkier little bungalows. Not as pretty as its sister concern in Ngwe Saung, but a dependable option nonetheless. **$–$$**

Shwe Ya Minn
Chaungtha
Tel: 042 42127
A friendly, efficiently run guesthouse on the road running behind the beach, popular mainly with foreign backpackers. The tiled rooms, in well-shaded single-storey concrete blocks with tiled roofs, are nicely maintained and close to the sand. English spoken and the staff are helpful. The only downside is it lies a 20–30-min walk from the village. **$**

NGWE SAUNG

Ambo
Ngwe Saung.
Book through Yangon office at the Ambo Hotel, Saya San Rd, Bahah township
Tel: 01 548 526 (Yangon); amboco.com
A budget resort, but a very comfortable and well-situated one, only 10 mins on foot from the village. You have a choice of differently sized rooms –

the biggest ones are large enough to accommodate families. All have pleasant wood floors, fans, fridges and sea views from their balconies. **$$**

Bay of Bengal
North side, Ngwe Saung
Tel: 01 667 024 (Yangon); bayofbengalresort.com
This gorgeous designer resort at the north end of the beach is the perfect place for a wind down. Its bungalows are spacious, breezy and beautifully styled with exposed-stone walls and rich, dark tropical wood floors running to huge verandahs (garden or sea-facing). The pool is huge, the staff enthusiastic and location spot-on. **$$$$–$$$$$**

Emerald Sea
South side, Ngwe Saung
Tel: 042 40394; emeraldseahotel.com
Small beach-side resort offering good value for money. Its bungalows come in four grades but are all pleasantly styled and furnished, and provide plenty of privacy. There's a generous-sized pool and restaurant specialising in fresh seafood, plus a spa and massage room. **$$$**

Shwe Hin Tha
North side, Ngwe Saung
Tel: 042 40340
Budget rooms or delightful sea-facing bungalows, with palm-lined walls, chunky wood beds, thick mattresses and colourful bedspreads, ranged around a palm grove right next to the

sands. Easily the best-value place in the resort. **$$**
Sunny Paradise
North side, Ngwe Saung
Tel: 042 40227; sunnyparadiseresort.net

International-grade complex offering formulaic comforts, from ocean-facing bungalows to a curvi-form pool overlooking the beach. The rooms, offered in a dozen different

categories, are mostly in double-storeyed blocks attractively designed in traditional Burmese style. **$$$$–$$$$$**

BAGO DIVISION

BAGO

With Yangon only a little over an hour away by road, there's no real reason to spend a night in Bago – you can easily visit the town in a half day en route to Kyaiktiyo. The main disincentive, however, is that its hotels are uniformly downbeat and grubby.
Bago Star
Kyaikpun Pagoda Road, Oatha Myothit
Tel: 052 23766
Though not much of an accolade, this is the ritziest place to sleep in Bago, hence its inflated room rates. Accommodation comes in high-pitched wooden bungalows, crammed together in a leafy garden, but without outside space. Inside, they're dingy and not all that spacious, and the air-con units are noisy. Don't even think about a dip in the murky hotel pool. **$$**
Emperor
8/2 Min Street
Tel: 052 21349
Pick of the budget bunch – better maintained than the competition and with fine views from its rooftop of the

city's pagoda-studded skyline. **$**

TAUNGOO
Myanmar Beauty II, III & IV
Pauk Kla Gyi Street
Tel: 054 21270
Welcoming guesthouse on the edge of town offering three categories of rooms. Go for a "IV" if one's free: they have lovely wooden interiors and views from their deep, old-fashioned verandahs over open rice fields and fruit orchards. Jungle trips are offered to watch working elephants. And the breakfasts are superb. Note that Guest House I in town is nowhere near as appealing. **$–$$**
Royal Kaytumadi
Royal Kaytumadi Street
Tel: 054 24761; kmahotels.com
This extravagant Burmese palace-themed resort hotel on the lakeshore ranks among the classiest mid-range places in the country. The rooms are spacious and equipped with modern amenities, and the location is a delight. **$$$**

PYAY
Lucky Dragon
772 Strand Road, Sandaw Quarter
Tel: 053 24222; luckydragonhotel.com
This is a modern, efficiently run resort on the peaceful far side of the river, with smart, spacious bungalows. White walls and dark-wood floors set the tone of the stylish interiors, and there's a great little pool with a Jacuzzi enclosure. The perfect base from which to visit the nearby ancient ruins, and excellent value. **$$**
Mingalar Garden Resort
Flying Tiger Garden, Aung Chan Thar Quarter, Near Phayagyi Pagoda
Tel: 053 28661; mingalargarden.com
This small-scale resort on the outskirts of town consists of semi-detached, teak-floored bungalows ranged around an artificial lake. They come in three styles: Burmese; Japanese; or European; and are fitted with modern air-con units. There's a quality restaurant on site, and the option of dining on a romantic floating platform. **$$**

MANDALAY & ENVIRONS

MANDALAY
Ayeyarwady River View
Strand Road, between 22nd and 23rd streets, Thirimalarlar West, Aung Myay Thar Zan Township
Tel: 02 72373
Modern, multistorey hotel on the edge of the city facing, as its name implies, the river (though there's a shanty town between it and the water's edge). Pitched primarily at Chinese businessmen and tour groups, but with good discounts for walk-ins. **$$$**
Hotel by the Red Canal
417, corner of 63rd & 22nd roads, Aung Myae Tha Zan Township
Tel: 02 68543; hotelredcanal.com
This should be your first choice in Mandalay if you can afford it. One of only a handful of true boutique hotels in Myanmar, it fuses regal Konbaung tradition with modern designer chic. Rooms come in four categories, set in cultural styles of Myanmar's main ethnic groups. The location, just east of the Palace complex, is tranquil, and

there's a relaxing kidney-shaped pool to lounge by when the heat gets too much. **$$$$**
Mandalay City
26th Street, between 82nd and 83rd Street, Chanayetharzan Township
Tel: 02 61700; mandalaycityhotel.com
Set in a secret garden away from the brouhaha of downtown Mandalay, the City is a relaxing, good-value haven that allows you to be in the thick of the action but not be bothered by the bustle of big streets (although the call to prayer from the mosque to the rear can wake you at 4am). Its 12-metre (40ft) pool is a welcome heat beater; the rooms are plain, but clean and spacious. **$$–$$$**
Mandalay Hill Resort
9 Kwin (416B), 10th Street
Tel: 02 35638; mandalayhillresort.com.mm
Sparkling Thai-owned resort hotel at the foot of Mandalay Hill, built in royal Burmese style, with multi-tiered pagoda roofs and antique brass *chinthe* grinning from the

terraces. Once inside it's a rather less distinctive, international-style four-star, whose trimmings include a large pool, fitness centre, tennis court and spa. **$$$$–$$$$$**
Peacock Lodge
5, 61st Street
Tel: 02 33411; peacocklodge.com
This is much the best budget guesthouse in the city – both for the size and cleanliness of its rooms, and warm hospitality of its hosts. Good-value breakfasts and dinners are served in their garden restaurant under mature mango trees, and the friendly owners are on hand to help advise with travel plans and sightseeing arrangements. **$–$$**

PRICE GUIDE
Prices are for a double room in high season.
$$$$$ = over US$200
$$$$ = US$120-200
$$$ = US$70-120
$$ = US$30-70
$ = under US$30

Queen
456, 81st Street, Between 32nd & 33rd
Street, Chan Aye Thar Zan Township
Tel: 02 39805; hotelqueenmandalay.com
Dependable mid-scale option offering
four categories of room in a 7-storey
tower block at the southwest edge
of the city. The location's not great
(you'll need to jump in a cab to get to
the sights), but the rooms are clean,
comfortable and spacious, and the
breakfasts terrific. Complimentary
internet in the lobby. **$$**
Royal Guest House
41, 25th Street
Tel: 02 31400
Best of the rock-bottom options: comfy

beds in clean (but cramped) rooms,
decent breakfasts and a cool rooftop
terrace with sunset views. **$**
Rupar Mandalar
A-15, Corner of 53rd & 30th Street, Chan
Aye Thar Zan Township
Tel: 02 61555; ruparmandalar.com
Gorgeous boutique resort on
the eastern outskirts of the city,
comprising 20 teak-lined bungalows
grouped around a lovely pool. Ruby-
coloured silk drapes and vases of
fresh flowers offset the dark-wood
interiors, and the place is crammed
with beautiful arts and crafts. Top-
notch facilities include a spa, tennis
court, fitness room and Jacuzzi –

though such luxury comes with a hefty
price tag. **$$$$$**
Sedona Mandalay
Corner of 26th and 66th streets,
Chanayetharzan Township
Tel: 02 36488; sedonahotels.com.sg
This Singaporean-owned four-star
occupies a prime position overlooking
the Royal Palace's eastern moat –
the views from its pricier upper-floor
rooms over the water to Mandalay
Hill are magnificent. The fittings and
furniture of its standard rooms fail to
live up to the pink-marble grandeur
of the lobby, but they're a good size
and the hotel as a whole delivers the
essentials. **$$$$**

AROUND MANDALAY

MONYWA

Shwe Taung Tarn
No.70 Yonegyi Quarter
Tel: 071 21478
The only budget guesthouse in
Monywa worthy of note. Its rooms
range from basic to grubby (ask for one
in the newer garden blocks to the rear
and you may get away without betel-
stained walls and rank carpets), but
they rustle up a better-than-average
fruit salad breakfast. **$**
Win Unity
Yone Kyi Or, Bogyoke Road
Tel: 071 22438; winunityhotel.com
A campus of recently built red-tiled
chalets in the style of a 1960s motel at
a quiet spot on the lakeside. What the
rooms lack in character they make up
for in cleanliness, and the large, well-
maintained pool, set in landscaped
gardens, is a real plus. Good value. **$$**

PYIN U-LWIN (MAYMYO)

Aureum Governor's House
Ward 6 Governor's Hill, Mandalay-Lashio
Highway
Tel: 085 21901; aureumpalacehotel.com
This sumptuous re-creation of the
original governor's residence stands
among Myanmar's grandest buildings,
complete with wood-panelled walls
and a colonial-style verandah wrapped
around the building. Only five guest
rooms occupy the main house; the rest
are in more run-of-the-mill bungalows
dotted through the grounds. The only
catch: it's owned by a Burmese tycoon
with close links to the former military
dictatorship. **$$$–$$$$$**
Grace 1
114A Nan Myaing Road
Tel: 085 21230
Good-value rooms with high ceilings,
bathtubs, TV and fans in a deservedly
popular budget guesthouse. Quite far

from the town centre, but transfers can
be arranged free of charge. Room rate
includes breakfast. Recommended for
families as the garden is large enough
to run around in – though some of the
rooms are very worn. **$**
Kandawgyi Hill Resort
Nandar Road
Tel: 085 21839
An affordable, downmarket version
of the Aureum Governor's House this
early 1920s mansion is a classic
throwback to British times, with a
verandah surveying flower-filled
gardens. Like its grander sibling, the
resort offers a few rooms in the main
building or chalets in the grounds.
And it's well placed for the National
Botanical Gardens. **$$$**
Pyin Oo Lwin
9 Nandar Road
Tel: 85 21226; hotelpyinoolwin.com
Opened only in April 2011 and
within easy walking distance of the
Botanical Gardens, the Pyin Oo Lwin
looks set to become the town's most
popular hotel. Its 20 red-tiled, lavishly
furnished chalets are all done out
in teak and arranged in landscaped
gardens. They've also got fireplaces –
a godsend on chilly winter evenings.
$$$–$$$$
Win Unity
8 Nandar Road
Tel: 085 23079
The best alternative if the nearby
Pyin Oo Lwin is fully booked, though
it's far less ritzy. The rooms are also
more simply furnished in pine, but
impeccably clean. **$$**

MEIKTILA

Honey
Panchan Street
Tel: 064 23588
This yellow-painted former colonial

residence on the lakeshore is
Meiktila's most commendable place
to stay. It offers large, air-con, en-suite
rooms with lake or garden views –
some have squat rather than Western
toilets. Rates include breakfast, served
on a gazebo overlooking the water.
$–$$
Wunzin
49A Than Lwin Road
Tel: 064 23559
You also get lake views from this
ex-government-run place, which is
the best fallback if the Honey has no
vacancies. All but a handful of its 30
rooms and suites, ranged in a double-
storey block set back from the water's
edge, come with air conditioning. Bring
plenty of mosquito repellent. **$–$$**

NAYPYIDAW

Pending the completion of a second
economy "Hotel Zone" in Naypyidaw,
budget accommodation is non-
existent, although the two places listed
below offer 50 percent discounts to
their rack rates if there are no official
delegations or parliament sessions in
progress.
Aureum Palace
Hotel No.1, Hotel Zone
Tel: 067 420 706
Pitched at visiting businessmen and
government cronies, the Aureum
is the capital's premier hotel. It's
owned by Tay Zay, one of Myanmar's
most notorious tycoons, whose
business empire is backed by the
junta. The rooms, dotted around the
shores of a pear-shaped artificial
lake, come in several categories,
and most have teak furnishings and
floors – though they're otherwise
lacking Burmese character. There's
a pool, spa and fitness centre.
$$$–$$$$$

Royal Kamudra

Hotel 10, Hotel Zone
Tel: 067 420 760; maxhotelsmyanmar.com/royalkamudra
This newly built five-star looked bleak and unfinished when we called but should be a lot easier on the eye when the trees and vegetation grow. Set in 30 acres of grounds, its executive rooms, suites and villas are palatial and luxuriously furnished. Facilities include a spa, fitness room and huge pool. Owned by a firm with links to the regime. **$$$–$$$$$**

BAGAN REGION

Accommodation close to the archaeological zone is divided between three main areas. Old Bagan is closest to the principal temples and riverfront; most of its hotels are pricey, high-end places patronised by tour groups. Further south, Bagan Myothit (New Bagan) offers the widest selection of mid-range places. Budget travellers, meanwhile, tend to congregate in Nyaung U, the site's modern service town, which has less character but offers the best value for money in the lower brackets. The following selection avoids all places with links to the military regime.

Gardens at the Tharabar Gate hotel

OLD BAGAN

Aye Yar River View

Nr Bupaya Pagoda
Tel: 061 60352; baganayeyarhotel.com
True to its name, this long-established resort, which recently underwent a major refit, occupies a prime position on the river bank. The richly furnished rooms enjoy sweeping vistas over the waterfront or the temples, and it's well placed for sightseeing. Puppet and music shows offer distractions in the evenings, or you can swim in the lovely curvi-form pool. **$$$$**

Hotel @ Tharabar Gate

Nr Tharabar Gate, Old Bagan
Tel: 061 60037; tharabargate.com
Swathed in lush greenery, the Tharabar is a relaxing oasis away from the heat and dust of the temple trail, but within easy walking distance of some of the best sunrise and sunset points. Its 84 rooms and suites in traditional-style brick and thatch bungalows, with teakwood floors and verandahs, are beautifully furnished in traditional Burmese art and crafts. The gardens are filled with scented flowers and the pool's well kept. **$$$$**

Thande

Old Bagan
Tel: 061 60025; hotelbaganthande.com
Built for the Prince of Wales' visit

in 1922, the main building in this characterful riverfront resort is the only colonial-era residence of note in Bagan, and its position right on the waterfront is hard to beat. Go for one of their teak-lined deluxe rooms for the best river views. There's a good-sized pool and restaurant. Amazing value considering the location. **$$**

Thiripyitsaya Sanctuary

Old Bagan
Tel: 061 60048; thiripyitsaya-resort.com
Smart resort comprising an open-frame reception area leading to a dining terrace with tables facing an enormous pool. The "standard" rooms are plain and a little worn looking, but serviceable. Book one of their lovely suites and you'll be able to savour the sunsets from your own private verandah. **$$$$–$$$$$**

BAGAN MYOTHIT (NEW BAGAN)

Arthawka

160 Cherry Road, New Bagan
Tel: 061 65321
Large, good-value rooms with wood floors and white walls, ranged on two storeys around a central salt-water pool. The bathrooms are a bit run-down, but the friendliness of the staff is ample compensation. Scheduled for renovation in 2012–2013. **$$**

Kaday Aung

Hninn Pann Street, Hteeminyin Block, Kyansittha Quarter, New Bagan
Tel: 061 65070; baganhotel.com
If their rates are maintained through the boom of the coming years, this place will offer unbeatable value in the mid-range bracket. Scattered under tamarind trees around a trefoil-shaped pool, its rooms, designed like elevated huts in local brick, are secluded and quiet, with polished wood and rattan interiors. In the cheaper "standard"

options the beds are on the floor. All have air-con and outside space. **$–$$**

Kumudara

Corner of 5th & Daw Na Street, Pyu-Saw-Htee Qtr, New Bagan
Tel: 061 061 65402; kumudara-bagan.com
Impeccably well-run mid-scale hotel boasting a pool, restaurant and fine views over the archaeological site. You can swim while enjoying the sunset light on the pagodas. **$$–$$$**

Thazin Garden

New Bagan
Tel: 061 65044; thazingarden.com
Three classes of room, all tastefully decked out in high Burmese style with teak floors, gorgeous handicrafts on the walls and private verandahs, are available at this low-key resort. Set amid palms and greenery on the site's southern outskirts, there's a lovely pool, and candlelit dinners are served on the lawn next to a crumbling 13th-century pagoda. **$$$**

Thiri Marlar

Thiri Marlar Street
Tel: 061 65050; bagan-thirimarlar-hotel.com
You won't find a better-run, better-value budget place to stay in Bagan than the Thiri Marlar. With their varnished wood floors, comfy beds and neatly tiled bathrooms, the rooms are immaculate and relaxing. Breakfast is served on a wonderful roof terrace with views of the distant temples. Bike rental and internet are also on offer. You can even book online. **$$**

PRICE GUIDE

Prices are for a double room in high season.
$$$$$ = over US$200
$$$$ = US$120-200
$$$ = US$70-120
$$ = US$30-70
$ = under US$30

Amazing Bagan
Golf Course
Tel: 061 60035; bagangolfresort.net
Off the main drag at the end of a long, tree-lined avenue next to the golf course, this quiet resort has three kinds of rooms in its pagoda-roofed main block, and more tranquil, brick bungalow-style apartments dotted around the grounds. The pool is one of the largest and best maintained in the area. **$$$**

Golden Express
Midway between Old Bagan and Nyaung U, near Htilominio Temple
Tel: 01 226 779 (Yangon); goldenexpresstours.com
Clean, functional, reasonably sized rooms in an atmospheric location deep in the archaeological zone. There's a small pool and garden terrace, where you enjoy breakfast as hot-air balloons drift overhead (the hotel's next to the launch site). Plain, but great value. **$–$$**

New Park
Tel: 061 60322; newparkmyanmar.com
Popular backpacker guesthouse down a side street off the main drag. The lower class of rooms are dingy, but the superior ones have hardwood floors, air con, hot water and sitting areas out front facing a central lawn. Best value in this bracket. **$**

Thante
Anawrahta Rd
Tel: 061 60315; Email: nyaunguthante@gmail.com
This is a reliable mid-price option, handily situated a short walk from the market, just off the main road. The large, clean rooms are arranged in blocks of four around a good-sized central pool and well-kept garden – you can float on your back and watch the squirrels chase blue-headed lizards through the palm trees. There's even a bakery and ice-cream parlour on site. **$$**

Popa Mountain Resort
Tel: 062 69169; myanmartreasureresorts.com
Luxurious mountain boutique retreat set in National Park boasting fabulous views of the Taungzalat Monastery. Forget the scruffy standard rooms, which open onto woodland, and splash out on one of the superior hardwood bungalows, whose verandahs have the best of the panoramic vistas. Facilities include a small but refreshing infinity pool, terrace restaurant and bar. The resort also offers activities including trekking, horse riding and birdwatching – though it's owned by a high-ranking associate of the former military regime. **$$$**

SHAN & KAYAH STATES

Accommodation is abundant around Inle Lake, especially at the upper end of the scale. A string of glamorous boutique resorts and five-stars, complete with stilted cabins or traditional Burmese-style bungalows opening on the lawned gardens, line the northeast and northwestern shore. Budget travellers, meanwhile, congregate in more functional, affordable guesthouses in the nearby town of Nyanghshwe, just inland but only a short boat ride away from the open water.

Golden Island Cottages
Nampan
Tel: 081 29390; gicmyanmar.com
This was the original stilted resort on the lake, and it enjoys a location that's perfect for sunrise views over the adjacent floating village. The rooms are a decent size and most have outdoor sitting space, but they're otherwise plain by comparison with the more modern competition. There's a restaurant and bar. **$$$$**

Inle Lake View Resort & Spa
Kaung Daing
Tel: 081 23656; inlelakeview.com
Ultra-stylish rooms set in 24 acres of well-watered grounds on the western shores of the lake. Rich, dark teakwoods and silk dominate the luminous interiors. Premium Lake Side villas have rain showers and their own petal-strewn bathtubs. Ingredients from the resort's own organic gardens dominate the Pan-Asian menu of the restaurant. **$$$$–$$$$$**

Inle Princess
Magyizin Village
Tel: 081 29055
The beautiful wood and terracotta architecture of this exquisite resort on the eastern shore of the lake fuses local Shan and Intha style with contemporary boutique chic: polished teak walls and floors; jade ceramic tiling; and pebble-lined open-to-sky showers. Laze on the deck of your own spacious villa, enjoying uninterrupted sunset views across the water, while you look forward to a herbal massage in the spa. **$$$$–$$$$$**

Inle Resort
Magyizin Village
Tel: 09 515 4444/521 1888 (mobile); inleresort.com
Another dreamy boutique resort, with traditionally styled chalets opening on to the water. Next door to the Inle Princess at the northeast corner of the lake, it has the feel of a Burmese palace thanks to the extravagant tiered roofs rising above its pillared dining hall. The spa here is especially lovely. **$$$$–$$$$$**

May
85 Myawaddy Road, Nyaungshwe
Tel: 081 209 417
Clean, comfortable twin-bedded rooms in a great little budget guesthouse run by a warm couple close to the town centre. The location's peaceful for most of the day and night, though expect to be woken at 6am by chanting monks if you forget your earplugs. Breakfast is served on a sunny terrace. **$**

Myanmar Treasure Resort
Maing Thauk Village
Tel: 01 399 334 (Yangon)
myanmartreasureresorts.com
The only hotel on Inle still blacklisted, because it's owned by a close affiliate of the military junta, which is a pity because the place is fabulous, with its own organic gardens, lotus ponds and gorgeous stilted chalets facing the lake. **$$$$$**

Princess Garden
Mine Li Street, Nyaungshwe
Tel: 081 209214
Outstandingly pleasant guesthouse in a rural setting on the edge of town. Its modern bungalows have verandahs facing the canal and rice fields. The pool's a major attraction, as is the unfailing hospitality of the hosts and staff. Complementary drinks in the afternoon, free bikes, and bargain rates. **$$**

Pristine Lotus
Khaung Daing
Tel: 081 209317; pristinelotus.com
The newest of the Inle's spa resorts is a veritable lakeside paradise. Hot springs supply the split-level wooden chalets, fitted with spiral staircases leading to a mezzanine deck where you can unwind after boat trips. Vibrant coral-, purple- and lemon-coloured silk complement the rich teak and whitewash colour schemes. The Balinese-style spa has Jacuzzis set into natural rock; and the gourmet restaurant is a breezy, relaxing place to dine. **$$$$$**

KALAW

Amara Mountain Resort
10/182 Wingabar Street, Kalaw
Tel: 01 652191 (Yangon); amaragroup.net
Pinch yourself and you could be in the Home Counties of England. Dating from 1909, the Amara's half-timbered houses have been lovingly restored and now hold 10 light, airy rooms with four-posters and open fires, set around a central lobby and pool at a wonderfully elevated spot above the valley. Birdwatching trips, mountain biking and a round on the 9-hole golf course are optional extras. **$$$**

Eastern Paradise
5 Thirimingalar St, Kalaw
Tel:081 /50315
Lovely family-run guest house: clean, balconies with hill views, and great breakfasts including Burmese doughnut and sticky rice with a pot of proper tea. **$**

Golden Kalaw Inn
64 Natsin Street, Mineli Quarter
081 50185/50311
A welcoming little budget guesthouse offering very cheap rooms that open on to a lovely common verandah overlooking the town (great for sunsets). The couple who run it also arrange dependable, good-value trekking trips in the area; and their cooked breakfasts are copious. All in all, a much better option than the dodgy Golden Lily next door. **$**

Hilltop Villa
Ward 3, Bogon
Tel: 081 50346; Email: superworld@mptmail.net.mm
Attractive pine-lined bungalows in a delightful setting with fabulous views of the Shan Hills from their west-facing balconies. The restaurant is not impressive, however. Long flights of steep steps lead through the gardens to the rooms. Close to the train station. **$$–$$$**

Pine Hill Resort
151 Oo Min Road, Kalaw
Tel: 01 548 109/240 853; Email: Pinehill@myanmar.com.mm
Plenty of old-world atmosphere lingers in this characterful hotel on the outskirts of Kalaw, 10 minutes' walk from the town centre. Comprising wood and stone chalets scattered amid well-tended gardens around a central colonial-era house, the rooms are large and have relaxing verandahs looking on to the lawns. Restaurant and bar on site. **$$**

HSIPAW

Mr Charles
105 Auba Street
Tel: 082 80105
This long-established guesthouse on the north side of the town is the backpacker hub for the region's trekking scene, and virtually every budget traveller who sets foot in Hsipaw makes a beeline for it. The eponymous owner offers a choice of variously priced rooms, from cells with hard beds, thick partition walls and shared toilets to fully en-suite with thicker mattresses and balconies. Eggs-to-order breakfasts are served in the yard-cum-driveway. Cycle hire; internet café; tours and treks organised. There are plenty of places to eat nearby. **$**

KENGTUNG

New Kyaing Tong
Mineyan Road
Tel: 084 21323
Recently built three-storey government-owned place on the hillside above town looking across at the pagoda and lake. Its 108 rooms come in three categories; all have bathrooms with showers, minibars and air-con. And there's a so-so outdoor pool. **$$**

Princess
21 Zay Dan Kalay Road
Tel: 084 21319
The most comfortable hotel in this Golden Triangle town, with modest but clean rooms and décor that's as quirky as the owner (pictures of Paris?). Electricity is intermittent, but they have a generator. The location is ideal for early-morning trips to the market. **$$**

Private Hotel
5 Airport Road
Tel: 084 21438
Comfortable one-storey hotel near the airport, located on a quiet avenue within walking distance of the town centre. **$$**

Sam Yweat
Kyaing Lan 1 Road & Kyaing Lan 4 Road
Tel: 084 21235
Colourfully painted, if otherwise spartan, rooms with big windows and flat-screen TVs. Fine for a couple of nights if you're out trekking all day. **$**

PINDAYA

Conqueror
Singong Quarter
Tel: 01 448 1211 (Yangon)
www.conquerorresort.com
Stylish resort hotel at the foot of the caves, comprising luxury split-level suites made of hardwood or less pricey bamboo stilt "huts" scattered in well tended gardens around a central restaurant and pool. Each has a fireplace and verandah. The restaurant serves Shan and Burmese food. **$$$**

Golden Cave Hotel
Shwe Oo Min Pagoda Street
Tel: 081 66166; goldencavehotel.com
This modest hotel close to the entrance to the caves has clean, comfortable rooms with balconies facing the hill, or more spartan "standard" ones. All have hot water, but only their "superiors" are equipped with TVs, fans and minibars. **$–$$**

Pindaya Inle Inn
Mahabandoola Street
Tel: 081 66029; pindayainleininn.com
Wood-and-bamboo-thatch or brick-built chalets, set amid manicured landscaped gardens. Light, airy, glass-walled restaurant with al fresco dining terrace and lakeviews. Close to the caves. **$$**

LASHIO

Lashio Motel
No.1 Quarter, Railway Station Road
Tel: 082 21702
A popular option with visiting foreign tour groups, this large motel is well placed for the early-morning produce market. The rooms are all air-con, spacious, with mini-bars and views over the city. The restaurant's no great shakes, but there are plenty of alternatives in the area. **$–$$**

KACHIN STATE

MYITKYINA

United
38 Thit Sat Street
Tel: 074 22085
You're not exactly spoilt for choice when it comes to accommodation in Myitkyina, and this Chinese-style hotel is just about the best option. Rooms are basic but comfortable enough for a night in transit, and there are plenty of local restaurants nearby. **$$**

BHAMO

Friendship

PRICE GUIDE

Prices are for a double room in high season.
$$$$$ = over US$200
$$$$ = US$120-200
$$$ = US$70-120
$$ = US$30-70
$ = under US$30

Letwet Thondaya Road
Tel: 074 50095
The better value of Bhamo's two hotels makes a pleasant stopover if you're travelling up or down-river on the slow boat. Its rooms are spacious and have sitting areas, tea- and coffee-making facilities and clean bathrooms. Everything's spick and span and the management speaks English. **$**

Grand
Post Office Road
Tel: 074 50317
There's nothing grand about this modern Chinese-style place beyond the tinted glass in its lobby, but it's the best fallback if the Friendship is fully booked. **$**

Malikha Lodge
Mulashidi Village, Putao
Tel: 09 860 0659/ 840 1065; malikhalodge.net
This exclusive boutique hideaway often proves the highlight of luxury trips to Myanmar. Hidden deep in the jungle overlooking a river, with glimpses through the giant bamboo forest of distant snow peaks, each of its massive designer bungalows is centred on a teak hot tub and cosy woodburner. The vibe is one of a posh house party, with gourmet food and butler service, and whitewater rafting and trekking trips to fill the days. Alas, it's

phenomenally pricey, and owned by one of the arch-cronies of the military junta – thus still subject to sanctions. **$$$$$**

Putao Trekking House
No.424/425, Htwe San lane, Kaung Kahtaung, Putao
Tel: 09 8400138; putaotrekkinghouse.com
The mid-scale alternative to Malikha Lodge is a lovely teak-built hotel with immaculate wood-lined rooms. As the name implies, they're hiking specialists and nearly everyone arranges packages to include treks of varying lengths. Bookings and permits have to be sorted in advance through local travel agents. **$$$$**

RAKHAING & CHIN

Mya Guest House
51/6 Bowdhi Street
Tel: 043 22358
In an annexe tacked on to a colonial-era building, the rooms in the Mya are large and clean; tasty breakfasts are served in an alfresco dining area. **$$**

Noble
45 Main Road
Tel: 043 23558
Generally grubby, cramped rooms with pillows like bricks and musty bathrooms, but the rates are low for Sittwe and staff unfailingly polite and helpful. Fine for a night. **$$**

Shwe Thazin
Main Road
Tel: 043 23579; shwethazinhotel.com
The most commendable transit stop in Sittwe, though that's not saying much. Passably clean rooms, with OK beds

Ngapali beach

and bathrooms; indifferent service. Not a patch on its namesake in Mrauk U. **$$**

Mrauk Oo Princess
Aungdat Creek
Tel: 043 50232; mraukooprincessresort.net
The village's most luxurious accommodation, favoured by visiting high-end tour groups. Its 21 stylishly designed and furnished wooden villas, conceived in regal Arakan style, are dotted around lush gardens and lily ponds, and enjoy views over the rice paddy to distant blue hills. There's a spa but no pool. Rates cover full board. **$$$$$**

Nawarat
Tel: 043 24200 ext 50257
Close to Shittaung Pagoda, the Nawarat is a well-run motel-style

place offering simple, clean rooms with decent beds, hot water and … Manchester United bathmats. The staff are friendly and breakfast is included in the price. **$$–$$$**

Prince
Tel: 043 24200, ext 50174; mraukuprincehotel.com
A hot contender for "Myanmar's Best Budget Guest House", this family-run place on the edge of town gets rave reviews from travellers for its beautiful, leafy garden setting, welcoming hosts and romantic wood-floored chalet rooms, which have high ceilings and piping-hot water. The home-cooked food is terrific too, and the owners run tours to the Chin villages upriver. Breakfast is included in the room rate. **$**

Shwe Thazin
Sunshaseik Quarter
Tel: 043 24200, ext 50168/50239; shwethazinhotel.com
Comprising a couple of dozen tastefully furnished wood cabanas ranged around a central restaurant, this is the best-value option in Mrauk-U, and a lot nicer than its namesake in Sittwe. The rooms are light and airy, with traditional textiles and woodcarvings lending a Burmese feel to the décor. Quality restaurant. No pool, but bargain rates for the level of comfort. **$$–$$$**

Amata Resort
Tel: 043 42177/01 665 126; amataresort.com
Stylish, double-storey wood cottages set in a garden right behind the beach. The rooms are gorgeous and reasonably priced for the level of luxury, but you may want to give the restaurant a miss; another gripe is that

they charge rip-off rates for cycle hire and other extras. **$$$$–$$$$$**

Amazing Ngapali
Tel: 043 42011; amazingngapaliresort.com
This resort of Arakan-styled two-storey villas scores highly among the package tour groups who make up most of its clientele for its boutique charm, breezy location and smiling staff. Some adore the wild location, on Ngapali's quieter north beach. Others find it too far from the main cluster of restaurants – a half-hour cycle ride south. **$$$–$$$$**

Bayview Beach Resort
Tel: 043 42299; bayview-myanmar.com

Arguably the hippest of the new resorts, Bayview offers minimalist European chic enlivened with splashes of Burmese silk and gilt. The garden bungalows are delightful, but you may as well splash out on a sea-facing one – worth the extra for the sunset views alone. Spa; watersports; day trips. **$$$$–$$$$$**

Sandoway Resort
Tel: 043 42244; sandowayresort.com
Constructed from local hardwoods, stone and marble, Sandoway's 57 villas and cottages occupy 500 metres/yds of prime beachfront, shaded by gently tilted palms and

flowering shrubs. The resort is part-Italian owned and is run to an extremely high standard. There's a huge pool, library, seafood restaurant and glam cocktail bar. **$$$$–$$$$$**

Yoma Cherry Lodge
Lintha Village
Tel: 043 42339; yomacherrylodge.com
Cosy, British-run boutique guesthouse with oodles of Arakan architectural charm, a well-tended beachside garden and sun terrace. Laundry service, wi-fi, cycle hire plus free airport transfers in a funky vintage Super Dodge coach. **$$–$$$**

MON, KAYIN STATE AND MYEIK

KYAIKTIYO

Golden Rock Hotel
Yathae Taung, Kyaiktiyo
On the slope of Mount Kyaiktiyo, about 1.2km (0.8 miles) from the top.
Tel: 057 70174
Wrapped in wild tropical greenery, this places enjoys a delightful position and has well-aired, spacious rooms with wooden floors and simple décor – some have great views of the Rock. The only catch is that it's a good hour from the summit, which means an early start to catch the sunrise. **$$**

Golden Sunrise
Kinpun
Tel: 01 701 027 (Yangon); goldensunrisehotel.com
In peak season, many visitors opt for accommodation down in Kinpun village, at the start of the official pilgrimage trail, where rooms are more plentiful and cheaper – in which case you won't do better than this lovely little Belgian-run hotel on the outskirts of town, whose elegantly furnished rooms look across leafy gardens and mango trees to the distant mountains. Everything's impeccably clean, and the staff courteous and efficient. **$$**

Mountain Top
Kyaiktiyo Mountain
Tel: 01 502 479 (Yangon)
You're a stone's throw from the Rock here and optimally placed for sunrise and sunset. The rooms are simply furnished but bright and clean. There's a lounge and restaurant and breezy terrace where guests can watch the pilgrims filing to and from the shrine. Bags of atmosphere, but by definition not the most peaceful of spots. **$$–$$$**

HPA-AN

Golden Sky
2 Thida Street
Tel: 058 21510

A recently built place near the riverfront pagoda and jetty whose main draw is the magical view through a huge picture window in the upstairs lounge area – a timeless vista of river, pagoda, karst mountains and paddy fields. **$–$$**

Soe Brothers
2/146 Thitsar Street
Tel: 058 21372
This modest guesthouse in the town centre is where most backpackers end up in Hpa-an. It's ultra-basic (shared bathrooms and toilets) but very cheap, well-scrubbed, welcoming and a good source of information on local trekking and sights. **$**

Zwegabin
Hpa-an–Mawlamyine Road
Tel: 058 22556.
Swanky motel on the outskirts of town boasting fine views across the surrounding paddy fields to the eponymous peak. Nicer than anywhere in the centre, though you'll need some form of transport to get around. **$$**

MAWLAMYINE (MOULMEIN)

Attran
Mandalay Ward
Tel: 057 25764/25765
Located on the banks of the Thanlwin River, the Attran consists of 30 attractively furnished bungalows, with large bathrooms. It's a perfect location for sunset views, which you enjoy from the fabulous teak terrace in front of the restaurant, or out on the water in the hotel launch. They also offer Burmese traditional massage and fishing pitches on request. You pay extra for the location and view here, but it's worth it. **$$–$$$**

Cinderella
21 Baho Road, Sitkei Gone Quarter

Tel: 057 24860; cinderellahotel.com
Recently refurbished mid-scale hotel near the park and GPO, offering 22 air-con rooms, wi-fi and 24-hr electricity (a real plus in this town). You can't miss the place: it's painted in powder purple. **$$–$$$**

Mawlamyaing Strand
Strand Road, Phat Tan Quarter, Mawlamyine.
Tel: 057 25624/24787; mawlamyaingstrandhotel.com
The town's top hotel, set back from the riverfront close to the main market area. Ranged over four floors, the rooms (all air-con with wi-fi) are spacious and good value, though lacking outside space. Only opened in 2012, so the furnishings are in good order. **$$–$$$**

MYEIK REGION

Andaman Club
Thahtay Kyun Island
Tel: 01 956 4354 (Yangon); andamanclub.com
Originally set up by the military dictatorship as a money-spinning casino resort for high-rolling Singaporeans and Malays, this once stylish hotel – the only one on the pristine Myeik Archipelago – is now under private management but has lapsed into a dire condition and is nothing like the luxury eco-lodge it bills itself as. The diving outfit is shoddy and food hit-and-miss. Overall, poor value for money, though the location can't be faulted. **$$$$$**

PRICE GUIDE

Prices are for a double room in high season.
$$$$$ = over US$200
$$$$ = US$120-200
$$$ = US$70-120
$$ = US$30-70
$ = under US$30

EATING OUT

RESTAURANTS

Perhaps because of the amount of oil that's used in its curries, Myanmar sometimes gets a bad press for its food, which is singularly undeserved. Sampling the country's distinctive hybrid cuisine – which fuses Indian, Chinese and Southeast Asian influences – actually proves among the highlights of any trip, even in more remote areas where you'll be limited to cooking that makes few concessions to Western taste buds.

Eating out in Myanmar

In most of the country's market towns and cities, the standard place to eat is a small, canteen-like restaurant where traditional Burmese curries and rice are the mainstays. Prepared early each morning, the dishes – which will include a few vegetarian options as well as meat and seafood – are typically displayed on a hot plate behind a glass screen, at the back of a no-frills, brick or cement-floored cafeteria. With the help of the staff, you simply indicate which main dish you'd like and they'll plate it up and bring it

Tea stall, Bogyoke market

to your table, along with a host of side dishes containing white rice, steamed vegetables, soup, dips, nuts, crunchy noodles, soy sauce and salt, to name but a few of the extras.

In such places, you'll rarely spend more than $7–8 per head for a filling meal. Stick to lunchtimes to reduce the risk of stomach upsets (although rarely re-heated the following day, the food tends to be kept warm until the evening, by which time it may have started to turn bad).

In the evenings, rough-and-ready, Chinese-style BBQ joints – *a'gin zein* – are the most common local eating option. The meats, seafood and vegetables are displayed on skewers; you select what you want and the cook will grill it in front of you while you wait, then serve it with a selection of side dishes, and maybe a cold beer if you're lucky.

Noodle shops are another Myanmar institution. Again, they tend to offer few frills, but the food will be fresh and tasty, and totally authentic.

Most Burmese teahouses also serve a range of light bites and snacks. While out on street corners of Mandalay and Yangon, you'll encounter innumerable stalls selling snacks such as samosas, Burmese pancakes – both sweet *(bein moun)* and savoury *(moun pyar thalet)* – and a range of delicious deep-fried bites served with dipping sauces. In addition, Indian and Chinese restaurants are numerous.

By far the widest choice of places to dine, however, is to be found in tourist destinations such as Bagan, Inle Lake and to a lesser extent Ngapali Beach, where dozens of small restaurants offer foreigner-oriented meals, from lighter, less spicy renditions of Burmese dishes to authentic stabs at Thai, Italian and French cuisine.

Here, you'll be presented with a menu, and table service is the norm. Bills are settled at the end in cash – only rarely are plastic cards accepted, and in such cases assume there will be a supplement of at least 4 percent added on as a transaction charge.

Tipping has become the norm in tourist restaurants if you've appreciated your service (see page 334) but not in regular Burmese places.

Drinks

Consumption of alcohol in general, and of beer in particular, is on the rise in Myanmar. Local brands of light lager such as "Myanmar Beer" and "Mandalay Beer" are ubiquitous, and in the resorts you'll be offered international brands brewed in Thailand, including San Miguel, Tiger and Singha. Neon-lit "beer stations", where local draught lagers are sold by the pitcher or glass, are the places most locals go for a tipple.

The country also produces some decent New-World-style wines these days, most of it grown in the Shan Hills around Pyin U Lwin (Maymo) and Taunggyi (near Inle Lake). Red Mountain (redmountain-estate.com), whose vineyard overlooks the shores of Inle Lake, is the stand-out estate: their Sauvignon Blanc has been particularly successful for the past few years. But the output from the nearby Myanmar Vineyard (Myanmar-vineyard. com) is not far behind.

As far as soft drinks go, you'll be spoilt for choice. Most proper restaurants offer freshly squeezed juice. Bottled water is available just about everywhere, though it is never strictly "mineral water" as it often says on the label. Always check the seal before opening.

YANGON

Thanks to the presence in the city of so many ethnic groups, the former capital offers by far the most diverse choice of places to eat in Myanmar, ranging from hole-in-the-wall noodle joints to Michelin-starred restaurants. With French and Italian cuisine featuring prominently on the foodie circuit these days, this is also somewhere you can indulge in a break from Burmese cooking.

For a quick bite, head for Barbecue Street in Chinatown (between Chinatown's Mahabandoola and Anawrahta streets), where rows of *a'gin zein* grills sizzle through lunchtime and evenings with everything from rib steaks and spicy chicken fillets to pigs' tails and quails. And it's not just for carnivores: tofu, broccoli, water chestnuts and fresh beans are also on offer.

Yangon's famous teahouses are also great places to refuel on a budget. Spaces to gossip, read the paper and people-watch, they're a cornerstone of the local social scene. The city has literally hundreds of them – all shabby and crowded, but offering a fascinating window on everyday life. A couple where you are more likely to find English-speaking staff are *Thone Pan Hla*, just west of the Sule Pagoda downtown, and *Lucky Seven*, at 164 West Shwegondaing, just north of the Shwedagon Pagoda, which serves a mean *mohinga* in the morning. Chinese teahouses whip up a choice of meaty rice dishes while the Burmese variety tends to stick to noodles; Muslim places typically specialise in freshly fried lamb,

chicken and vegetable samosas.

Aung Thuka
17 (A) 1st Street, West Shwegondaing
Tel: 01 525 194
An authentic, no-frills introduction to Burmese cooking, conveniently situated just three blocks north of the Shwedagon Pagoda, across from the entrance to the Savoy down a small side street. There are no menus or tablecloths, or even walls. Just take your pick from the selection of curries and salads in pots ranged on the long counter at the back, which will come with the usual bowls of sauce, soup and veggies. The venison is recommended, but everything's packed with flavour. You'll be hard pushed to spend $5. **$**

Feel Myanmar Food
124 Pyidaungsu Yeiktha Street
Tel: 01 725 736
Packed with as many locals as foreign visitors, this ranks among the top Bamar restaurants in Yangon. Forget the menu, just pick from the huge range of fish, chicken and vegetable curries bubbling away in the buffet, and take your meal outdoors for an informal vibe, or stay in for a more conventional restaurant experience. Great prices. And they do a passable cappuccino. **$–$$**

Green Elephant
3 (H), Block 801, 27th Street, Aung Daw Mu Quarter
Tel: 01 537 706; greenelephant-restaurants.com
Popular mainly with foreign tourists and expats, *Green Elephant* provides a perfect introduction to Burmese cooking, as they go easy on the oil and

spices. Meals are served in a double-storey, open-sided wooden dining hall. Reservations recommended. **$$–$$$**

Happy Café & Noodles
62 Inya Rd, Bahan Township
Tel: 01 705 620
Spicier and sharper in flavour than their Shan equivalents, Kachin noodles are often served mixed with pickled bamboo shoots, and this unpretentious place in northern Yangon, where expat Kachins come to dine, is the best place to sample them. For the main ingredient, choose from tender chicken wing or pork rib. **$**

Le Planteur
22 Kaba Aye Pagoda Road, Bahan Township
Tel 01 541 997; leplanteur.net.
Refined, exquisitely presented French cuisine prepared by a Michelin-starred chef, and served in a candlelit garden under a craggy old cashew tree. Get there early enough and you can have a pre-dinner drink in the sexy, red-velvet-lined lounge. For mains, try the leg of pork with honey or melt-in-the-mouth lobster in lotus stems, and for dessert, the sublime chocolate gateau if it's on. The wine list is the best in the country. Pick-up and drop-offs in a vintage British car by arrangement. Reservation essential. **$$$$**

L'Opera
62 D, U Tunein Street, Mayangone Township
Tel: 01 665 516; operayangon.com
Served alfresco on the lawned grounds of a double-fronted British-era villa, on the banks of a small lake, *L'Opera* serves the most succulent, authentic Italian food in the city – fresh pasta with shrimps and courgettes, spaghetti in truffle sauce, imported Tuscan cold cuts, wood-fired pizza and wonderful saffron risotto. They also have a full list of quality Italian wines. **$$$$**

Mandalay
Governor's Residence Hotel
35 Taw Win Road
Tel: 01 229 860
After a kafir-lime mohito in the lobby, settle at a table in the grounds of this splendid former colonial mansion for a feast of Pan-Asian cuisine, against a background of live Burmese classical music. The cooking is

Noodle salad, Downtown Yangon

TRANSPORT
ACCOMMODATION
EATING OUT
ACTIVITIES
A – Z
LANGUAGE

Strand Grill

world-class and the atmosphere memorable, but brace yourself for an eye-popping bill (around $100/head if you order a bottle of Red Mountain wine). **$$$$**

Pandonmar
78C Inya Road
Tel: 01 536 485
One of the gastronomic highlights of Yangon has to be a Burmese or Thai meal in the lantern-lit garden at *Pandonmar*, a 19th-century house on Inya Road. Everything's fragrant and filled with unexpected flavours, from the gourd fritters to the Bagan-style pork in bean paste and creamy river prawn curry. Owner, Mr Sony, is an attentive host. **$$**

Parisian Bakery & Café
132 Sule Pagoda Road, Kyauktada Township
Tel: 01 387 298
A delectable assortment of Gallic pastries and cakes – from strawberry tart to chocolate gateau – served by a legion of uniformed waiters in a blissfully cool air-con dining room. And they do top-grade Myanmar coffee from a proper espresso machine. **$$**

Prome
Pyay Road
Currently one of Yangon's hottest *a'gin zein* (literally "grilled stuff") joints – a cut above your average BBQ hut, serving sushi, soups and salads in addition to specialities such as crunchy pigs' tails and crispy fried sparrows. Be sure to round your meal off with their sweet and peanutty ice *kachang* – a perfect palate cleanser. **$–$$**

Sandy's Myanmar Cuisine
Kandawgyi Palace Hotel, Kan Yeik Tha Road, Dagon Township
Tel: 01 249 255
For once, cooking as inspirational as the location. Although it's pricey by local standards, quality is assured in this famous Bamar restaurant, where you'll be wowed by the local flavours while gazing over the water at the amazing Karaweik Barge. Kick off with a starter of duck eggs and minced prawns, then try the boiled snake-head fish in moringa leaves, leaving room for the delicious *shwegyi*, a traditional dessert made from rice flour, sugar cane and coconut. **$$$**

Sabai @ DMZ
Dhama Zedi Road
Toned-down, tourist-friendly Thai cuisine (including a great green chicken curry, tasty stir-fried pumpkin and a mean *pad thai*), served in a spacious and airy dining hall. Dessert is on the house. They've an equally nice branch on Inya Road. **$$–$$$**

Sky Bar
20th floor, Sakura Tower, 339 Bogyoke Aung San Rd, Kyauktada Township, Yangon
Tel: 01/255 277; www.sakura-tower-yangon.com/sky.htm,
This aptly named bar on the 20th floor of Yangon's tallest building is a fabulous place to drink or dine while enjoying panoramic views over the city. Both Asian and Western dishes are featured on the eclectic menu, along with cocktails, wine and draught beer. **$$$–$$$$**

Strand Grill
92 Strand Road, Dagon Township
Tel: 01 243 377
Just the place if you're really pushing the boat out. The Strand's signature restaurant serves Belle Epoque food to match the architecture. The lobster thermidor, prepared with a hint of English mustard and real Parmesan, is legendary, but the deer and lamb are no less memorable. And don't miss the head chef's cheekily named starter: the doughnut (a ball of foie gras and truffles deep fried in breadcrumbs). **$$$$**

Shwe Li BBQ
Nar Nattaw Street
This super cheap, no-nonsense BBQ joint is usually packed by 6pm. The food is consistently good. Give their Chinese dumplings and friend noodles with pork and cucumbers a go. Menus in English. Open evenings only. **$**

Thiripyitsaya Sky Lounge
Sakura Tower, 339 Bogyoke Aung San Road, Kyauktada Township
Tel: 01 255 277
Sip an iced cappuccino or tangy coffee float while admiring 360-degree views of the city from the top of a 20-storey skyscraper. **$$$**

BAGAN REGION

Old Bagan holds the lion's share of upscale restaurants, several of them benefiting from prime sunset locations overlooking the river. Nyaung U is more geared towards budget travellers, and like its hotels, offers much better value for money if you can be bothered to travel out there by taxi.

Aroma 2
Yar Kinn Thar Hotel Road, Nyaung U

"No good, you no pay!" is the slogan of this delightful little Indian curry house on "Restaurant Row". But it is, so everyone does. At candlelit tables on an earth floor, you can tuck into generous portions of tasty but mild, Tamil-style curries and rice served on glossy banana leaves, with freshly squeezed papaya juice and a host of different chutneys and dips. Get there

well before 7pm to avoid a long wait for your meal. A tad pricey by Nyaung-U standards, but worth the extra. **$–$$**

Black Bamboo
Yar Thin Thar Street, Nyaung U
Presided over by a French patron, *Black Bamboo* is a tranquil garden restaurant where you can drop by for fragrant coffee, fresh muffins and home-made ice cream (the best in

Bagan), or a full-scale meal. Try their tempura, delicious aubergine curry, or sunny salads. **$$**

Green Elephant

Yamonar (River View), Thiripissayar Quarter, New Bagan.

Tel: 061 65182; greenelephants-restaurants.com

Fine Burmese and Shan cuisine – steamed Ayeyarwady fish with lime and chilli, crispy duck or the house special, Bamar chicken curry – served at a magical spot on the riverbank. Diners sit in an open-sided pavilion, approached via a long teak boardwalk – an unforgettable sunset venue, though the views and black-tie service come at premium rates. **$$–$$$**

Moon

North of Ananda Temple, Old Bagan

Tel: 061 60481

Coloured fairy lights and Pathein parasols create a pretty scene at this popular vegetarian restaurant in the old walled city, where you can refuel after the heat of the Bagan Plains with tangy green papaya salad, cooling pumpkin soup, guacamole-chapatti or a wonderfully creamy coconut curry. **$–$$**

Queen

Wetkyi-in Village, Nyaung U–Bagan Road (Main Road)

Next to the Bagan Princess Hotel, this small, family-run restaurant does a roaring trade thanks to its charming service, delicious, freshly cooked food, relaxing ambience – and low prices. As well as tasty local standards, such as river fish or country chicken curry, they also do pizzas, pancakes and other foreigner-friendly staples – all in generous portions, served on lovely black lacquerware trays and terracotta crockery. Free internet. **$**

San Thi Dar

Myinkaba village, south of Old Bagan

This unassuming little place on the roadside at Myinkaba makes a perfect pit stop if you're cycling past after a temple tour. Don't be fooled by the rough tables and rustic setting. The vegetarian Burmese food is top notch, the family welcome second to none, and prices are rock bottom. **$**

Star Beans

Near Tharabar Gate, Bagan-Nyaung U Rd (Main Road), Old Bagan

Tel (mobile): 0973 033 816

If you're staying in one of the nearby five-stars, you'll probably eat much finer food at *Star Beans* than back at your hotel – for a fifth of the price. A mix of French and Myanmar cuisine dominates a well-focused menu. Be sure to order the smoky aubergine salad, which is perfect with a crunchy baguette. And their grilled fillet of river fish is to-die-for. **$$**

Yar Pyi

Near Tharabar Gate, Bagan-Nyaung U Road, Old Bagan

A warm family vibe prevails at the *Yar Pyi* in Old Bagan, where you'll be waited on by a chatty father-and-daughter team. Backstage, the cook (Mum) rustles up simple but flavoursome Burmese dishes, with a range of fresh salads (Dad shops at the market each morning). Kids will love their coconut rice and fried noodles. And they do a wicked pumpkin soup. **$**

MANDALAY AND SURROUNDINGS

Although it lacks the cosmopolitan variety of downtown Yangon, Mandalay's restaurant scene has improved vastly over the past few years and now offers some stylish dining options as well as the standard local stalwarts.

City Café

66th Street, Mandalay

Only a short walk from the *Red Canal Hotel*, this funky American-bistro-style restaurant serves a wide selection of European and Asian food (grills, burgers, salads, fresh fruit salads, draught beer and imported wines) to a mostly young, well-heeled, local crowd – hence the relentless FM rock soundtrack. **$$**

Green Elephant

3 (H), Block 801, 27th Street, between 64th & 65th streets, Aung Daw Mu Quarter

Tel: 02 61237

Settle at a candlelit table in the beautiful garden of a colonial mansion for a romantic supper of fine Chinese, Burmese and Thai-inspired cuisine. You're paying primarily for the ambience, but the food's dependably good. Popular with large tour groups, so get there early. **$$$**

Ko's Kitchen

282, corner of 19th & 80th streets

Tel: 02 69576/31265

Fine Thai cooking in a worn old Art Deco building close to the west side of the palace complex, beside the moat. Again, popular with tour groups, so an early arrival is recommended. **$$**

Lashio Lay

65 23rd Street

Rough and ready canteen near the central market serving tasty, totally authentic, Shan cuisine to a discerning local clientele. Ask your friendly hosts to help you choose from the dishes simmering on the steam table. **$**

Spice Garden

Hotel on the Red Canal

417, corner of 63rd & 22nd roads

Five-star north Indian food served on

Restaurants and boats on Taungthaman lake

RESTAURANT LISTINGS
Prices for a full meal, with drinks, per person **$$$$**= over US$40 **$$$** = US$20–40 **$$** = US$10–20 **$** = under US$10

benched tables overlooking the hotel pool, or inside a smart timber-framed, double-storey dining room. Go for one of the tandoori options, prepared by chefs in front of you, or the creamy Mughali chicken curry. Plenty of veg alternatives, and the service is courteous, but prices are top whack for Mandalay. **$$$**

Too Too
27th Street, between 74th and 75th streets
Ask a local where you can try proper local cooking and they'll direct you to this simple, wood-fronted restaurant down a quiet backstreet to the south

of the palace. It whips up an array of rich, not-too-oily meat, veg and fish curries, served with all the trimmings on formica-topped tables. No beer. **$**

The Club Terrace
25 Club Road, Quarter No. 5
Tel: 085 22612
Dine on a leafy terrace of a mock-Tudor colonial-era bungalow in the shade of big red Pathein parasols. The mostly Malay and Thai food is consistently excellent (try the chicken in ginger and fried asparagus special if it's on),

prices restrained and beer served in ice-cold frosted glasses. **$$**

Golden Triangle
MandalayNLashio Road
Just a couple of minutes' walk from the clock tower, this bakery café, housed inside a pillar-fronted Raj-era building where you can people-watch on the verandah from comfy wicker chairs, makes a perfect pit stop for coffee and cake – or a decadent glass of strawberry juice. It's patronised almost exclusively by foreign tourists, but the prices are reasonable. **$**

SHAN AND KACHIN STATES

All of the lake resorts have pricey restaurants attached to them, usually offering views of the water from luxuriously designed teak dining halls. For cheap eats, try the nightly market at Mingala market in Nyaungshwe, where you'll find a string of stalls dishing up steaming bowls of Shan noodles, grilled meats and fish from the lake.

Green Chilli
Hospital Rd, Mingalar Qtr, Nyaungshwe
Tel: 081 209 132
This is one of the most beautifully designed restaurants in the village, with a dining room featuring a high-pitched terracotta-tiled roof and smart teak furniture. The Pan-Asian menu is dominated by authentic Thai dishes, the food is as attractively presented as the décor, and the staff unfailingly attentive. Try one of their green curries, juicy kebabs or owner, Kaythi's, melt-in-the-mouth green onion balls. Pricey

for the area, but worth it. **$$**

Inthar Heritage House
Inn Paw Khon village, Inle Lake
Tel: (mobile): 09 4931 2970;
intharheritagehouse.com
Built with reclaimed antique timber amid verdant paddy fields, IHH is a resplendent specimen of local Intha architecture, and the food served in its restaurant is no less wonderful. It's one of the places around the lake where you can sample authentic Intha recipes, handed down by the cooks' grannies. Profits from the centre's restaurant, gallery, book and gift shop support rescued Burmese cats (over 40 of them live on the ground floor). Pop in for a coffee on the sublime lake-facing verandah if don't fancy eating. **$$**

Min Min
Yone Gyi Street, Nyaungshwe
A pristine little restaurant on the main street, run by a couple who are genuinely hospitable – a rarity in this

tourist-driven town. The Burmese food is carefully prepared, fresh and wholesome, and the eponymous owner a mine of info on the local area. **$**

Viewpoint
Taik Nan Bridge
Near main bridge & canal, Nyaungshwe
Tel: 081 29062
By far the poshest place to eat on the lakeside, looking over rice fields and the local jetty. It specialises in fusion Shan cuisine, given a funky Gallic gastro twist and served in great style by waiters who bring your meal to your table in miniature teak boats. Try their acclaimed braised beef or Shan tapas. Pricey, but few regret the splurge. **$$$**

Everest Nepali
Aung Chan Thar Street
Delicious Indian and Nepali basics – such as *dhal baht* and chicken masala – served alongside a handful of foreigner-friendly salads in a welcoming family restaurant. **$–$$**

Pyae Pyae
Union Highway
Simple, unpretentious Shan noodle joint patronised mainly by locals. Don't miss the house speciality, clay-pot noodle soup (featuring a wondrous mix of ingredients, including some exotic hill mushrooms). Smiling service and proper local prices. **$**

Kiss Me
Zaw John Road
A very pleasant riverside pavilion restaurant whose modest appearance belies the high quality of the food, appreciated particularly by the town's hip young things. Order a selection of spring rolls, fritters and salads, which come with an array of zingy sauces. **$**

Fried snacks and sweet tea at a local tea stall, Taung Tho market

Selling snacks at a roadside teashop, Nyaungshwe.

PINDAYA

Green Tea Restaurant
Shwe Oo Min Cave Road, Singaung Quarter
Set in a large, wooden colonial house
by the lake, with lovely views over the
water, the *Green Tea* does first-rate
Burmese and Shan meals, especially
fish dishes, as well as a handful of
Western options. Order anything with
avocado (a local speciality) and you
won't go far wrong; they even serve
avocado juice. **$$**

TAUNGGYI

Golden Kite
Yone Gyi and Myawaddy Road, behind the
Hotel Amazing
Tel: 081 29327
The last thing you expect to come
across in Taunggyi is an Italian
restaurant, especially not a good one,
but prepare to be amazed. Granted,
it's a bit of a tourist trap, but the pizzas
and pasta taste like the real deal,
and the views are magnificent. Some

Burmese dishes are featured on the
menu too. **$$**
Sein Ngwe Shein
Inn Chan Village, Taunggyi
This is a good option if you want
to escape the tourist scene and
eat real local food in a wholly local
environment. The snake-head
soup is a winner, and tilapia fish in
tomato curry is amazing. Or try the
steamed tilapia stuffed with garlic,
ginger and onions. Family-run, and
a refreshing change from the local
resorts. **$**

WESTERN MYANMAR

MRAUK U

Moe Cherry
Alay Zay Quarter
Popular mainly with foreign
backpackers, the *Moe Cherry* is a
welcoming, family-run restaurant just
east of the palace walls specialising
in tasty Burmese and Rakhaing
standards at prices that don't dent
the pocket. Their delicious pork curry
with mini fried potatoes is a perennial
crowd pleaser.
River Valley Restaurant
Minbar Gyi Road
Tel (mobile): 0985 02400
Pleasant, impeccably clean
restaurant-cum-beer bar on the main
road between the ferry jetty and town,
serving mainly Rakhine dishes and
cold beers. It's the smartest place in
the village, and well situated close to
the river. **$$**

NGAPALI BEACH

Family Ngapali
Ngapali Beach

Sumon and her sisters do a terrific
grilled squid and butter-garlic lobster,
best enjoyed with their out-of-this-
world dipping sauce of lime, garlic and
chilli. Cheerful service, big portions
and restrained prices. **$$**
Moonlight
Ngapali Road
Great beach tucker served by
an enthusiastic and hospitable
husband-and-wife team. Try one
of their fillets of grilled fish from
the bay, drizzled with delicious
house ginger-lemon sauce, or
coconut prawn curry served in a
coconut shell, rounded off with
"banana fired with rum" (banana
flambée), and peg of Burmese
brandy. **$$$**
Ngapali Kitchen
Ngapali Beach Road
The most popular place on the strip,
whose fame rests primarily on its
knock-out seafood curry, grilled
lobster and house chips, which
go down a storm with its mostly

European clientele. Local and family-
run. **$$$**
Silver Full
Ngapali Beach, near the Amata Resort
Tel: 09 4965 3790
Top-notch seafood at reasonable
rates, including jumbo tiger
prawns, caught fresh each day
(it's one of the few places in the
resort that will bring the fish to
your table before it's cooked).
Owner Ko Thant Zin Naing does
Red Mountain wines at lower than
average tariffs. Guaranteed no
MSG. **$$$**

RESTAURANT LISTINGS

Prices for a full meal, with drinks, per
person
$$$$= over US$40
$$$ = US$20–40
$$ = US$10–20
$ = under US$10

ACTIVITIES

ENTERTAINMENT, FESTIVALS, SHOPPING AND SPORTS

ENTERTAINMENT AND NIGHTLIFE

Aside from a half dozen bona fide nightclubs patronised mainly by expats and the country's elite, evening entertainment in Yangon and Mandalay tends to be low-key, limited to male-dominated beer gardens, downbeat karaoke dives and old-style tea shops. Outside the main cities, everything shuts by 9pm, or earlier. That said, if you're on a pre-arranged tour, chances are your holiday company or hotel will have laid on some form of cultural entertainment for the evenings. This usually consists of truncated (ie "foreigner friendly") recitals of classical Burmese music and dance, or puppet shows.

Discos, bars and pubs

Yangon's nightlife is the most dependably lively in Myanmar, thanks to the handful of small clubs attached to the city's five-star hotels, where a mixture of rich kids, bored expats, government cronies and movie industry movers, shakers and starlets shake their stuff on weekends, watched by tables-full of restless young men. Most double as pick-up joints for sex workers, and close earlier than clubs in more developed countries. For those after a less brassy atmosphere, and who can do without expensive imported liquor, **19th Street – a narrow back lane in the old enclave of Latha Township** – is lined with beer terraces, bars and barbecue joints where both foreigners and locals hang out through the evening.

Yangon

BME2
350 Ahlone Road, next to Summit Park View Hotel
Owned by a Wa drug baron, the Bone Myint Entertainment 2 – BME2 for short – is the hippest hangout in central Yangon. Expats rub shoulders with Yangon's bright and beautiful, while a house band clanks out covers. When it closes at 12.30am, everyone trogs up to BME1, near Aung San Suu Kyi's house, whose VIP rooms are the special attraction.

DJ's Bar
Inya Lake Hotel
37 Kaba Aye Pagoda Road
Tel: 01 662 866; www.inyalakehotel.com
In its own separate block next to the main hotel, DJ's is one of the main stomping grounds for the city's hip, young and rich set.

LV
Kandawgyi Hotel
Recently revamped club in an ultra-smart five-star where the DJs spin deep house for a mostly well-heeled, local clientele; the $10 admission includes one drink.

Mr. Guitar Café
22 Sayasan Road
Tel: 01 550 105
Run by a famous Burmese musician, this place serves up live soft rock, light bites and a wide choice of imported liquors. Open 7–11pm

Music Club
Grand Plaza Park Royal Yangon
33 Alan Paya Lan
Tel: 01 250 388
This complex in the hotel's basement remains one of the hottest live music clubs in town featuring touring DJs and live music from a Filipino house band, plus private karaoke rooms. Open 7pm–midnight.

Pioneer Music Bar
Yangon International Hotel
330 Ahlone Road, Dagon Township
Tel: 01 229 224;
www.hoteljapanyangon.com
One of the most popular discos in the city, especially on weekends, when they host nightly fashion shows and live bands. $5 admission covers a drink. Open 8.30pm–midnight.

Zero Zone Rock Restaurant
10 Gi Ze Road, Chinatown
Famous for its fashion shows and dance performances, Zero Zone is a rooftop joint that gets rave reviews for its BBQs and karaoke, though it's more overtly a pick-up joint than most.

Theatre

The best place to experience traditional Burmese dance and music – known as *pwe* – is on the city street or pagoda grounds at festival times. If your visit does not coincide with a festival, however, there are two public theatres in Yangon and smaller establishments in Mandalay which have various performances, including some showcasing the country's lively puppet tradition.

The National Theatre
Myoma Kyaung Lan, Yangon.
Performances of *pwe* are often staged at the National Theatre, along with concerts by international artists. Check with your tour rep or staff at your hotel to find out what's on while you're in town.

Karaweik Hall
Kandawgyi Lake, Yangon
Made in the form of two giant gilded karaweik birds, the floating restaurant on Kandawgyi (Royal)

Lake lays on nightly recitals of classical Burmese music and dance, in uncompromisingly lavish surroundings. Shows start at 6.30pm and cost K20,000/US$25/head, which includes a sumptuous buffet supper.

Mandalay Marionettes
66th Street, between 26th and 27th streets, Mandalay
www.mandalaymarionettes.com
Popular with backpackers and tour groups alike, delightful puppet shows take place each evening at Mandalay Marionettes. From 8.30pm.

Moustache Brothers
39th Street, between 80th and 81st streets, Mandalay.
The Moustache Brothers' famous satirical show is an institution in Mandalay. A brand of traditional theatre known as a *yeint*, which combines clowning with dance and puppetry, it's staged by three moustachioed locals who were imprisoned for poking fun at the government. They're now only allowed to perform for foreigners.

Cinemas in Yangon

The Burmese love movies. There are more than 50 cinema halls in Yangon, about a third of them in the downtown area. In addition to Burmese-language films, the Motion Picture Corporation shows carefully selected foreign features on a regular basis, including movies from India, Hong Kong, North America, Europe and Japan. Seating 700 people, the **Thamada** is the grandest venue, and presents English-language and other foreign films on a regular basis. The Junction Cineplex and Junction Center are spanking-new multiplexes in gleaming American-style malls, screening the latest blockbusters.

Junction Cineplex
Junction Square Shopping Centre 2nd Floor, Between Pyi Road and Kyuntaw Road, Kamayut Township
Tel: 01 527 055

Junction Center (Maw Tin)
Corner of Anawrahta Road and Lanthit St, Lanmadaw
Tel: 01 225 244

Thamada
5 Alanpya Pagoda Road, Dagon Township
Tel: 01 246 962

Thwin
309 Bogyoke Aung San Road at corner of 35th Street, Kyauktada Township
Tel: 01 272 594

FESTIVALS

January (Nadaw/Pyartho)

Kachin Manao Festival (Kyitkyina, Kachin)
Traditional *manao* "totem poles" form the focus of tribal dances by Kachins dressed in traditional finery.

Ananda Pagoda Festival (Bagan, Mandalay)
Thousands of pilgrims descend on Bagan's greatest temple for this month-long religious celebration, when a funfair and market accompany the worship. Monks wait in a long line for their alms bowls to be filled.

Naga New Year (Sagaing)
Most of the Naga tribespeople from Sagaing and Chin states are Christian, but their exuberant New Year's festival, marked by spectacular group dances and animal sacrifices, harks back to their animist past.

February (Pyartho/Dabodwei)

Maha Muni Pagoda Festival (Mandalay)
This intense Buddhist festival venerates the country's most adored statue, a massive gold seated Buddha enshrined in the southern suburbs of Mandalay. Copious quantities of incense are burned in large fires.

Salone Festival (Tanintharyi Region)
Traditional dances, feasts, rowing and diving competitions mark this government-sponsored homage to the region's Moken "Sea Gypsies", staged in Majungalet Village on Bocho Island in Myeik – one of the few occasions when foreigners are allowed on to the Mergui Archipelago.

March (Dabodwei/Tabaung)

Shwedagon Pagoda Festival (Yangon)
Yangon's magnificent stupa becomes the centre of a week-long period of intense veneration, attracting huge crowds from across Myanmar.

Kakku Pagoda Festival (Inle)
Marriages are fixed, deals struck and pwe performed in the lively fair that precedes the Pa O people's annual New Year celebrations at the extraordinary Shan stupa site near Inle Lake.

April (Tabaung/Tagu)

Thingyan Water Festival (Country wide)
Perhaps the quirkiest of all Myanmar's festivals, and certainly the sauciest, is this hot-season bash, when girls get soaked to the skin by water-throwing admirers.

Thanaka Grinding Festival (Rakhine)
While the women of Sittwe grind the roots of *thanaka* wood, the men play instruments, sing and dance in this festival dedicated to the fragrant paste worn by most Burmese women.

Shwemawdaw Pagoda Festival (Bago)
Singing and dancing competitions are the key part of this annual temple festival in the monument-laden former capital.

Myanmar New Year Festival (Country wide)
Buddha images are bathed in *thanaka* water as older Burmese retreat to monasteries and temples to pray.

May (Tagu/Kason)

Wesak (Buddha's Birthday)
Celebrated by the watering of Bodhi trees at temples and monasteries around Myanmar, Wesak marks the day of the Buddha's Enlightenment. Musical troupes accompany the stream of locals carrying pitchers on their heads.

Chinlone Festival, Mahanumi Pagoda, Mandalay
The national *chinlone* (a local version of "keepy-uppy") competition, attracting the country's finest exponents.

August (Waso/Wakhaung)

Taungbyon Festival, nr Mandalay
For eight days running up to the full moon, this small town upriver from Mandalay is transformed with an intense, hedonistic *nat* worship festival.

September (Wakhaung/Tawthalin)

Tooth Relic Ceremony, Pyay
The culmination of three days of celebrations, the famous molar is paraded on elephant back around the riverside town of Pyay before returning to its temple for another year.

October (Tawthalin/Tadingyut)

Kyaikhtiyo Pagoda Festival (Mon State)
Streams of pilgrims climb the sacred mountain in Mon State to venerate the famous Golden Rock Pagoda at this auspicious time.

Phaung Daw U Festival (Inle Lake)
This flamboyant festival on Inle Lake

lasts for two weeks and features a re-created royal barge with a gigantic *karaweik* bird mounted on its prow.

November (Tadingyut/ Tazaunmone)

Matho Thingan (Yangon)
Monks are offered newly woven yellow robes in this nationwide festival.

December (Tazaunmone/ Nadaw)

Kayin New Year Festival
Colourful traditional dress is donned by Kayin (Karen) people to mark their New Year.

SHOPPING

Nearly everywhere you visit in Myanmar will have markets (*zei*) selling traditional handicrafts and other potential souvenirs, and these are great places to spend your money as you can be sure most of it will reach the local people who most need it. In addition, upscale hotels nearly all have souvenir boutiques, selling similar merchandise at inflated prices. Either way, you're most likely to have to pay with cash.

Another rich source of things to take home is the concessions lining the stairways to Buddhist pagodas, which specialise in quintessentially Burmese religious paraphernalia, from incense to mini Buddhas and prayer beads.

Among the well-heeled urban middle classes, however, modern air-con, multistorey malls are the preferred places to shop. There is an ever-increasing number of them springing up in Yangon and Mandalay, though for obvious reasons – and because their prices are higher than those of similar shopping places in Bangkok and Singapore – they tend to frequented by few foreign tourists.

Malls sell at fixed prices. The same certainly can't be said of Burmese markets and souvenir shops, where you'll have to bargain hard to gain a fair price: start at roughly 50 percent of what the vendor asks and work up from there, and don't be afraid to walk away (or even feign walking away) if you think he/she is asking too much.

For sheer variety, you can't beat the country's largest shopping area, Yangon's **Bogyoke Aung San Market**, which holds around 2,000 shops under one roof, offering a massive selection of antiques, fake antiques, arts and handicrafts, in all price brackets. It opens from 9.30am

to 4.30pm, Monday to Saturday.

There are also **open-air markets** across Bogyoke Aung San Street, at the corner of St John's Road and Pyay Road; and east of the Botataung Pagoda. The **Theingyi Indian Market** is just off Anawrahta Street. The biggest and oldest market in Yangon, it sells household wares, textiles and traditional medicine and herbs. The **Thirimingala Market** in Ahlone Township at the northern end of Strand Road sells fresh fruit, vegetables and meat and provides some good photo opportunities. There's also a **Chinese Market** at the corner of Mahabandoola Street and Lanmadaw Road. Separate **night markets** are open on specified streets after dark; the best ones are in Yangon's Chinese and Indian quarters.

The entrances to the **Shwedagon Pagoda** house large bazaars – of some length, in fact, covering both sides of the stairways. The one at the east entrance is the most interesting; among the items frequently sold are puppets, drums, masks, toys, brassware and metal goods, including swords. The bazaar at the pagoda's south entrance is notable for wood and ivory carvings – though bear in mind many countries ban the import of ivory.

At regional markets across the country, particularly those in eastern Shan State, you may come across parts of endangered animals for sale – such as rhino horns, ivory and tiger claws. Bear in mind that the purchase of such items is illegal, and that you may face a stiff fine, or worse, if any are discovered in your luggage on arrival back in your home country.

Augustine Souvenir Shop
23 (A) Attiyar St (Thirimingalar St) Kamayut, Yangon
Tel: 01 705 969; www.augustinesouvenirshop.com
This sumptuous emporium is crammed with quality antique silverware, lacquer, woodcarving, metalwork, colonial furniture, stone figures and traditional porcelain.
Nandawun
55 Baho Road, Ahlone, Yangon
Tel: 01 221 271; www.myanmarhandicrafts.com
This is the largest privately owned craft centre in Myanmar, offering a huge range of tapestries, silk, authentic tribal costume, paintings on silk and cotton, as well as woodcarving, lacquerware and other craft forms.
J's Irrawaddy Dream
1st Floor Strand Hotel, 92 Strand Road, Yangon
Tel: 01 392 471
Locally woven and dyed fabrics

are J's mainstay, but they also sell handicrafts such as lacquer, and stock stylish dresses for women.
FMI Centre
Among the most popular of Yangon's air-con malls, and conveniently situated next to Bogyoke Aung San Market.

Mandalay

Mandalay's **Zegyo Market** (at 84th Street, between 26th and 28th streets) opens early in the morning and remains open until dark. The **Kaingdan Market** fruit and vegetable market is found by walking a couple of blocks west from the Zegyo. The cheapest market for household goods is in Chinatown between 29th and 33rd streets. The **night market** is on 84th Street between 26th and 28th.
Sein Myint Artist
42 Sanga University Road
Tel: 02 26553
Sells gorgeous silk *kalagas* and has an interesting gallery with paintings and carvings.
Yadanapura Art Centre
RM(6), BLOG (B-3), Malikha Shopping Complex, Yadanar Road, Thingangyun Yangon
Tel: 01 564316; yadanapura.com
This government-run enterprise has a good selection of quality handicrafts, jewellery and paintings.
Soe Moe Momento World
No.469, 84th Street near the Mayae Son Won Pagoda, Kyauk Sit Tan Road, Mandalay
Tel: 02 70558
Soe Moe stocks a vast selection of traditional handicrafts, from embroidery to bronze deities – some of them made on site. The prices are nominally fixed, but you can usually negotiate discounts.
Mandalay Marionettes
66th Street, between 26th & 27th streets, Mandalay
Tel: 02 34446; mandalaymarionettes.com
Puppets make great presents if you've any children to buy for, and this place stocks the widest choice in Myanmar.
Shwe Pathein
276 Strand Road, corner of Kon Zay Dan Street, Ward (3), Yangon
Tel: 01 370803
Showroom and sales outlet for traditional Pathein parasols.

Inle Lake

All the local hoteliers and boatmen on Inle Lake will know the location of the five-day market, hosted by the different settlements around the lakeshore in rotation. Most tourists make a beeline for the Ywama floating market, but it's a lot less authentic-feeling these days than the one at Inthein. Local specialities include Shan shoulder bags and textiles made from lotus silk.

Bagan

Most of Myanmar's best lacquerware is made in Bagan, specifically the village of New Bagan (Bagan Myothit), the residential area 8km (5 miles) south of the archaeological zone. There are literally dozens of outlets dotted around the ruins, but three dependable favourites include: Chan Tan (Main Road, Myinkaba), Ever Stand (between Old Bagan and Nyaung U); and Golden Bagan (Khyae Main Road, Old Bagan).

Booksellers in Yangon

It's worth browsing the bookstalls set up along main streets in both Yangon and Mandalay, the largest conglomeration of which is to be found on Bogyoke Aung San Street, and on side streets west of Sule Pagoda Road, where original and photocopied out-of-print titles can often be found.

Monument Books
150 Damazedi Road, Bahan Township Tel: 01 537 805; www.monument-books.com
This is Yangon, and Myanmar's, number one bookstore, with an impressive range of fiction and non-fiction titles in English. They also have a branch in Mandalay at 45B, 26th–68th St (tel: 02 66197).

Bagan Book House
100, 37th Street, between Mahabandoola and Merchant roads Tel: 01 377 227
Specialises in antique and collectable books.

Myanmar Book Centre
55 Baho Road, corner of Baho and Ahlone roads (Near Eugenia Restaurant), Ahlone Township Tel: 01 212 409; www.myanmarbook.com.
The country's largest stockist of books about Myanmar, housed in delightful colonial-era premises.

SPORTS

Sports are a popular diversion in Myanmar. Soccer matches are played almost weekly at Aung San Stadium, home of Yangon FC. More typically Burmese, however, are the sports of chinlone (a local version of

A Burmese boxing match

The following description of Burmese boxing is taken from Forward magazine (1 August 1964), as quoted by author Helen Trager in her book We, The Burmese:
"The head is used for butting, either to stop an opponent's rush or to soften him up while holding him fast in a tight grip. The hands are used not only for hitting but also for holding. The elbows are used to parry an opponent's blow or to deliver one in the opponent's side. The knees are used for hitting an opponent who is held fast, or they may be used to deliver blows while the boxers are apart. The feet may trip an opponent or at least keep him off balance, or they may be used to stop an opponent's rush with a well-executed flying kick.
"These tactics are commonly employed by Burmese boxers. To deliver the blows effectively, however, the boxer has to master his footwork, which is also considered

important in another branch of art of self-defence, Thaing. A Burmese boxer has to know where to place his feet, how to advance, how to retreat, from what position to jump into the attack, and how best to evade the blows of the opponent. In close combat the Burmese boxer has to be well acquainted with techniques of wrestling.
"...To safeguard the boxers from accidents, there are rules against scratching, biting, pulling hair, and hitting or kicking an opponent in the groin. The fingernails and toenails of boxers have to be kept properly trimmed. A boxer who is down may not be kicked or hit in any way...
"The match is decided at the sign of blood. Each boxer is allowed to wipe away the blood three times before he is declared the loser. A match may also be decided when one of the boxers is too hurt to continue although he may not be bleeding."

"keepy-uppy") and bando (traditional Burmese kickboxing).

Football

The Burmese are football crazy. The national game has tended to be eclipsed by the English Premier League, which is followed with near religious devotion across the country, though that may change in the coming years as the newly inaugurated Myanmar National League gathers momentum. In 2009, the MNL replaced the former Myanmar Premier League, whose 14 teams were all backed by (and named after) government ministries. Interest in the league was muted, but the new MNL has no government-affiliated sides and is proving a lot more popular with Burmese football fans. Top of the division for three consecutive years has been Yadanbon FC, based at the Bahtoor Stadium in Mandalay, with rivals KBZ FC, from Shan State, and Yangon FC close on their heels.
The creation of the new league reflects a desire on the part of the Burmese government to promote football as the national sport, and eventually compete in international tournaments. Cables published in 2008 by WikiLeaks showed that regime cronies and other tycoons were encouraged by the junta to set up MPL teams with incentives such as gem- and jade-mining concessions.

It remains to be seen whether the national squad can improve on their dismal performance in the World Cup qualifiers of 2007 when they lost 7-0 to China. The team were temporarily banned from the 2018 qualifiers after a match between the national side and Oman had to be abandoned when fans pelted the pitch with rocks, shoes and water bottles.

Burmese boxing

To the unfamiliar Westerner, Burmese boxing appears to be a needlessly vicious sport. Boxers may use any parts of their bodies in attacking their opponents, and a match is won by whoever draws first blood. You can see matches in Mandalay at the training facility on 76th Street between 27th and 28th streets. Bouts are also held throughout the country at temple festivals.

Chinlone

A non-competitive team sport combining dance moves, martial art and great skill, chinlone is the national game. It's played by groups of six people, traditionally using a ball woven from rattan, which participants moving in a circle pass between each other using stylised kicks or hits from six designated points of contact: the top of the toes, the inner, outer and soles of the feet, the heel, and the knee. Players take it in turns to go into the centre to "solo", where they try to pull off as many cool moves as they can. When the ball drops to the floor, the play is over and starts again. Rather than winning or losing, the essence of *chinlone* is style.

Chinlone festivals are held across the country, the largest of them lasting weeks and attracting hundreds of different teams.

The matches are held on circular, beaten-earth rings and accompanied by live commentary from an announcer who calls out the names of the players each time they strike the ball, and who entertains the crowd with witty word play as he does so. Live Burmese music provides an inspirational soundtrack: the best teams are able to kick and move in time, gaining extra admiration for keeping in rhythm with the orchestra.

Both men and women play *chinlone*, as do children, and there's no age limit – it's not unusual to see three or four generations of players in the same team. A solo performance version of the sport also exists, called *tapandaing*. Travelling on luxury steamboats on the Ayeyarwady River, you might catch a demonstration by one of the country's top performers, such as Su Su Hlaing, Myanmar's number one female *chinlone* player, or Ko Maung Maung, undisputed master of the notoriously difficult "mandala move".

Golf

Myanmar's long connection with golf dates back more than a century, when British traders created an 18-hole course at Thayetmyo on the right bank of the Ayeyarwady in central Myanmar. This antique course now features as a must-play on golf tours of the country, as does the state-of-the-art Yangon Pun Hlaing course. Designed by Gary Player in 2000,

Cycling, a popular way to visit the temples, near Dhammayangyi temple, Bagan

Pun Hlaing serves as the venue for the Myanmar Open, a cornerstone of the Asian Tour. The country's number one course, however, is Mingalardon (royalmingalardongolf. com), set amid 115 hectares (286 acres) on the outskirts of Yangon. Other international-standard courses are to be found at Ngalipi, Bagan, Mandalay, Pyin U Lwin and Taunggyi (Ayethaya) near Inle Lake.

Be warned that if you're lucky enough to get a round on any of these, you'll need to get up at the crack of dawn to enjoy it – the heat on shadeless expanses of grass can be excruciating after 10am.

Outdoor activities

The outdoor scene in Myanmar is still very much in its infancy, and for the most part sports such as whitewater rafting and diving are the preserve of high-end tourists. That said, trekking is gaining widespread popularity in certain tourist centres.

Trekking

Kalaw and – to a lesser extent – Hsipaw are the principal hubs for trekking in Myanmar. Operators offer a range of itineraries, from short day treks to multi-day hikes as far as Pindaya and even Inle Lake. Nights are spent at monasteries and in hill-tribe villagers en route where you can interact with locals in their own homes.

As restrictions ease and the Wa insurgency subsides, another area worth considering is the hinterland of Kengtung in the Golden Triangle region of eastern Shan State.

With more time and a flexible budget, the spectacular mountains in the far north around Myanmar's highest peak, Hkakabo Razi, are also within reach of two-week treks from the town of Putao, where several agencies are on hand to arrange porters, provisions and transport to and from the trailhead.

Trekking trips are best arranged through an accredited local tour operator, though smaller agencies may also offer a similar package. For a list of local trekking agencies, see page 336.

Whitewater rafting

The headwaters of the Ayeyarwady River offer superlative whitewater rafting, though the sport remains a highly niche one. Often dubbed the "Everest of Rivers", the Maykha, a tributary of the Ayeyarwady River, is the whitewater hot spot, and one of the world's most extreme multi-stage routes – a nonstop sequence

of rapids surging through narrow gorges flanked by pristine jungle. For guests staying at the luxury Malikha Lodge near Putao (malikhalodge.net; see page 316) there's also the softer option of the Nam Lang River, which flows through some wonderfully wild forest and canyons, passing rarely visited tribal villages en route. You can combine a rafting adventure there with a testing hill trek.

Cycling

Due to popular demand, bicycles are available for rent at most locations where young travellers congregate. The environs of Bagan, Mandalay and Nyaungshwe are particularly suitable. The bikes are not necessarily the latest models on the market, but they come very cheap. Almost any guesthouse can get you one. It is also possible to bring in your own bike.

Alternatively, book a pre-arranged cycle tour from a specialist operator such as Spice Roads (spiceroads. com), Grasshopper Adventures (grasshopperadventures.com) or Velo Asia (veloasia.com).

Diving and snorkelling

The Myeik (Mergui) archipelago, one of the least explored coastal zones of Asia, holds considerable promise for divers, with an astonishing array of sites and sea life inhabiting some of the world's best-preserved coral reefs, all with superb underwater visibility. However, restrictions still limit travel on the islands to a single, extremely pricey five-star option – the Andaman Club (andamanclub.com) – on Thahtay Kyun Island (see page 317).

The alternative is to book a live-aboard diving cruise from the Thai resort of Phuket, where a handful of crews have permits to operate across the Burmese border.

For the less experienced, Ngapali Beach in Rakhaing State has some great snorkelling sites around the islands offshore. Most of the hotels in the resort can arrange boat trips to spots such as Pearl Island, where you can swim around a coral reef teeming with colourful fish. See Scuba diving agencies, page 336.

Hot-air ballooning

It's possible to fly over the ancient ruins of Bagan in a hot-air balloon. Flights take place at sunrise or sunset and last for about 45 minutes. More details appear on page 208, or go to Eastern Safari's website (www. easternsafaris.com) for booking arrangements and a selection of inspirational photos.

A – Z

A HANDY SUMMARY OF PRACTICAL INFORMATION

A

Addresses

The grid-planned centres of major cities, including Yangon, adopt a numbering system that works from east to west – and north to south, too, in the case of Mandalay. Corner addresses appear as, for example, "2nd and 24th St".

Admission charges

For foreign tourists, entry to major archaeological and cultural sites, including those at Bagan, Bago, Maruak-U, Pyay (Prome) and monuments in and around Mandalay, is by a $10 government ticket. These tend to be valid for a period of three to five days, and cover most of the places of interest in any given location. You can pay in foreign currency or the equivalent in kyat. An additional K300–500 may also be levied for cameras and camcorders.

Other sights that tend to charge foreigners for entry include large religious complexes (such as the Shwedagon Pagoda; $5) and museums ($5). In all these cases, Burmese nationals enter free, or for a much reduced charge.

B

Budgeting for your trip

If you're travelling on a pre-arranged tour, where all the transport and accommodation costs are covered by the price of your holiday, your main expenses are likely to be dining and shopping. If you're not fussy about your surroundings, it's easy to find a filling meal for less than US$10. Allow around $10–15 per head for a two-course meal in a regular, mid-scale restaurant, or $20–40 in a five-star hotel. The most upmarket establishments may cost a little more than this. Breakfasts are usually included in your hotel tariff, but it's sometimes worth checking. How much your souvenirs set you back will depend on your ability to haggle, but as a rule of thumb count on around $10–15 for a puppet, or $100–200 for a top-notch lacquerware bowl.

Independent travellers will also need to factor in accommodation costs: allow around US$30 for a double room in a good-standard budget hotel. Transport costs are generally quite low, particularly the buses, but any internal flights will rapidly increase your expenditure.

C

Children

Unless you're lucky enough to be travelling on a luxury tour, staying in five-stars and moving between destinations by air-con tourist vehicle or air, visiting Myanmar is not an easy option for families. The relentlessly hot and humid climate, uncomfortable public transport, unfamiliar food and absence of dedicated facilities for children mean you'll have to be

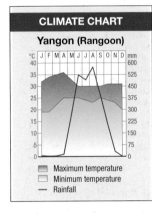

CLIMATE CHART

Yangon (Rangoon)

- Maximum temperature
- Minimum temperature
- — Rainfall

resourceful. You'll also have to bring a supply of nappies to see you through your trip – they're unavailable outside Yangon and Mandalay – though dealing with disposables causes inevitable problems in out-of-the-way locations, where refuse collection is non-existent.

Having said that, the Burmese love children and will do everything to make them comfortable, to the extent of taking them off parents' hands at every opportunity.

If you're travelling independently with children under 7, consider renting a car and driver for the duration as journeys by bus, in particular, can be long and gruelling, with no toilet facilities and few stops en route.

Sights in Myanmar that your children will love include the marionette shows in Mandalay (see page 325) and the massive reclining Buddhas at Bodhi Tataung, Bago, Yangon and elsewhere. They'll also enjoy the vibrancy of local markets, and trips by boat on the rivers and around Inle Lake.

Climate

Like all countries in South and Southeast Asia's monsoonal region, Myanmar's year is divided into three seasons: there are regional variations, but essentially it is hot and wet from May to October, cooler and dry from November to February, and hot and dry in March and April.

The Southwest Monsoon brings rains beginning in May, which are most intense between June and August. This is a time of high humidity – especially in the coastal and delta regions – and of daily afternoon/evening showers, as winds carry the moisture in from the Indian Ocean. The central inland region is drier than other parts of the country, but is also subject to much rain during this time. Travel during the rainy season can quite often be interrupted due to flooded roads and railway lines; it is made even more difficult as this information is not always made available through the media.

In October, the rains let up. From November through to May the Northeast Monsoon brings mainly dry weather, particularly away from the south. The cool season (November–February) is the most pleasant time to visit. The average temperature along the Ayeyarwady plain, from Yangon to Mandalay, is between 21°C and 28°C (70°F and 82°F), although in the mountains in the north and east, the temperature can drop below freezing and snow can fall.

The hottest weather occurs during March and April, before the rains, with temperatures in the central plain, particularly around Bagan (Pagan), climbing as high as 45°C (113°F).

The annual rainfall along the coasts of Rakhaing (Arakan) and Tanintharyi (Tenasserim) ranges from 300 to 500cm (120 to 200in). The Ayeyarwady Delta gets about 150 to 200cm (60 to 100in), while the central Myanmar region, between Mandalay and Bagan, and the surrounding areas, averages 50 to 100cm (20 to 40in) of rain each year. In the far north, the melting snows of the Himalayan foothills keep rivers fed with water.

When to go

The best time to visit is during the relatively cool, dry winter months between November and February. This is peak tourist season, when the skies are blue for days on end and night time temperatures are pleasant. Up on the Shan Plateau around Inle Lake, you may even need a fleece in the evenings. Travel anywhere between May and early October is problematic: roads are routinely washed away, rail lines flooded and cyclones wreak havoc on the coastal plains and delta area.

Myanmar's festival calendar is jam-packed and you're sure to come across some kind of celebration during your trip, whenever you chose to come. The biggest events are Yangon's Shwedagon Pwe in February and raucous Thingyan in April, a nationwide knees-up when lots of drinking, singing, dancing and throwing of water marks the start of the Burmese New Year.

What to wear

Dress in Myanmar is casual but neat. Unless you are conducting business, you won't be expected to wear a tie anywhere. Long trousers for men and a dress or long skirt for women, lightweight and appropriate to the prevailing climatic conditions, is the generally accepted mode of dress for visitors. Quick-drying clothes are a good idea for visits during the rainy season or Thingyan (the "water festival"). There is no law against shorts or short skirts, but this type of clothing is not common in the country outside the trendy clubs of Yangon.

A sweater or jacket should be carried if you plan a visit to the hill stations or Shan Plateau, especially in the cool season. Open footwear, such as sandals, is acceptable, but remember to remove footwear when entering religious institutions. An umbrella would be a worthwhile investment during the rainy season. Bring a hat for sun protection.

Crime and safety

Although no dependable statistics on the subject exist, most travellers will affirm that Myanmar is a safe and welcoming place to travel. Muggings and petty thefts may have increased since the decline in the country's economic fortunes over the past couple of decades, but they're still rare – and much less frequent than in more developed Asian countries. Even so, take the same precautions as you would at home: don't wander about unfamiliar parts of Yangon or Mandalay on your own at night. Keep your passport and other valuables under lock and key at all times.

In addition, it's advisable to avoid all demonstrations and large gatherings, and don't take photographs of soldiers, police, military installations or equipment.

Customs regulations

Tourists are allowed duty-free import of limited quantities of tobacco – 400 cigarettes, 100 cigars, or 250g (8oz) of pipe tobacco as well as two litres of alcoholic beverage, and a half-litre bottle of perfume or eau de cologne and articles for personal use. Any foreign currency in excess of US$3,000 should be declared on arrival, but you won't be required to obtain clearance for valuables such as a laptop, DVD recorder, camera or mobile phone.

Items prohibited from import into Myanmar:

Counterfeit currency
Pornography
Narcotic and psychotropic substances
Toy guns and remote-control toys
Firearms
Live animals/birds

Prohibited exports

Stone-Age implements and artefacts
Fossils
Antique coins
Bronze and clay pipes
Palm leaf manuscripts and *parabaike* (folding manuscripts)
Inscribed stones and bricks
Inscribed gold and silver plates and other objects
Historical documents
Religious images and statues
Carvings or sculptures of bronze, stone, stucco and wood
Frescoes and fragments of frescoes
Burmese regalia and paraphernalia

Departure tax

A flat departure tax of US$10 is levied at check-in. Make sure you keep a nice crisp dollar bill for the purpose. In addition, travellers on domestic flights have to pay a fee of K1000 (just over $1).

Foreign currency

Foreigners may bring in as much foreign currency as they wish. Amounts in excess of US$2,000 or its equivalent must be declared on the Foreign Exchange Declaration Form (FED). However, the import and export of Burmese kyat is forbidden, and the export of foreign currency is limited to the amount declared upon entry.

Formalities both on arrival and departure are now quite easy as long as you do not lose the various forms you have been given upon entry.

D

Disabled travellers

Mobility-impaired travellers will find Myanmar a difficult proposition. The roads and walkways are mostly in an abysmal state, other wheelchair users a rare sight and access to public buildings such as railway stations, museums and archaeological sites frequently problematic.

As ever, the success of your trip will depend to a large extent on forward planning. The following websites may provide some useful pointers:
www.able-travel.com – Global info for adventurous travellers
www.disabledtravelersguide.com
www.globalaccessnews.com – Disabled travellers share their experiences
www.flying-with-disability.org – Advice for planning a flight.

E

Embassies and consulates

Consulates and embassies in Yangon

Despite the fact that Naypyidaw is nowadays the official capital, most of the foreign embassies and consulates remain in Yangon. As far as the consular services of your own country go, bear in mind that embassy officials are usually not allowed to travel freely outside Rangoon without prior permission from the Burmese government, except to a limited number of destinations, and that as a result assistance in an emergency may be restricted or delayed.
Australia, 88 Strand Road
Tel: 01 251 810; www.burma.embassy.gov.au
Bangladesh, 11/B, Than Lwin Road, P.O Box 70
Tel: 01 515 275
Canada n/a
China, 1 Pyidaungsu Yeiktha Road
Tel: 01 221 280; www.mm.china-embassy.org.
France, 102 Pyidaungsu Yeiktha
Tel: 01 212 520; www.ambafrance-mm.org
Germany, 9 Bogyoke Aung San Museum Road, Bahan Township
Tel: 01 548 951; www.rangun.diplo.de

India, 545/547 Merchant Street, Kyauktada Township
Tel: 01 243 972; www.indiaembassy.net.mm
Laos, NA1 Diplomatic Quarters, Taw Win (Franser) Road
Tel: 01 222 482
Malaysia, 82 Pyidaungsu Yeiktha Road
Tel: 01 220 249; www.kln.gov.my
Nepal, 17 Natmauk Yeiktha Road
Tel: 01 545 880.
Singapore, 238 Dhamazedi Road, Bahan Township
Tel: 01 559 001; www.mfa.gov.sg
Sri Lanka, 34 Taw Win Street
Tel: 01 222 812; www.slembyangon.org
Thailand, 437 Pyay Road, Dagon Township
Tel: 01 222 784; www.thaiembassy.org/yangon
United Kingdom, 80 Strand Road (Box 638)
Tel: 01 380 322; ukinburma.fco.gov.uk/en
United States, 110 University Ave, Kamayut Township
Tel: 01 536 509; burma.usembassy.gov
Vietnam, Building No.70-72, Thanlwin Rd, Bahan Township
Tel: 01 511 305; www.vietnamembassy-myanmar.org

Burmese embassies and consulates abroad

Australia
Embassy of the Republic of the Union of Myanmar,
22 Arkana Street, Yarralumla ACT 2600
Tel: 02 6273 3811
www.myanmarembassycanberra.info
Canada
Sandringham Bldg, 85 Range Road, Suite 902-903, Ontario KIN 8J6, Ottawa
Tel: 1 613 232 6434
South Africa
Embassy of the Republic of the Union of Myanmar,
201 Leyds Street, Arcadia, Pretoria, South Africa
Tel: 27-12-341 2556
www.myanemb-sa.net
United Kingdom
Embassy of the Republic of the Union of Myanmar,
19A Charles Street, London W1J 5DX
Tel: 020 3397 4463
www.myanmarembassyuk.co.uk
United States
Embassy of the Republic of the Union of Myanmar,
300 'S' Street, NW Washington DC
Tel: 202 332 3344
www.mewashingtondc.com

Electricity

The standard electrical current is 230-volt/50 hertz.

Etiquette

In common with most Asian countries, the Burmese are quite formal (by Western standards) in the way they engage strangers, especially foreigners, and anyone of a different gender. You'll find them painstakingly polite, considerate and gentle – and appreciative of those who respond in a similar fashion, particularly in homes and places of worship.

When introduced to people in Myanmar, it is considered good manners to call them by their full title and full name, beginning with "U" (the equivalent of "Mr") and "Daw" ("Mrs", "Ms" or "Madam").

It is particularly difficult for a Burmese to address a Westerner only by his Christian name, even when they are close friends. Thus Ko Kau Reng will never call his friend "Ronnie", but will address him as "Ko Ronnie" or "Maung Ronnie". Similarly, Nancy would be called "Ma Nancy". Ko Kau Reng expects that he, too, will be similarly addressed.

Business etiquette

Handshakes are nowadays the conventional greeting between businessmen. You shouldn't, however, offer your hand to a woman, unless an associate offers you hers first, in which case it's fine to shake it; all other physical contact should be avoided.

Business cards are used widely and, as in most of Asia, should be exchanged on first meeting. Use both hands to present and receive them (it demonstrates respect), as does taking a few seconds to read the details. Do not put the card in your pocket straight away as this may also be deemed disrespectful.

Dress should be conservative. Lightweight suits for men are acceptable, ideally worn with a tie. Women should ensure that skirts are of knee length or lower. Although the majority of business people dress in suits or formal shirts when meeting foreigners, some – and nearly all politicians – still wear the traditional *longyis* or *htameins*.

Temple etiquette

A Buddhist place of worship is unlike its equivalent in the West. You might find a devout Buddhist in deep meditation on any temple platform, but you might also see whole families eating their lunches in front of a Buddha image. You will see lines of monks walking slowly around the stupa, but you may also observe hordes of children happily running around. The temple ground is where every Burmese village or city neighbourhood congregates in the evening. But don't let the "everydayness" fool you. This is sacred space, and there are certain rules you must keep in order to show your respect.

Throughout the country, wherever you enter religious grounds, you must remove your shoes (or sandals) and socks. Proper clothing should also be worn at a temple: especially, no short skirts for women, and no brief shorts.

If you watch the pious Buddhists who climb to the terrace surrounding a stupa, or who wander through the passageways leading around a temple's central *cella*, you will notice that they always turn to their left. By keeping the sanctuary on the right, they follow a universal "law", moving in the same direction as the sun across the sky.

No shrine souvenirs

Pagodas and temples are usually beautifully decorated, and most Burmese are pleased if you are inspired to photograph their shrine. But photos should be your only souvenirs. Although many Buddhist structures seem to have a surplus of small Buddha statues that no one appears to care about, these are still venerated images.

G

Gay and lesbian travellers

Homosexuality is technically illegal under section 377 of the Burmese penal code, and punishable by up to 10 years' imprisonment. Although the law is rarely enforced, in June 2007 a European national was sentenced to seven years for "committing homosexual acts".

Attitudes to same-sex relationships, whether gay or lesbian, remain conservative and shrouded in stigma and superstition. Many Burmese believe that being gay is a form of cosmic punishment for having had a bad relationship with a woman in a past life. Young men attracted by other men may be dispatched to a monastery to have their sexual orientation "corrected"; rape is also commonly used against lesbians for the same purpose. And ambiguously worded laws are routinely deployed by the authorities to harass anyone suspected of "dubious acts".

For fear of being ostracised by friends, work colleagues and family, lesbian, gay, bisexual and transgender (LGBT) Burmese rarely openly admit their sexuality. Apart from the odd "Queeny Boy" working clubs in Yangon, the only obviously transgender people you're likely to come across are the oracles who perform at *nat pwe* festivals, such as the one at Taungbyon near Mandalay. And there are as yet no hundred-percent gay venues anywhere in the country; cruising areas, where they exist, tend to be well hidden.

Myanmar's conservative attitudes have had serious health implications. The Burmese government asserts that HIV levels among gay men are around 29 percent, suggesting an infection rate 42 times higher than the rest of the population. The Rangoon-based NGO, Aids Alliance, estimates that fewer than 20 percent of the people needing anti-retroviral treatment are receiving it.

Even so, as Myanmar slowly modernises, public attitudes seem to be shifting – at least among the privileged classes. In 2011, a LGBT-oriented TV programme, Colours Rainbow TV (tvnews.colorsrainbow. com), was launched online in Yangon, with monthly news bulletins, interviews and features. And there's even talk of Yangon and Mandalay hosting the country's first ever Gay Pride parties in the near future.

Utopia Asia
www.utopia-asia.com
Detailed scene reports and gay steers, mostly for Yangon.

Purple Dragon
www.purpledrag.com
LGBT-oriented tour operator.

Mandalay Travel
Mandalaytravel.com
Myanmar-based gay-and-lesbian-friendly travel agent.

Human Rights Institute of Myanmar
The organization behind Colours Rainbow TV.

International Gay, Lesbian, Bisexual, Transgender and Intersex Association
Igla.org
LGBT news and views from around the country.

H

Health and medical care

Health officials require certification of immunisation against cholera, and against yellow fever if you arrive within nine days after leaving or transiting an affected area. Proof of smallpox vaccination is no longer required.

All visitors to Myanmar should take appropriate anti-malarial precautions before entering the country, and should continue to take medication throughout their stay. The risk is highest at altitudes below 1,000 metres (3,000 t) between May and December. Many upcountry hotels have mosquito nets, but any hole makes them worthless. Bring your own mosquito net and carry mosquito coils to burn while you sleep.

Perhaps the two most common hazards to visitors are sunburn and intestinal problems. The best way to prevent sunburn, especially if you're not used to the intense tropical sun, is to stay under cover whenever possible at midday, and, if you do go out, wear a hat or carry an umbrella. You'll see many Burmese, especially women and children, with yellow *thanaka*-bark powder applied to their faces to help screen out the sun. If you find yourself sweating a lot and feeling weak or dizzy, sit down (in the shade) and take some salt, either in tablet form or by mixing salt in a soft drink or tea.

Nearly every Westerner (especially first-timers) travelling in Myanmar and eating local food comes down with diarrhoea at some point during their stay. This can be uncomfortable and inconvenient. A good solution is to carry charcoal or Lomotil tablets. Better still, stay away from unfamiliar foods wherever possible.

Health standards in much of the country are still relatively low. Don't ever drink water unless you know it has been boiled or is sold in sealed bottles. All fruit should be carefully peeled before being eaten, and no raw vegetables should be eaten. Amoebic dysentery is a danger to those who are not careful.

It is best to discuss your travel plans with your personal physician with regard to recommended immunisation (tetanus, hepatitis, typhoid) and the specific anti-malarial drug needed. If you require any medication, it is best to bring along a sufficient supply.

For longer stays, and if your travels should take you to outlying areas, consider bringing your own medical kit as your specific prescription or drug may not be available.

Travel insurance

Travel insurance gives you the peace of mind that – in the case of unforeseen circumstances – you will be compensated for any loss of property and expenses incurred from the interruption and cancellation of trips, and for medical and other emergencies as spelt out in the specific policy.

Travel insurance usually includes cover for damaged and lost luggage – although most airlines do pay compensation against such claims; loss of deposit (for travel arrangements) – and compensation for flight delay and cancellation. Insurance policies also carry provision for hospitalisation and emergency evacuation to the nearest locality for proper treatment.

Medical treatment

Several hospitals in Yangon admit foreign nationals in emergencies. However, because of the generally lamentable state of the country's health-care facilities, travellers requiring serious care are generally air-evacuated to Bangkok; ensure your insurance covers such an eventuality.

Asia Royal General Hospital
14 Baho Street, Sanchaung Township, Yangon
One of the few hospitals in the country offering international-standard medical services.
Tel: 01 537 296; www.asiaroyalmedical.com
International SOS Clinic
Dusit Inya Lake Resort
37 Kaba Aye Pagoda Road, Yangon
Tel: 01 667 879; www.internationalsos.com
Full outpatient and emergency services, delivered by a professional team of expatriate and national doctors.

Pharmacies

Yangon has several pharmacies, all with 24-hour counters:
May Pharmacy, 542 Merchant Street.
AA Pharmacy, 142 Sule Pagoda Road.
Global Network, 155 Sule Pagoda Road.
Outside Yangon, pharmacies are few and far between.

I

Internet & email access

Internet access is readily available in Yangon and Mandalay, and in busy tourist centres such as Bagan and Inle Lake, but much less so elsewhere (only 25 percent of Burmese have a dependable electricity connection and the cost of a computer lies well beyond the reach of most local families). Connection speeds tend to be too slow for browsing, but are generally adequate for sending and receiving emails; power surges and failures are commonplace. Wi-fi is all-but standard at most high-end hotels these days.

To find your nearest internet point, ask at your hotel first – if they don't have a computer or wi-fi facility they'll be able to direct you to the nearest internet café. Note that at the time of writing, Skype and other internet voice-call providers were banned, and numerous sites blocked by the government, though following the democratic reforms of recent years such restrictions are expected to ease.

L

Left luggage

Because of the risk of terrorist attacks, there are no left luggage facilities in train or bus stations, or any other public places in Myanmar, though hotels may agree to store baggage.

Lost property

It's unlikely you'll gain any help from the Burmese police if you lose anything valuable while you're travelling in the country – though most insurers require some form of documentation from the local police to underwrite any loss. If in doubt about the paperwork required to make a claim, contact your insurers direct by telephone or email.

If you lose your passport, rest assured that some form of emergency travel documentation may be issued by your embassy or consulate in Yangon. The process will go much more quickly if you can provide a photocopy of the lost passport

and visas. In any case, contact the embassy to register the loss as soon as possible; you may be required to return to Yangon immediately to make an application.

M

Maps

The best all-round map of the country is Nelles *Myanmar (Burma)* 1:1,500,000, which is printed on both sides of coated paper. It's clearly drawn and includes shading of the major contours, as well as inset plans of Yangon, Mandalay, Bagan and Mrauk U. Rendered at slightly smaller (less detailed) scale of 1:2,000,000 is Periplus Editions *Myanmar Travel Map*. The third contender is the more graphic *Burma (Myanmar) Road and Physical Travel Reference Map* published by ITM at a scale of 1:1,350,000.

Free maps of major Burmese cities and tourist destinations are handed out by Myanmar Tours and Travels in Yangon (see page 000). You can also obtain free paper maps of most large cities and towns from the Myanmar-based cartographers, Design Printing Serices (www.dpsmap.com).

Media

Newspapers & magazines

Co-sponsored by the Ministry of Information and Myanmar army (Tatmadaw), the English-language edition of the government-run daily, the *New Light of Myanmar*, features endless reports on visits by the generals to factories, schools and religious institutions. Foreign news comes from agencies such as Reuters, via the government censors. You can peruse the online edition at myanmar.com/newspaper/nlm.

The Myanmar Times (mmtimes. com) is marginally more open and eclectic, but still stops short of being critical of the government. Like every other publication in Myanmar, it has to submit to pre-publication censorship imposed by the Press Scrutiny and Registration Division, whose Draconian rule explains why the country has so few dailies (the Ministry cannot process any more overnight).

The International Herald Tribune and other international newspapers are sometimes available at hotel news-stands, along with weekly news magazines. If you're desperate for reading material, used magazines can be purchased inexpensively from street vendors.

Radio & television

Myanmar broadcasts three free-to-air channels, all of them run by the government. The MRTV-4 channel hosts global sports, news and documentary channels, including National Geographic, BBC World, CNN, ESPN and Fox Movies.

The advent of the internet has posed all kinds of problems for Myanmar's government censors, not least the maverick Democratic Voice of Burma (DVB), which broadcasts online at www.dvb.no from its base in Oslo, Norway. Begun as a shortwave radio station in 1992, it launched a satellite news channel in 2005 – just in time for the 2007 saffron revolution, coverage of which by its free-ranging "VJs" brought DVB to the world's attention and inspired the hit movie, Burma VJ.

Visitors carrying shortwave radios will be able to pick up BBC Radio (www.bbc.co.uk) and Voice of America (VOA, www.voanews.com). The shortwave frequencies change according to the time of day; see their respective websites for further details.

Money

Myanmar's official currency is the kyat (pronounced "chat"), which comes in denominations of K1, K5, K10, K20, K50, K100, K200, K500, K1,000 and K5,000. For foreign visitors, however, the US dollar serves as an alternative. Most hotels and travel agents charge in dollars, and you'll also need them for air and rail tickets, and to pay admission charges for major sights. For just about everything else – including souvenir shopping, bus travel and meals in independently run restaurants – you'll use kyat.

Either way, expect to have to carry large bundles of cash. With a few exceptions, nowhere accepts credit or debit cards, or travellers' cheques. And there are as yet no ATMs from which to draw local currency.

Over the past decade, the official rate of exchange has wavered between K5.75 and K7 to the dollar. However, no one pays any attention to this, not even banks and exchange counters at airports, where rates are over 100 times more than the official government rate (between K750 and K1,350 for US$1).

With banks now offering the best

exchange rates of all it's no longer necessary to change money on the black market. Avoid dodgy money changers who approach you on the street. They may offer higher rates but could well short-change you. Hotels and accredited money changers in places like Bogyoke Aung San Market in Yangon are other good places for foreigners to change their currency. Haggle over the rate, and count your kyat carefully before handing over the dollars. You should also make sure there are no rips, tears, creases or holes in any of the kyat. If there are, they won't be accepted.

Dollar bills also have to be in **perfect condition**, and ideally issued no earlier than 2008. Again, check when you first purchase them back home that they're all mint, or something close to it. The higher the denomination the bill, the better the exchange rate.

Service charge & tax

International-standard hotels levy a government tax and a service charge of 10 percent each; some restaurants impose a 10 percent government tax only. Rumours were circulating in late 2012 that these rates will soon be hiked to 20 or 30 percent, which will add dramatically to the cost of a holiday in Myanmar.

An additional departure tax of US$10 is levied on all domestic flights; it has to be paid in cash when you check in.

Tipping

Tipping isn't as yet the norm in Myanmar, and not expected, though this is bound to change as tourism becomes more widespread. That said, a small consideration of K100 at monasteries and remote religious sites will always be welcome.

O

Opening hours

Business hours for all government offices (including post offices) are 9.30am–4.30pm Mon–Fri, 9.30am–12.30pm Sat. Shops open between 8am and 6pm. Restaurants open at 8–9am, depending on whether they offer breakfast, and close at around 9pm.

In Yangon, the main government travel agent and tourist information service, **Myanmar Travels & Tours**, opens 8am–8pm seven days a week.

P

Photography

Burmese are generally happy to pose for photographs, though as a courtesy it's always a good idea to seek permission first – easy enough through simple gesticulation and smiles. People also love to see the photo you've taken afterwards on the preview screen.

However, avoid photographing any military personnel or police. And never point your camera at a barracks, army vehicle or anything that could possibly be deemed strategic.

On longer trips, it's always a good idea to back up your images on to a memory stick or portable drive – though you may have to use a computer in an internet café or hotel to do this. And don't forget to bring your charger and spare battery – and re-charge frequently.

Postal services

The Yangon General Post Office (Tel: 01 285 499) is located on Strand Road at the corner of Bo Aung Gyaw Street and is open 7.30am–6pm Monday to Friday. All other post offices are open 9.30am–4.30pm Monday to Friday, and 9.30am–12.30pm Saturday. They are closed Sunday and public holidays.

The only exception is the Mingaladon (Yangon) Airport mail sorting office. It is open round-the-clock daily, including Sunday and holidays, for receipt and dispatch of foreign mail. Ordinary letters and postcards will be accepted here at any time. Registered letters can be taken at the airport postal counter only during normal government working hours.

For larger parcels, DHL is a faster and more reliable method of posting – though a far from cheap one. Their main office in Myanmar is at 7A Kaba Aye Pagoda Rd in Yangon (open Mon– Sat 8am–6pm; tel: 01 664 423; www. fastforward.dhl.com).

Public holidays

All offices are closed on the following days:
4 January Independence Day commemorates the date in 1948 that Burma left the British Commonwealth and became a sovereign independent nation.

12 February Union Day marks the date in 1947 that Aung San concluded an agreement with Burma's ethnic minorities at Panglong in the Shan State.

The Union of Myanmar (Burma) flag, which has been carried by runners to each of Myanmar's state capitals, is returned to Yangon amid the roar of hundreds of thousands of people from all over the nation.

2 March Peasants' Day honours the working population.

27 March Resistance (Tatmadaw) Day commemorates the World War II struggle against Japan. It is celebrated with parades and fireworks.

1 May Workers'/May Day The working people's holiday.

19 July Martyrs' Day is a memorial to the country's founding father, Aung San, and his cabinet who were assassinated in 1947. Ceremonies take place at the Martyrs' Mausoleum, Yangon.

Non-Buddhist religious holidays: Minority groups celebrate holidays not on the Burmese calendar: the Hindu festival *Dewali* in October, the Islamic observance of *Bakri Idd* with changing dates, the Christian holidays of Christmas and Easter, and the Kayin (Karen) New Year Festival on or about 1 January.

S

Smoking

Smoking has been banned since 2007 in all hospitals, clinics, stadiums, schools, colleges and universities. The sale of single cigarettes is also outlawed. However,

Area codes

Yangon: 01
Bago: 052
Lashio: 082
Mandalay: 02
Mawlamyine: 032
Monywa: 071
Myitkyina: 074
Pathein: 042
Pyay: 053
Pyin-U-Lwin: 085
Sagaing: 072
Sittwe: 043
Taunggyi: 081
Taungoo: 054
Thanlyin: 065

no one takes much notice of the law, and it's rarely enforced.

T

Telecommunications

The country code for Myanmar is 95, the code for Yangon is 1 (01 when dialling in the country) and 2 (02) for Mandalay. Myanmar has direct satellite links to seven countries: Japan, Hong Kong, Singapore, Thailand, India, UK and Australia. Siemens of Germany has installed additional satellite communication lines that have brought telecommunication connections up to Western standards.

When dialling from outside the country omit the 0 in the area code. IDD (International Direct Dialling) is easily available in major Yangon and Mandalay hotels and at kiosks; costs are based on US$ rates plus a service fee. From the smaller towns it may be possible to call Yangon but not overseas.

The Central Telegraph Office (Tel: 01 281 133), located one block east of the Sule Pagoda on Mahabandoola Street, is open from 8am to 9pm Monday to Saturday, and from 8am to 8pm Sunday and public holidays.

Mobile phones

There is no international GSM roaming facility for mobile phones in Myanmar. Phones brought in from outside the country may officially be subject to temporary confiscation at the airport, to be returned upon departure (though in practice this rarely, if ever, occurs). You can, however, purchase local Burmese SIM cards and top-up card for around US$20 and use these to make national or international calls and texts.

Time zone

Myanmar Standard Time is 6 hours and 30 minutes ahead of Greenwich Mean Time. If you come from Bangkok, you will have to set your watch back half-an-hour upon arrival in Yangon.

Toilets

Outside quality hotels, toilets tend to be of the basic squat variety. And don't expect them to be as clean as you may be used to back home. Paper

is rarely provided (though it's available in most general stores) and will block the drain. A tap on the wall (or outside) is used to fill a small plastic hand bucket, with which you're then supposed to sloosh yourself.

Tourist information

The only official source of tourist information is Myanmar Travels & Tours (MTT), whose head office at 118 Mahabandoola Garden St (tel: 01 371 286; www.myanmartravelsandtours.com) is the best place to arrange permits for the more off-track parts of the country open to visitors. They also book airline and rail tickets, but offer little in the way of useful, practical information beyond handing out town plans and leaflets. MTT maintains no offices abroad.

Since 1991, dozens of private officially recognised tour operators have set up business in Yangon, Mandalay and elsewhere. They are more flexible than Myanmar Travels & Tours, and are quite eager to please.

Travel to certain areas requires hiring the services of an approved tour operator. Other areas are strictly off-limits. The "official list" (viewable on the MTT website) distinguishes between areas open to individuals and those restricted to package tours.

Tour operators

You can save a lot of money by arranging your holiday through a Burmese company rather than one based in your country (nearly all foreign tour operators use Burmese firms as ground agents in any case, adding a mark-up on top). Local travel agents are also essential if you wish to visit permit-only areas of Myanmar, such as the far north of Kachin State.

Recommended tour operators in Yangon
Abercrombie & Kent
64, B-2 Shwe Gon Plaza
Tel: 01 542 949; www.abercrombieandkent.com
Asian Trails Tour Ltd.
73 Pyay Road, Dagon Township
Tel: 01 211 212; www.asiantrails.info
Columbus Travels and Tours
586 Strand Road
Tel: 01 229 245; www.travelmyanmar.com
Diethelm Travel
I Inya Road
Tel: 01 527 110; www.diethelm-travel.com

Exotissimo
#0303 Sakura Tower
339 Bo Gyoke Aung San Street
Tel: 01 255 266; www.exotissimo.com

Good News Travels
4th Floor, FMI Centre, 380 Bogyoke
Aung San Road.
Tel: 01 375 050; www.
myanmargoodnewstravel.com

Myanmar Himalaya Trekking & Culture
Summit Parkview Hotel, 350 Ahlone
Road
Tel: 01 227 978; www.myanmar-explore.com

Myanmar Shalom
No.70, 31 Street, Pabedan, Yangon
Tel: 01/252814
www.myanmarshalom.com

Inspiration Myanmar
6 Shwe Ghondine Road, 1st Floor,
Bahan Township, Yangon
www.inspirationmyanmar.com

Recommended trekking agencies in Myanmar

Mr Charles Guest House
105 Auba Street, Hsipaw
Tel: 082 801 105

Harry's Trekking House
132 Mai Yang Road, Kengtung
Tel: 084 21418

Putao Trekking House
424/425 Htwe San Lane, Kaung
Kahtaung, Putao
Tel: 09 840 0209; www.
putaotrekkinghouse.com

Scuba diving agencies

Heritage Travels & Tours
www.myanmarheritagetravel.com

Myanmar Elite Tours
www.myanmarelitetours.com

Phuket Scuba Diving
www.diving.phuket.com

Moby Dick Adventures
www.moby-dick-adventures.com

Tours
A typical 18-day package tour will
take in the main highlights: Yangon;
Mandalay and around; Inle Lake;
Ngapali Beach; with a night or
two on a luxury cruiser down the
Ayeyarwady.

Travelling independently, or on
a tailor-made tour, gives greater
flexibility, allowing you to explore
less frequented corners of the
country.

Either way, to cover much
ground within the 28 days allotted
by a tourist visa, you'll have to take
at least a couple of flights, and
have a rented car and driver at
your disposal for much of the trip
– all of which is much more easily
arranged through an agent than

by yourself. Because agents also
get hefty discounts from hotels,
airlines and car companies, it may
not even work out much more
expensive.

One sure-fire way to save money
is to travel as part of a group in a
minibus accompanied by a guide –
the most common option for tours
arranged abroad.

Tour operators in the UK

Audley Travel
New Mill, New Mill Lane, Witney,
OX29 9SX
Tel: 01993 838925. www.audleytravel.
com

TransIndus
75 St Mary's Road and the Old Fire
Station, Ealing, London W5 5RH
Tel: 0844 879 3960; www.transindus.
co.uk

Tour operators in Europe

Indochina Services
Steinerstrasse 15
Haus A, 2. OG, 81369
München, Germany
Tel: 089 219 0986; www.indochina-
services.com

Tour operators in the US

Asia Transpacific Journeys
(tailor-made and package tours)
2995 Center Green Court, Boulder,
Colorado 80301
Tel: 1 800 642 2742; www.
asiatranspacific.com

Indochina Services
870 Market Street, Suite 923,
San Francisco, CA 94102 USA
Tel: 415 434 4015; www.indochina-
services.com

Diving operators

Dive Asia
Tel: (66) 76 330 598 (Thailand)
www.diveasia.com

Santana Diving & Canoeing
Tel: (66) 76 294 220 (Thailand)
www.santanaphuket.com

South East Asia Liveaboards
Tel: (66) 76 340 406 (Thailand)

V

Visas & passports

Visitors to Myanmar of all
nationalities must present a
passport valid for a minimum of six
months after the proposed date of
entry, and a tourist visa obtained
in advance at one of the country's
overseas embassies or consulates

(a list of which appears on page
331).

An entry visa for tourists (EVT)
is valid for a maximum of 28 days
and entitles you to enter the country
only via an international airport, not
overland.

Applications procedures,
processing times and costs vary
from country to country but appear
in full on the relevant Myanmar
embassy website. Anyone listing a
media job can expect a prolonged
wait and should consider declaring
a suitably vague alternative, such as
"consultant" or "teacher".

Note that children above seven
years of age, even when included on
their parents' passport, must have
their own visas.

At the time of writing, business
visas for most foreign nationals were
available on arrival – check on the
embassy or consulate websites prior
to departure.

W

Weights & measures

Myanmar has retained many of the
old weights and measures in use
during the British colonial period.
1 viss (peith-tha) = 1,633g/3.6lbs
1 tical = 16.33g
1 cubit (tong) = 0.457 metres/18ins
1 span (htwa) = 0.23 metres/9ins
1 furlong = 201 metres/659ft
1 lakh = 100,000 (units)
1 crore = 100 lakh

The tin, or basket, is used to
measure quantities of agricultural
export goods. The kilogram equivalent
differs for rice, sesame, and other
goods.

Women travellers

Women travelling alone will find
themselves rarely hassled when
compared to other countries in
the region. Still, single women
may find it more comfortable to
travel with a companion. There are
no restrictions on wearing shorts
when visiting temples in Bagan,
particularly those in ruins or that
have been reconstructed. However,
brief shorts or skirts, or skimpy
clothing is frowned upon and women
will probably feel more comfortable
wearing long trousers or an over-
the-knee skirt. The traditional *longyi*
that the Burmese wear is a good
alternative.

LANGUAGE

UNDERSTANDING THE LANGUAGE

Survival Burmese

The Burmese language is tonal, like Chinese and Thai. The way in which a word is pronounced affects its meaning: a single syllable, given different stress, may carry several distinctly different meanings.

This may sound daunting, but in fact tones by themselves rarely obstruct survival communication. Other factors such as correct pronunciation of the vowels and consonants and having the proper rhythm are also important, however.

In the following list of words and phrases, accent marks are used: (no mark) – low even tone (:) – long falling tone (.) – short falling tone (') – glottal stop or creaky tone. The (') sign at the end indicates a glottal stop (like a final "t" but softer). The only way to know exactly how they sound is to have a native speaker say them for you to hear.

An "h" beginning a word indicates aspiration: "hk" is like the English "k" in Kate whereas "k" is closer to the "k" in skate. Sounds such as "hm" and "hn" resemble "m" and "n" but without the "breathiness". "Ng" is a sound not found at the beginning of English words. It does occur frequently in the middle of words such as "ringing" or "singing". Practice by first saying the whole word and the gradually cutting off the first two letters until you are saying "nging".

Ana-deh

Every language contains expressions which don't lend themselves to translation. Burmese is no exception. The essence of Burmese courtesy stresses encouraging the other person to agree with you. Not imposing on others is the basic principle of "ana-deh". The venerable Judson dictionary explains the term well as, "to be deterred by feelings of respect, delicacy, constraint, or by fear of offending". While all these feelings exist in Western countries, the concept as a single idea does not, or else there would be a word for it.

"Ana-deh" must be learned and felt inwardly. It is true art to meet another person at a halfway point where neither side will lose face in the confrontation.

In the Westerner's dealings with Burmese authorities, he or she will often encounter this "ana-deh" approach to problems, coupled with a marked aversion to making a decision that will cause someone difficulty (such as turning down a visa extension application). In some cases, it can lead to considerable delays. Westerners must be patient and try to understand what other forces are influencing the individuals concerned.

Conversation

How are you? *nei kaun: dha la:*
I am well *nei kaun: ba deh*
I am not well *nei thei' ma kaun: bu:*
How're you doing? (informal) *beh lo leh:*
That's good *kaun: deh*
I like it *chai' teh*
Do you understand? *na: leh la:*
I understand *na: leh ba deh*
I do not understand *na: ma leh bu:*
Yes *ho' keh.*
Yes (politely by male) *ho'keh.hka mya.*
Yes (politely by female) *ho'keh shin'*

Local ladies and goat, Bagan.

Yes (answering a call politely by male)
hka-mya.
Yes (answering a call politely by
female) *hka-shin'*
That's true *ho' ba deh*
That's right *hman ba deh*
No, that's not so *ma ho' ba bu:*
Please repeat *pan pyaw: ba oun:*
Speak clearly *shin: shin: pyaw: ba*
Why? *ba pyi' lo. leh:*
Never mind *nei ba zei*
It doesn't matter *kei'sa. ma shi.
ba bu:*
What is it? *ba leh:*
Do you know Burmese? *bama lo
ta. dha la:*
Only a little *neh: neh: pa: pa: ba beh:*
I speak very well *kaun: kaun: ta.
ba deh*
Are you English? *ein:galeik. lumyo:
la:*
No, I'm not English *ein:galeik. lu
myo: ma ho' bu:*
Where do you come from? *beh ga.
la dha leh:*
I come from America *ameiri.kan
ga. ba*
Goodbye *thwa: meh*
Take care *kaun: kaun: thwa:*

Accommodation

Is there a hotel near here? *di na:
hma ho-te shi. la:*
Can I see the room? *a-kan chi. ba
ya zei*
Single room *ta yau' hkan:*
Double room *hna yau'.hkan:*

Dining

What do you want to eat? *ba sa:
chin dha leh:*
Is there...? *...shi. dha la:*
I'll eat... *...sa: meh*
Pork curry *weh. tha: hin:*
Chicken curry *cheh. tha: hin:*
Beef curry *a-meh: hin:*
Fish curry *nga: hin:*
Shrimp curry *bazun hin:*
Noodles with curry *kau' hswe:*
Vegetables *hin: dhi:*
Fruit *thi' thi:*
Fermented tea leaf salad *la peh.
thou.*
**Fermented noodles with
fish broth** *mo: hin: ka:*
What do you want to drink? *ba thau'
chin dha le?*
I don't want to drink. *ma thau' chin
bu:*
I'll drink... *...thau' meh*
Coffee *ka pi*
Black tea with milk and sugar *la
peh. yei.*
Plain green tea *la peh. yei jan:*
Hot water *yei nwei:*
yei *Water.*

bi ya *Beer*
hin: jo *Hot soup*

Directions and places

Where is the...? *...beh hma leh:*
Where are you going? *be go thwa:
ma lo le:*
Railway Station *mi: ya ta: buda yone*
Theatre *yo' shin yone*
Hotel *ho teh*
Post Office *sa dai'*
Bank *ban*

Time

When will you go? *beh do. thwa:
ma leh:*
What time will it start? *beh
ah-chein sa. ma leh:*
One o'clock *ta na yi*
Two o'clock *hna na yi*
Airplane *lei yin byan*
Train *mi: ya ta:*
The bus will leave. *bas. ka: twe. me*
Trishaw *hsai'ka:*

Shopping

How much is it? *be lau' le:*
Lower your price. *sho. ba ohn:*
The price is too high. *zei: mya: deh*
Lower some more. *hta. sho. ba ohn:*
Expensive *zei: chi: deh*
OK/good *kaun: ba bi*

Health

Dentist *thwa: sa ya wun*
Doctor *sa ya wun*
Hospital *hsei: yone*

Book binder in Yangon

Pharmacy *hse: zain*
Where is the...? *...beh hma leh:*
Call the doctor. *sa ya wun ko pei: ba*
I am ill. *nei lo. ma kaun: bu:*

Numbers

one *ti'*
two *hni'*
three *thone:*
four *lei:*
five *nga:*
six *hchau'*
seven *hkun/hkun–ni'*
eight *hyi'*
nine *ko:*
ten *ta-hseh/hseh*
eleven *hseh.ti'*
twelve *hseh.hni'*
thirteen *hseh.thone:*
fourteen *hseh.lei:*
fifteen *hseh.nga:*
sixteen *hseh.hcau'*
seventeen *hseh.hkun*
eighteen *hseh.hyi'*
nineteen *hseh.ko:*
twenty *hna-hseh*
thirty *thone:zeh*
forty *lei:zeh*
fifty *nga:zeh*
sixty *hchau' hseh*
seventy *hkun-na-hseh*
eighty *hyi' hseh*
ninety *ko:zeh*
one hundred *ta-ya*
one thousand *ta htaun*
ten thousand *ta thaun:*
hundred thousand *ta thein:*
one million *ta than:*
ten million *ta ga dei*

စာအုပ်အမျိုးမျိုးချုပ်သည်
BOOK BINDING

FURTHER READING

General interest & travel

Collis, Maurice. *Lords of the Sunset.*
A tour of the Shan States.
Kipling, Rudyard. *Letters From the East.* The author's travels through Asia.
Amitav Ghosh. *The Glass Palace.*
Prize-winning novel whose plot shadows a century of Burmese history.
Rory MacLean. *Under the Dragon: A Journey Through Burma.*
Poignant travelogue focusing on the lives of four Burmese women.
Theroux, Paul. *The Great Railway Bazaar: By Train Through Asia.*
Amusing account of the author's railway adventures.

General history

Thant Myint-U. *The River of Lost Footsteps: A Personal History of Burma.* A highly readable account of the country's chequered history, both ancient and modern, by a high-ranking Burmese émigré.
Orwell, George. *Burmese Days.*
Bittersweet novel about British colonial rule.
Shway Yoe (Sir J.G. Scott). *The Burman: His Life and Notions.* A gold mine of cultural information from a 19th-century British colonial official.
Collis, Maurice. *Last and First in Burma.* An account of the country during and after the war.
Stilwell, Joseph. *The Stilwell Papers.*
Edited and arranged by Theodore H. White. New York: William Sloane

Associates, 1948. "Vinegar Joe" in his own words.

Contemporary Myanmar

Aung San Suu Kyi. *Freedom from Fear & Other Writings.* A collection of essays by and about the Nobel Peace Prize winner.
Mya Than Tin, editor. *Encounters on the Road to Mandalay.* A collection of interviews with ordinary Myanmar citizens.
Peter Popham. *The Lady and the Peacock: The Life of Aung San Suu Kyi.*
Biography of Myanmar's Nobel-Prize-winning political leader.
Zoya Phan. *Little Daughter: A Memoir of Survival In Burma and the West.*
Phan, a native Karen, became the face of a nation enslaved after this gripping 2009 memoir was published.

Arts & culture

Falconer, John et al. *Myanmar Style: Art, Architecture and Design of Burma.* A photographic survey of major design components in both traditional and contemporary Burmese design.

Other Insight Guides

Companion volumes to the present title cover the Southeast Asian region comprehensively and include *Bangkok*, *Laos & Cambodia*, *Indonesia*, *Malaysia*, *the Philippines*, *Singapore*, *Southeast Asia*, *Thailand* and *Vietnam*. The Insight Step by Step series of itinerary-based guides includes *Step by Step Bangkok*.
Insight's acclaimed laminated Fleximap series includes *Vietnam/ Laos/Cambodia*, *Ho Chi Minh City* and *Bangkok*.

Send Us Your Thoughts

We do our best to ensure the information in our books is as accurate and up-to-date as possible. The books are updated on a regular basis using local contacts, who painstakingly add, amend and correct as required. However, some details (such as telephone numbers and opening times) are liable to change, and we are ultimately reliant on our readers to put us in the picture.

We welcome your feedback, especially your experience of using the book "on the road". Maybe we recommended a hotel that you liked (or another that you didn't), or you came across a great bar or new attraction we missed.

We will acknowledge all contributions, and we'll offer an Insight Guide to the best letters received.

Please write to us at:
**Insight Guides
PO Box 7910
London SE1 1WE**
Or email us at:
insight@apaguide.co.uk

TRANSPORT · ACCOMMODATION · EATING OUT · ACTIVITIES · A – Z · LANGUAGE

CREDITS

Insight Guide Credits

Project Editor
Tom Le Bas

Series Manager
Carine Tracanelli

Art Editor
Tom Smyth

Map Production
Original cartography
Cosmographics, updated by
Apa Cartography Department

Production
Tynan Dean, Linton Donaldson and
Rebeka Ellam

Distribution
UK
Dorling Kindersley Ltd
A Penguin Group company
80 Strand, London, WC2R 0RL
customerservice@dk.com

United States
Ingram Publisher Services
1 Ingram Boulevard, PO Box 3006,
La Vergne, TN 37086-1986
customer.service@ingram
publisherservices.com

Australia
Universal Publishers
PO Box 307
St Leonards NSW 1590
sales@universalpublishers.com.au

New Zealand
Brown Knows Publications
11 Artesia Close, Shamrock Park
Auckland, New Zealand 2016
sales@brownknows.co.nz

Worldwide
Apa Publications GmbH & Co.
Verlag KG (Singapore branch)
7030 Ang Mo Kio Avenue 5
08-65 Northstar @ AMK
Singapore 569880
apasin@singnet.com.sg

Printing
CTPS-China

© 2013 Apa Publications (UK) Ltd
All Rights Reserved

First Edition 1980
Ninth Edition 2013

INDEX